Bitters in the Honey

Tales of Hope and Disappointment across Divides of Race and Time

Beth Roy

The University of Arkansas Press

Fayetteville   1999

03   02   01   00   99   5   4   3   2   1

Designed by Liz Lester

☉ The paper used in this publication meets the minimum
requirements of the American National Standard for Permanence
of Paper for Printed Library Materials Z39.48-1984.

Library of Congress Cataloging-in-Publication Data

Roy, Beth.
     Bitters in the honey : tales of hope and disappointment
across divides of race and time / Beth Roy.
          p.   cm.
     Includes bibliographical references and index.
     ISBN 1-55728-553-5 (cloth : alk. paper). —ISBN
1-55728-554-3 (paper : alk. paper)
     1. Central High School (Little Rock, Ark.)—History—20th
century. 2. School integration—Arkansas—Little Rock—
History. I. Title.
LC214.23.L56R69   1999
379.2'63'0976773—dc21   99-23950
                                                   CIP

Acknowledgments

Bitters in the Honey was six years in the making. If it takes a village to raise a child, it takes an army to write a book. To the following, my most ardent thanks:

In Little Rock, Jerome Muldrew was a guide who literally and figuratively escorted me through the history and halls of Central High School. Dottie Woodwind, too, nurtured me with hospitality and good stories. On my first trip to Little Rock, Becky Jenkins accompanied me to the initial interview with Gov. Orval Faubus and helped by charming him with her acute questions and forgiving manner.

Closer to home, the manuscript was read in many, many drafts by a splendid group of authors who have met together over many years for mutual support and critique. Andrea Altschuler, Karen Branson, Mary Anna Colwell, Margarita Decierdo, Sandy Freitag, Matthew Hallinan, and Katie Nash have put their charmed touch on the work at various points along the way. Andrea, Karen, and Mary Anna read every word of every draft; their ability to come up with yet another new and helpful suggestion was truly amazing.

A long list of other people read the manuscript and commented in abundant detail: Mary Adams Trujillo, Juliana Birkhoff, Roberto Chené, Pete Daniels, Helen Helfer, Shelby Morgan, Beverlee Patton, Rose Saginaw, Claude Steiner, and Donald Wilkinson. Their ideas and experience sparkle between the lines of the work.

Barbara Howell placed her gentle touch on the project, copyediting the manuscript and then making me cry by refusing payment as her way of supporting what I was doing.

Nobody has read the text in more detail or debated the concepts with more intellectual vigor and emotional encouragement than Mariah Breeding. Without her my life as well as my work would be much the poorer.

There would have been no text to read had it not been for four women who transcribed the interviews. Jeanne Gahagan, Mary Hudson, Ellen Murland, and Pat Ward spent many hours transforming miles and miles of audio tape into pages and pages of written dialogue. Their sensitivity to the nuances of the stories they heard, not to mention their endurance, provided a secure foundation for the writing of *Bitters.*

At the very beginning of the project, I was fortunate to be introduced to Melba Pattillo Beals and to have access to dialogue with her at crucial moments. The honesty, wisdom, and passion that infuse her book helped illuminate mine.

Every writer entertains a fantasy of being adopted by the perfect agent. Michele Rubin is that agent. She took up this project and stood by me through the dicey times, her unwavering commitment to the work bolstering my own at moments when mine needed bolstering. I thank also my old friend, Barry Tarshis, who connected me with Michele and nurtured the early stages of the project.

Through much of the time I've been interviewing and writing *Bitters,* I've also had the extreme benefit of working with a multiracial group of colleagues at the National Conference on Peacemaking and Conflict Resolution. The opportunity to work intensively on the most crucial issues of diversity in an atmosphere of love and respect has enriched my thinking and my spirit more than I can say.

Finally and above all, my warmest thanks go to my many interviewees, who allowed me to intrude on their time and their lives, who greeted me so generously and talked with me so openly. This book is dedicated to their continuing growth and happiness.

Contents

ONE
Stories of Central High

It was the *high school . . . a wonderful, idyllic . . . Andy Hardy kind of high school.*

—Wesley Pruden Jr.

When I passed by Central High School, I just said, "Well, I've got a high school, too. I love mine. I hope you love yours."

—Jerome Muldrew

Little Rock is a pretty place. Green and gently rolling, the city has spread westward over the years since it gained notoriety, growing along the Arkansas River out from the old downtown district into hilly suburbs filled with gracious homes. The central city has had its ups and downs, like so many urban centers in America during the second half of the twentieth century. Today, it has a certain vibrancy as high-rise buildings bustle in the daytime with office workers.

But that vibrancy is thin. Attempts to fan the few remaining sparks of retail life downtown have met with little success. At the bed-and-breakfast inn where I stay there is a little tree just outside the dining room window. The tree is hung with bird feeders, and a Peterson's *Guide to Southern Birds* lies near-to-hand on the table. My hostess told me she got the tree cheap when the city dismantled a failed pedestrian mall that had briefly closed Main Street to through traffic. Today, cars once again flow past seedy stores, places with a role in the history of Little Rock, now quietly surviving in a commercial backwater, places like Jimmy Karam's Men's Clothing Store.

If you drive due south from downtown, you cross over the freeway and pass a cluster of grand old Victorians surrounding the governor's mansion. The Quapaw District dates back to the mid-nineteenth century. Its lovely Victorians housed the growing professional elite of the city at a time when Little Rock was becoming a center of commerce, banking, and government.

To reach Central High School, you turn right on West Fourteenth Street. Almost immediately the grand homes of the Quapaw District give way to small houses of brick and clapboard which line straight but rolling streets. The school is the next large structure you reach, barely a dozen blocks west of the governor's mansion and many worlds away.

When I first flew into Little Rock, I headed in my rental car straight for Central High:

> It was *the* high school. . . . You've been there; I'm sure you drove by it and saw it. It's a beautiful school. It's quite large; there were 627 members of my graduating class in 1953. [Wesley]

Images of the building have become permanently wedded to the history of civil rights struggle in America: Nine black teenagers clutching their schoolbooks, surrounded by helmeted soldiers with bayoneted rifles at the ready, walk proudly past the decorative fishpond and up the grand double staircase rising above the inscription "Little Rock Central High School." The momentous procession seems dwarfed by the arches and statues adorning the brick facade of the four-story building they are about to enter.

Central High's location—just east of the Union Pacific Railroad tracks—reflects a significant part of the story of civil rights in Little Rock. East of the tracks is the wrong side of the tracks, the poorer part of town. Even the grand homes of the Quapaw District contained boardinghouses and small apartments until gentrification rediscovered its glories a few years ago. At the time of the confrontation at Central High School in the mid-fifties, most of the east Little Rock area was shared by black families and working-class whites separated into neighboring enclaves:

> We would always say that you could tell where the white neighborhood ended and the black neighborhood started because the pavement would just stop in the middle of the street. And when we first moved over here in this area, the streets were nothing but mud, and there were ditches on both sides of the street. And couldn't but one car pass at a time. [**Marian**]

Today, the area is almost exclusively black.

The school building itself dwarfs the surrounding neighborhood. First opened in 1927[1] Central High's appearance promised great things to children of modest means. "Did you graduate from Central?" I asked Wesley Pruden Jr., the person who'd described the school as *the* school. A white man in his late fifties, Wesley is the son of a minister who played a prominent role in the events there. Today he is a well-known journalist in the East. "I did," he replied, and quickly amended, "It was *Little Rock* High School. Those of us who graduated from Little Rock High School always correct that. We never approved of their changing the name."

What was the significance of the name change? For years, Little Rock High School was *the* high school, the only one in town, many people told me. Actually, it was not the only high school; it was the only high school for white students. Black students were served by Dunbar High, a proud and well-respected institution built in the 1930s using the same design as Central, albeit a quarter its size. By the time the crisis hit in 1957, two new high schools had been built: Horace Mann replaced Dunbar as the blacks-only high school in 1955, and Hall High opened in the fall of '57 with a small white student body drawn from the affluent new suburbs west of the tracks.

When Wesley said Little Rock High was *the* school, his meaning was more than arithmetic:

> It was really kind of a wonderful, idyllic . . . Andy Hardy kind of high school.[2] Very good musical programs. Fine athletic teams, which people in that part of the country tend to measure their schools by. Every year there were dozens of scholarships, always several scholarships to the Ivy League schools. People did very well.
>
> I think that was one of the *many* underlying reasons for a lot of the bitterness toward the white establishment about the way the whole desegregation thing came about. Because it was felt by the people in the middle-class, working-class neighborhoods that fed Central High School, that Central was being sacrificed on behalf of this new high school out in the richer part of town.

What the world saw of desegregation in Little Rock was a morality tale about power and race. They saw a grand institution whose doors needed quite literally to be breached by force in order for children of all races to attend school together. What many white citizens of Little Rock saw was also a story about power, but of a very different sort. Their story was about class, about an abuse of privilege by affluent people within their own community. Little Rock High had offered children from families of modest means a chance "to do very well," even a possibility of a scholarship to an Ivy League school. Americans have little vocabulary with which to express class distinctions. Ask an American what class she is and the betting is good she'll reply, "Middle class." Higher education is one of the few places that encodes class gradations in a nuanced way. We all know how a high-school dropout differs from an "ivy league" graduate, whose life chances can in turn be easily distinguished from those of the alumnus of the local state institution. On the other hand, public high schools can be places where class lines are blurred; everyone attends together, whatever their ultimate destinies may turn out to be.

Many young white people in Little Rock experienced their school that way; again and again people commented to me that their classmates came from throughout the city (neighborhood often being another marker of class position), that teenagers of all economic circumstances rubbed shoulders and shared the opportunity to improve their prospects in society. To attend Central High was, it seemed, to experience the American dream of unlimited opportunity. When those in power ordered Central High to desegregate while protecting the "privilege" of the new suburban school to remain all white, they revealed a nasty truth: that everyone was not equal after all—everyone white, that is. Some people responded with bitterness, not only toward the black champions of civil rights, but toward the white establishment as well.

Interactions between issues of race and class, and of gender as well, characterize the drama of Central High. Too often when we Americans talk about race, we separate it from other aspects of life and, having done so, remain mystified about why race continues to play so volatile and distressing a role in our society. As I listened to the many stories of Little Rock, I heard common themes, differently described, of how seemingly unconnected identities based on race, class, gender, generation, geography, all fit together to form a dynamic construct with deep significance to both political and personal life. Formed of a multitude of interrelated, unexamined assumptions, this construct describes a world in which inequalities of power are natural, and individuals compete for well-being as individuals at the same time they occupy distinct social locations replete with social roles and expectations.

For black youths in the community, the pieces fit together rather differently. To be "not white" was to be undeniably located in a group, with no confusion about the fact that that group's position in society determined each individual's chances. Central High was, therefore, a story of collective efforts to make social change leading to greater choice and access to resources, two things many of their white peers took for granted. Jerome Muldrew lived near Little Rock High and attended Dunbar in the 1940s. Every day he walked past those grand portals on his way to school, while his white neighbors, boys he played with in the streets, went in. I asked him how that felt to him, and he said:

> When I passed by Central High, Little Rock High School, I just said, "Well I've got a high school, too. I love mine. I hope you love yours." . . . I had a lot of pride about my school. I thought it was just as good as Little Rock High.

At the time I first interviewed him, Jerome had taught at Central High for twenty years. The conversation went on awhile, and the rapport between us grew warmer. When I asked him how he'd felt when the school was desegregated, he admitted feeling a little differently than he had first indicated:

> I was anxious to join the fight. I was very anxious, because this is what I thought should happen. Why should I have to pass by one school in order to go to another? I loved Dunbar; I look back now and appreciate learning of the black experience, but in reality I live in a multicultural, multiethnic society. In order for me to function successfully, integration of the schools is a viable solution. I was and still am an integrationist at heart.
>
> That's the bitterness I have, [even though] I thought my teachers were real great and that compensated for not attending Central High. But when I read integration was about to take place in Little Rock, I was very proud we were chosen to play this part in the civil rights movement.

Confrontation at Central High

Memories of the past are complex and variable things. Recollections of things from different moments are like sheer scrims on a stage, layers of consciousness that shift in relationship to each other, revealing now one aspect, now another, depending on particularities of light and perspective. How Jerome remembers himself feeling as a high-school student is different from how he remembers himself feeling as a young teacher contemplating a court order to desegregate the school he had walked past daily. The stories of desegregating Central High that I heard were all heartfelt, often impassioned, sometimes laced with regret, more often with bitterness. They frequently differed from each other in substance and in detail. How and what I was told informed me as much about the feelings and social position of the speaker as about the events she or he described.

One story among the many I heard is the one often labeled "The History of Desegregation at Central High." It is a version gleaned from the printed record and, almost everywhere except in Little Rock itself, the one most commonly retold. I recount it here as a sort of base-line narrative, not because it is the "true" version, but because it is the one most likely to resonate with the reader's own recollections.

Both school officials and civil rights activists considered Little Rock to be a good place to begin desegregating public schools.[3] It was the capital of a border state with a reputation for "moderate" race relations. White citizens outnumbered blacks two to one, unlike many places in the deep South where the proportions were reversed. Little Rock was experiencing a postwar economic boom, with businesses moving in from out of state and thereby creating a stake in a peaceful society. The school board, while weighted toward a segregationist position, was composed of "reasonable" people and was headed by a liberal superintendent from Missouri, Virgil Blossom. Whatever their underlying sympathies, the school authorities were willing to uphold the law of the land. The courts, too, offered reasonable promise of cooperating with change. The NAACP had successfully used the courts to challenge inequities in pay for black and white teachers a few years before.

Finally, the new schools being built were seen as an opportunity to introduce change, since change was afoot anyway. The new high school out west, Hall, was due to open in fall 1957, suggesting a certain symmetry: it would be all white; Horace Mann to the east would remain all black; Central would be integrated. A very modest plan (named for the superintendent, the Blossom Plan) was drawn up by the school board in negotiation with the NAACP: a handful of black students—in the event, there turned out to be nine of them—were to enroll in Central in 1957. The starting date, at first set considerably later, was moved up through court orders initiated by the NAACP.

Over the summer of '57, resistance to the plan mounted. Ten days before school opened, Georgia's governor Marvin Griffin visited town and spoke passionately about the need for desegregation to be stopped in Little Rock, lest it take hold throughout the South. The day before school opened, Gov. Orval Faubus called out the National Guard, for the purpose, he claimed, of maintaining "peace and order." On the next day, a smallish crowd of about three hundred white people formed outside the building, noisily watching as the Guard admitted teachers and white students. The black children stayed home while the NAACP asked for guidance from the court. The federal judge opted to take the governor at his word. If the Guard were there simply to maintain peace and order, then there was no reason not to continue with the desegregation plan.

On Wednesday, September 4, the second day of school, the crowd had grown to about a thousand strong. Eight of the black children were escorted to the door by ministers from both black and white churches. They were turned away by stony-faced Guards. The ninth student, a slightly built girl named Elizabeth Eckford, had not gotten word of the plans; she came alone by bus (the parents had been told not to accompany their children, lest their presence "induce" greater violence). Armed Guards barred her way, and she wandered back through an increasingly hostile crowd, alone and weeping, until a middle-aged white Quaker woman pushed her way forward and escorted the traumatized child back to the bus.

Jockeying quickly began in an effort to convince Governor Faubus to call off the Guard and let the students enroll. On September 20, a

Friday, three weeks after school had started, the Guards were with-drawn. The following Monday morning, the nine students were escorted to the side door of Central High by city policemen, and they attended classes for the first time. But the mob in front of the build-ing got wind of their admittance and massed threateningly. Police offi-cials decided it was too dangerous for the black students to remain in their classes; by noon they had spirited them away in fast-moving automobiles.

The level of violence that Monday finally convinced President Eisenhower to intervene. By Tuesday evening, the 101st Airborne marched into town, and on Wednesday morning the nine students proceeded under guard up the grand front staircase of Central High and attended classes.

Struggles continued all year, in the streets around the school, in the courts, in political discussions both locally and nationally, and inside the school itself among the students. Nonetheless, Ernest Green, the only senior in the group of nine, succeeded in graduating that May. When school was due to reopen the next fall, the legislature passed a bill allowing all Little Rock high schools to be closed. Closed they remained throughout 1958–59—except for a football season which went forward with its usual elan and success. Finally, in fall of 1959, with a new, more integrationist board of education and legislature elected, the schools reopened.[4]

Meanwhile, Little Rock's reputation had been transformed from genteel to nasty. The intensity of resistance that was mounted took many people by surprise. "Nobody, nobody anticipated the trouble that followed," said Evelyn Armon, a black woman who was a school administrator in the district for forty-nine years. "Nobody."

> I don't know exactly how to put this but it wasn't until after that trouble started that we really realized how deep the feelings here were. See, these were people that we had, businessmen that we had traded with, and [there were] positive signs. . . .
>
> [It] was kind of a shock, you know. It just made you think—they liked us, to be very blunt, they liked us as long as we stayed in our place. And that reaction of the community was a shock. It really was, that these people . . . got out there with such bitterness.

Narratives and Essences:
Getting Beneath the Surface

Any story can be told in many different ways; history is no exception. It is simply a narrative told from a particular perspective, containing within it many theories and arguments. Evelyn's story began with an expression of surprise, and surprise is a good indicator of a theory or set of assumptions that has just been contradicted. She thought "they liked us," a theory of peaceable race relations, but discovered "they liked us as long as we stayed in our place," a discovery of a very different set of social arrangements. How desegregation came about in Little Rock, why it was constructed in the way it was, why people ranging from the governor to students in the school behaved the ways they did, all form strands of the narrative that can be emphasized or overlooked, interpreted or subjectively reported.

This notion of multiple stories can lead one in several directions. Some people maintain that there is no objective truth, because every individual's experience gives rise to a different truth. Others maintain that some versions are mistaken and others accurate. As I listened to the many versions of Central High's history, I felt ever more strongly that neither assertion was exactly right. Storytelling is a political act.[5] How we portray the past, ourselves, and our fellows can defend or contest social arrangements. Often, I found "errors" in my interviewees' accounts; they placed the National Guard in the wrong place at the wrong time, insisted people were where they couldn't have been at a crucial moment; announced that one of the Nine was an outsider planted inside Central High for strategic reasons, while other people attested to that very "outsider" having been born and reared right up the street. It is precisely in these distortions of "fact" that political arguments reside.[6] "Memory fails," wrote Karen Fields:

> leaving blanks, and memory collaborates with forces separate from actual past events, forces such as an individual's wishes, a group's suggestions, a moment's connotations, an environment's clues, an emotion's demands, a self's evolution, a mind's manufacture of order, and yes, even a researcher's objectives.[7]

"Any mistake is meaningful," Fields argues. "[M]emory 'tainted' by interest is a dead-serious party to the creation of something true. The 'mistakes' it may embody represent an imperfection only in light of the particular purposes scholarship has."[8] Any and every account of a shared history like the history of Central High School has stories to tell us that go beyond the obvious facts of what happened, when, and to whom. The many choices people make of structure and omission, like their memories of events and their recollections of their lived experience in the form of anecdotes, all contain meanings which we can and should mine for deeper understandings of our shared world. In the aggregate, those multiple meanings constitute a unitary reality, best described not by "what happened" but by a complex and interacting set of dynamics: intricate dances of power negotiation, small and frequent acts of political decision that serve to construct personal identities, silences and inaction that assert implicit understandings of rights and privileges.

But all stories are not equal, nor is injustice relative. Wrongs *are* perpetrated. Scholars and activists have labored for many years to understand white racism in terms that would lead to effective antidotes. Yet racism is still with us, hard and strong. One finding of my study in Little Rock is that white racist attitudes continue unabated, their forms and codes changed since the fifties, but not their intensity. If we are to make change happen, we must account for that tenacity, for it goes beyond poor education or bad character. We must seek insight instead into deeper issues of power relations, and especially into the ways social relations of all sorts—especially race, class, and gender—are internalized so as to promote acceptance of social structures which may privilege some over others but are genuinely in the interest of a very few.

I believe that attitudes and personal feelings are tightly linked to social conditions as they are lived by individuals. What we think and feel, how we interpret our lived experience, is deeply informed by who we are as social creatures at a moment in time. Psychology itself, I believe, that most personal of arenas, is a social construct, because the beliefs and attitudes we learn in the course of social interaction, at home and in the world, so fundamentally shape the direction of individual lives and the feelings we have along the way. The lessons we learn, especially those that appear in memory later as "truths," are not accidental. Instead, they mediate social relations of power and hierarchy with great force and constitute a concrete link between individual consciousness and social structure.

If one posits (as I do) that individual emotions and attitudes are linked to social life and that they reflect something real in lived experience, then it becomes a reasonable premise that white racism is linked to something problematic in white lives. Too often in the American discourse on race we condemn those with whom we disagree, and the disagreements mount. A desire for a color-blind society causes some people, both whites and people of color, to wish to overlook continuing inequalities which are, sometimes, close to invisible to those not directly disadvantaged by them. At the same time other whites believe that demands for justice are disingenuous, that in fact they are demands for privilege. Meanwhile, people of color wishing to right racial injustices may see white resistance as a morally crude power play in defense of indefensible privileges. In all these cases, I believe those involved miss the crucial point: that we cannot get beyond the matter of race until we have come to terms with it. To do that, we must stop demonizing those who stand against social change and instead understand the perspective from which they speak. The challenge I took on in beginning this study was to listen to the life histories of white people from Little Rock who, passively or actively, resisted desegregation in Arkansas and to unpack their view of themselves as the true sufferers in order to understand what it is they do truly suffer that somehow goes unexpressed in other forms.

For me, the task was truly a challenge. I began this project because I care deeply about racial justice. In 1954, when the Supreme Court handed down the decision ordering school desegregation, I was a thirteen-year-old resident of Fort Worth, Texas, and about to be a high-school freshman. The school I attended was, of course, segregated. A transplanted northerner and a Jew born while the holocaust raged through Europe, I regarded Jim Crow as an inexplicable wrong, and I welcomed the prospect of its demise. My childhood had been filled with the terrifying knowledge that people existed who might slaughter me based on accidents of my birth, and I identified deeply with what I believed was a comparable wrong done to African Americans. I could do nothing to affect the course of fascism in Europe, but in Texas I could act. To do so represented to me a profound opportunity, a glimmer of hope that humanity might be redeemed from the evil of genocide.

That summer before my freshman year, a small group of local people came together to begin to prepare the ground for what we hoped would be peaceful and speedy change. I joined enthusiastically; over the summer I called many of my friends inviting them—indeed, expecting them—to take part. One or two came to a meeting, but every one of them eventually declined to participate. Quietly, they explained that their friends would never forgive them; their parents asked them not to, fearing economic reprisals; their own truest feelings lay elsewhere. As my freshman year got rolling, I looked around and discovered myself to be the lone white high-school student participating in the group. Others among my peers spoke up bravely in classes or in conversations with friends. But I was surprised and disappointed that they did not choose to work actively to right what they agreed was a wrong. I was even more deeply distressed to find how many of my classmates defended the system of separation.

As it happened, Fort Worth's schools were not desegregated for thirteen years. By then, I had graduated, left for college in the east, married a man from India, and gone to live in a little village north of Calcutta. By then, Central High had happened, too, and people of good conscience, people like my parents and the members of our small group, used data showing how severely local business had suffered economic injuries in the aftermath of the resistance in Little Rock to persuade the business community of Fort Worth to cooperate with school desegregation.

For many years after I returned from India in the 1970s, I watched the racial climate of America grow hot and cold. I became a counselor, helping people make all sorts of changes in their lives. Mediating conflicts (some of them involving racial issues) became a central aspect of my practice. Then came the eighties and the nineties. American race relations seemed to me to deteriorate markedly. The gulf between whites and people of color grew wider, understanding more and more strained. My children grown, I returned to the university in the mid-eighties to earn a doctorate in sociology, because I wanted to study instances of social conflict in different contexts and cultures. Along the way, I began using oral history as a way of pursuing my theoretical bent. If individual subjectivity is grounded in social reality, then I wished to explore those theoretical questions that concerned me using the concrete vividness of personal stories. Little Rock had influenced me deeply; newly arrived in the northeast from Texas, I had watched the drama unfold on television and asked again and again, "Why so much hatred? How have we failed? What could we have done differently?" In my heart of hearts, though, I think I most truly asked, "What's wrong with those people?"

Four decades later, after twenty-five years of hearing people's most intimate stories in therapy and mediation, that judgmental question still echoes in my mind, only now I know it is the question that is wrong. My work with people has given me more and more insight into the constructive side of conflict, and helped convince me that a theory of the dynamic relationship between subjectivity and objectivity, the notion that what people feel makes sense, that emotion is always grounded in realities of life, is both accurate and useful. To start with that premise is to search deeply for an understanding of the real differences that divide people in conflict, dignifying those differences by naming them and delineating their interconnections, and from that standpoint negotiating reasonable solutions to real problems. This approach is self-fulfilling. To believe there is something concrete at root of seemingly irrational and possibly intractable conflict leads to a search which, more often than not, yields genuine solutions.

If I wish others to change—and I fervently do—I understand that I, too, need to do something different, to move beyond judgment into a deeper exploration of why white people, good people, mistakenly and vehemently blame fellow Americans of color for all sorts of improbable things. It is in that spirit that I invite my readers to hear stories, painful as they may sometimes be, from across divides of race that seem to grow ever deeper over time.

■ ■ ■

This project has taken me quite a journey. I began in orderly academic fashion formulating a list of civic leaders from whom to request introductions to people who had been touched by the drama at Central High. I wrote and called, and then traveled to Little Rock to speak with them. They listened, interested, polite. Those in the white community shrugged and said, "I don't know anyone; I'm new in town; I wasn't here back then." The closest I came was an occasional individual who said, "Gee, I think I vaguely remember hearing that someone or other had graduated from Central High that year. Who could that have been?" I approached Governor Faubus; he was only too happy to talk, but not about introducing me to others who had played roles in the drama. In the black community, I more easily found people who had been leaders back then, for there had been less out-migration from Little Rock—and, I suspected, there was more pride, less shame in the roles they had played. It was also a smaller community; people knew exactly who was where when back then, and now. Eventually, just by hanging around, I began to find slim links to others who'd been involved, to white students in the school at the time, to friends of the governor, to the children of school officials, and so on. One person directed me to others, and slowly my list of interviewees grew like the snowball so often referred to by academics to describe this type of sample selection.

With limited means at my disposal and a desire to listen deeply rather than broadly, I chose a relatively small number of interviewees (about sixty in all) who had lived the history of Central High from a variety of positions. There are many other ways to approach a study like mine. Random selection of interviewees, investigation based on standardized questionnaires, explorations from other more institutional perspectives, would yield useful but different insights. I knew that for every interview I did I was not doing many possible others. But I was relatively unconcerned with randomness and, much as I would have liked to continue the conversations endlessly with many other people, I accepted the limitations of my means. For what I was after was exploring a common set of relationships, having as much to do with dynamics and processes as with the informational content of people's stories, and I believed that any person's story would lead me there. I was therefore willing to accept the relative narrowness of a snowball sample. I did, however, make an attempt to cover certain bases. While my primary objective was to understand those who most mystified me, white people who resisted desegregation, in order to understand the wider context I also interviewed white integrationists and members of Little Rock's black community. However different the experiences of blacks and whites in America, our society is one and our fates depend profoundly on each other. I believe that white lives in this country cannot be understood outside the context of black lives, because whiteness is so deeply assumed by white people to represent "normality." It is only when the scope of vision is expanded to include the lives of people of color that we can see the hidden assumptions which most influence our construction of reality and therefore our choices. Moreover, it is evident from the white interviewees' own stories that their lives were intimately intertwined with the black people who served them, who challenged them, who existed unnoticed in every aspect of their daily activities. All those transactions were intrinsic to the drama of Central High, and because they were the point of intersection of two very different realities, I knew I could not begin to do credit to the stories of whites if I didn't also understand the lives of blacks.

Many of the names I use in this book are fictitious. Most of my interviewees were uneasy about being identified, worried that what they had to say would be unpopular with their peers and neighbors, or embarrassing to themselves. I have sought to protect their confidentiality, often using pseudonyms (indicated in the text in boldface the first time they are mentioned) and disguising details. In some cases, however, people played roles that cannot be disguised; some of those people eventually withdrew from the study, while others generously agreed to let me use their true names. I have quoted the interviews at great length, because I know there is nothing I can write that comes anywhere close to the richness, texture, and honesty of the spoken word. Writing this book, I imagined myself in a long and intricate conversation, a continuation of the actual conversations that constituted the interviews themselves. To be sure, in the written version I am privileged, for I have ultimate editorial say (although a number of people whose stories appear below have read the text and argued points with me in ways that are reflected in the final version).

Early in my project, I decided not to try formally to interview the nine African-American students. It was a confusing choice. On the one hand, their view of events was crucial to any reconstruction of the history. Who else but they knew the details of what happened that year as they lived them? But the Nine share a peculiar circumstance: they are both injured individuals and public personae. Their experiences were intensely hurtful on a personal level. Others were experiencing social change; they were living a nightmare. At the same time, their experiences are public property. When I began interviewing people, the stories of the Nine had been told many times by other people: Mrs. Elizabeth Huckaby, the vice principal; Daisy Bates, the head of the NAACP; film companies and journalists and scholars. As I formulated my project, I learned that some among the Nine had reached moments in their lives when they wanted to tell their own stories. Melba Pattillo Beals was writing a book. Ernest Green was working with Disney to film his version. Others were tired, burned by public appearances, doubtful of the benefits to them of participating in the study.

It seemed to me they were right. I, a white woman, could perform a very particular role: to explore the stories of other white people who had lived a moment in history by which I, too, had been shaped. I knew from previous studies how much the "stars" of a drama draw the eye, often eclipsing the reality that many other players are central to the plot, however much they may be seen to be—and see themselves as being—peripheral. So it seemed a reasonable premise to concentrate on unnamed participants in the drama of Little Rock, both black and white, and to rely on published and produced accounts of the Nine's experiences as they themselves chose to portray them.

What follows is therefore not a history of school desegregation in Little Rock, but rather many histories of some people's experience of that past time and, in the context of their life stories, many treatises on their wishes and disappointments, resentments and satisfactions, passions and distortions both then and now. It is often hard to read disparate versions of seemingly singular events without seeing them as competing for truth. I urge you to read each story as a facet of a greater whole, a single dance in a ballet with structure and meaning, even though the overall design may not be obvious when viewed from a particular seat in the audience nor from the perspective of an individual dancer. Grounded in the past, the recollections of Central High's desegregation I heard are truly about the present, about searing social issues which endure through time, which affect us all, but which *can* be changed. I seek to make a contribution to change by exploring several interlocking themes:

- Why many white Americans have come to believe they lack agency to change the conditions of their lives;
- How racial identities and attitudes interlock with class and gender identities in ways that often invest race with responsibility for that which is problematic in other arenas of life;
- And, finally, how emotion and beliefs, individual memory and community discourse work to translate social structures of power into the dynamics that shape race relations in America today.

TWO
The Big Gate

Little Rock has always had very good race relations.
—Wesley Pruden Jr.

*They thought the Negro wasn't protesting. . . . But you ought to
go and listen to them down at the big gate.*
—Reverend Rufus Young

To the outside world, the crisis at Central High sprang full-blown
from the pages of a newspaper or the screen of a television set. But to
the people who lived the crisis in Little Rock, it was a moment in a
continuum of time reaching back before their births to a collective
past. I begin, therefore, not with accounts of 1957, but with life stories
from the times before, in order to sketch the context, a sort of scaf-
folding on which the history of Central High was built. Interweaving
fact with myth, family stories with collective ones, tales told by elders
with data learned from books, the accounts which follow are no less
accurate than those in the official histories—and for purposes of this
work, more informative.

Wesley Pruden Jr.

I met Wesley Pruden in a cafe in Washington, D.C. A dapper white
man, soft-spoken and erudite, he wove a pretty tapestry of Arkansas
history that veered back and forth from the personal to the social:

> My family arrived in Arkansas in 18—. Well, my father's
> family arrived in 1840. Some of the family on my father's
> mother's side arrived in the late eighteenth century. There were

only three hundred, I think three hundred white families in the state when we first got there.[1]

Where did they come from?

North Carolina and Georgia.

And before that? What's your European heritage?

English. We're English. My father's family's been in North America for about three hundred and fifty years. One branch went to New England. I have a relative who was one of Cotton Mather's associates. But the good branch went south, to North Carolina.

What's wrong with the other branch?

Well, they're close to the Yankees. That's a joke more than anything else.

They were quite well-to-do by the standards of the time in North Carolina. They owned land and owned a fishery on the coast. I'm not real sure why they came to Arkansas. We believe they were headed to California, actually, or at least somewhere in the West.

You have to understand that Arkansas was populated in many ways like Australia. It was a lot of riff-raff. The western migrations all went practically due west. Tennessee was settled by North Carolina, and Arkansas was settled by Tennessee. It goes that way.

Until early this century, the eastern third of Arkansas was a swamp, almost impenetrable. You had to cross the Mississippi River, and once you crossed the river you were worse off than you had been, because you still had forty, fifty miles of swamp, with lots of snakes and alligators. As a result, the wagon trains got to the river and, if they were going west, they either went north through Missouri, or they went south through Louisiana, which left Arkansas a backwater. Plus the fact that Oklahoma, which is on the western side of Arkansas, was Indian territory; it was set aside for the five Indian tribes. So once you got there, you either had to stay, or get out the way you came in. As a result Arkansas was largely unpopulated compared to the states around it well into this century. And the frontier really didn't close until this century.

My father was born in 1908 in the little town of Alexander, Arkansas, which is practically a suburb of Little Rock now; it's about fifteen miles away. But when I was growing up, it was quite remote. He had heartbreaking stories to tell about two little brothers who died while he was a child. One of them died of diphtheria, and I don't know what the other one died of. But mostly they died because there was no doctor in the community, and there was no way to get to the doctor in Little Rock, which today would be very close, but in those days it was a half-a-day's ride in a buggy.

So that colored the way people thought about things. They're very insular people. I know when I was a kid growing up and went to school in the forties, in the war years, one of the things we were taught is that Arkansas alone among the states could be so totally self-sufficient that you could build a wall around the state and we could survive, because we had everything we needed. I don't know whether that's true or not, but it certainly does give kids a very interesting view about themselves and about the people they live among.

And the truth of the matter is that psychologically a wall pretty much was erected around the state.

Outside observers in the early part of the last century corroborated Wesley's version of Arkansas history. Charles Daubeny, a professor from Oxford University in England, visited a family not forty miles away from Little Rock in 1837, and described its head, a man named Walker, as "one of the best specimens of an American yeoman, with somewhat of a Presbyterian cast about him." Less sympathetically, a French observer at the same time, Joseph Latrobe, commented, "Many a man, born and educated for better things, but who, living badly or freely in the old states, lastly mortgaging his estate and plunging irrevocably in debt, made over his debts to his older son, stole a horse, and off to Arkansas!"

Buried amid Daubeny's glowing descriptions of yeoman life in Arkansas is one reference to another side of things:

> Where the negroes [sic] are chiefly employed in farming concerns, and are not numerous, the institution of slavery assumes something of a patriarchal character, and

each proprietor may be regarded in the light of a country
squire, having much time at his disposal, and exercising a
species of feudal sway over his dependants.[2]

Widely overlooked by visitors at the time and by historians in the twentieth century was the existence of a small but growing black population. Although there were few if any large slaveholdings, many of the
white yeoman families owned one or two slaves. By the time Arkansas
became a state in 1836, the Missouri Compromise of 1820 had ensured
the legality of slavery within its borders. When the Confederacy formed
twenty-five years later, Arkansas joined, not without some controversy.
Out of a white population of 325,000, minimally 40,000 men went off
to fight with Johnny Reb, while 6,000 enlisted with the federal troops.[3]
By that time, about one in three Arkansans was black.[4] Many were
occupied with mining and with cotton cultivation which had by then
expanded into Arkansas.

Reverend Rufus Young

When I talked with Reverend Rufus Young, a black man in his
eighties, retired minister of a Little Rock church that had played a role
in desegregating Central High, I got a picture of Arkansas at once different and in other ways strikingly similar to Wesley's:

> I was born out in the country. Born and reared out there on
> my granddaddy's farm, my granddaddy who was a slave. Twenty-
> one years old when he was set free. He was donated a one-
> hundred-and-sixty-acre tract from the state—at that time if you
> fenced in and cleared up a certain area in a certain length of time,
> they gave you a deed to it. So my granddaddy got a deed to that
> in 1877. It's been in the family ever since. That's where I was born
> and reared, out there on Granddaddy's farm.
>
> Went to school out there until at least eighth grade. Wasn't
> anybody in grade with me out there so I ... came out to Dermott,
> Skye School in Dermott. Chicot County Training School, that's
> where I finished high school.

We were sitting in the living room of Reverend Young's home in
North Little Rock. Shelves of books lined one wall, and stacks of

magazines dotted the furniture. Mrs. Young apologized for the clut-
ter, explaining they were in the middle of sorting papers. She left us
to talk, by the sounds that reached us keeping busy nearby in a back
room. The phone rang frequently, but Mrs. Young only rarely interrupted the flow of our conversation to consult her husband.
Meanwhile, Reverend Young moved from one recollection to another,
chuckling deeply as he spoke, attentive to my reactions and questions.
He was that rare combination of an accomplished storyteller and a
sensitive listener.

As he described his education and I observed his books and papers,
I asked him where the premium on education had come from in his
family, which led him to tell me about his grandfather's second wife:

> Strangely enough, my granddaddy never went to school a day
> in his life. He was twenty-one years old when he was set free. And
> my grandmother— Of course, really it was my stepgrandmother.
> My real grandmother, my daddy's mother, died before I was born
> so I didn't know anything about her. But my real grandmother
> couldn't have been any more dear to me than my stepgrand-
> mother. Even though she'd never been to school, she was about
> two years old when she was set free. She'd never been to school
> but two months in her life. We all marvel now at how much she
> was on top of things. Of course, she said herself that some super-
> intendent down there wanted her to teach. She had never been in
> school but they wanted to hire her to teach school. . . . [laughs]
>
> I recall that a Baptist preacher came to our church—there
> were two churches in that community: African Methodist
> Church and Missionary Baptist Church. Well, he was Baptist.
> And he wanted to come up here to go to school at the Baptist
> college. One local Baptist preacher criticized him that he had to
> go to school to learn how to preach. "God call you to preach, you
> open your mouth and God'll fill it." Well, my grandmother
> responded to what he had said. She said, "Yes, God will fill it. Just
> as full of air as he can get. Come on y'all and let's give this man
> some money to go over there and go to school."
>
> She had never been to school too much in her life, but she
> had got insight into the value of education in one's life. When I
> left, Grandpa wanted me to go to school. It's gotta be Grandma's
> influence.

And where were your parents at that time?

My father died when I was four years old. He was living there on Grandfather's place, that's where I was born, with my mother. But he was out selling logs one time, December. Contracted pneumonia. At that time they didn't know how to treat pneumonia. He died of pneumonia at the age of thirty-five.

Both black and white people died for lack of care. Both black and white people earned their living cutting and selling wood. Both demonstrated a certain yeoman-like entrepreneurial spirit, although under very different conditions. Both moved from country to city, following an upward class trajectory in the first half of the century.

Wesley, too, had grounded his life story in his father's experience of urbanization. Settling first on a poor vegetable farm, they'd turned to the timber industry for sustenance. "Arkansas's always been a great timber state, even now three quarters of the state is covered with timber, more timber now than there was in 1900, interesting enough." Finally, in 1927 the family moved to Little Rock. "My grandfather thought his prospects would be better," Wesley said, "and then they always lived there."

Like Reverend Young, Wesley's father became a minister, and he, too, eventually played a prominent role in the crisis at Central High. When the conversation turned to the topic of race relations, both agreed that their shared history contained injustices, but when it came to the question of who was disadvantaged, their stories diverged wildly. Wesley had claimed:

> Little Rock has always had very good race relations, in part because it doesn't have the large black population that some other southern cities do. I don't know what it is in Little Rock; it's probably around 20 percent, I guess. As opposed to Memphis, which is about half and half, and New Orleans which is probably predominantly black. The cities that had the trouble is where you had about a fifty-fifty split.
>
> But anyway, the race relations were always good. Even after the trouble started, the anger of the white segregationists was not at the blacks. It was at the white power establishment. I always thought that if they had desegregated the other high school when that school was built around '53, '54, it was built

with the desegregation process in mind, and they were going to sacrifice Central and they felt they could keep Hall either all white or mostly white. Had they gone the other way, had the people who were promoting desegregation taken the view that we will set an example, I don't think anybody would ever have heard of Little Rock.

The working-class neighborhoods felt like people in the more affluent neighborhoods were saying, "This will be good for you; do it." And it made everybody very angry.

Plus the fact that there is no question that in 1957 attitudes were very different than they are now. And I've never made any apology for my father or for my friends there who had attitudes that by today's standards are quite puzzling, baffling, not even understandable. Because that's just the way it was.

Young people today, in my own family, my nephews, have asked me, "Well, what did you think about segregation?" And the answer is, I didn't think about it. It was just the way it always was, and it was like, we don't think about it being Sunday morning when it's Sunday morning. But I think it's foolish to judge previous generations by our own. I mean, Jefferson owned slaves. It's true he also gave us our country, you might say. God knows what later generations are going to think about us, some of our silly attitudes.

If I were explaining to a man from Mars, or even someone from California, I would say it's important to keep that in mind, that it was a class, very much a class thing that fed the desegregation effort.

At the time of desegregation, most white Arkansans believed, as Wesley did, that race relations in their state were amicable. Indeed, back then many black citizens had agreed, too. It was a view I heard echoed in Evelyn's surprise at the uproar outside Central High. But few African Americans then or now thought desegregation was more about white class distinctions than about race, and, however peaceable they described things as being, nobody black and of sufficient age was without stories of Jim Crow and their personal injuries. I asked Reverend Young about his experiences of black-white relations growing up in rural Arkansas in the early years of the century, and he first explained how few whites there were in his world:

Out there in the country, see, only one white family lived
out there. He was sort of the straw boss, the nephew of Bill
Martin, big farmer, and he owned a farm out there adjacent to
our farm. He and his wife lived out there, sort of overseer of the
farm. But didn't have any contact with him, though.

It didn't take much contact for the few whites around to make a
big impact on the young Rufus:

Where race relations were concerned, first, in those days you
had to have a license to hunt. [When I went to get one,] there
was a line of colored people to get a license from the white family
that gave them out. [The white woman] was filling out that form.
And when it got to the point it said, "Color," she looked at me
and she wrote, "Yellow." [laughs] I was one of them yellow niggers. Well, I laughed about that, because that was the first time,
that incident passed on in my memory.

How old were you then?

I was about in my teens, about fourteen, fifteen, something
like that.

What did you think about that?

How ridiculous it was, she didn't know how to classify me.
All she had read on there "colored." Colored. That's what they
called you, colored. Didn't call you nigger, called you colored.
There wasn't but five races, and I guess I knowed I wasn't a member of the yellow race.

Stories rolled off the reverend's tongue, and as they rolled on they
became progressively less funny and more painful:

But my real first contact with what I'd call a real experience
of racism, they had a postmaster there in Dermott, a postmaster.
[...] You was afraid to ask him, if you had a penny coming back,
you afraid to ask him for your change. He took a lot of pennies
like that. One day—I saw this with my own eyes—a boy, he
hadn't been tampered with at all, he was black. He looked out
there and said, "Boy, how come you so black?!" "Well, I don't
know sir." "Tell me, you black devil!" Well, that just sort of grind
me on the inside, when he talked to the boy like that. "Devil
made you black."

Then they had a man, a ticket agent there at the railroad station. He was quite a racist. He hated black folks, seemed like.
Wouldn't sell you a ticket. Sell white folks tickets first. He
wouldn't sell you a ticket, walked in there. However near the time
[for your train], he'd wait on white folks but he wouldn't wait
on you. Then you'd have a close call trying to get on a train, see.

Those were minor incidents, the first real incident was when
I got on the bus. I caught myself a Southern Pacific bus, they didn't
have any Trailways or Greyhound buses running at that time. But
Southern Pacific had a bus, it was Southern Pacific Railroad. . . . I
was on a bus that morning, paid my fare, and you had to sit in the
back, your seats were on the back of the bus. 'Course whites got
to sit both front and back. If a white got on before you did, and if
they filled up they could sit from front to the back, all the way
back. So at that time they wouldn't sit two to a seat. One would
sit here and one would sit here and one would sit there and you
couldn't sit down by one of these. You had to look out one of them
vacant seats. [chuckles]

I got on at Dermott and I got a seat. Got up there around
Dumas somewhere, got crowded. The operator made me get up
and give a white man my seat and put me back there with the
luggage. They had a luggage compartment, didn't have a luggage
compartment up under there like they have now, but it was in
the rear of the bus. You opened the door and you go back and
have some seat they let down from the wall and you sit back there
with the luggage. So that wasn't fair to me, I paid the same fare
that the white man paid and then I had to get up and give him
my seat and go down and sit with the luggage. Being out from
the country, I hadn't made that a custom.

I got up there to Little Rock, went down there at the railroad station and there was a cafe across the road, think they
called it White Eagle. But we couldn't go in the front, we had to
go around and come in the kitchen, they cooked back there and
they served us back there in the kitchen. [laughs]

Reverend Young's stories had a clear progression of points: from
"funny" anecdotes of white ignorance, to white insults of black people,
to unjust actions endured. Now Rufus told me of his own growing
anger:

Well, I had two similar experiences down in Baton Rouge, Louisiana. It was the Greyhound bus then, it was in the forties. That other'd been back there in the thirties. In the forties I got on a Greyhound bus there in Baton Rouge to go on over to Hamlin, Louisiana. Same thing. 'Course they had a sign up there, only the operators supposed to move that sign, it was moveable, but the black folks sit behind that sign, whites sit in front of it.

So there were about five or six vacant seats there and no seats vacant behind that sign. I had to stand up and moved down to a vacant seat. So I stood up there and looking down at the vacant seat and the operator, he looking through the rearview mirror to keep an eye on me. He thought I was going to sit down in one of those vacant seats, which I did.

Soon as I hit the seat, he hit the brake. Boom. Jumped up and, "Get up from there! Get back there behind that sign!" [laughs] I could see what Rosa Parks felt down there in Birmingham and Montgomery, Alabama. But I didn't have the nerve she had. Made me mad as it made her.

So I got back there. He was saving those seats for—we got down the road there, I guess about eight or ten miles, about ten or twelve white kids got on going to school. Saving their seats for them. [chuckles]

Then we got to Hamlin, I changed to go on into Jackson, Mississippi. Same situation. Whites sitting one to a seat. One to a seat, two seats on this side and one to a seat, two seats on that side. And so four people were taking up the space for eight people. If they had moved up and sat together that would have left two seats back there for blacks to sit, but they sat one to a seat and we blacks standing up there. It was hot, August. That's when I really got angry. For the first time ever I sensed the reason for a big cause.

White man sitting there right by me, he had his Bible out reading. I couldn't sit down there while he read the Bible. I just imagined he must have been a preacher reading the Bible. I'm a preacher and I couldn't sit down there by him. I said, if that Bible tells him to treat me like he treat me, away with that Bible.

If I had any money, I'd have gotten off that bus and bought the biggest car I could find. [laughs] Then it came to me that's the reason why our folks will buy a big car. They criticize black folk for buying a big car, but I appreciate why they'd buy a big car. They will do that. Of course, if I had any money I'd have done that same thing. [laughs heartily] [. . .]

In Birmingham, Alabama, I tried to transfer my insurance [policy]. Got the address to one of the main buildings downtown. They had four elevators. So I went to the first one, the elevator came down, had a black operator and nothing got off but white. The black operator did that— [gestures with his thumb to the side] So I stepped over to the next one. It came down. Nobody got off but white. Black operator did that— [gestures again] So I stepped over to the next one. It came down. Nothing got off but white. Black operator. [gestures, laughs] I said, "What's going on here?" So the fourth one, it came down. Black and white got off of that one. [laughs] So when I got on, nobody got on but me. I talked to the operator, I said, "Is this the only elevator black can ride?" He said, "Yeah, and sometimes white folks crowd them off of this one. Makes me so damn mad I don't know what to do." [laughs] The irony of the situation was, they could ride with blacks on that one, but they couldn't ride with them on the others. Crazy.

As Reverend Young catalogued injustice after injustice, he also described a common component of the experience of discrimination. Externally, in his visible behavior, he capitulated to necessity. He might consider refusing to comply, but he didn't "have the nerve." That self-condemnation, I thought, hinted at psychological scars left by what was a reasonable strategy, given the reality of violence suffered by black people who historically had stood up to white racism. How Reverend Young did express his noncompliance was in ridiculing the racist mores he was forced to accept. I commented on that internal dynamic and he characterized it brilliantly:

So there was a good deal of rumbling and protest going on among black people during this period you're speaking of? People were complaining?

Oh, yeah. They do what you call complain down at the big gate.

Down at the big gate?

Now that's an expression that came out of a story. One Negro said, "I cussed that old boy out."

Says, "You did?"

"Yeah, cussed him out."

"What did he do?"

"He didn't do nothin', I cussed him out."

So he decided he's going to cuss him out, too. [But] that boy beat him up. Went back, told his friend, "I thought you said that old boy didn't do anything. When I cussed him out, he beat me up."

"Where did you cuss him?"

"I cussed him to his face."

"I did better than that. I cussed him down at the big gate."

So always been protests down at the big gate, where they couldn't hear what you said. Down at the big gate. Always did. That kind of cussing going on, where you're grinnin' when you ain't tickled and scratchin' where you don't itch.

[When the Supreme Court ordered desegregation] then all these white politicians, they'd get up and make statements, "We're getting along all right. If these outside agitators didn't come in here, well, everything all right." They thought the Negro wasn't protesting out loud, because they were protesting down at the big gate. They thought they were satisfied, happy with the way it was. They ain't never been satisfied or happy with the way they were treated.

But you ought to go and listen to them down at the big gate. When they get up there in front of you, they smile and scratch whether or not they itching. Grin when they not tickled. That what you call Uncle Tomming, that's a method of survival. Surviving in the situation. So they mistook that for their being satisfied, but they weren't satisfied.

"Little Rock has always had very good race relations," said Wesley. As I listened to Reverend Young describe the strategic manner in which vulnerable black people protested, "down at the big gate," it made more sense to me that both blacks and whites would be surprised and aggrieved by the drama at Central High. Black people had learned long since to mute their anger, sensing that below the surface of "good race relations" there lay another reality. That blacks protested "down at the big gate," unheard by whites, colluded with the commonly held illusion among whites that black people were content with the status quo, an illusion promoted by their peaceable day-to-day transactions with black servants in their own homes. But while black people strategized in self-defense, white people viewed the resulting silence as peace, not submission. Most white people did not believe themselves to be capable of violence; they believed those who were, were a contemptible minority. But at the same time they had no comprehension of how influential the violent minority were. The very real history of brutality by whites affected the everyday consciousness of blacks and constrained their expressions of disaffection at the society that treated them unequally.

Jerome Muldrew

Jerome Muldrew illustrated this point early on in our conversation. A generation younger than Reverend Young, Jerome's experience of being black in Arkansas reflected the changing times in which he came to adulthood. Muted but not silenced, Jerome's protest was eventually heard well inside the "big gate."

Several people suggested I talk with Mr. Muldrew for reasons that were not altogether clear to me. Nobody was able to name a particular role he had played in the drama of Central High. But he was currently a teacher in the school, as well as someone who seemed to evoke a marked respect from his peers in the African-American community of Little Rock. I called him, and he agreed to see me, although on the phone I couldn't quite tell what he felt about talking with me. He spoke without much emphasis as we made a date to meet at the school on a Friday afternoon, at the end of the last day of summer session.

Although I'd circled Central High in my rental car as soon as I arrived in Little Rock, this was the first time I had been inside the building. I made my way to the office, gaping at the grand dimensions and art deco adornments of the corridors. Expansive like everything else in the building, the office was divided in half by a long counter. I informed a secretary that I was looking for Mr. Muldrew, and she asked me to wait, gesturing toward a row of chairs across the room. After a few minutes, a short, unassuming-looking man approached the counter. He gave no hint of recognition. The secretary spoke quietly to him, and he completed some business with her before he looked my way. Greeting me without a smile, he proposed we talk in a counselor's office. I thought we were in for a cool conversation.

We went through some doors, and Jerome asked a man seated behind a desk for the use of a room. "OK," he said, "but they'll be locking up promptly at 3:30. You'll have to be sure to be out of the building by then." Jerome nodded confidently, although my heart sank a bit. It was well after two o'clock by then, and I hoped our talk would be longer than an hour—although Jerome's cool manner had begun to make me doubtful about my chances.

We settled into a small, barren room behind the office, and Jerome began without prompting to tell me about himself:

> My father was a shipping clerk. He was actually multi-talented, held various occupations; he was a chef for the Arkansas School for the Deaf and Blind, a Pullman porter for the Missouri Pacific Railroad, and a musician. My mother was a housewife. I'm the youngest of five children, and we're an all-boy family. Basically, we were all born and raised here in Little Rock.
>
> We lived out in the west section of Little Rock, in a salt-and-pepper neighborhood, out the vicinity of Pulaski Heights and Stifft Station. And we were raised in a pretty pleasant environment, a healthy biracial environment. People got along well together.
>
> And maybe except for some bitter feelings in 1926, before my birth—1926, there was a black that was lynched in Little Rock during that time, at Ninth and Main Street. He was Lonnie Dixon. So, we did have some little flare-ups, some flare-ups of that type, during that particular period.

I had heard stories of this lynching before, although never described as a "little flare-up." The lynching had happened some months before Jerome was born. I wondered how it had affected his consciousness growing up, and I asked when he'd heard about it:

> I was aware of that story as a child, I knew what was happening. It's very vague in my mind; the details are unclear. I'm

sixty-six years old, I was born in 1926. So this was handed down, the story handed down, you know, by word of mouth from parents, neighbors, and so forth. [. . .]

It was published during that particular period. Now, I wasn't reading, but they kept old newspaper clippings of what was occurring as far as Little Rock was concerned and I was introduced to it orally and reintroduced to it when I learned how to read and write. So, we knew about it, it was just a thing everybody in Little Rock [knew]. I think he was lynched at Bethel Church, on Ninth and Broadway, a black church.

The story I heard about that lynching was that they thought he had committed a crime, but it turned out it was the wrong man—

That's right.

—that he had not.

He had not, that's true. I heard about that when I was a child.

I began to comprehend that the phrase "little flare-up" suggested something substantive. The story gave dimension to Reverend Young's account of black people's reticence, demonstrating how a common understanding of danger came to be shared by everyone in the black community, just as the rising and setting of the sun was known to everyone, and its meaning, like sunrise—like Sunday morning—was self-evident: life was "pretty pleasant," but it could turn ugly. The lynching was "little" in that it was a symbolic act, a sharp threat to the community which never materialized into wholesale acts of brutality but made perfectly clear the possibilities.[5] How Jerome understood that lesson, what he subsequently made of it, was the story he went on to tell me. But first he recounted his experiences in his family and as a young man:

I attended Dunbar Junior High, Dunbar Senior High, and Dunbar Junior College. The Dunbar High School building housed three levels of education. But my education was interrupted. In May of 1944, I was drafted into the army. I served in the segregated army. I was with the engineering corps, and I attended drafting school. My company was a dump truck company, so there was no use for my schooling after I even graduated from it. So I was placed as a clerk, I worked there as a clerk.

I also was, I was, I am or was talented. I got that from my father. He formed a band called "Oliver and His Blue Rhythms" in the late twenties and thirties. This was during the jazz movement in America and heyday of West Ninth Street, known as "The Line."

And I was a part of the Seventh Service Command, what we called Special Service. We formed a quartet entertaining other GI's. Seventh Service Command. [. . .] I was a singer, so we formed a swing quartet—fellows from all over the United States. And we performed shows and this type of thing.

Jerome was shipped out to Japan and Okinawa, where he was stationed when the atomic bomb was dropped on Hiroshima and Nagasaki, and the war ended. Those experiences in the military influenced his future substantially. All but one of his brothers had also been drafted (the oldest son was exempted), and Jerome went on the tell me about the aftermath for him and his family:

> We all came through . . . , and that was a blessing. Number one that we were returned, and also a blessing that we were all educated under the GI Bill of Rights. And all of us have received college educations.

> *Your oldest brother, too?*

> Yes, yeah, he went to college, also. All of us graduated from Philander Smith College [a traditionally black college located in Little Rock].

> *Were you the first generation in your family to go to college, or did your parents go to college?*

> My father attended college, Philander Smith College, but he did not complete college. My mother did not attend college. So, that's right, umm-hmm, first in my immediate family. We were the first to *graduate* from college, I'll put it like that.

> *Clearly there was some value you got in your family about—*

> Oh, yes, definitely, oh yes, my father was well educated. He also taught music and the like, and we were very devoted to edu-

cation. As children, we always had some kind of library in our house, whether it was a beat-up set of encyclopedias or not, we'd have something to read, always, in our house. And we were very devoted to education.

We also had a lot of community organizations during that particular period, too. My father was head, you know, just in our neighborhoods of organizations [that] dealt with church work, recreation, this type of thing. [. . .] We were all members of a church, the Christian Methodist Episcopal Church, and Baptist, and so forth. We were Protestants.

Jerome grew up in a family where goals and values were consistent with the community in which he lived. It was, in his description, a "healthy biracial environment." But in the greater outside world that he encountered during the war, Jerome met quite another reality. For many African-American men, the Second World War marked a turning point. Not only did it underscore ideological contradictions between serving in a segregated army while fighting anti-Semitism and injustice in Europe and Asia, but it also gave men greater access to education than their parents had had. I wondered what effect on other levels Jerome's war experiences had on him:

> *When you came back from the war, what was your feeling at being back in Little Rock?*
>
> To me, I had a good feeling coming back to Little Rock. It was in the forties, '46, spring of '46 I came back to Little Rock, and I went back to school immediately, almost immediately.
>
> *You didn't have any questions about going to school?*
>
> Oh, no, no, we knew all the time we were going. [laughter]
>
> *Did you know you were going to be a teacher?*
>
> No, I really wanted to be a lawyer, that's why I majored in the social sciences rather than just one specific area. And, of course, I didn't go to Law School. I guess I wasn't that ambitious or something.
>
> But anyway, we graduated from college and I didn't intend to teach. Since I didn't go to Law School, I wanted to do something with this education, and so I decided I would teach, and I

taught in the public schools, and also coached football, basketball, track. And I went back to school later on and received my
master's degree from University of Arkansas in Fayetteville . . .
in education.

When I got out of the service, I really didn't have any problems, we didn't have any racial problems, in our immediate city,
other than we were accepting, I guess, we accepted segregated
facilities—that is, riding on the back of the bus, sitting in the
balcony of a movie, drinking out of colored and white fountains,
riding at the front of the train.

We all were asking ourselves, what, you know, what is the
place for the Negro, where is it, you know? When you ride the bus,
it's at the back of the bus [chuckles], when you're in the movie, it's
in the balcony of the movie, so there was all this movement of
people around. [chuckles]

By this time in our conversation something magical had happened. Speaking in a calm, uninflected way, Jerome had captivated
me. Partly, it was his droll humor, which had both bite and sweetness
to it. But also his emotional understatement somehow expressed a
depth of feeling that had me leaning forward, hearing in his frequent
pauses and repetitions of words and phrases not uncertainty, but
rather a carefully constructed articulation of a complex reality. He,
too, seemed to be warming to our conversation. Positive as his account
of white-black relations had so far been, he gradually began to talk
about the painful parts more fully and with more outrage:

But I did want to mention this, during the war when I was
a high-school student at Dunbar, we did have a serious problem
existing on West Ninth Street when one of our black soldiers was
killed by a Little Rock policeman. Name of Sergeant Foster.
Needless to say, these black troops were moved out of Little Rock
hours after the killing occurred. And our reaction was, as kids,
first horror and later anger. In protest, we made up a song to the
tune of "Let's Remember Pearl Harbor," and we changed the
words to "Let's Remember Sergeant Foster." This was our way of
protesting as black and Negro high-school students. So, I think
that would be one of the keys to us when we were in high school.

Second thing that happened to us in high school was the fact that we had some *strong* teachers, black teachers at Dunbar, and they were willing to stick their necks out for themselves and us. Dr. John Lewis was the head of the faculty during that particular period, and we won a teachers' salary dispute in Little Rock. I was a student in high school, I think that was '42 or '43. It was a battle for equal salaries for teachers of African descent, and Thurgood Marshall was attorney for the teachers. Some of our teachers were fired, they just simply lost their jobs, later they were re-hired, years and years later they were re-hired. One, Rosemary Walker, taught me biology then—teachers taught everything, too. She was really a foreign language major. And Dr. Gibson, Reverend Gibson, who taught me math, he also was on the firing line. Gwendolyn McConaco was on the firing line, Dr. Lewis, Mrs. Sue Cowan, Morris Williams, all our teachers were on the battlefield for a just cause.

We won that case. And that gave a very strong impetus to what could be done in a moderate climate. Now, we really didn't, we weren't oppressed like say people in Montgomery, where you had a large black population. We were oppressed but it was never the type of thing that would create violence.

Jerome's story was a finely tuned mixture of forbearance and resistance. Life was peaceful, not as bad as in Montgomery. But at the same time he was deeply influenced by the tragedy of Sergeant Foster and inspired by the teachers' victory, the first overt activism in which Jerome had taken part, an encouraging training ground for what was to come. The war experience layered a consciousness formed at home, which in turn was layered on a tradition of everyday acts of resistance to racial injustice. Protest at this level took the form of prideful attitudes and small acts of rebellion.

Jerome went on to tell me how black and white youths had played together: "We'd play Sunday baseball together. And played football together." Moreover, they'd made mischief together, too, which was, one might suppose, even more a bonding experience: "We'd slip into the boys' club down there, play all we wanted to." In light of that camaraderie, I asked how it felt to walk past Central High every day on his way to Dunbar while his white sport-mates went inside:

Well, to tell the truth, we were very proud of Dunbar. Dunbar was the only black high school in Arkansas. And we had a lot to be proud of.

When I passed by Central High, Little Rock High School, I just said, "Well I've got a high school, too. I love mine. I hope you love yours." [laughs] That type of thing.

Even if you had white friends, there was no discussion, we even played together, came back from the service we palled around—we didn't pal around together, but we were on good speaking terms and this kind of stuff.

As Jerome struggled to name the quality of "pals/not-pals," he began to describe more and more deeply the "not-pals" side of the picture:

We did have some problems, some fights, some white-black fights on the streetcars, you know, and occasionally . . . they would overpower us because the fact that you had all white policemen. So, there you have it, that same ingrained discriminatory ———— It was sort of futile to physically attack them, but I think we outsmarted them.

What kind of things would cause friction on the streetcars?

Seating. For example, I might not feel that good that day. I might not feel like sitting on the back of the bus. And there'd be a seat in the white section, nobody'd be sitting there. You could sit there, the conductor would come back and tell you to move out of that seat. Well, now he's got a confrontation right there. See, this is the type of thing that would do it.

It's funny, funny about color. The posted ordinance read, "White passengers seat from the front and colored passengers seat from the rear." The problem would arise when a light-skinned African American was mistaken for a European American and sat from the front. My mother was light skinned, and she got on the bus and she sat wherever she wanted to, they would never even question her ethnicity. [laughs] She didn't do it on purpose, but she could, if she got tired now, she'd sit right down there. And even some of the white passengers who didn't know any better, would offer her a seat. [laughs] But that was my mother, you know, my natural mother. [laughter]

*Did it happen when you were with your mother? Did you
end up sitting in the back while she was in the front?*

Yeah, yeah, oh, sure. You know, I wouldn't raise anything,
I'd say, That's good. Sit right down.

It happened in hospitals, when she was a patient in Arkansas
Baptist Hospital, even after most barriers of segregation were
torn down in Little Rock. The white patients would question
whether or not I was her son when I would come see her, even
when we had integrated wards.

Jerome noted these injustices and contradictions long before he
could act overtly to bring about change. Agency consists of a state of
mind that precedes action, an acknowledgment of wrongs done, a
willingness to engage in everyday acts of protest. It is an uncomfort-
able state in which to exist, because it involves the dual consciousness
of wrongs to be righted and of a certain powerlessness to make them
right. I asked Jerome how he'd handled that dilemma, if he'd consciously sought acts of rebellion:

Yeah, definitely. Yeah, I was rebellious. You would rebel
against the system, in your own way.

*What were other ways in which you were able to rebel?
Maybe one way was to have so much pride in your own school.*

Yeah, I did, I had a lot of pride in my school, which I
thought, I thought it was just as good as Central. I didn't know
it was, I didn't know [laughs] it was inferior to Central until the
1940s. But [laughs] I thought it was a pretty good school.

*Did you become convinced that it was inferior after that
time, or do you still think that it was comparable?*

I'd say it was inferior only in the facilities. This extended to
the labs, science labs, the animals that they work with in biology,
chemicals, so forth and so on. I think they were better equipped
than we were.

My brother always played a little football, and there was a
rumor—I think it was more fact than fiction—that the Dunbar
team would have to use Central High, uh, Little Rock High
School's practice uniforms to play their games in. And then

they'd wash 'em in the school laundry and send 'em back on Monday so [the white team] could practice in 'em again.

I think it was only a lack of equipment that was involved in the situation, because our teachers were well qualified academically. Our teachers graduated from some very fine schools. You know, you couldn't get a Ph.D. from Philander or Tyler Deager or Fisk, but you could get one from Columbia. And we had Ph.D.'s there, we had people with master's degrees teaching us. And then the black schools, like Fisk, LeMoyne, Talladega, Tuskegee, Hampton, all these schools were real strong schools. And those people were well-qualified professors in those schools.

Of course, you had a mixed faculty in those schools, all those schools you had mixed faculty, you had white and black teachers in those schools. So, I don't think that the human quality, as far as teaching and instruction is concerned, I don't think they had as much to teach with as the white teachers over here at Central High.

Jerome may have "complained down at the big gate"—even now, I suspected, he had resentment he was not expressing to me—but I was surprised at how good-natured his complaints in fact were. At the same time his strong will to make justice happen was clearly evident.

But when change did hit Little Rock in the form of desegregation, Jerome found himself marooned out of town. Others were crowding in through Reverend Young's "big gate," complaining with purpose where they could be heard, and Jerome yearned to join them:

> I was teaching in another area . . . in Arkadelphia, Arkansas [a college town southwest of Little Rock]. . . .
>
> I was anxious to join the fight. I was very anxious, because this is something I wanted to happen. I didn't see why I had to walk by Central High School, although I loved Dunbar, but I really don't see why, I look back and say I don't see why I had to go past this school in order to go to another school.
>
> Because that's a bitterness that I have towards that, but, you know, the fact that the school was, I thought the teachers were real great and so forth. I felt that compensated for not going there. And I guess it did, but when I heard, when this first started happening, I was very, very—and still am—integrationist at heart.

I noticed a shift in the mood of Jerome's account. Where before he had taken a prideful stance, insisting his school was as good as "theirs" (as it was in terms of scholarship, according to all accounts), as soon as real change was in the air, Jerome remembered himself as experiencing indignation at the injustices he had nonetheless endured. This, I thought, was a codicil to his earlier answer to my question about rebelliousness. When no change had been in prospect, focusing on his pride in Dunbar was an act of protest. But Jerome associated memories of bitterness with the moment when redress came to appear possible. In the days when he walked past Central High as a student, when no challenge to the unjust status quo was afoot, it was the more powerful act to praise Dunbar. With the advent of court-ordered integration, acknowledgment of the bitterness he'd felt passing by Central High became politically potent. Amazingly, resentment and all, he continued to feel a sense of ownership in the larger community he shared with the white population of Little Rock and of Arkansas:

> I was really proud of Little Rock, too, in that Little Rock was chosen as one of the places where this type of experiment of human engineering could take place. You know, [when] they started, it was a toss-up between Nashville, Tennessee, and Little Rock, Arkansas. Plus the fact, I said, It ought to do pretty good in Arkansas. I said, Up there in a little ole country town like Van Buren, Arkansas, or Fayetteville, I said, they're already busing the few blacks that are up there to these white schools. I said, It seemed like they doing pretty good! And I said, That's in Arkansas.
>
> So, I felt confident that this [desegregation] would be successful, and I was anxious to come up in Little Rock, back to my home town, I was very proud to come back to see the progress that was being made in education. And that's really the way I felt. I didn't feel, I guess I didn't have sense enough to be afraid. I didn't fear any problems.

Jerome and I went on talking intently, moving forward in time, talking deeply about contemporary problems of multicultural education. Meanwhile, time in the literal sense went by, and suddenly I noticed the clock. It was 3:15, and I remembered we had to be out of the school building very soon. Thoroughly engaged by what Jerome was saying, I asked if we could continue our conversation at a later date. Negotiating an appointment as we went, we gathered up our possessions and moved briskly to the front doors, a long bank of them opening onto the grand front staircase.

At least, they would have opened if they hadn't been securely padlocked. We checked our watches. We still were five minutes shy of the 3:30 deadline. But the custodians were working to a different clock; they were gone and we were locked in. Jerome went from door to door, rattling the clunky chains and padlocks with which they were secured, finding all of them indeed locked. Setting off for the side doors with me in pursuit, he soon discovered that they, too, were fastened with no-nonsense padlocks.

"Oh, well," he said. "We'll phone security to come let us out," and off he went at a trot, down a staircase, through a labyrinth of corridors. Hurrying after him, I began to notice odd signs we were passing: "101st Airborne: Turn in uniforms here." "National Guard gathers on the second floor." Gradually, I realized they must refer to actors in a film that was in production at the moment. Based on the story of Ernest Green, the one black student who graduated in 1958, the movie was made by Disney. I was hearing a good deal of suspicion and complaint about this project. People were skeptical of its "biases"—both Ernest's and Disney's. White people seemed more likely to question Ernest's perspective, black people Disney's. Some people had told me how painful it was to see uniformed troops surrounding the school again. Now, however, in our flight through the basement corridors, these signs of today's depiction of yesterday's drama seemed bizarre in the extreme.

As we rushed through the hallways, I was struck by the absurdity of our position. Jerome had just been telling me how it had felt to be locked out of Central High, and here we were locked in. The stories I was hearing about the history of the place, stories laced with memories of media representations, were shadowed by the signs and symbols of this new media representation that had just somehow become part of my own story. The layering of realities and representations I had come here to understand was instead beginning to boggle my mind. At last we arrived at Jerome's office, a crowded and windowless cave clearly

shared by many teachers. Jerome dialed a series of numbers, only to
find that security, like the custodians, had taken a hike. It was, after all,
a Friday. It was, moreover, the very end of the summer session, a break
before school proper began.

Jerome was beginning to appear uncharacteristically perplexed,
although still, characteristically, determined. He paused briefly, and
dashed off to try the cafeteria windows. Again, I gathered up my equipment and hurried after him. The cafeteria was huge, the site of some
of the most notorious scenes involving the Nine's torment and retribution. We tried a few doors with growing discouragement and finally
gave up. Back we ran to the office, beginning to get the giggles, which
didn't, however, deter Jerome from hatching his next idea of what to
do. I couldn't at the moment imagine anyone I'd rather be locked in
the bowels of Central High with than activist, optimistic Jerome.

This time he dialed downtown, the district headquarters. Listening
to Jerome's side of the conversation, I realized he was having some
trouble making our plight clear. When at last he'd convinced the person on the other end that we had tried all reasonable exits and they
were indeed barred, he paused for a long beat, listening with a look of
growing astonishment on his face. At length he held the phone away
from his ear and said to me, "They don't have keys to the padlocks, and
they can't reach any of the custodians on the phone." Meanwhile, the
clock ticked closer and closer to five, when, we feared, even the people
downtown would abandon us. At last, we agreed to wait by a certain
door, to which they would send either a custodian with a key, or, lacking one, a handyman with a padlock cutter.

We retired to the given door, and we waited. And we waited. And
we waited. We were talking animatedly, so it was no hardship to wait.
But gradually we wondered if we were perhaps being bested by one
of those bureaucratic solutions that rely on neglect. Finally, Jerome
gathered his incredulity in hand and darted off in the direction of the
cafeteria once again. I waited where I was, not sure whether perhaps
the men's room were in that direction. Pretty quickly, though, Jerome
returned, beaming, and gestured to me. He led me into the cafeteria,
through rows of tables, toward a far corner where, lo and behold!, one
unlocked door had been overlooked. We walked blithely through it,

Jerome-the-man shaking his head in relief while Jerome-the-teacher shook his head in dismay at this slip-up by the custodians. We bid each other a warm good-bye, promising to meet again later to continue our conversation.

Sally Simpson

On the day Central High School was desegregated it was filled with the kinds of white Arkansans in whom Jerome had, before our adventure, just been expressing his faith. Because Central was "*the* high school," alumni of the class of '58 reflected the range of people populating white Little Rock. **Sally** typified her classmates. A decade younger than Jerome and growing up a stone's throw from his childhood home, she lived the white counterpart to his experiences of segregation.

Sally's story as she told it to me, however, started not with race relations but with protestations of normalcy. When I called Sally and asked if I could come interview her, she first demurred that she was just an ordinary person and had nothing interesting to tell me, and then, at my insistence that ordinary people were precisely the ones I sought, she shyly agreed. But she refused to let me come to her home, which was "far away" in a suburb outside of Little Rock. Instead, she joined me at the inn where I stayed. My innkeeper obligingly vacated the premises, turning over to me the dining room so we could use the breakfast table overlooking her pretty reclaimed tree.

Sally arrived exactly on time, carefully dressed and still apologizing for not having played a more prominent role in the desegregation drama. At length, we settled in at the table over tea and tape recorder, and I asked her to begin by telling me about her family:

> Well, I had a real good family life. You know, it was a little turmoil here, a little turmoil there. But everybody has a little turmoil here and there. I have two younger brothers. . . .
> Now my family, as far as a family, my mother and father and brothers and I were a tight unit. But, my grandparents and aunts and uncles and all that are just kinda—They just didn't have good relationships. And I guess that was why I wanted my family to be, you know—

We went to my grandparents' house and it was a pleasant experience. But nobody else was ever there. You know, the uncles and stuff, every once in a while someone would be over. But it was, OK, Marilyn's family is going to be here. And Marilyn's family is gone and Samantha's family is going to be here.

Did you spend holidays together?

Holidays? No.

What kind of work did your parents do?

My mother worked off and on at, I guess, clerical work, secretarial stuff. My father worked for the railroad. He was, well, he did lots of things, he was a switchman, but my father also did odd every things, all the time, you know. He baled hay in the summer, he—well, he always wanted to make a lot of money, and he never did. He was always too much of a good guy. [laughs]

What kind of education did your parents have?

My mother had two, I think they both had two years of college.

And their parents?

I don't know about their parents. I know my grandfather on my father's side made lots and lots of money. He was in insurance. He was with the railroad. He died at a very young age, what I call a very young age. He was fifty-two. Had leukemia and died of leukemia. I don't know if he had college degrees or not.

But lots of people didn't have, quote, college degrees, they might have gone to college for a while in that particular group. My grandfather and my grandmother on my father's side didn't, she never worked. She was the lady of the house. We didn't have a real good relationship because she had two daughters and my father. And the girls could do no wrong and he could do no right. And we just didn't have a very good . . . we weren't over there much. [laughs] Didn't have a real good relationship with them.

Plus, it was really crazy because the reverse was true of the grandchildren. Her grandsons, which were her daughters' children, could do no wrong. And, you know, "Well, Sally, what do you want?" But, anyway—

Then my mothers' parents, Papa had several businesses, shops, in Little Rock, in the downtown Little Rock area.

How would you describe your biological family's class position as you were growing up?

As I was growing up, how would I describe them? Probably, oh, I can't think of the names—"Happy Days."

Happy Days? What is that? Lower middle class?

Probably middle, middle class. I mean, we never owned a home. We always rented. But, I never wanted for anything. I mean, I never had everything I wanted but I never wanted for anything. I don't think we ever had two cars. Not until after I was gone and my brother was gone and all that kind of stuff. Daddy bought a house, oh gosh, after I was married. So I had nice clothes. I had dance lessons. My brothers did Little League and they had all their uniforms. I mean, we didn't have everything we wanted but we had what we needed. We were happy with it.

Sally's family's class position was strikingly similar to Jerome's. After a year or two in college, her father, too, worked a variety of jobs, including one on the railway. But I was getting a rather different sense of the quality of her life from the one Jerome had conveyed. Where he had portrayed his father as talented and successful in his pursuits, Sally spoke of her dad's disappointments, never making the money he hoped to. He was downwardly mobile compared to her grandfather's financial achievements, lacking some of the markers (two cars, a home of his own while raising his kids) of the middle-class lifestyle she nonetheless claimed. But her brothers did have uniforms which Jerome's brother was made to borrow, a symbolic evocation of the difference race made. There were other differences connected to race. Both fathers worked for the railroad, but Jerome's dad was a porter and Sally's a switchman, a typically racialized division of labor. I wondered if race hadn't influenced another subtle matter on a social level: Sally hinted at turmoil and disunity in her family, happy though she might have been. Many among my African-American interviewees expressed a feeling of solidarity that existed in the black extended family and community, an experience which was less commonly articulated by white Little Rockians. Sally had experienced a sort of fragmentation, manifested in the absence of holiday gatherings and her adult sense of the child-she'd-been recognizing the politics of grandparental favoritism by gender. Sally came of age in a time when many white, middle-class families were breaking apart, moving from tight-knit extended structures to nuclear units more autonomous and less assisted by older generations.

If her family typified something in its trajectory from extended to nuclear, Sally's experience of race relations was also characteristic for white people in Arkansas at the time. I asked her what kind of contact she'd had with black people growing up, and she replied:

> Well, a black lady took care of me when I was little. See, we didn't have any money but we had somebody who came in and took care of me. And I guess took care of the house a little bit, and stuff like that. So, it's kind of an irony of sorts. I mean, well not an irony, it's, I guess, it's what you decide to spend your money on. [. . .] But I remember Faith, and she would take me down to the playground and we would play. Oh, I loved Faith. And I can't remember how old I was, probably—when I started school, I don't remember much more about Faith. But I remember going to the playground with her and hugging her neck. She'd always bring me little prizes, and she lived out in the country and was poor but she, I don't know, she'd bring me little stuff.

> *Did you know if she had children of her own?*

> Yes, she did. She got married, I kind of kept up with her, not one on one, but I'd say to Mother, "Whatever happened to Faith?" And she'd say, "She's living at so-and-so and she's married and she has five or six kids." You know, I still have my pictures of Faith.

> *What about in your neighborhood where you lived?*

> In my neighborhood where I lived, I guess, well, when I was in junior high school there was a black area of town. I lived over here, and it's on the east side of Little Rock. I lived down close to Roosevelt Road and there was a black section of town and then there was the school. And so there was this wad of kids and I was kind of on the end of the bunch. We'd start out, the kid across the street and such, and we'd walk and pick up kids along

the way. Because we walked to school. I mean, it wasn't, you know, twelve miles in the snow and sleet.

We'd walk to school, and we would walk through the black section of town. And then we would walk on and get to school. But we were always, you know, in a group. Basically, made sure that we didn't go through the black section of town without a group. But, I mean we were walking, we were grade school kids, we were walking from Roosevelt Road, which would be Twenty-fifth Street up to right around where the freeway is, which is what? We were walking a good distance. But we just made sure there was always a bunch of us, but we weren't afraid to go through that area of town. Nobody messed with anybody. We didn't mess with them and they didn't mess with us.

Would you have been afraid to go through that part of town by yourself?

Probably. But it really wasn't a bad section of town. It was just because everything was segregated. You were the white folks and they were the black folks. Then when we moved and I was in junior high and high school—no, I was in high school, we lived two doors down on the edge of a black district. But they did their thing and we did our thing. No, I was never afraid to live that close to them. But then, it was a different time. It's not like, you know, they were, I mean, it wasn't like they were afraid to do anything. It's just that it was a different time. People weren't mean and people weren't violent and people weren't, I don't know, people just weren't.

And now, it's like, you know, you look at somebody cross-eyed and they go, "OK, you want to fight?" I don't think so. But I remember that they did ride in the back of the bus and there were colored signs, and it said colored. You know, for the different bathrooms. And the different water fountains. But I don't really remember being afraid.

Do you remember ever thinking anything in particular about those signs that made the separation?

No.

You just accepted that bathrooms and the like should be separate?

Yeah, that's their bathroom, that's my bathroom.

Sally was younger than Jerome, and she lived in the poorer part of town, the very area where "the pavement would just stop in the middle of the street," denoting the border between white and black residences. Those differences may well have accounted for her very different experience of race relations in her neighborhood. This was not Jerome's "healthy biracial environment." Sally's public world consisted of wary separateness, an absence of fear based on an absence of contact between white and black youths. I thought the difference may also have been about gender; girls may not have enjoyed the sort of cross-race camaraderie boys achieved through sports. What was to me Sally's most striking commentary on race relations, though, was her story about Faith, her family's maid. Unlike Jerome's encounters in the street, a public space where sometimes there was harmony and sometimes trouble, Sally's relationship with Faith took place in Sally's domestic territory where Sally was confident of a wholly warm meeting of the races. This theme, of white people forming opinions about race relations based on encounters in their own homes, where they were employers and black people servants, occurred very often throughout my interviews.

Another aspect of my conversation with Sally evoked a common theme with both black and white people, and that was about religion. "My religious background is Methodist," Sally told me. "Probably, quote, a backsliding Methodist."

"Do you belong to a church now?" I asked.

> Yes. I don't go a lot, but I belong. As far as that's concerned, I just, we moved . . . I grew up in a very large Methodist church. When I went to college, I sort of slipped. Didn't go much. I got married, not in the church, we ran off and got married. We would go on occasion. I mean, the children were baptized in the church. You know, I have some pretty strong, when I grew up, I mean, I was there every Sunday, every Wednesday, every Sunday morning, every Sunday night, every function, every thing.

> *Because that was important to your parents or to you? Or both?*

> Probably both. Because my father never went to church with us very often because he always worked on weekends. But Mother would go. And she would go in the mornings. I guess that was

where the only socializing that we ever got to do was in the church. So, you know, we went to church.

Church represented community and was the province of the women. Whatever people's spiritual beliefs and needs, the institution of church often played this role in the lives of both white and black people. As an institution that was both public and yet delineated a very personal social circle, church also often defined racial boundaries and was highly instrumental in forming racial attitudes, as Sally's next story demonstrated:

When we moved out to the country we went to a very small little church. It was called Fall Hills Methodist Church. I mean I'm talking small, I'm talking twenty-five people in the whole congregation—that's the kids, the adults, the elders, the whole bit. And that was fine. We went every Sunday. We loved it.

And then one of the larger churches that was in one of the black areas of town, and getting to be a really rough black area of town, decided that they needed to move their congregation. So they negotiated with, I don't know, the hierarchy in the Methodist Church, and this, that, and the other. And then they discussed it with our congregation that we would merge.

Because we were a little tiny church, but we had a lot of property, a big hunk of land. So, they needed the hunk of land and, quote, we needed them. Well, one of the stipulations of the merger was that we would retain our identity as far as this would mean, you know, Fall Hills would be kept in the name. So it would be known as Fall Hills Delta Methodist. Well, fine.

Our paperwork got done as far as merging, and building and money. And then all of a sudden it became Delta Hills Methodist Church. And I really took offense to it. And we, you know, that's where our membership was 'cause they combined them. We never went back. I'm sure it's a lovely church. I mean, I'm sure it's nice. Well, it was sufficient with the name change because there was a lot of confrontation, and it just wasn't a pleasant scene.

Was some of the controversy because it had become an integrated church?

See, it wasn't an integrated church.

The black congregation didn't move?

Uh uh. . . .

I see.

Delta Hills was, I mean, they may have had their, quote, token blacks.

But they pulled the church out of the—

Right, out of the black area of town. I don't know if they were fleeing the black congregation or if they were fleeing the black community. Probably that because the Methodists, you know, do not discriminate openly . . . In some of the uppity, snootier churches, they have blacks. I don't know because I haven't been involved in that particular part of it.

Sally's understanding of what constituted discrimination was interesting and complex. She implied a certain sympathy with the choice to move a primarily white church out of a black neighborhood, a different act in her mind from moving to exclude black church members. But the newly merged church was not integrated, suggesting that racial exclusion is what in fact happened. In a subtler and more ambiguous way, she implied that only upper-class congregations *were* integrated, and her use of the words "uppity" and "snooty," plus her disclaimer of involvement, made clear her feelings about such groups. Her quarrel with the merger was partly about losing the intimacy of a twenty-five-member congregation, partly about what she perceived as an unjust use of power: from the mystified way the transaction was accomplished by "I don't know, the hierarchy in the Methodist Church" to the final insult of reneging on the agreement to keep the word "Fall" in the name. Her withdrawal from the church was both a way to avoid "unpleasantness" in the form of "confrontation," and also an expression of disaffection with the changes and the process. In this sense, her act of leaving the church was a protest "down at the big gate." Many months later I met with Sally and her husband, **Bill**, and we talked about their own flight from city to suburb, another act of power taking, this time explicitly around issues of race.

But for the moment, Sally embedded in a seemingly innocent answer to a routine question a half-joking and very characteristic defense of her racial attitudes. "Where did your ancestors come from?" I asked, and she replied:

> Probably England. As far as my side of the family, they're basically English. But as I understand it, I have Scotch, Irish, English, Swede in my background and a smidgen of American Indian. We were gregarious. We don't discriminate. [laughs]

Jane Emery

Sally may have been a typical white child of Arkansas. Jane Emery, also white, wasn't sure she qualified as an Arkansan at all. Transplanted in early childhood from a very different part of the country, she represents a category of Little Rock society that was growing apace at the time of desegregation, new "Yankee" settlers. Different though she was, Jane nonetheless struggled to define herself in relationship to the same categories and social structures her classmates referenced. I asked whether she had been friends with Sally and her circle at Central High:

> No, they were in a much more popular, elite cheerleading group, I would say. [...] Not that I was an outsider, but I think everybody in high school feels they're an outsider. They were much more an elite cheerleading group.
> The South is very traditional that way, so you really need to be in a cheerleading group. And I couldn't stand to cheer for anything, I had none of that interest.
> My closest friend was also [part of] a small female nerd group. [laughs] And I was in that group. My friend ... was from an old southern plantation family that lived in Scott, Arkansas, which is a rural area. But old, old plantation. So she had a lot of money, and she was in the country club, but she wasn't in Sally's circle. She was also kind of outside, but she had money and we didn't have money—I suppose more than we ever let on. But I always felt much more identified with the working class, or lower middle class probably they were. Not the real elite.

Jane greeted me at the door of her modest West Coast tract house wearing well-worn jeans and a white shirt. Wiry, reddish-haired, a sociology professor in a California university, she quickly communicated an intensity of purpose that swept me into the interview almost before I could get my tape recorder running. Jane's home shouted individuality. It was neither neat nor messy. Objects filled the shelves and covered the surfaces, and it seemed likely that each one held a chapter of Jane's times and travels. I suspected things had come to live where they were, not because she'd thoughtfully set them out for display, but because that was where they'd landed when she unpacked. The net effect was a little overwhelming, but charming, interesting, provocative.

My sense of Jane as a traveler was confirmed as she introduced herself further:

> I'm not southern in heritage and I think that's important. If you've lived in the South you really need to be there, born and reared in several generations to be a good southerner. So my family had moved there in 1944 from Buffalo, New York. I was born in '41, I was around four, so it was somewhere in that time frame.
>
> My family's heritage is from Kansas, so there's a real pride in being from Kansas. My grandfather fought in the Civil War, [for] the North. Kansas was brought in as a free state with Missouri being a slave state. My relatives were from the eastern part of Kansas—John Brown and all that sort of thing. I guess the family's always had on my father's side a pride of being involved in the Civil War from the North.
>
> My mother's family's also from eastern Kansas. They moved to Buffalo after they married. My father was a medical school professor, and he moved to Arkansas because his health was failing—he was having heart problems and wanted to get out of Buffalo's miserable winter. So he moved to Arkansas.

Jane's mother was a teacher who was prevented from teaching in a time when married women were barred from the classroom:

> My mother was very bitter and frustrated because she couldn't teach once she got married, and that was in Kansas. When we moved to Arkansas she tried to get a teaching job, and in order to keep expenses down, the school boards didn't want to hire any women who were what they considered too old, who

might be retiring soon. She was over forty-eight. As I recall the story she could teach for substitute pay, as long as she got less pay [than regular teachers]. So, my mother began teaching somewhere in the end of the forties, early fifties, and then taught until she finally did retire.

What Jane had told me so far located her in a variety of social matrices. She stood at a complex intersection of classes: not an elite "cheerleader," but friends with an elite southerner from plantation society. She herself, she claimed, was more working class, or lower middle class, although her father was a Ph.D. physiologist who didn't let on to being as well-off as he probably was because, she later told me, he himself had childhood roots in poverty. Since I hadn't asked Jane anything about her class origins, all this explanation suggested a good deal of concern with who exactly she was, and the answer in class and social terms involved a good deal of ambiguity. It was also interesting to me that Sally, whose switchman father did a working-class job, had labeled herself middle class. But Jane, whose professor father was to me clearly middle class, veered toward a self-definition of working class. Together, they demonstrated familiar unclarities in Americans' understandings of class status, and ways in which such definitions are often more emotionally strategic than sociologically factual.

Much less ambiguous was Jane's suggestion of her family's position around several controversies. They were on the side of the North in the Civil War (many people expressed positions about race by reference to their ancestors' loyalties in the Civil War). They were "bitter and frustrated" about her mother's experience with prejudicial schoolboard rules, which suggested some indignation about discrimination toward women. Overall, she sketched a set of beliefs about justice that led me next to ask what messages she had gotten from her Kansas-rooted family about segregation:

> I guess that was something I wanted to discuss. I mean, it's such a part of the South but it's never, it's so taboo you don't even discuss it. So I don't remember my parents ever discussing segregation *per se*. They would discuss the issues or the problems that black people had. [...]
> My father had a number of employees at the medical school

[where he taught] who were black, and they typically had the maintenance jobs. So there were a number of blacks that worked for, or with, him.

And I remember that he would often loan money to them because there was no way if they needed money, even a small amount, they could go to a bank and get money and they were often on such marginal living. And so I remember that my father would always loan them money, and that's probably one of my first memories, you know, in terms of doing something for people.

And then, well, we would later have a black person who helped in the house one day a week.

The mention of a servant sent Jane off on a digression, more finely delineating her class position:

I grew up in a more working-class neighborhood with middle-class educated parents. But my parents always acted like we didn't have very much money, primarily because my father grew up extremely poor. I knew I wasn't hungry like some of my friends might be, and I'd a friend with a dirt floor in the house, and there were houses not too far when I was in grade school that didn't have plumbing. We're talking white people much less poor than the black ones.

The whole South has always been very poor, so certainly in the forties and fifties it wasn't uncommon for kids—I can even remember them coming to school barefoot. We were in a poor white region that began to develop a little bit, a little bit more. Certainly poverty was real—when you talk about poor kids or country kids—and a lot of people talked about their country kin. So there was a lot of that kind of feeling, that it was rural and that it was poor, and the blacks were in other areas. There were no blacks in that immediate area at that time. They were just known as poorer than the people around us.

Both the content and the manner of Jane's description of her neighborhood suggested discomfort. She started sentences and interrupted herself. She spoke quickly, in a sort of rush to sort out contradictory experiences and complex thoughts. Where her conflicted class position and her ambivalence about race coincided were, predictably, in her feelings about her family's black maid:

We did have black help, as I said, once a week. And there was one interesting story. The first day [Denny] came to work, my mother fixed lunch and we were—my father would help start the laundry; the joke is my father would start the chores and we would all finish them, OK. And we did wringer washing, OK. So, he would fill up the tubs and all that sort of thing.

And so, anyway, we were getting ready to eat lunch and my mother set Denny a place at the table and she looked really strange, because that was not common to eat [together]. And she said, I'll do it in the dialect if you like, she said, "Ahh's never eaten next to a white man before. But I'll do it, I'll sit next to the doctor."

OK. And I just say that because I think there was never any question in my parents' mind that that was not what you would do. We're all working together, we're all going to eat together. It was some time before I realized how—I mean there were poor black women [who] had to eat, frankly, at a far back room and on paper plates, because they didn't want to contaminate the good china, or whatever.

So, I think my parents treated blacks with some equality, but there's no question you can't grow up in that region without a lot of prejudice.

This phenomenon of my white interviewees talking about their racial feelings in terms of how they observed their parents treating their black maid made sense; the gulf between blacks and whites was so wide that most white people didn't notice any other contact with black people, a condition that was not reciprocal for black southerners. The prototypic experience of passing each other on a public street, for instance, was described by whites as placidly unremarkable, by blacks as an exercise in acute consciousness of social rules and physical dangers. The employee-employer relationship whites did experience was a perfect fit with how they imagined their society to be: yes, there was a "natural" racial hierarchy, but it was a benevolent one. Whites held power, but wielded it in a kindly fashion. Publicly, Jane's parents were silent in debates about desegregation or, presumably, other discourses of race. Privately, they respected their black employees. Although Jane and most of her white peers saw these two realms as wholly separate, the stories I heard about Little Rock made clear very significant ways their private and their public actions did in fact link up.

Jane was at one and the same time talking history and theory, and also remembering childhood experiences laced with her own and her family's reactions to racism. She strained to distinguish her upbringing from that of her peers and to include herself in the racist milieu in which it all took place. I'd asked if her parents spoke with her about race and prejudice, and she'd said they hadn't. Yet their attitude toward Denny did speak to her; it clearly conveyed important lessons—as did her mother's fear later when desegregation grew near:

> I don't remember my father ever mentioning it [Denny's hesitancy to eat with the family] except that as he got sicker (he had heart problems) Denny would be with him a lot more. There was a real mutual respect [between them]. I think that's what often happens with some of the poor blacks when they work with—my father had some prestige in the community. It was a mutual kind of thing. I think she really liked—he respected her and she respected him.
>
> I think that happens a lot in the South, that some of the white people would, quote, treat blacks much more like them, like the people that worked for them, and loan them money and do things for them. But that didn't mean that they ever considered them so equal they would put them in the same schools.
>
> So, the idea of education and schools never really came up, although my father was always concerned about education and he gave money to one of the first, I think it was one of the first, but it was a black school that was set up as a high school and college to educate blacks, I think in Mississippi, and it was one where they could work for their tuition. And my father gave them money.
>
> Later, my father died in '57 just before this [desegregation], summer of '57, and my mother was very worried because it was in the paper. . . . And my mother was very worried that people would—people sent a lot of hate mail in '57 and '58. The Capital Citizens Council sent a lot of garbage to everybody and she was so worried that they would find out that my father had given money to the black school and might in some way retaliate. I mean, there was that much hostility just because you had done

anything positive for blacks. There was this feeling that you might get hostility. So she was just worried, I think as a widow it just made her more vulnerable.

Vulnerability to social pressure and its defiance was a strong theme in Jane's story. In parallel with Reverend Rufus Young and Jerome Muldrew, she, too, experienced pressure to conform to mores she found problematic, although, significantly, the coercion was social rather than physical. Unlike the two men, however, because the traditions that compelled her were less obviously oppressive, she had correspondingly less clarity about her choices. As she went on to tell me her memories of growing up in Little Rock, the tensions and contradictions of her position grew more and more vivid:

> What I remember in second grade—and I've asked several other people and they don't recall it—but I have a vivid memory of this big blue chart with our names written on it. And you got checks and then gold stars and on every Monday the teacher called the roll and you had to say, "Yes, Ma'am," or, "No, Ma'am," whether you'd been to church or Sunday School, and they'd call roll that way. [...]
>
> Second grade . . . , I said, "No,"—honest thing to say—and people looked at me and stared—I mean, by the time we'd been through a couple weeks. And I think the teacher talked to my mother. And we went Easter Sunday. And the class clapped, because finally I had a check.
>
> But you know it was just glaring to see this blue chart and everybody had checks and gold stars. And I didn't. I had X's or whatever.
>
> Same thing happened third grade, but social pressure took over. After about the third week, I don't know why, you can guess what I said: "Yes, Ma'am." No problem, as long as you said yes, they never checked up. They were off my back.
>
> So I always say the good Christians taught me my first lying lesson, right?

Contrary to reputation, small children have a strong desire for integrity, so that lesson took a toll:

Do you remember what you thought about that at the time?

Well, I really felt the need to be honest at the time, which is interesting. I know by the third grade, at least by the fourth grade, it made me feel better to say—well, I definitely had been to Sunday School. And I could at least say, "Yes, I go to a Methodist church." I took pride that it wasn't fundamentalist, particularly as I got older. The Methodist church was OK and my aunt was a Methodist missionary so that fit in, you know. So I could be a Methodist and go through that.

As Jane grew into her pre-teen years, the dynamic continued, although the rewards changed. Instead of gold stars, church attendance earned her service badges for her sweater, which in those days was a major mark of status. So, too, did the problems created by going to church grow in seriousness:

My father was very authoritarian, a patriarch, OK. It was just so clear that he would have nothing to do with religion. And being in the South people always knocking on your door, like you might have Jehovah's Witness here, it's constant. If they find out you're a new person in the neighborhood and you don't have a church, and my father would just be so definite about—he might let them in, if they're a neighbor, but he just made it very clear he had no use for it. And he liked to poke fun at them. I mean, a virgin birth to a physiologist is just—and so I just knew that all that was ———

Well, once I went to vacation bible school, and that was fun in the summer, you do that in the summer. And I went with a Baptist friend who lived across the street. And she kind of helped push me, "Go forward," when they were singing their song. She said, "Well, just go forward."

And I guess the message got to me, and I thought, Well, sure I guess I should, you know, I've been saved; I better go do this. And I remember going forward and then they said, "We're going to tell your parents how wonderful this is that you found Christ," or whatever they say. And I thought, My god, you know, I didn't know you were going to tell my father!

And I remember I was very worried about it and my friend

said, "Oh, you know, Pastor So and So will just come and have chicken dinner with you on Sunday," and I thought, Oh, no! He doesn't want to come to our house!

So luckily they just called, and they said that I had come forward and said Christ had come to me or whatever, and I remember my mother asking me about that, because of the guy had telephoned. And I remember denying it.

So it obviously was very strong because I remember saying I had gone forward but I hadn't really accepted Christ or something, you know. I kind of covered myself. But I remember lying and feeling guilty, so that says something. That was fifth grade, so I was like ten.

So I knew, I was obviously scared of my father's reaction. I mean he wouldn't have done anything physically, but he was mentally—he could play mind tricks. I wouldn't say he would psychologically abuse me, I'm not saying that, but you know, it was so important I didn't want him to think I was—think badly or put me down or ridicule me or something.

Jane was caught. She could lie and pretend to her friends and teachers, but in doing so she put herself in jeopardy of her father's judgments and authoritarianism, and so she ended up lying to her family as well. An outsider to her peers, like them yet different, she accommodated convention where she could, walking thin, unsteady tightropes between belief systems. Her awkward discomfort with the community in which she found herself could not have contrasted more sharply with the childhood experiences my next interviewee described.

Mahlon Martin

After my first round of conversations with people who had been directly involved in Central High the year of desegregation, I began to think about other groups: people who had been students in the other high schools and at Central in other years. Mahlon Martin was one of the people I'd consulted for introductions within the African-American community. I knew he was a little younger than the class of '58. I called to ask if he'd talk with me, and he agreed, as gracious as he'd been generous on our first visit.

Mahlon was the executive director of the Winthrop Rockefeller Foundation. We met at his office, a grandly appointed room on the second floor of an elegant Victorian in downtown Little Rock. Mahlon seated himself next to me in one of the comfortable wing-backed chairs on the "visitor" side of his large mahogany desk. A handsome man nearing fifty, his salt-and-pepper hair cropped close, elegantly attired in a gray suit and blue shirt and tie, Mahlon quickly told me he was recovering from a bad bout with cancer. That information was like an emotional filter tinting our talk, for me adding poignancy to much of what he said, for him, perhaps, promoting an inclination to talk deeply and personally.[6]

Mahlon had mentioned before that he'd had the opportunity to attend Central High after the crisis had ended, and that he'd chosen not to go. I began our interview by asking when that had been and how he'd made his decision:

> It was '60. [...] I'm not sure that was a real conscious, gut, ethical kind of decision. I probably ought to start by saying during the crisis itself in 1957 I was in sixth grade, finishing elementary school. Both my parents and grandparents in numerous ways were very protective of the environment I grew up in, and so I was really sheltered in large part from what was going on.
>
> *Would you tell me a little bit about your family?*
>
> My father passed, I think that year, in '57. I had a very strong grandmother—my father and grandfather passed within two months of each other—but I had a very strong grandmother who lived next door; I lived with my mother at home, which again was next door.
>
> We had a kind of extended family, in the sense that next door to that was an aunt and a cousin, so I grew up in a kind of extended family environment: three homes that are next to each other. My grandmother was an extremely strong little person, a teacher by profession. By '57 she had retired, but really, because my mother had to work after my father passed, was the one that kind of raised us on a day-to-day basis.
>
> And she and my mother were in so many instances, now as I look back, very protective of us in the sense of being exposed to what one would consider racism, the impacts of racism. I

guess I recall—my mother worked at Dillard's [a big department store]—going down and seeing the black and white water fountains. But even there I was shielded as much as possible and grew up maybe naive in terms of the real issues going on around us.

I mean, you couldn't be totally isolated. In fact, I remember during that time, '57, '58, friends of mine and I would walk to the Boy Scout meeting, which was about a mile from home. And I remember an effort one evening on the way to school where a group of young white kids, I don't think they really tried to hit us as I look back, but tried to scare us as if they were going to run over us in the car. And it was somewhat upsetting.

But that as I look back was my only minor confrontation with any of that.

Did you read that incident at the time as racial?

Oh, yes, certainly. I think that, even though I was sheltered, you couldn't live here and not know something was going on and what was going on. I think it was more kids being devilish than anything else, using words and, you know, calling us names and acting as if they were going to run over us.

What did they call you?

Nigger. Yeah. But it wasn't something that was a life-shattering experience.

And so I say that only to say by being sheltered it may not have been the kind of issue with me it might have been with some other folks in a different environment.

Mahlon's portrait of life growing up in a protected black community resonated with Sally and Jane's descriptions of life in an almost wholly white world. All three children experienced the racially segregated worlds of home and community into which they were born as fundamentally safe. But where Jane's nuclear family had migrated away from their kin and Sally's was isolated by family politics, Mahlon's was still extended, grandparents, aunts, and cousins all living side by side and appearing as major characters in the child Mahlon's life. If the children had different experiences of private life, their sense of public space was also different. Mahlon was protected from contact with a white world his elders assumed would be hostile and which indeed proved itself to be so. Sally knew well the boundaries between her streets and "theirs," and she also assumed she could move through African-American spaces without harm. Jane understood that her father had contact with black people at work, a context in which he was their superior and acted with generosity. But she herself had no memorable contact with black people except one loyal maid. All three of them, nonetheless, "knew something was going on," and, while what they thought that was differed significantly, all three of them correctly comprehended their own racial community's reading of reality.

These themes were evident in Mahlon's discussion of his decision about high school. Even when speaking of memories that may well have been painful, he spoke in an even tone, freely, without the hesitations and alterations characteristic of so many interviewees' speech. He struck me as a man accustomed to speaking both often and carefully. He knew what he wanted to say and said it precisely:

> And so by the time I reached high school, I had become fairly popular at school. I was very active to some extent in athletics: I liked to play baseball and we had just started a baseball team in high school. I was active in the band, had a number of close friends that lived in my neighborhood, most of whom probably would not have been asked to attend Central, who were average students, wound up doing very well in life, but were not honor roll students and what-not. And I just chose without a whole lot of fanfare to want to stay with my friends and go to Horace Mann.
>
> My mother was one who would not have pushed me one way or the other. In fact, she shared with me later in life that she got calls from people that encouraged her to encourage me to go. But she simply took the position then and related to me later that that was a decision that she wanted me to make, she wanted me to be happy. So it wasn't like it was one that was of great magnitude at the time. But it was simply my choosing it.
>
> And I think in retrospect at least for me it was a good choice. I wound up being student council president, enjoyed my high-school career, and had probably many more close relationships in terms of friends from that experience than I might have had had I gone to Central.

Mahlon paused in his own story to reflect on the implications of his personal experiences for the African-American community at large. The losses he feared he would have suffered had he attended Central High paralleled the losses he now recounted occurring in the larger social sphere:

> Interestingly, and I think part of our problem now is, part of the negative impact, although I think equal housing and the results of it have been good generally, but I think in the minority community what it has done is take out of the neighborhoods many of the leaders that were there years ago that provided leadership, that set moral standards, that set ethical standards for the neighborhood.
>
> I can't name all of them, but I can remember, for example, I grew up playing baseball. Most black doctors sponsored teams. Most of those in the community who had respect, regardless of their employment, their vocation, although I remember many mail carriers at that time, my father was a postman, that were active as voluntary coaches in baseball programs, were active as Scout leaders, kind of set the moral tone in the community. I was active, even though I didn't belong to the church next door, in a [church youth] group. . . . In fact, I wound up leading a group of kids when I got to be an older teen. But there were plenty of activities within the neighborhood that provided opportunities for kids to do things without having to be exposed to the other problems. You had, for example, an all-black Junior Deputy Sheriff Baseball program, and while separate, it still provided that environment, and those protections, because your exposure was limited.
>
> I can go through the neighborhood now, and while many of them have passed, you can kind of walk through it and see the older leadership, people who stayed in the community, in the neighborhood and provided that.

Mahlon's walk through the neighborhood might also be a walk through the century. In his mind's eye, he sees the community as it was. On the ground, he sees it as it now is. The turning point was not exactly midway through the century, but was close: 1957. Mahlon's story of his years coming up contrasted so sharply with Reverend

Young's story of the first half of the century. For Reverend Young, the narrative themes involved progress from slavery to farm to university. The journey from country to city was overlaid with continuing discrimination and racism. It also mirrored the contours of Wesley's father's life, and of Sally's family, white folks struggling upward, not altogether successfully.

More than anyone else in my study, Mahlon was the individual whose personal climb upward was most dramatic. His life story in the decades following the fifties was a paradoxical paradigm of the ambitions of his white cohorts. They believed their opportunities were limited only by their personal capabilities. Mahlon achieved the success most of them did not, but unlike them he did not take personal credit for it. I opened the door to this part of his story with a wrong assumption:

> *Tell me about your experience after high school. Was college your first integrated experience?*
>
> Well, in fact, I went to a predominantly black college. I went to Philander Smith College [in Little Rock].
>
> As I mentioned to you earlier, and I think that's part of my health problem, but my father and grandfather passed two months apart; my father passed first in '57, and my grandfather, that's his father, passed two months to the day after that. And I was one of two kids in my home, the oldest of two sons. And as a result of that, probably as much in my own mind as anybody telling me, I felt a responsibility to become the man of the family.
>
> And as a result of that wound up, I guess, taking care of my grandmother, who became really an adoptive parent right after I graduated, a little before I graduated from high school. Which created a situation, I had a number of scholarships, and I often ask myself was it my fear of leaving home, or was it really I wanted to stay home and take care of her? But I did choose to stay home for that reason. That was my reason at the time.
>
> And so I went to Philander Smith, not because I liked Philander Smith, in fact at the time I went, they'd just stopped requiring students to wear neckties every day. So it was a rather stiff environment for me. And I hated it the first year, but I wound up liking it. But I went because I was here and at least

Philander had a reputation as being a pretty good academically oriented college. I went there for four years.

Graduated from Philander, I went to work in the insurance business, and kind of ran into the same thing I'm talking about. I was the first black hired by something called the American National Group. All of them were primarily debit oriented, where I had a debit [or client list] I collected, and I sold insurance. But my debit was clearly restricted primarily to blacks. I realized real quickly I couldn't sell much insurance, particularly not the better kind of insurance, within my debit.

I was hired being told that the company really wanted to begin to deal with, up to the administrative level, to start to be inclusive of minorities. But after two years of fighting that debit—and I realized number one that I was not an insurance salesman because I had a real problem getting people to purchase something that they couldn't afford, and more often than not that's what I wound up trying to do—but after two years of that I also realized, in fact was told, that while the company still wanted to promote minorities, they were not quite ready to do that. Because the next level up would have been to make me assistant manager or district manager, which would have—there were not enough minority debits to restrict a manager to only a minority area.

And so I really left that job with not very much to do. And had a couple of friends in construction, worked with them. And then happened to one day run into a friend who had been very active when I played ball and with our family, and he suggested I come down to the city of Little Rock and I did, and went to work with the city and spent most of the rest of my life there in numerous positions. [. . .] Spent three years as city manager and then went to state government and six years there.[7]

As I look back, I'm not naive enough not to know that at least individually my race has been beneficial to me. I've happened to be in the right place at the right time when decisions were made that it was time to actually address and do something with minorities. Having been there, I was able to be recipient of that.

So, often, it's somewhat of a dilemma for me in the sense that personally it's been beneficial but I see so many others, and friends and others, who have been negatively impacted. And I guess all of those personal experiences color how I look at what's happening in the schools.

How exactly has your personal experience formed your view?

It's probably made me a bit more hypocritical, or, well, maybe a bit more, a bit less optimistic about the future.

And I say that because the position I'm in now and the last two positions have afforded me an opportunity to actually be involved in circles [in which] very few of us are involved. I see how decisions are made, see how selective people at that level are in terms of who gets involved, really understand the criteria for selection to participate at that level.

So it's made me probably more cynical in terms of what I had hoped integration would lead to in this country, and that is a real acceptance of people regardless of the color of their skin. And I'm a lot less optimistic that our human frailties will ever allow us to do that. And that's just not black and white, I mean that's culturally, that's worldwide, I mean we look around us and see that situation as evident from a cultural standpoint, a religious standpoint around the world.

It was at this point in his story that Mahlon connected his own success in life to the debacle at Central High School, modestly but sagely relating the personal to the political:

What you've been describing is how the history of race relations in America has impacted your family and others. Is there something that you think is particular to your experience here in Little Rock, that came directly out of the desegregation struggle in '57?

Oh, I think *clearly* my having been city manager was a direct result of '57. I'm not sure I'd say that with the state position, but with city manager there is no doubt in my mind.

In what sense?

In the sense that that's what tore down the small-knit group . . . who [once] ran this community. [. . .]

There was a time in this city when seven, eight people actually made decisions that affected everybody. They owned the banking institutions, the financial institutions, they owned the real estate companies, and they could literally do that. In fact, I've been in a room with someone when I heard them pick up the phone and call and say, "If that asshole fool does that, he'll never get another line of credit in Little Rock." That's been years ago, but there was that kind of power.

That no longer exists. There are leaders and there are folks who can certainly influence things, but they're not five or six people, I don't think. And I've been around most of those who have been identified in that role, who, on any given issue could go in a room and decide this is where the city's going. And what I guess has been interesting is watching the frustration on their part of not being able to maintain what they saw as a real powerful structure in the past. [. . .]

It was '57 [that changed that], because I don't think anybody recognizes the economic impact both the state and Little Rock suffered as a result of '57. Most folks who were around at that time, particularly those generations my age and a little bit older, still live under the shadow of that. Even when that's not the issue they think it is, they see it, everybody they meet not from here, as people who equate us back to Central High. And a lot of that's true. I mean, I've had people tell me even when they've gone traveling overseas, the only thing people can recall about Little Rock is 1957.

I think much of what happened from '57 until even today is a direct result of that. We still live under that long shadow. The problem is [laughs] we want to create that different image, but we still also want to do business as usual. And the two things tend to clash every so often.

In the end Mahlon's account pointed back, like a circular depiction of a complex history, in the direction with which Wesley had started: to issues of class and power. So layered were the steps along the way, however, that I thought more of a drunken spiral than a two-dimensional circle. The many stories I heard about the lives surrounding the narrative of Central High wove back and forth from the most personal realities to the most political, from domestic realms to public ones.

I've noted that the place in childhood where the races intersected was different for children of the two races: for whites it occurred in the safety of their own homes, for blacks in nasty encounters in the public streets. This asymmetry helped to form notions of rights and entitlements in a world more or less one's own. Personal transactions like these, acts of generosity toward blacks by whites, acts of discrimination on blacks by whites, repeated throughout life, formed and reinforced worldviews which, sometimes through personal acts of disobedience, sometimes through public acts of challenge, were also continually re-negotiated.

These personal experiences intersected dynamics on other levels. For both black and white people in Arkansas, lives in the first half of the century were shaped by two structural forces: racial inequality and changing economic opportunities. How race affected black lives is obvious: from mailing a letter to finding a doctor, from taking a walk to getting a university degree, Jim Crow dictated both your objective chances and your subjective experience if you were black. If you were white, race seemed a benign influence, simply a description of a way of life. In fact, though, white lives were influenced by racial definitions far more profoundly than appeared on the surface. For racial mores intersected both with class distinctions and with gender roles to form a thick matrix of the possible and the plausible for white people, too.

On an economic level black and white people experienced very different horizons but similar dynamics. Both left the farm for the city; both hoped for and experienced improvements in economic status and well-being. Moreover, both white and black Arkansans— and Americans in general—regarded their economic lives after the Second World War with optimism, believing that the dim days of the depression were over and better times lay ahead. But as the desegregation of Central High School approached reality, black people believed nothing was assured them; do what they might, success could always be taken away, especially since success meant leaving traditional black communities which offered a measure of protection. Their best route to well-being, therefore, lay in political directions. White people, in contrast, felt that upward mobility was their individual due. Just as the segregated South seemed as unquestionable as the fact that Sunday was Sunday, so too the notion that hard work and right behavior would inevitably lead to greater well-being and status seemed incontrovertible.

When nine black students entered Central High by the front door, that act represented for both white and black people a resounding change, not just in social arrangements, but also in fundamental ideologies of rights and privileges. Until that moment the two communities had met wholly on white terms. For whites, desegregation rattled the supposition that white rights defined society. For blacks, it opened doors to places both promising and perilous.

The political door it opened for Mahlon Martin was both. When he passed through it, he walked through the shadows of two characters who strode the stage of power in 1957 with bombast and huge effect, two cronies named Jimmy Karam and Orval Faubus.

THREE
Inside the Gate

If I'd a thought it'd help Faubus, I'd a done it. . . . I was a big shot in those days.

—Jimmy Karam

One way it would have been political suicide, the other way was survival.

—Orval Faubus

In 1980 when Orval Faubus published his memoirs in the form of a big two-volume set of clippings and political lore, he called it *Down from the Hills*.[1] "He was an old country boy from up at Huntsville," Faubus's friend Jimmy Karam described him, "and hardly out of Huntsville but to Little Rock, and so I liked him."

Orval Faubus and Jimmy Karam were cronies, two ambitious boys come to the city to make good. They typified their times and also played a significant role in shaping them. Their stories were a central piece of the context for the drama at Central High. If the stories in chapter 2 are views from a personal perspective, Jimmy and Orval's narratives describe the public world of political contention. Taken all together they sketch a complex matrix of experiences, actions, and interests that help make sense of the Little Rock debacle. In particular, they demonstrate ways in which racial hierarchy also defined a social hierarchy among whites. In this context, opposition to civil rights for black people was equally an effort by some whites, not just to defend their own place in society, but also to re-situate themselves in a rapidly changing social geography. Coming "down from the hills" to an expanding industrial scene, Faubus and Karam joined together to defend an old racial power order which they themselves did not overtly support, for the purpose of establishing a competitive advantage in a newly emerging class order. All in all, power was the name of the game they played, power in both its political and its personal forms.

Wesley Pruden described Arkansas as a backwater populated by riff-raff, disenfranchised settlers who found their way to an ungenerous land and somehow remained there. The Faubuses were descendants of those same early settlers, the branch who farmed the mountainous crags of the Ozark and Ouachita Mountains. The Karams were recent immigrants with a parallel history in a very different frame.

When Arkansas became eligible for statehood in 1831, the question of slavery was hotly debated, and big cotton cultivators prevailed. In 1836 Arkansas joined the slave-owning region of the United States.[2] Rural Arkansas is divided, as Wesley suggested, into two distinctly different regions, hills to the west and north, lowlands to the east. Swamps along the Mississippi River were drained and plantations established, and with them grew the prevalence of slavery. But in the Ozarks where the Faubuses lived, farmers, trappers, and lumberjacks continued to live the yeoman life in counties virtually devoid of black people. Between the two extremes lay a stratum of small burgs where poor whites and blacks scratched out a hard existence on tiny farms. It was from the furthest extremes of these regions that Orval Faubus and Jimmy Karam emerged to be blown together by a gathering wind.

Jimmy described their first meeting to me in some detail:

> I had never met him until he ran for governor the first year against [incumbent governor Francis] Cherry. He was a great underdog, and they were talking about him going to some little college up here in Arkansas, Commonwealth or whatever.
>
> But anyway, he was very much an underdog, and I like underdogs. I never met the guy, but he was speaking at Pine Bluff at a baseball stadium there and he had a microphone, and the wind was blowing, and the papers would blow away so I went up and held the papers for him. I never met him before.
>
> So I held the papers there for him to where the wind wouldn't blow them away. He's a likable person, a likable person. So I got to know him and like him and that's how I first met him.
>
> *Was it solely because you liked him that you became so supportive of him and played such an important role in his election?*
>
> He just has a fine personality. He's a country boy from up here at Huntsville, and he never had been down to the big city until he, I think, was put on the Highway Commission or some

kind of commission here, I don't know. But I just liked him; he's got real personality.

In his autobiography, Faubus, too, recounted this story of his first meeting with Jimmy. Arriving late for the most important speech of his campaign (his driver had gotten lost and taken him to the wrong place), he found himself alone on the field of a ballpark, facing dark bleachers on which he could dimly make out ominously shadowy figures:

> A lone, bare microphone, almost spectral in appearance, stood some twenty feet from the high fence separating the park area from the bleachers. There was no lectern, no table or desk for papers, no individual with instructions, assistance or guidance. Except for the microphone I stood alone in the empty field.
>
> With a breeze blowing just holding the loose leaves of my speech would be some problem. . . . I looked around for a stone or other object to hold them in place on the ground. The most suitable object I found was an empty soft drink bottle, which was certainly not the best for the purpose because of its tendency to roll. . . .
>
> As I was weighting down the documents I was, all at once, conscious of a presence by my side. "Here, Orval," a voice said, "let me hold those for you."
>
> The presence was Jimmy Karam of Little Rock. I don't know why he was there. Whether he came as a helper, a spy, out of curiosity or whether the Lord sent him, I never knew. I did not inquire then or in the years to come. His help was sufficient for the moment.[3]

Political actions often arise from personal identities—and vice versa. Identity is not a singular thing; it takes many forms and it is constructed out of deeply internalized ideological messages. Jimmy portrayed himself as bonded with Orval Faubus against an ill-blowing wind, two outsiders from the hills allied to beat the odds. To Orval, Jimmy was a useful instrument, not someone to trust unquestioningly, but helpful nonetheless. Faubus had many allies, of course; Jimmy was not very prominent among them. Besides, Jimmy had a certain reputation; it probably didn't do for Faubus to embrace him too enthusiastically. But the governor's description of their meeting contains within it many of the tensions of his political life to come: alone, negotiating

menacing forces he can't quite comprehend, dependent for help on
people from whom he feels (and strategically maintains) a wary distance, yet plunging ahead doggedly on his ambitious course. There is
also a theme of power in both men's stories. To Orval, Jimmy is lowly,
literally stooping helpfully at his feet, so insignificant that the soon-to-
be-governor need not trouble himself to figure out whether his helper
is angel or spy. By the time they met Jimmy was an established businessman in Little Rock. But he was also the child of immigrants, and conscious as he was of having lifted himself by his own bootstraps, he
identified strongly with Faubus's quest to do the same. "He had never
been down to the big city," Jimmy said. "He was very much an underdog, and I like underdogs."

In the complexities of their relationship and the strategic telling
of its story, Orval and Jimmy lay down themes of history unfolding
in their time. If their meeting was the prologue for a drama of national
significance, then there waited in the wings a third character, another
country boy made good: Dwight Eisenhower. As the two cronies from
Arkansas forged their alliance, they played for power against a president who, contrary to his own beliefs and desires, administered racial
reforms while spearheading a redistribution of authority between
state and capitol.

Jimmy Karam

Evelyn, the African-American school administrator, had talked
about Jimmy when expressing her shock at how white people in Little
Rock turned against the black community outside the doors of
Central High School:

> Oh, it was just a disgrace! Of course, that was the news every
> day, you know, what was going on up there. I think the com-
> munity was in shock, I think the community was in shock. . . .
> And folks said, "Not Jimmy Karam."

Later, she elaborated her view of Jimmy:

> They called Jimmy Karam . . . a friend to black folks. He ran
> the store, many of his clients were black people. We have a col-
> lege now called UALR, the University of Arkansas at Little Rock,

which at the time was a two-year junior college and was not connected with the university system. It had a football team, and
Jimmy Karam was a young man, and he was the coach of the
team. Very liberal man, or so we thought. There came a time for
them to play a team that had some black players on it. The administration, as I understand, objected, or some of the alumni, or
some of the people connected with it, and he said, "No, if they're
on the team, I want them to play." That further projected him as
a very liberal person.

But, as things progressed and they began to angrily get into
mobs outside the school, he was supposed to have said, "I'm out
here because my daughter is in there." Something to that effect.

See, there were parents outside the school. And the point
was consistently made that a school is for children, students and
their teachers; the parents don't belong there.

But he made this significant statement. I just have to hear a
statement one time. "Just let them come on, and we'll give them
the kind of integration they want, we'll show them." Now this
was Jimmy Karam, a businessman, that had many black [cus-
tomers], he respected the younger men in the teaching profession, you know. And he had good merchandise.

Well, that was kind of a shock, you know. It just made you
think—they liked us, to be very blunt, they liked us as long as
we stayed in our place. And that reaction of the community was
a shock. It really was, that these people got out there with such
bitterness.

In the many accounts of the drama I heard, Jimmy's role lay somewhere between evil eminence and court jester. Governor Faubus is
often held responsible for having created the crisis. If so, then Jimmy
was widely described at the time as his operative, a gray presence at his
side, the man behind the scenes who directed the mob in the streets.[4]
Evelyn's reaction to Jimmy's behavior exemplified the sense of surprise,
of role reversals and inexplicable betrayals that lace through the story
of Central High. Jimmy Karam was a "friend to black people" who
lined up with the mob. He was a parent who violated the right of students and teachers to occupy their school without interference. To
Evelyn, he was a white man who was friendly toward blacks only as
long as they stayed "in their place."

As I talked with Jimmy and Orval, and with many others from the white community of Little Rock, I came to see the struggle as Evelyn had, as a fight for the definition of place. "Place" was an important concept in the South of that time. When the chains of slavery were broken, there arose a brief period of black Reconstruction in the South, followed by a highly successful white reaction against growing black political and economic power.[5] One element of that reactionary campaign was to promote a morality of "place." Black people were no longer confined geographically to the plantation, but they could be bound by social chains to a very clearly defined social location. Over the years, a sense of "place" was internalized by both whites and blacks, although by different means and in different ways. Each group came to define its social terrain in reference to the other's. Segregation came to represent a renewed ordering of the universe, a way of naming social hierarchies, racial and other, and each individual's location within them.

Jimmy's "place" in Little Rock society was vividly articulated by the setting in which we met: his store. A men's clothing establishment in the heart of a fallen downtown, full of clothing racks, but tellingly underpopulated, the place was more an institution than a commercial enterprise. Jimmy's desk was tucked away behind and perpendicular to the counter where he was not immediately visible to the customers (had there been any), but where he could see everything. His spot formed a sort of enclave; squeezing in beside the counter, I was invited to take an ancient leather chair, and thereby to participate in the court Jimmy held daily from eleven to three.

Jimmy made me pursue him for an interview. I'd sent him material about the project, and he'd returned it, unopened. I'd telephoned him before, during, and after my visits to Little Rock, and he'd refused to talk with me. Finally, I'd decided to brook the lion in his den. I'd appeared unannounced at his store, packet of material in hand, dressed in my most southern-ladylike outfit. Jimmy looked me up and down, took the envelope I held out to him, and said gruffly, "Look around for a few minutes."

I wandered among the racks, while he went on talking to a pony-tailed boy and his father, to whom he was clearly dispensing some largesse or other (a summer job, perhaps). Man and boy left, showering thanks behind them, and Jimmy nodded to a salesman, who told him that the usual rep was recovering from a hysterectomy (many tumors, but none malignant) and would be back to grace Jimmy's establishment soon. More glad-handing preceded the conclusion of that piece of business, and then I was summoned.

I sat down, and Jimmy immediately launched into the story of how he went to New York with his friend Faubus in 1959 and was saved by Billy Graham. I protested that I needed my tape recorder, which, of course, I hadn't brought with me since Jimmy had point-blank refused to talk with me. Now he'd apparently changed his mind, and we made an appointment for the next day.

The eldest son of immigrant parents, his father Lebanese and his mother French, Jimmy grew up in poverty in Lake Village, Arkansas, a small town almost on the banks of the Mississippi River and barely twenty miles from Dermott, where Reverend Young went to school. Lake Village was, in Jimmy's memory, evenly divided between black and white population. Just as Faubus's early history read like a prototypic American myth—boy from the farm struggles to get education and goes to the city to gain fame and power—Jimmy's story, too, depicted an American success story, but in a less popular version. Where Orval followed the plow, Jimmy followed a peddler's cart from which his father sold the pots and pans and sundries that farm households required. Orval may have been true-blue and salt-of-the-earth, but Jimmy's story of growing from immigrant roots was equally emblematic of American reality, if less well told.

Now pushing eighty, Jimmy was a handsome dark-skinned old man with a sparkle behind his glasses, a mouth full of slightly too-perfect teeth which he flashed in not-quite-believable smiles, a hearing aid filling one ear (he fiddled with it frequently), and a well-rehearsed and self-vindicating story to tell. The wall behind him told part of the tale. Above a full row of shelves crammed with ancient papers and files and supplies (as well as a large bottle of mustard closed with tinfoil, a giant-sized pair of tennis shoes, and other flotsam and jetsam of fifty years at the same site) were large framed photographs of Billy Graham and other celebrities of the revival circuit. On the top

shelf were his awards (a silver bowl for winning a football champion-
ship, a plaque proclaiming him Little Rock's Man of the Year in 1949,
a clock with coins for hour markers that, he told me, was given him
for his membership on the state banking commission during Faubus's
tenure). Noticing me noticing these artifacts, Jimmy immediately
linked them with the story he wished to tell:

> And he was elected governor and 'course I thought did a
> good job. He made me state athletic director, and put me on the
> War Memorial Stadium board, and put me on lots of boards:
> state banking commission, I was bank commissioner here for
> six, eight years, I don't remember. [Gestures to the wall of
> plaques behind a shelf of trophies.] I think that's it up there with
> that money on the damn thing.

If Faubus was responsible for Jimmy's elevated status, Jimmy quickly
let me know how he had been important to Faubus in return. In
Jimmy's story desegregation played a minor role to the centrality of
his friend Orval's ambitions:

> And then integration started, you know. And in order to be
> elected—Faubus didn't know anything about blacks, there's not
> one black where he's from. Not one in Madison County. He never
> saw a black person until he come to Little Rock. He didn't know
> anything about black people. And I *knew* black people; I was born
> and raised with them and liked them very much.
>
> But to get elected governor, he had to make a stand, at least
> he felt he did. And he came out against integration and won by
> 73 percent or 71 percent, or by an enormous—whatever.

Having situated himself as Faubus's friend, taken his place, so to
speak, at the governor's right hand, he turned to his role in the drama
of Central High. Quickly, he labeled himself "Innocent Bystander"—
and a wronged bystander at that:

> Now, the reason that they picked me out, I was well known.
> Everybody knew me. I had been a football coach and put them
> on top of the heap, and in the clothing business, and where there
> was excitement, anything going on, I was there. Everybody knew
> me, everybody. And with my reputation in those days, they could
> accuse me of anything. Yeah, anything they wanted to. So they

were sure it was me. [In a tone of indignation:] I had no more
to do with those people going out there than you did, and you
weren't even here. But I was there, so they singled me out.

Who is "they"? Who singled you out?

The newspaper, the mayor, fellow I didn't like in politics.
Anybody else, they would believe most anything about me,
because I was a rough and tough guy. I mean, I don't care what
it was, I got in the middle of it.

*Are you saying you hadn't in fact had anything to do with
the drama up until that point?*

Nothing, nothing, nothing. As I told you, I was on the
Urban League for years, ever since I was in Little Rock. And had
many, many, many black friends.

But they had to choose somebody that they could point to
and everybody would know. And that's why they picked me.
Because I was—like I say, if I'd a been what I am today [i.e., a
practicing Christian], they'd never mention my name. No. But
they wanted to have somebody everybody'd believe anything. In
those days I went to the horse races, I went to—anything to do
with excitement or something, I did.

As he elaborated on what he'd been before, he appeared to be not
so innocent after all. But even his sinning was well meant and
redeemed by confession, and in any case not the particular sin for
which the world blamed him:

It was not a good life, but was the only thing I knew. I was
seeking happiness and peace and freedom and I thought if you
did that, it'd make people look up to you. Which was a stupid
mistake. But without Christ you can't help it. My wife, I'd go to
her as I did my mother before, on bended knees, "Please forgive
me, I don't know why I did this." I'm talking about when I'd go
out and do wrong. And when I got up and started back out,
Satan would be doing the same thing. And I'd try to quit. . . .

That's the only reason to single me out. Only reason, because
people'd believe most anything about me.

[But] you didn't have to start the ruckus out there. They
were there. And I went out 'cause there's a crowd there.

So who did *start the ruckus out there?*

Well, a town called England, Arkansas, eastern Arkansas, south Arkansas, strong segregationists. Strong, strong. Those are the very people that fought me. It was because I was a foreigner. Very, very same people—the Ku Klux Klan, where I'm from, my people are Catholics, too, beside being foreigners. One was bad enough, but then the both of them was—the Jews didn't have a problem like we had.

So, I had to come out fighting, I had to fight. I know I didn't have to, but I felt like I was gonna force someone to respect my parents, my mother and me, I was gonna make 'em. Well, you can't do that. But I didn't know that, and whatever it took, I was going to try to do.

Did you recognize any of the people in that crowd from your earlier days?

Oh, I knew lots and lots of people. You talking about that day at school? I knew lots of people. See, I was one of 'em, I was tough and rough as anything you'd ever seen.

They were people from Little Rock?

Yeah, I think. That's me in that picture, me out there.

The ambivalence of Jimmy's position is well expressed in his notions of who comprised the mob. The mob were out-of-towners, those same racists who had plagued his own youth. He, too, was an out-of-towner, but a refugee from persecution. Yet he pointed proudly to his own face in the crowd of those he anathematized as outsiders and racists, even while he scanned a photograph to identify for me the people who were locals from Little Rock.

I pressed the question of where he, Jimmy Karam, stood in all this:

What did you think, in your heart of hearts, about the integration of the high school?

I had no problem; in fact, I fought for equal opportunity. In my football team, the only one in Arkansas that ever played against 'em at that time. I coached blacks in football, I was raised with 'em. [...]

[Faubus] didn't know anything about blacks. He never saw a black before he come to Little Rock. Never saw one.

Now, the stand he took, I would have to say, it was the only stand he could take and be elected. I don't know this, but I imagine politicians do whatever they have to do. To be elected. I know that's why he took—he didn't know 'em. And like I say, I think he won by . . .

I just got a card from Governor Faubus. We're good friends. I like him a lot. I don't see him much now. And we stayed friends. I liked him a lot, he's a good man. He didn't know what would happen with this thing. But he was a politician, and a master politician he was, in his day, a good politician. And he, I'm sure, was sincere about that. . . .

[Aside to someone else: "Hello, young man, good to see you. I'm looking forward to your mom and daddy's fiftieth anniversary. This young woman here is interviewing me, here."]

But I was the point man that they got on. Because everybody knew me and I was rough and tough in those days. I wasn't a mean guy, but I was seeking peace and happiness and freedom and respect and all those kind of things.

Here's an article that suggests you were doing more than that . . .

I showed him a clipping he himself had handed me a few minutes before. It was a story about Jimmy's involvement in a racially provocative incident. He read for a moment and explained:

My presser, a black friend, worked for me, so I had him get his son and daughter, and dress them up, little babies. One was about five or six, the other was about seven or eight, and I had them go out to Hall, Hall was the new high school here. And I dressed them up real nice and had a big sign printed: PLEASE LET MY CHILDREN GO TO SCHOOL, or something, I don't remember exactly what. Let's see.

Why did you do that?
Just to be mean. Just to be ornery.

Who were you being mean to?
Anybody.
It wouldn't make any difference. If I'd a thought it'd help

Faubus, I'd a done it, if I'd a thought it'd help. You know, I was
a big shot in those days.

See, I had the sign, "Let my children go to that school," or
something like that.

Repentant sinner though he portrayed himself to be, Jimmy was
surprisingly unrepentant about some things. His "prank," staging a
bogus demand by black people to breach the so-far unchallenged walls
of the new, still-segregated high school, was bound to elicit outrage
from white people in the affluent suburbs. He insisted the act was
merely mischievous—and then unguardedly implied it was an
attempt to help Faubus ("If I'd a thought it'd help Faubus, I'd a done
it") to whom his own interests were closely tied ("I was a big shot in
those days").

Jimmy's theme (voicing beliefs in equality of the races while acting to impede its implementation, claiming all the while that it was
he who suffered injustices) was one I heard again and again from
white interviewees. Indeed, it was echoed by Governor Faubus himself, he who most often is held responsible for the debacle of 1957.

Orval Faubus

If Jimmy and Orval shared an identity as small-town outsiders
challenging the inner sanctum of power and prestige, they had in
common two other characteristics as well: a tortured set of contradictions in their definition of self in relationship to established society, and an unconflicted conviction in the naturalness of their desire
to be accepted within that very same establishment.

Orval Faubus was born in 1910, in a hamlet called Greasy Creek
high in the craggy mountains. The year Orval, the first child, was born,
his father, Sam, homesteaded one hundred and sixty acres—the same
size holding granted to Reverend Young's grandfather in the south-
eastern quadrant of the state forty-five years before. If you drew a line
from the Faubus farm to the Young farm, it would bifurcate Arkansas
diagonally, its mid-point squarely in the city of Little Rock where
Governor Faubus and Reverend Young faced each other across a different line in 1957.

Nobody could have predicted that Faubus would end up on the

side he did. Neither of his parents had much formal schooling, but Sam Faubus was a self-taught intellectual and a follower of Eugene V. Debs, the socialist leader who advocated democratic workers' participation, equitable distribution of wealth, and, in the First World War, pacifism. Sam went to prison during the war, when his eldest son was seven, for his refusal to fight. Orval's middle name was Eugene.[6]

Eldest of seven children, Faubus grew up in a cabin that expanded as the number of his siblings grew. The governor gave me a copy of his war memoirs, *In This Faraway Land,* when I last met him, a few months before he died. In a preface entitled "Background of the Writer" he sketches an idyllic account of his early years, filled with stories of community life, wakes and barn-raisings, births and celebrations, and aid to the ailing:

> Here in this rough house, situated on a narrow bench of the mountain, bordered by truck patches and small fields, all surrounded by the encompassing hardwood forests, were born my four sisters and two brothers. As in my birth, mother was "waited on" by the country doctor who rode horseback from his home in Combs the two miles to our place, carrying in his saddle bags whatever medicines and instruments were used. He was assisted by neighbor women who were summoned whenever "the time had come."[7]

Like Abraham Lincoln, an icon to whom Faubus compared himself throughout his political career, he split logs, helped his dad bring in the crops, and walked miles to school, eventually gaining the elevated position of country schoolteacher.

When the United States entered the Second World War Faubus signed up, even though by then he had a wife and child and could easily have been exempted. Perhaps this early contrast with his father's resistance to *his* war foreshadowed other differences to come in 1957. In one of our conversations, in the course of telling me how honest he was throughout his time in politics, and thus how true he'd always been to his father's principles, he paradoxically invoked his war experiences:

> Well, I was always taught by my mother and dad to be honest, and I had seen people in politics get into trouble because they hadn't abided by the rules; they'd done things that were off-color.
> But the main thing was, I went through three hundred days

of combat with the front line infantry in World War II. There were personal friends of mine, buddies that I loved, in every cemetery from Normandy to the German border. Our casualties were 180 percent of the original strength. In fact, I just got a letter and the obituary of his wife from one of my buddies that lives in Missouri. And when the war was over, out of the one hundred and eighty-seven men that crossed the Channel in Company F, he was one of only four that were left.

Now, I know a lot of people would dispute it and say, "Oh, that's too damned pious and that's not right," but when anything like that [i.e., something shady like bribery] came up throughout my administration, I did the right thing, 'cause I had the thought, Those fellows are looking down on me up there, that lost their lives. And they say, "Yeah, look what we died for, and you son of a bitch, you're betraying us, you know, by taking up with these things." Excuse the language, but that's kind of military language.

It took some doing to get Faubus elected and make Jimmy into a big shot. Although his political life had begun before the war—he'd served in the elected office of circuit clerk and recorder—it was when Faubus returned to his home in Madison County that he began to seek public office in earnest, surprising many when he won the governorship in 1954. Jimmy was right when he described Faubus as the underdog; many seasoned politicians considered his first gubernatorial race a fool's errand. To everyone's surprise, the young outsider from the hills forced the incumbent, Francis Cherry, into a runoff. For white voters race barely figured into the campaign. Cherry was a "moderate," declaring in anticipation of the Supreme Court desegregation decision "we will have to abide by the decision handed down because that will be the law."[8] If race was not among the hot issues, tensions between rural and urban Arkansans were. Cherry favored industrialization and proposed taxation plans that farmers believed would disadvantage them, especially poultry farmers concentrated in the northwestern part of the state, Faubus's home territory. Faubus ran on a populist platform, defending the little guy, although he had already been a figure in state government, brought to Little Rock to direct the Department of Highways by Cherry's predecessor, the liberal governor Sid McMath.

None of these controversies had much to do with Eugene V. Debs or socialism. Nonetheless, forced into an unexpected runoff and running scared, Cherry launched a McCarthyite attack on Faubus. In the mid-1930s Orval had briefly attended an institution called Commonwealth College. ("He was a great underdog," Jimmy had said, "and they were talking about him going to some little college up here in Arkansas, Commonwealth or whatever.") Located in the hills a hundred miles from his home, it was a brief experiment in left-leaning alternative education supported by Sam. Orval stayed a very short time, leaving when he discovered that the college was not accredited and its degree would not be honored in many places. In addition, he later claimed, he had been distressed to discover that the place had communist affiliations.[9]

Faced with Cherry's exposé Faubus first denied he had ever been to Commonwealth College, even though there was clear documentary proof that he had been. Not for the last time his political future was saved by someone who later became his enemy. Outraged at Cherry's anticommunist smear campaign, the editor of Little Rock's progressive daily paper the *Arkansas Gazette,* Harry Ashmore, contacted Faubus, advising him to tell the truth and writing the speech in which he ultimately did so. The speech—the very one in the ballpark that launched his association with Jimmy Karam—was a huge success and helped to carry Faubus to victory.[10]

In his autobiography and elsewhere, Faubus represented himself as having been surprised by the communist presence at Commonwealth and shocked at a speech condemning marriage:

> One of [the speaker's] remarks, made with conviction and fervor, was "Marriage under capitalism is nothing but legalized prostitution!"
> I immediately thought of my mother who had loved only one man, married him and been true to him all her life. I said nothing during or following the lecture but I had heard enough. Soon afterward I departed the college without paying any tuition or taking any courses.[11]

I wondered how it could have happened that he'd arrived at Commonwealth unprepared for a communist affiliation, given his father's previous support for the place. In my first meeting with him, I asked him about his attendance there and heard a story with a rather different emphasis:

> I wasn't there very long, but I learned some while I was there.

> *How did you come to go there?*

> Well, my father was an old-time socialist and he was on the mailing list for that college. I'm sure that's how the literature came into my hands. And it offered, well, you could go there and work to pay your tuition. And of course, you lived on the college, and you'd have to do the work, and you got your food and lodging and the schooling.

> It was out in the country west of Mena, over in Polk County. Very beautiful place, out there. I didn't stay very long because it was a divided, about a third of the faculty and students were members of the Communist Party and another third were Socialist—and of course, I wasn't prejudiced toward them; my father had been one—and the other unaffiliated. When they organized, I belonged to the unaffiliated group, but I could learn a great deal by observation and watching the others.

> They had a very marvelous library; they took all the daily papers in Arkansas and got the papers out of New York and Washington. I read two or three books while I was there by Upton Sinclair. You know, he was a liberal writer who had been classified as such, was the Democratic nominee for governor in California at one time. But they united against him and defeated him.

> *What kind of mark did your experience at Commonwealth leave on you?*

> Caution.

> *Caution about what?*

> Well, with your associates—see, I was taught in the hills that you were known by the company you keep, and you should not keep bad company. I mean, that was drilled into me over and over again, you know.

> Strangely enough, I never did use it as an argument, but some of the segregationists did. They said, "They want to force

us to associate with these people that we don't think are as good as we are or that have criminal records, or so and so." But you know, there's good and bad in all people, all groups.

For Orval Faubus, all roads led back to a defense of his record on desegregation. Many people had told me of the ex-governor's wealth, claiming he had emerged from office with a nest well feathered. I was surprised, therefore, to find him living in a modest tract house in a suburban town an hour out of Little Rock, surrounded by little hyperactive dogs belonging to his second wife. A grandbaby's playpen lay against the picture window, and the governor's bronze nameplate proudly decorated the mantelpiece.

Faubus was a handsome old man, charming, quick-minded, filled with vivid memories and endless stories. All the other southern governors who interfered with school desegregation sooner or later made public apologies for their stance. Faubus was the exception. We chatted while I set up my equipment, and the elegant old politician let me know he was not going to change his mind today. I expressed interest in the town of Conway where he lived.

> This is the fastest growing county in Arkansas. There are about forty-six housing developments around here.
>
> *Why is it growing so fast?*
>
> Problems in Little Rock. They live out here and work down there.
>
> *What are the problems in Little Rock? [I asked naively.]*
>
> Schools. The same problems that I had in '57 and '58.

I gasped, admiring the skill with which he had just launched our talk in precisely the direction he wished it to go. He continued:

> Like, our next-door neighbor there is a Nebraskan. Came down here when Missouri-Pacific Railroad moved one of its big facilities up there to North Little Rock. So he came on down, left his wife and children up there to finish the school year. But he learned enough about their problems in Little Rock School District that he didn't want any part of it. So they got a residence

up here, and his children go to school here, and he commutes back and forth. We can hear him every morning at six o'clock revving up that car, getting ready to take off.

What are the problems in the schools?

Busing. They're spending three or four hundred thousand dollars a year to send children to school in taxicabs. It costs more to run a bus line. That's because of the federal court's order to have a certain amount of integration, race mixing, proportionate. So they have to go over here and get black students and take them way over yonder, and then go over there and get other students and take them in the other direction. They sometimes pass each other. And the buses have increased. There was a piece in the paper today about the number of buses they have in Little Rock. It's ridiculous.

I could easily believe that an extraordinary proliferation of buses had taken place, because I had just driven into town past a yard filled with rows and rows and rows of sparkling new orange buses. Paradoxically, Conway is a place where school buses are manufactured. Paradoxes seemed to cluster around Faubus like lint, as if he sat at the center of some mammoth static electric field.

Not least among them was the one I confronted as his interviewer. Researchers are never objective, and my own history was a strong presence during my conversations with Faubus. To me, watching the Little Rock struggle unfold as a teenager, Faubus was the villain of the piece. I saw him as a segregationist die-hard, backward, defending wrongs I strongly wished to right. Sitting beside him on the sofa in his suburban home, I could not maintain my hostility, nor did I wish to because I knew the story was more complex than my earlier blanket condemnation allowed, and I knew it was precisely those complexities I needed to hear and to decipher. Some people from Little Rock's African-American community had already begun to alter my thinking about the man, because they saw him more dimensionally at the same time they disapproved of his actions. When, for instance, I'd asked Evelyn, the registrar in the black high school, what her most vivid memories were of the fateful year, she'd replied:

Now, what I can remember about '57–'58 is that the students were placed in the school not at the beginning but three weeks after school started. And there was some financiers and people of influence who had convinced Governor Faubus, who was from the hills area, I guess, and limited in his knowledge and education, I'm gonna say that, and they had convinced him that he didn't have to have desegregation.

I'm not really sure that he was real fully committed to the idea that he shouldn't have it. But he had the power, they had the money. They knew within their hearts that eventually we would have desegregation.

This reference to an alliance between power and money was intriguing, given Faubus's early reputation as the common man's friend and the current simplicity of his lifestyle. But before I could question Evelyn more, she hastened to correct the impression that she might not hold Faubus personally responsible:

But let me say this, still talking about '57–'58, I feel that Governor Faubus set the tone. All he had to say was, "Well, I'm really not for it either, but that's the law. We are going to be a law-abiding state. If the law says that the students will go in to the schools, they will go in."

Instead, you know what he said? "The people don't want it."

"Caravans will descend from the hills," and I'm quoting him, "and there will be bloodshed."

As a result, they did descend, they came from everywhere.

In another of those little (but significant) paradoxes of history, Evelyn went on to mention a glitch in Faubus's program:

Well, the first day, he had the National Guard, ring them around the school, this was '57–'58. And he said, "Let in no blacks." But he forgot that there was a custodial staff and a cafeteria staff, so they had no one to cook or clean for them that day.

No blacks in the first day. So then he had to rearrange that and say, "Well, let these in, they work in the cafeteria."

Evelyn took a certain wry satisfaction in the unintended consequences of Faubus's actions, evidence of the invisibility of black working people.

Jerome Muldrew, who as a boy had walked past Central High every day on his way to the black high school and as an adult taught at the integrated school, had his own moments of amusement as he recollected his feelings about Faubus:

> *When the problems started, when Faubus called out the*
> *National Guard and the mobs formed and all that, were you sur-*
> *prised by that?*

Yes, I was. Then, of course, I really got angry, because I wondered how in the world could a governor of a state exert that much power over the state, and then defy the president of the United States. Your president of the United States is being flouted by this man from Greasy Creek, Arkansas, somewhere. And I asked, How can this happen? I was angry for that reason.

The second thing, I was angry because Faubus had skeletons in his closet before he became governor of Arkansas, in that he was affiliated with this Commonwealth School, up there, I think it was Mena, Arkansas, and they were accused of communism. And the people rallied behind him, and that's how he really got into office, because Governor Cherry's propaganda and stuff backfired and worked for him.

Although, ironically, and this is a paradox, the South, you know, we weren't supposed to vote, blacks weren't supposed to vote in Democratic primaries until 1961. Because we weren't allowed by the Democratic Party to vote in Arkansas, the blacks. But we were voting, anyway. . . . We voted right after World War Two. But they didn't eradicate that law from the Democratic Party, I think, and you can check through other sources, until 1961. But, I do know that, in a sense, blacks were voting illegal as far as the Democratic Party was concerned. . . . If you won the Democratic election in Arkansas, that was it. You were governor.

Jerome told the tale of Faubus's election with as much relish as outrage. Jerome's story had been filled with examples of steady and quiet resistance to segregationist policy in the South, and here was another one. Arkansas, like the rest of the South, was a one-party state; the only vote that mattered was the primary, because the Democratic "candidates" for office ran unopposed in the general election. Various stratagems were used throughout the South to disenfranchise blacks, and this one was common, to deny them the right to vote in the

Democratic primary, which was, legalistically, a private affair. But every action has its reaction, and in this case an act of oppression created an opportunity for rebellion. Jerome was telling me with some glee that they had surreptitiously voted anyhow. The joke was that they had thereby helped elect Faubus, believing him to be a liberal because he was associated with Commonwealth College, and thus they had enabled him to do exactly what they feared his opposition might do: thwart desegregation.

So, both blacks and whites voted for Faubus during that particular period. So, when this came up, I was really appalled to see how he turned against [his original constituency]. Here, him an underdog, and winning an election like that, it just shattered my belief in humankind, somehow. Then I said, well, all of a sudden now this man is just going to turn like this on people who actually helped him to win an election?

How did you explain that to yourself?

Well, I just simply signed it off as being politics. And I said that it was politically expedient for him to do what he did, in both instances. Because he knew he had enough plurality to win when he was at Commonwealth College, and he would have enough plurality to win if he turned to Satan. Because you see, we were considered a moderate state, but then, if you're a moderate state it meant that you can turn either way, you could either become a segregationist, or not-a-segregationist.

Now I feel that what he was doing was what most politicians would do. But as a nonpolitical thinker during that particular time, I was hurt by his action. I really was. I didn't want to see one human turning like that from another human. But then, as I grow older, I can see that certain things bring about certain quirks in individuals.

So, I still don't think that he was just a bad person, but I do think that he was very greedy, and he was very gullible for power. And I think he misused his power when he stood up to Eisenhower like he did. And having talked to him, too, had gone up to Washington. Eisenhower would've bent over backwards to have made some kind of an appeasement. Then he came right back and decided he would do what he did.

Reasons and Records

Remembering Jerome's indignation and listening now to Faubus talk of the past, I got a very different picture of Eisenhower's role and relationship with the governor. Faubus addressed Jerome's charges as if he had been present when they'd been made—as if, indeed, they were very familiar to him and his rebuttal a well-rehearsed theme:

Many of my critics accuse me of doing what I did for political reasons. Because it did turn out to be a very one-sided issue politically. But that wasn't the case.

I was serving my second term. I'd already been elected, had defeated the strongest segregationist in the state in being re-elected, renominated, and then re-elected. We had passed a program which increased teachers' salaries, and the black teachers got a bigger increase than the white teachers, because they deserved it. There was some discrepancy. Their salaries were generally lower for doing the same work as the white teachers. And working with my education department we eliminated that disparity before I left office. Schoolteachers were as happy as they've ever been in many years.

Business was happy because we had an industrial program that was being highly successful in the state. Union labor was happy with me; it was classified in *Time* as the brightest spot in the Union for union labor in Arkansas. The AFL-CIO was the first to merge in Arkansas when they decided they would merge, from two separate organizations to one. The REA [Rural Electric Administration] coops were my strong friends; I had helped them win some battles with the private power companies.

There wasn't any group in Arkansas that was formidable politically but what was happy with me. That was the situation.

Now, my fear was the problem, the crisis could hurt me, because in politics, you do something to displease people and they remember it a lot longer than the ones that you please. It's just a fact of life in politics, and maybe it shouldn't be, but that's the way it is. So, I was concerned that it would hurt me.

But when there is a crisis of that kind, the worst thing a leader can do is to become known as a do-nothing. So I decided what my course what be: I would prevent violence, and if that meant barring the students from the schools on a temporary basis in order to keep the peace at the time until they settled down, then so be it. And that's what I told the federal authorities.

He didn't do what he did for political reasons, he claimed. But he did fear he'd be politically harmed if he didn't do what he did—even though what he did, he insisted, was done for the right reason: to prevent violence. Besides, he went on to assure me, his actions flowed easily from his political philosophy, as attested to by some folks with authority (in the course of their doing something very like what I was doing now, interviewing him):

> Well, I've been interviewed hour after hour by a couple of fellows who are writing books and a biography, and one of them has declared me a true democrat: in other words, let the people decide. Provide the governmental machinery so that the people can decide.
>
> Now, this is in keeping with Thomas Jefferson's philosophy which went into the founding of the government of the Union in the beginning. If something is come about because of public sentiment, which in the long run can't be denied, then I don't think it can be stemmed by authority or by law short of absolute dictatorship. And dictatorship, you know, is the most distasteful form of government that there can be. Benevolent dictators, yeah, they can do a better job for a while, but when you get a bad one there's no way to remedy it.
>
> Now, the people in the great majority will at times make mistakes. But as long as they have the privilege of making the decisions for themselves, they can correct that error when it becomes apparent to them. So that in the long run, my firm belief has always been that in the long run to let the people decide for themselves and let them by their own actions solve their own problems, you know, that are local problems, that that is the best.
>
> And that is the philosophy which I held and that's the system that I tried to uphold, and that's why I opposed so strongly the federal courts' decisions dictating to the people what they should do. I think that's a violation of the U.S. Constitution and the division of powers. Sure, it becomes established as law over a period of time; if the executive branch takes it up and enforces it, there's nothing that the people can do to thwart it.

Shaking myself free from the magnetism of Faubus's oratory, I calculated that he had so far articulated three justifications for his actions: political expediency (" . . . because in politics, you do something to displease people and they remember it a lot longer than the ones that you please."); peacekeeping ("I decided what my course what be; I would prevent violence. . . ."); principle (". . . my firm belief has always been that in the long run to let the people decide for themselves and let them by their own actions solve their own problems, . . . that is the best"). As he talked with me, I noted how deftly he blended Jeffersonian democracy and socialist populism to articulate what was essentially a states' rights argument. After all, he suggested, in the context of the times and the specific struggle over desegregation, the point was the clash between federal and state authority. "And that's what I told the federal authorities," he'd said with emphasis, having just finished telling me what he'd told them was that he had a right to bar the students from the schools to keep the peace, to overrule a decision made by the people's elected representatives on the Little Rock School Board based on his own assessment of something that might happen, but had not yet happened.

While Faubus spoke philosophically, I sensed something a good deal less dispassionate behind his words, a more personal compulsion he had not so far articulated. What that might be was not clear, but it evoked shades of Jimmy, comfortably ensconced in his retail kingdom, talking of his humiliation at the hands of villagers very like Orval portrayed himself to be (and, I suspected, was not, given his upbringing by a self-educated, socialist father). Jimmy had said, "I had to come out fighting. I felt like I was gonna force someone to respect my parents, my mother and me," and I wondered whether Faubus, underneath the rhetoric, might not be saying something very similar.

When I returned after two years of interviews, I wasn't sure the governor remembered me. He must have picked that up, because he immediately referred to my origins in Texas: "It was Fort Worth you came from, wasn't it?" he asked. We settled in on the same settee, with one fewer little dog in attendance. Faubus looked tired, although he was just as elegantly dressed as he'd been the first time we met, just as courtly, just as in control of the conversation. He quickly told me he was recovering from surgery for prostate cancer, and I had the hunch he wanted a chance to talk more fully.

Still, he started off once again disclaiming responsibility for the confrontation at Central High, but in rather different terms. Once again exhibiting his knack for addressing the very issues in my mind I'd not yet voiced, he launched into an analysis of the relationship between local, state, and federal authorities:

> Now there were two things could have prevented the Central High School crisis: If the school board had said, Now this is our local problem; this doesn't concern any of the rest of you anywhere in Arkansas, and in any other school districts in this area. This is our local problem; we're going to handle it the best we can. And said no more than that. But instead here was all this boasting that this was going to be the great example for everybody else. . . .
>
> Now, the second thing that could have prevented it, if the federal government had forsaken its cowardly, hypocritical attitude and assumed the responsibility, if the federal authorities had assumed responsibility for a federal court order, then we wouldn't need to have a crisis. They could've sent in some of their U.S. marshals; they could have deputized some others, and if it had an attorney general at the head of the Justice Department who had been honest enough and forthright to call the governor and say, "Now Governor, we have a federal court order down there to integrate the school. I know it's not your problem, it's not your duty to enforce federal court order. It's my duty to do it, and we're going to move in, we're going to do it the best we can. I'll be hopeful that maybe you could give us some cooperation, but at least not cause us any difficulty with solving the problem."
>
> I would have accepted that. There wouldn't have been anything to be done about it but let them go ahead. Then there wouldn't have been any crisis. But here was this idea, and it's hard to explain, hard to understand, there was this idea that these people were going to be overnight heroes: Patterson, Ashmore [Hugh Patterson, publisher, and Harry Ashmore, editor, of the liberal *Arkansas Gazette*], thought that they'd be written up nationwide and around the world as having solved this problem. And here was a federal government that wouldn't lift a finger.

What had become of Jeffersonian philosophy? He'd waxed eloquent on my last visit about the rights of the little fella to self-determination (even comparing Little Rock favorably to the plight of citizens in communist domains). Now, however, he cried foul because the feds hadn't sent the marshals in sooner and relieved him of his thankless position. Which was the philosophy that guided his behavior at the time, that a stronger or a weaker federal authority was needed? I wondered whether he had in fact acted in fall 1957 to solicit federal intervention or to thwart it:

Did you protest to the Justice Department?

Oh, yeah, I called the Justice Department three times on my private line and asked to speak to Attorney General Brownell or someone who could speak for him.

When was the first phone call?

Oh, must have been ten days or two weeks before the crisis, the first one. They never did return a phone call. So, I wondered what their attitude was going to be, what they were gonna do. What I wanted to know from them, anticipating the possibility of trouble, even the probability, was what were they willing to do to keep down the trouble and if disorder broke out, what were they willing to do to control it and restore order. So finally on the second day before school was to open, a member of the Justice Department appeared in Little Rock.

Who was that?

His name was Caldwell. He's a native of Arkansas. In fact, his father was the librarian for the Arkansas State Supreme Court, who was on my side all the way; that shows you the divisions that they had then. So he wanted to see me secretly. So my receptionist worked it around and got him into the office without—'cause a lot of people didn't know him, anyhow.

Faubus suggested that his conference with Caldwell would not have been popular with his supporters and therefore required secrecy. While publicly he challenged Eisenhower and the federal government for the right of white Arkansans to control their state's racial destiny, privately he beseeched that same authority to relieve him of the political conundrum he faced. But he got nowhere:

And we conferred for more than an hour; it might have been less that two hours. And I tried to explain all these things to him, and the possibility even the probability of difficulty. And I said, "Doug, now you're from the Justice Department, what can you people do, what will you do, to restore, to maintain order here and to restore order if it gets out of hand?"

He said, "Governor, we can't do a thing." He said, "We can't do a thing until we find a body." Which is a legal terminology that there must be a transgression before they can move in.

But I was afraid that there'd actually be a body. And that's when I really got teed off with them, because, of course, I was already unhappy with the Justice Department and Brownell—they wouldn't return my phone call and wouldn't give me any advance information. I knew they had U.S. marshals, I knew they could deputize others, and they could have moved in and taken over the situation. . . .

I was put on the spot by the resolution in the Congress signed by all southern representatives except three and all the senators except two, the two from Tennessee [the Southern Manifesto in which congressional delegates from the South went on record in opposition to the Supreme Court desegregation decision]. And then the attitude of the Justice Department and the attitude of the school board, you know, they was letting this go ahead without disputing it, there's going to be an example. Everything!

So you're suggesting that you were put in an impossible position, that you were given the responsibility for solving a problem that you didn't really have the power to solve. . . .

Nor the responsibility for creating it.

But what became of your principles and your personal beliefs about the right thing to do about the racial question? Keeping the peace became the problem, not the problem of race in the public schools. What happened to your beliefs?

Well, they didn't change. I knew eventually that the integration would come if the federal government took responsibility to enforce it. But in times like that the primary responsibility of the chief executive is to maintain order, prevent destruction of property, injury to people, and even deaths. And this was the best way I could do it, perhaps the only way.

Faubus's way of doing it was to make inflammatory speeches, claiming (inaccurately as it turned out) that people were arming themselves and that "blood would run in the streets of Little Rock" if desegregation proceeded.[12] The night before school opened, he announced in a televised speech that he had posted the National Guard at the schoolhouse doors, to "act not as segregationists or integrationists," but "to maintain or restore order and to protect the lives and property of citizens," by ensuring that "the schools . . . for the time being . . . be operated on the same basis as they have been in the past."[13] But as dramatically as Faubus threw down the gauntlet, the federal government refused to pick it up.

Finally in mid-September, Faubus flew east to meet Eisenhower face to face, a meeting that grew from elaborate negotiations originated and conducted by Brooks Hays, Little Rock's congressman. In Brooks Hays's view, the discussions went reasonably well. Having been served with notice that the Justice Department was pursuing legal means to force the governor to withdraw the National Guard, Faubus seemed to agree to stop blocking the enrollment of the Nine if Eisenhower would slow down the whole process.[14] But the courts pressed forward with the existing timeline, and a week later Faubus withdrew the Guard and with it any state involvement in the students' protection. On Monday, September 23, the Nine entered the school by a side door to avoid the protestors massed at the front entrance, and the mob grew so threatening that city police had to effect a dramatic rescue. The next day, Eisenhower sent in the 101st Airborne. Once again, the school was surrounded by armed might, this time federal troops bearing bayoneted weapons. This time, the Nine began to attend classes on a regular basis, each one accompanied by a personal federal bodyguard. Faubus's worst fear and, perhaps, fondest hope had occurred. He had been overwhelmed by federal might, and the matter was out of his hands.

Accounts of the civil rights period often focus on the conflict between federal power and states' rights. It was a theme long woven through the annals of American history, and it crystallized once again in the context of school integration. But Faubus's story of his battle with Eisenhower gives another slant to this endemic center-state tension, suggesting an intriguing reversal. Faubus *wished* for federal intervention, even while his rhetoric asserted state control. Eisenhower tried to *avoid* federal action, even while his administration publicly supported racial change in the southern schools.

"Orval went around the bend and called out the National Guard," Harry Ashmore told me:

> and that forced the issue in a way that the white establishment had done everything they could to avoid, even though many didn't like it, accepting the limited integration plan, that was to avoid this kind of showdown with the federal government. And Eisenhower, who's the villain in the piece as far as I'm concerned, as much as Faubus, because this son-of-a-bitch would never support the Supreme Court decision. I think, had he done that in the period—it was three years after the Court decision came down. If we'd had some support from him—

By many accounts, Eisenhower had no heart for desegregation. He had resisted integrating the armed forces, despite pressures for an end to discrimination created by the sorts of experiences Jerome had recounted to me. Eisenhower was the product of a small town in Kansas, and it is helpful to remember that *Brown v. Board of Education* arose from a case in Kansas. Segregationist sentiment was not confined to the South. Eisenhower is widely quoted as saying, years after the Supreme Court decision, that his biggest mistake in office had been his appointment of Earl Warren as chief justice. The president had valued Warren for his conservative views and was irreconcilably affronted by the justice's turn to the left once on the court.

But the momentum of national change was at odds with the man—both the one who was president and the one who was governor. As corporations became increasingly national in scope, there grew a greater need for uniformity of conditions across state boundaries. That dynamic combined with a greater sentiment in favor of racial equity (arising in part, as Jerome had suggested, from the experiences of black servicemen in the war) to create a pressure for a decisive federal intervention. At the same time, Faubus had newly emerged on the Little Rock political landscape and expected to operate with the downhome hegemony customary to governors of Arkansas. His personal beliefs played a very second fiddle to his desire for power, and that desire was bolstered by some business interests. Faubus's buddy Witt Stephens, for instance, headed a utility company that had an interest both in industrial growth and in continuing control over regulatory legislation. Like Faubus, Stephens's personal views on desegregation were secondary to his strategic interests. By Mahlon Martin's description of how local power worked in Little Rock back then ("There was a time in this city when seven, eight people actually made decisions that affected everybody") it seems likely that a clear position in favor of peaceful desegregation on the part of that small coterie would have made a difference. But while some local businessmen may have wished to avoid a confrontation with the feds, as Harry Ashmore suggested, those who mattered simply wanted the governor to stay powerful— and beholden to their own largesse.

Faubus confirmed this view of things as our conversation stretched on into a dimming afternoon. I pressed the governor to tell me more about his personal opinions in the midst of all this cross-fire. He had insisted he was neither for nor against desegregation, and he'd expressed very contradictory views. But I began to notice a pattern to the way he spoke about the events:

> *I want to ask you a question about language. You've said repeatedly that you did not have a position against desegregation. And at this stage in the history you're presenting yourself as being not on either side.*
>
> Yup.
>
> *Yet you pretty consistently use the word "opposition" to mean the integrationists. At what point did the integrationists become the opposition?*
>
> After I placed the Guard at Central High School.
>
> *Not before that?*
>
> No. And it was headed by Harry Ashmore and Hugh Patterson, some other prominent figures in Little Rock, some of the business people that didn't want any disruptions because they were interested in making money and not the welfare of the schools or the kids.

I pressed the point, citing other places where he identified clearly with the segregationists. Why, I asked again, had he chosen not to provide the kind of leadership Evelyn had imagined? ("All he had to say was, 'Well, I'm really not for it either, but that's the law. We are going to be a law-abiding state. If the law says that the students will go in to the schools, they will go in.'")

> Oh, no, I wasn't going to do that, because it'd have been stupid on my part. The press used to come in and say, "Why don't you go out and tell these people that this is what ought to be done? There are some issues where the people are not well informed, but they'll listen to you and listen to your explanation and consider what you ask them to do."

> But in a situation of this kind, every person has got his mind made up. It'd just be like butting your head against a stone wall. It'd be the same as speaking to stumps. Well, I knew that. The press, you know these young fellows, didn't have enough judgment to realize that.

> So all I could do was to, I guess you'd say, roll with the tide and do the best I could. Because then I had influence with the segregationists and so I *did* keep down a lot of trouble.

> *So that was a strategic decision you made, to ally yourself with the segregationists?*

> Right. It wasn't philosophical. No, they allied themselves with *me* and I didn't rebuff them.

> *But you just said, "We will win" You included yourself in the "we." That suggests a more active alliance.*

> Somewhat.

> But you see if I hadda said, "You will win," they would have said, "He's not with us." And the sentiment was so overwhelming at the time.

> *But why was it more important for you to be accepted as an ally of the segregationists than accepted as an ally of the integrationists, given how polarized it was?*

> Well, one way it would have been political suicide, the other way was survival.

Attitudes of political cynicism are sufficiently integrated into the American psyche that it would have been easy for me to accept that last statement in the spirit in which it was offered. Faubus suggested that political survival was unarguably a sufficient motivation to do what he had done. Drawing myself up, I plunged into the hegemonic waters of the politically obvious and swam on, seeking deeper explanations of what induced Faubus to cling to office the way he had. He'd made it very clear to me that it wasn't about money, and his current circumstances gave that claim a ring of truth:

> I wanted to be a good governor, and 'course as Witt Stephens says, who became my friend and one of my main supporters and he was very, very rich, he always said, I didn't have any desire for money. Well, I didn't desire money over principle.

He had insisted he was not motivated by racism. His family background made that, too, a credible statement. As our afternoon together drew longer, I naively asked him to tell me why survival mattered to him:

> Well, I guess the same reason why any politician wants to survive.

> *I imagine there are different reasons why politicians want to survive.*

> I had things going that I wanted done. If I hadn't stayed in office the length of time I did, the State Hospital wouldn't have been rebuilt, the Children's Colony wouldn't have been built, educational television wouldn't have been established, 'cause I had to muscle it through the legislature. Roads and bridges. Also, taking care of the old folks; I got as much sense of satisfaction out of that, when those old people sat on their porch in their rocking chair and were happy and unconcerned, feeling confidence in me as the governor that I was going to do the right thing by them, that meant a lot.

> I used to travel from Little Rock up to my home area to vote and take a small plane up across the mountains, and I'd look down there at all those little houses out across the country and the roads leading into the town and you could see the cars moving in, and I'd hope all of them were going to vote. But they came from homes that were generally well satisfied with the service

they were getting from their state government. Well, that was important to me.

But I guess, to be candid, ego was a part of it, too.

What sense of satisfaction or of self did you get?

Out of the ego thing? I broke the records. And now I hold the record.

The record for?

Served the longest and elected the most times. And I think, in all sincerity and honesty, did the most good for the people.

Do you have any regrets? Is there anything you want to apologize for?

No. No, I've been asked that many times about the Little Rock situation. Now, I've said this and I'll say it again: I regret that it ever happened. I wish that it could have been prevented. But I don't know anything else at the time that I could have done that so successfully prevented property damage, injury to people, and deaths.

Because he did good for industry and maintained a good relationship with them, industrialists and financiers like Witt Stephens did not quarrel with his role in the Central High debacle. They made small efforts to contain the damage, but essentially they let events, including heavy intimidation of other business people by segregationists to remain silent, take their course. In the end, that proved to have been a mistake. Two years later, the Women's Emergency Committee studied the economic impact of the crisis on Little Rock, and it was their finding of the business devastation wrought that helped significantly to convince the community to elect a liberal school board and to move forward on peaceful integration.

At the end of our long talk, I asked Faubus how he felt about it all in retrospect:

You had a long career and did all kinds of things. How do you feel about the fact that the one thing you're known for in the outside world is your role at Central High School? And you're held in considerable disregard about that.

Yeah, I understand. But I don't think that's the majority sentiment. When this thing developed and they set up a private school [i.e., when the Little Rock public high schools were closed the year after the crisis], without even sending out any letters or anything, contributions came in from every state in the Union and eight foreign countries.

Look, Wallace was a segregationist. He's what some people would call a racist. I never was, except maybe by some who didn't know about the situation. Even Sid McMath and Henry Woods that opposed me in '62. A fellow wrote a book about me that he said one of the reasons was to give a more balanced viewpoint of Governor Faubus, and he interviewed all those people. McMath told him, he said, There wasn't a racist bone in Faubus's body. And all the other people that this man interviewed expressed the same opinion. But Wallace ran for president, seeking the Democratic nomination—can't remember the year now. He got a very significant vote in Indiana and in some of the other northern states. Then he went into the primary in Michigan, and Michigan and Maryland were the same day. There were fourteen other candidates seeking the Democratic nomination, including Muskie and some of the very prominent ones. Wallace got more votes than all of them put together in Michigan, and then he carried Maryland and that was the day he was shot and taken out of action.

So I'm not a rascal to a lot of people out there. I'll tell you a funny little story. Went to the southern governors' conference, Sea Island, Georgia, and a fella named Barron B-A-R-R-O-N was governor at that time of West Virginia. And this was a time I think that I was chairman of the conference. . . .

The Virginia State Fair was underway a few miles from Sea Island, where we were. And of course Barron invited all the governors to go over. Only four of us went, I think, and I was one of them. But I was glad I went, because when we got there the FFA boys, and I was the first FFA boy ever elected governor of Arkansas—Future Farmers of America—and the 4H girls, whatever they called them, they all had been divided up, and they had been assigned a governor. Well, mine were so pleased that I was there, and they got to show me through the exhibits and so on. And they were so pleased my wife was there, the girls. But I could see the disappointment in the faces of the others whose governor didn't appear.

But anyhow, then we went after that and were seated up in the stands and had, I guess what you call it, sulky racing, where you've got this one animal in shafts with a two-wheel vehicle and it's supposed to trot; if it breaks into a gallop that disqualifies it. And they were showing us that.

Over to our right was seated a bunch of officials from West Virginia. Legislators, state senators, and so on. And near the end one of them got up and came over and said, "Governor, I just got to come over and shake hands with you. And I've got a story I want to tell you."

He said, "In my district in West Virginia, there's an old lady named Jane that lives out in the country. And she's the political leader and advisor for that whole area. Everybody goes through her if they want to get some kind of favor from the governor or the state senator and so on. So everybody visits her.

"So I was out campaigning and I went by her house and I was visiting with her. And we were having a nice visit. And a big old black tomcat ran by, and she kicked at it and said, 'Get out of the way, Faubus!'" [chuckles]

And he said, "Aunt Jane, why did you name that old cat 'Faubus'?" She said, "'Cause he's a fighter."

This view of himself as fighting the powerful rang true as part of his motivation. As a boy from the hills, he had struggled against the odds to gain power, and throughout he was kept at a distance by those in the inner coterie. Arkansas is even today a small pond with a well-defined circle of power. Just as Jimmy Karam wanted respect above all ("I was a big shot in those days"), so Faubus desired to be taken seriously.

Jimmy's passion in this respect was formed by his experiences as an outcast: "I had to come out fighting. I felt like I was gonna force someone to respect my parents, my mother and me." Faubus, in contrast, represented his boyhood as an idyllic one of community companionship and acceptance. I wondered, though, whether there might not have been some contradictory themes. His father's politics could not have sat particularly well with many of his neighbors. To be a political radical is to embrace a certain identity, one at odds with the mainstream in which we all inevitably swim. Orval grew up inside a small town, but outside a worldview. His ambivalence about Commonwealth College may well have reflected the complexities of his own identity. Even in his relationship with his father, tensions remained unspoken but well acknowledged between the two. Harry Ashmore wrote about his experience of that aspect of the drama:

> When Orval betrayed the old man's teachings and thereby became a prime object of media attention, Sam Faubus refrained from denouncing his flesh and blood to the reporters who sought him out in his little house up on Greasy Creek. But, throughout his son's long career in the statehouse, he regularly wrote sharply critical letters that appeared in the *Gazette*'s "From the People" column over the signature Jimmy Higgins [a labor leader]. He identified himself only after I had moved to California, where I received a letter in his shaky handwriting saying he now felt free to tell me that he was Jimmy Higgins, and wanted to commend me in his own name for my stand against his erring son.[15]

I asked Faubus about this story; he laughed and said:

> Yes, I knew about that all the time. My dad has his opinions. Now, I did think he opposed what I had done, how I'd handled the situation. But he was for the social advancement, and he believed that full rights for black people and integration was all right. Now of course he lived in an area where there was no problem. If he lived in Little Rock, he'd be condemning what was going on to the nth degree.

Jimmy Karam was a misfit who made a kingdom in a clothing store. Orval Faubus was a prototype—the boy from the hills—who defied stereotypes but kept trying to fit them and was seen in the end to be the essence of the racist politician. The lives of both men defined social divisions and both were devoted to crossing those lines. Harry Ashmore wrote:

> Even as a little boy, Sam Faubus once pointed out, Orval could never stand to be looked down upon. As an

unexpected tenant of the Governor's Mansion he had ample reason to feel that the Little Rock establishment resented his populist assault on Francis Cherry, and tended to write him off as a rude demagogue. He suspected that the liberal Democrats, who should have been his political allies, didn't take him seriously. He saw, correctly, that when the Blossom Plan worked through to its conclusion the affluent whites in the suburbs would be largely exempt from integrated schools while the working-class whites in the downtown section would have to send their children to class with blacks. His most durable antagonist, Daisy Bates of the NAACP, believed that it was this personal resentment that pushed him into the arms of the segregationists. "I could see what was happening to Orval after he got in office," she once told me. "The liberals thought he was a political accident and wouldn't be there long, and they had little to do with him. When he put those troops around Central High it was the people in Pulaski Heights he was really trying to get at. I told Edwin Dunaway [president of Little Rock's Urban League]: You all may deserve Orval Faubus, but, by God, I don't!"[16]

What Orval and Jimmy both contested was their own place in a class system that included both material rewards, social status, and an identity that allowed self-respect. The forum for that contest was, almost incidentally, racial, because the burning question of the time concerned desegregation. Orval was convinced that he himself was not a racist, but "the people in the great majority" were. Without a second thought, he therefore allied himself with a position about which he had no strong conviction—either way. For the boys from the hills the fight was not about race but about power relations. But in fact it was about race, because the only contenders for class power they recognized were white, and so their own struggle up the ladder of power defined them as white. Thus black issues were incidental to them but crucial to so many others as the two cronies strategized in their own interest. We shall see how issues of identity and power were negotiated on many levels by many other white people also, throughout the story of Central High.

At the very last moment of my time with Faubus, he reintroduced questions of race on a very personal level, in a way he'd refused to do during the formal interview. I was packing up my tape recorder, the wires all undone and the tape removed, when the governor, regarding me speculatively, said, "You know, I have a classmate out there in California. Her name is Roy, too. She married a fellow named Roy."

"Oh, yes?" I said, a little distracted by wires and microphones. "Where was he from?"

"Somewhere out there," Faubus responded vaguely.

"Roy is my married name, too," I volunteered. "My husband was from India."

He smiled a little wryly. "I've run into several of those Indian people at the medical centers here and in Houston. Hard-working people. Know they've got a chance and work hard to make the most of it."

He looked at me with a mischievous glint in his eye. "L. C. Bates," he said, getting ready to quote the husband of Daisy Bates, Faubus's nemesis when she'd chaired the NAACP during the crisis in Little Rock. L. C. Bates was a prominent African-American journalist in town and someone Faubus had claimed as a friend when the dust settled in the sixties. "L. C. Bates," he continued, "once said (he shook his head winningly and chuckled), 'We can make opportunities for them, but I don't know what's going to get those guys off their behinds and doing something with them.'

"That's the thing about dark people," Faubus went on. "The ones from other places work hard, but . . ." His voice drifted away on a fertile silence, until, some tense moments later, I said good-bye.

FOUR
Cracking the Gate

*And the . . . segregationist groups were just rantin' and pantin'
about, picketing, . . . holding meetings, burning crosses . . .*

—Chris Mercer

*That's our feeling toward the blacks. . . . If they love us, we
love them.*

—Maddie Jean Blair

It's been a long, long struggle.

—Sara Murphy

Most conventional stories of history we encounter, whether in
popular representations or in text books, feature individuals (usually
white men) as the architects and builders of change. In the drama at
Central High, the most likely candidate for that role was clearly
Governor Faubus. Again and again, people I interviewed held him
responsible for what happened. My own memories of the times are
filled with commentaries I heard about his pivotal role. He was praised
or vilified, but universally seen as the man who made Little Rock's
experience what it was.

Faubus's presentation of himself in his own narrative ricocheted
between that view and a very different one. At any given moment he
might present himself as a decisive force for good, saving lives and
averting social upheaval, or alternatively as the sport of powers over
which he had no control, a victim rather than a history maker, help-
lessly squeezed between inaccessible federal power and irresponsible
local ambitions.

This question of individual roles relates closely to a central question about the nature of history. Who drives history? Who makes
change happen? Does history spring from the minds and hands of a
few powerful people? Or are ordinary folks, those whose names never
appear in the annals, the mobs in front of the school and the students

within, the true agents of history? My interviews in Little Rock often dwelt on this matter of agency in painful, personal detail. Most of the white people who talked with me, especially those who populated the school itself, portrayed themselves at best as innocent bystanders, at worst as the real victims of the piece. Black people, however, more often saw themselves as activists, making personal choices to reshape society.

Between those who acted like Governor Faubus and those acted upon like the students of Central High there existed a stratum of people who engaged the events of 1957–58 with intentionality and effectiveness. Their stories deepen the picture of what happened and why, and illuminate meanings underlying race relations today.

Chris Mercer

Chris Mercer is an African-American attorney who, as a young lawyer in the fifties, assisted Thurgood Marshall in filing the pivotal suits in federal court that led to school desegregation. One night over Chinese dinner, I asked him what he'd thought of the governor's behavior in 1957. "Did you think Faubus would do what he did?" I asked. "Was it a surprise to you?"

> No. That was socially and politically correct in the white world at that time. That was socially and politically correct. Faubus was doing what was socially acceptable.
>
> Though Arkansas had made some advances and done some things, I don't know that there was widespread acceptance or widespread acquiescence. When you've lived for so long over here and you've attained a certain level, you're basically afraid of the unknown. You've never had to do this. I don't know whether it was just bigotry on the part of folk or that you feel more comfortable in doing what you've been doing all along. To disrupt that becomes awkward. So a number of people would be just as happy if I just didn't have to deal with that. "I'm doing all right and I don't have to deal with that."
>
> And as a result you get people like Faubus in Arkansas and your boy down here in Alabama and your boy in Mississippi and your Maddox in Georgia. But they're out there rantin' and pantin' and so it may be embarrassing to a lot of people. They

just say, "Well, let them go on because it does not disturb my world."

You said, "Did you think Faubus would have done that?" I think that we were more surprised that Faubus went that far. Just to say something to placate people, fine and good. Faubus himself would say many, many times, you know, [it was] politically expedient: "I didn't really feel like that." Faubus had not, growing up where he had, a real exposure to blacks. He grew up in northern Arkansas. [. . .] Faubus came from a little place way up in the Ozarks called Huntsville. [. . .]

He was a poor boy, got to town and the limelight and in a position of power, and he was doing what was politically expedient. [. . .]

Sometimes you don't realize the implication of the act until it's over. I don't think that Faubus would have done what he did had he known it would have gained him such adverse notoriety. Many times you do things you don't realize the implication of what you did. I don't think that he would have done this if he had known that this was going to place Little Rock at the forefront of the resistance movement.

You would expect the resistance in Birmingham, in Atlanta, in Columbia, South Carolina. You would expect it in Jackson, Mississippi. These were places that you would expect the resistance movement. Little Rock was the last place in the world anyone would have thought that the world renown resistance would have come to the forefront.

But it would have been a holy bloodbath [in those other places]. There were no real killings and murders and people getting bitter. I'll tell you business and commerce and involvement in all the rest of the community was going on as if nothing was happening out at Central High School.

It took some doing for me to arrange a meeting with Chris, given my fleeting trips to town and his busy schedule. But I'd persevered, finally inviting him to join me for dinner. A tall man with a deeply lined face, Chris arrived carrying a heavy old battered briefcase. I thought, as his story unfolded, that bag was a pretty good metaphor for his life on the front lines. He marched to the table, shuffled through some papers, parked the briefcase at his feet and never once referred to it again as we talked for hours and hours. In story after story, as the wine flowed and the hour grew late, he recounted the depth of his convictions and the fury of the storms he had weathered.

I thought Chris's assessment of Faubus was surprisingly generous (especially in light of the latter's sweeping dismissal of black Americans in my final exchange with him). He saw the governor as uninformed about black issues. He believed his resistance to be politically motivated. At the same time, he recognized that things might have been worse, a point the governor himself had made to me more than once. As I listened to Chris try to sort out the contradictions in Faubus's actions, I thought his spirit of generosity might spring as much from his sense of participation in the history behind Central High's desegregation as from a simple willingness to forgive:

> I did a small amount of work in Fort Smith. And actually it wasn't so necessary to do much in Fort Smith because they didn't have that many blacks in Fort Smith and they'd always maintained a pretty decent high school, you know, there wasn't that much distinction.
>
> They were geographically segregated. Quite a few blacks lived on the north side. None were living on the south side of Fort Smith. They went on and integrated the north side high school and didn't have a problem.
>
> I know what they did in Fayetteville. This was the forerunner, before the Supreme Court decision on desegregation. When I went to school there in '49, the schools were not integrated. They only went to the eighth grade, and after you finished the eighth grade, that was the end of it. This is the seat of the citadel of learning, the seat of the university.

Chris was speaking of the small college town to the northwest of Little Rock where the University of Arkansas is located. While he talked, we opened our fortune cookies. "I didn't bring my glasses," Chris said as he struggled with the small print. I offered to read it for him, but he soldiered on, extending his arm to find a usable focal length: "You will finally solve a difficult problem that will mean much to you," he read aloud. I said I sincerely hoped so, and Chris smiled merrily as he plunged back into his story, elaborating the history of desegregation in Fayetteville:

A quite small black community they had up there. . . . The black community up there was a servant community. Some were left over from some of the people who went up to do common labor when they were building the university. Some stayed around there. You had maybe four or five hundred blacks.

[Nonetheless,] in Fayetteville [that] was a large black population for northwest Arkansas. Ferndale had one black family. Rogers didn't have any. Yellville didn't have any. You get a few blacks down there at Alma, forty miles down the ridge, and a few in Fort Smith.

But in any event, the [African-American] do-gooder ladies, you know, the little social clubs and the tea drinkers, thought it was just horrible that our kids here [in Fayetteville] would not have access to any school after they finished eighth grade, so the first thing they did, they petitioned the school board. They got the school board to provide them with a high-school education. And coach was out there looking over the rippling muscles on all these boys he thought he was going to have on down at the Fayetteville school, but they sent them down to Fort Smith! What they were doing was running a bus down there every day. That's seventy-one miles from Fayetteville down to Fort Smith. They'd run that bus down there, and they'd have to get up early in the morning and get back late at night, and people get to crying. It's very mountainous. I don't know if you've been up to Fayetteville.

The bus had an accident one night and hurt some of the kids. And the women said, "Now, that's just too bad having those kids ride like that. Not only is it too bad, it's dangerous." And what have you. "We're not going to have that." So then the school board said, "Well, it's too [expensive] to [keep] them [in a separate school] around here." So they paid for them to stay down in Fort Smith.

At the time, Fort Smith had Fort Chaffee, which was full of blacks, an army post. So they stayed down there. And as fate would have it, some of those little old pretty girls got seduced by some of those old boys out there at the camp, and they got pregnant. And the good sisters then really got up in the air. "Now, that wouldn't have happened if they'd been having the sanctity of home. And putting them off down there, we're going to have to do something about it."

So it took some adversity to bring about the end result, but behind all those experiences, they integrated the schools in Fayetteville prior to the 1954 decision. They went on and integrated schools there. They've been integrated ever since. So there were different motives, different techniques, and different procedures going on everywhere.

But you never had the turmoil about involvement because it was not in as great numbers, and they didn't have to do with much movement. No law suits had been filed. And some should have been filed in places where they hadn't been filed. They used Little Rock as an example, "OK, let's see what happens in Little Rock. Whatever they say up there we better do that, or if we don't, they'll do it to us down here." Little Rock has been the scapegoat down through the years.

Interestingly, that was precisely the complaint I heard again and again from white people in Little Rock, who were bitter about the bad reputation their city had earned—undeservedly, in their view. Often people said, "If you think we're bad, you should see those folks down there in Mississippi." On the other end of the spectrum from "bitter scapegoats" were the African-American women, the "do-gooder ladies" who drove the process of desegregation in Fayetteville. Their power to do so derived from a moral authority attached to good mothering. So, too, in Little Rock, women were potent agents of social change in all possible camps of the struggle.

Chris's story about the prior desegregation of the Fayetteville schools might have suggested that the process would proceed peacefully in Little Rock. His personal experience with integration also suggested optimism:

I went to Law School up at the University of Arkansas in 1949. And I wasn't the first one to go, you see. They admitted the first black student in February of '48.

That desegregation success was also dictated by expediency, Chris explained. The state was required to provide professional training for all students who desired it, and it was a good deal cheaper to integrate the existing institutions than to send the one or two black students who applied elsewhere.

But if the Fayetteville public schools and the University of Arkansas Law School were positive precedents, others were more problematic. "I worked with the Hoxie School District," Chris said. "Have you ever heard that name?" I had heard of Hoxie. Virgil Blossom, the superintendent of schools who authored the desegregation plan as well as a book about his troubled experiences thereafter, wrote of Hoxie as a positive example of integration:

> At Hoxie, a small town in eastern Arkansas, the School Board integrated approximately twenty-five Negro children into the white schools. When the segregationists demonstrated against integration, the School Board itself went into federal court and secured what has since become known as the "Hoxie type" restraining injunction against interference. The demonstrations ceased and school integration proceeded.[1]

Chris's version of what happened at Hoxie was a good deal more elaborate and dynamic:

> The significance of Hoxie was that the school board there was trying to integrate the schools because they really couldn't afford to maintain [separate systems]. They exchanged with Jonesboro with the high-school students, and they maintained a little elementary school, but the resources for the school district were so meager, they couldn't afford this elementary school and to pay the tuition for the high-school students to go down there. And one of the ways to eliminate this deficit was to integrate schools. They had schools there that could easily take them in.
>
> The thing that made them conspicuous, though, was that back in those days, many schools adhered to the prevailing economy. If it was agrarian, kids would be out during harvest season. So they had what they called a split term.
>
> So Hoxie was going to integrate its schools [in 1955] when the kids were going to go to school in the summer, so they could be out in the fall to help out in the harvest. This was prevalent throughout the South. And by virtue of trying to integrate its schools in the summer, it meant that it was doing so much sooner than the fall term when most people would be trying to go to school.

So it became very conspicuous. And the White Citizens Council and other segregationist groups were just rantin' and pantin' about, picketing, and zeroing in on that community, holding meetings, burning crosses, and all this sort of stuff. And I went up [there].

But what we did up at Hoxie—and this was unique—the Hoxie School District wanted to integrate because it could not afford to segregate. And it voted to do so, but there was so much outside pressure being put on people, who were not necessarily part of the school district but were working up the frenzy of people who were part of the school district. Open demonstrations, inviting people from everywhere. "We can't let this happen." "We got to keep this from going."

So the Arkansas Council on Human Relations, and I was involved with that, we went up there, and I went to Jonesboro, and I found a white lawyer that I thought would be sympathetic because of something he did when we were up at school at the university. . . .

I said, well now, Bill . . . might be sympathetic. I didn't know whether he was or not. Bill was an attorney. His dad was an attorney, and his wife was an attorney. His wife was a United States Magistrate. . . . So I went to Bill and I said, "Bill, these people over here want to integrate the schools but they are being prohibited from doing so because of all these demonstrations and they can't get nobody to represent them. Would you represent them?"

He said, "Yeah, but I don't know what to do."

I said, "I don't know what you do right now, but," I said, "I'll go back and research the law and find out something for you to do."

He said, "Well, if you give me some law, I don't know nothing about no law. If you give me some law, I'll do it."

So I came back, and I couldn't find any law directly on the point, but I found some law that I thought was apropos: that if you have a constitutional obligation to perform a duty, then you have a constitutional right to be protected in the performance of that duty. It was in one little obscure case. I went back and gave that to Bill, and Bill filed the petition in federal district court on behalf of the Hoxie School Board—this is before Central— on behalf of the Hoxie School Board to get an injunction against the White Citizens Council and these other segregationist groups who were demonstrating up there, to get an injunction to enjoin them from interfering with the Hoxie School Board in the lawful performance of its duty to integrate the school.

That worked. That became the landmark case, the Hoxie case. But it was on a little obscure law. It's the inverse of things, so if you have a constitutional obligation to do something, then you have a constitutional right to be protected in the performance of that duty.

Hoxie might have established a point of law on the basis of which the federal courts could act. But it paradoxically accomplished several other things that benefited the segregationist side. By the time the crisis in Hoxie was over, the Citizens Council was well established statewide. A doctrine called interposition, the idea that the state has the right to interject its authority between that of local officials and the federal government for the purpose of maintaining peace, was evoked and explored. A previous incident in Mansfield, Texas, in which desegregation was halted by mob action without intervention by federal authorities, was widely contrasted in Arkansas with the Hoxie experience and explained away as the result of national party politics (a theory that helped raise the dander of Arkansas Democrats). If Superintendent Blossom drew positive inspiration from the case of Hoxie, so also did Governor Faubus.[2]

Maddie Jean and Stanley Blair

If Chris helped construct the legal foundation for desegregation, my next interviewee helped shape its implementation. I was especially interested in talking with parents of children who were students in Central High at the time. In general, they fell in the category of people occupying the sidelines, but one clear and unexpected exception was **Stanley Blair**. Toward the end of one fall visit to Little Rock, someone told me about a couple whose daughter had been a Central High student that year. I called them right away, thinking I'd set up an appointment next time I was in town. "Come on over!" they said with such enthusiasm that I decided to risk missing my plane to see them on my way to the airport.

Stan and Maddie Jean lived in a little clapboard house in a very pleasant neighborhood bordering a big park. There was a chill in the air that day, but their house felt like a tropical rain forest. They were old and frail and, presumably, vulnerable to the cold, but blessed with really good central heating. The living room was cluttered and dusty, filled with newspapers and magazines and the detritus of years of living. Neither of the Blairs heard too well, and neither was too well endowed dentally, so conversation was a little iffy. But they made up in élan and humor whatever they lacked in physical equipment for communication.

There was some business with chairs. There were only two in the room, and Maddie scolded me away from either of them. "I sit there," she declared, pointing with royal good humor and resolutely hurrying her tiny frame to the spot, "and that one's his. Stanley! Bring a dining room chair." Stanley was a burly gray-headed man, scruff-faced and lined and merry.

When at last we were settled and the tape recorder on, they set about telling me their histories: where they were born (she in Alabama, he in Texas); how they'd met (introduced by a mutual friend in the little town where Maddie Jean lived and where Stanley was working for a real estate broker—"I was not particularly impressed," said Maddie Jean in a way that struck my ears as oft-repeated); how they'd come to live in Little Rock (Stanley was hired by a local developer).

In the midst of these biographical rehearsals, Maddie declared:

> Our kids all graduated from Central. Every one of them. And Marcia, now, could have gone to Hall 'cause we lived out this way, but we decided that was stupid. After all, the other three had graduated from Central.

Marcia, I knew, was a senior in 1957. Now I learned that she was the youngest of the four Blair children:

> Marcia would graduate from Central, too. And it worked out.
> I remember Stanley telling her—I thought you might be interested in this—he said "Now, honey, remember this, the innocent bystander is always the one who gets hurt. Now be careful." That's all he said, and I didn't say anything, 'cause I knew Marcia was going to behave herself, you know. I just didn't worry.

That seeming non sequitur momentarily preoccupied me. If Marcia were an innocent bystander, what worry was Maddie feeling when she instructed her daughter to behave herself? It seemed to me in combination her parents were giving Marcia some complex instructions: mix Maddie Jean's thought with Stanley's warning and you got an active rather than a passive definition of innocence. Maddie went on to reminisce about her own entrances onto the stage of history:

> Now, there were two things that I will tell you about Central, I was talking to Stanley about it, that I remember about that year particularly.
>
> Marcia had to take medicine for a little heart problem. And so she called me frantic, just frantic one morning. She said, "Momma, I forgot my medicine." And I said, "Well, I'll bring it to you."
>
> She said, "Well, I don't know whether they'll let you come or not." See, the National Guard was all around. I said, "I'll get your medicine to you, honey."
>
> So we decided where we would meet, at the side. I drove up and this National Guard came up, and I said, "I'm Mrs. Blair, my daughter is Marcia Blair. She needs her medicine and here it is. Now, she's coming out that door. Now you and I will walk up together, and you will watch me give her the medicine." [. . .]
>
> So we did, I think I even held his arm, I'm not sure, you know I never worry about things like that. And she came out and got the medicine and I went on.
>
> Then graduation night, Marcia [and her friend], . . . they had plans, Stan wasn't even here. He was in Shreveport or something on business. So I went with a close friend of mine. And so Marcia said, "Now, Momma, you've got to get my—oh you know—my cap and gown." And I said, "Well, Marcia, I can't get it from you up there [because the area where the students sat was guarded]." She said, "I'll be out on the field." I said, "All right, I'll walk down to the end of the field and you can give it to me. And then you get to go ahead and play games. But you be in by so-and-so." That was it.
>
> Well, we always said, "401 and Ernest." [laughs] That was all we ever said: "401 and Ernest." And Ernest was very nice, and

> Ernest behaved himself, and Ernest walked in by himself or with
> another boy, I have forgotten.

It took me a few beats to realize that Maddie was enumerating the
graduating class: 401 people and Ernest Green, the only black student
to graduate that year. With whom he walked down the aisle to receive
his diploma had been a highly controversial question, so Maddie Jean's
allusion was a thickly coded one.

Code for what? I wondered. Maddie's first forays into talking about
Central High were all about her own brushes with armed power, the
most vivid and dramatic aspect of the times—and also, perhaps, the
stories she thought would most interest me. But so far she'd told me
little about her own feelings. What had she thought at the time, I now
asked her, about the school's being desegregated?

> Well, I didn't think anything about it one way or the other,
> I had grown up with blacks. They're like white folks, some are
> nice, some are raunchy. Some are ladies and gentlemen, some
> are poor white trash, or poor black trash.
>
> My daddy [a pharmacist] waited on blacks and whites. I was
> brought up by a black nurse. Well, not really; we had washwomen
> and everything.
>
> But of course that was over in Alabama. So, I still get along
> beautifully with blacks because I like them personally. [...]
>
> I don't think anything about it one way or another. Socially,
> I do not go with blacks, but they come into my house, and they
> sit, and they talk with me if they need to, but that's because I'm
> more comfortable with white folks, and they're more comfort-
> able with black folks. Socially.

Maddie Jean told me she'd had "an awful lot" of contact with
black people connected with Stanley's work. "And it was never a problem," she insisted. "I mean, when we went out to eat, well, I just tried
to make them feel good. What else could I do?"

Stan now went on to elaborate his views, without reference to
Maddie's statement. Stan was in the unusual position of having had
a close relationship to Governor Faubus, including serving occasionally as a political advisor. But more importantly Stanley served during the crucial years as a lobbyist for the largest industrial developer

in the state. I remembered Evelyn talking about "some financiers and people of influence" who had shaped Faubus's politics, and I knew Stan's bosses were among those who, in Evelyn's descriptions, "had the money." I knew from Faubus himself that he'd done favors for them, and I was interested in what Stan might have to say about how that business worked. I asked him how much contact he'd had with the governor back then, and he said, "Oh, two or three times a day. I was speaking largely on behalf of my employer." Intrigued as I was by these relationships to power, I first asked about his views of the desegregation process:

> I had known [Faubus] real well and I frankly was surprised at the turn of events. 'Cause he was inclined to be a liberal. And nearly all of his acquaintances were liberals. And then the political atmosphere in Arkansas was about like it is now.
>
> There is a separation, geographically, of people east and south of Little Rock, and north and west of Little Rock. The social mores are still in place, and Little Rock was the focal point of a clash of attitudes. Generally speaking, and this shows some of my provincialism, generally speaking the people north and west of us geographically, they manifest a bigoted attitude that just didn't exist in Little Rock at that time.
>
> And 'course the governor was playing to all sides and the problem became locally a political problem when we had this very liberal school board here. Very liberal, law-abiding superintendent.
>
> And the people started choosing up sides, and it came down to our school board, and our superintendent said we would integrate as the courts had said we would. And all of the people in the state including those in the northwest and those in the southeast said they didn't want Little Rock to be the first place to be integrated, brought by court order. And so there became a philosophical conflict between our school board and the governor's office, the administration. And so it was politics, and we had a good school board. I didn't admire any of them particularly. All but one of them was in my Sunday School class.

> *Why didn't you admire them?*

> They were autocratic in their—they wanted to run the Little

Rock School District like they ran their private businesses: there would be no outside interference. They didn't classify themselves as political creatures and each one of them had his own private set of bias. And that came into play. It's almost impossible to describe verbally the attitudes, the feelings, and the bias, the prejudices that entered into Little Rock 1957.

Stan had started with a very objective description of the forces at play: bigoted rural folks, a law-abiding school board, a liberal governor. But as soon as his subjective view entered the picture, things became more complex. Like Maddie, Stan identified himself as a liberal, but at the same time he established himself as a critic of the "very liberal" school board and superintendent.

Stan went on to tell me about the various pressures on Faubus to change his position on desegregation. The "plantation class" in eastern Arkansas wanted to have at hand an uneducated and thus inexpensive black work force, he explained. Believing that desegregation in Little Rock would lead to their being forced to desegregate their own school districts and better educate black children, thereby jeopardizing the cheap labor force, they leaned on Faubus to resist federal intervention. In the event, it had worked just that way:

> There are fewer and fewer black folks that are plantation laborers now. They get educated and get out.

Maddie didn't altogether agree with Stan's analysis. She saw the same development more in terms of technological changes than educational ones:

> Well, they know that they got more mechanical things. It's not that they, it's more mechanical stuff. And one mechanical thing can take the place of about fifty [laborers]. Right, Stan?
> STAN: Yeah, cotton picking.
> MADDIE: Cotton picking and all that. That's what did that. Then they went up to Detroit. They're always at Detroit.
> STAN: Saint Louis.
> MADDIE: They were at Saint Louis. Saint Louis was the first stop. And then from Saint Louis up to Detroit. And they had a hard time, and a lot of them came back. And when they came back, why, there were no plantation jobs for them, so there was

nothing in the world for them to do but to work in the yards or in the houses.

And well now, my nurse, my brother's nurse, went up to Detroit, and she came back. She said that, she said, "They don't love you up there, Miss Maddie." [laughs] And that's all she said, "They don't love you up there. You're just a peg." And that's just something that apparently meant a lot to her.

She was at our wedding. Remember, Stanley? We were married at home, my momma and daddy's home, she came to our wedding. And the cook, everybody was there. I mean, you know, they were just part of the family. You take them on, too. [. . .]

I don't think anything about it one way or the other. The only thing that really bothers me is when they start shooting around or slinging pistols or flinging knives or stuff like that. But that happens everywhere. That's not just confined to here. I'm glad I don't have any children going to high school now! [laughs]

Stan squinted at my tape recorder. "Is this on?" he asked, pointing. I indicated it was, and he drew himself up for what I took to be an important statement:

Late in my career, I realized that one of the weaknesses between the blacks and the whites in the South, and everywhere else for that matter, was communications. And there still isn't good communication between the blacks and the whites. Here, or Los Angeles, or anywhere else. My ability to get along with black folks was, I was able to communicate with them, and understand their communication.

I was able to pick up, in my stay in Mississippi, and then later in Alabama, some of the lingual aberrations of our black people. A lot of the white folks that worked alongside or closely with the blacks understood that. But the average man in the street, the average white man in the street didn't understand the meaning of their patois. They use different words for different activities. [Long pause] The word love doesn't mean the same thing.

What do you mean, Stan?

Well, the black people, particularly the young black people —and they still do—identify love with sex and lust. [chuckles] That didn't sit well with the white folks.

As I sat trying to figure out what I was supposed to say next, Maddie leapt in with ribald enthusiasm, once again damning with faint praise:

> Well, a lot of white folks identify that the same way, Stanley.
> STAN: That's right, that's right.
> MADDIE: True.
> STAN: Those of us that identified it the same way can understand the blacks, too. [laughter]
> MADDIE: [Howls] You know what I'll be calling you!
> STAN: I know.
> MADDIE: With that thing off, please. [nodding toward the tape recorder and laughing heartily]

But seriously, Maddie Jean continued:

> No, anyway, you really did, Stanley, you could communicate well. And I can communicate well, but that's because I've been brought up with them, and I really love them a lot. I think I always have. There have been moments, of course. But you find that anywhere.

By this time, Maddie and Stan had made very clear to me how they viewed their personal race relations and in the process given vivid expression to a common white southern attitude: loving dehumanization. That established, I thought we'd reached a moment to shift gears a bit. Realizing I still knew very little about their reactions to the dramatic events at Central High, I asked them what they'd thought when Faubus called out the National Guard. Stanley replied:

> Well, I was, at that particular time, that particular segment of time I was in New York. I first heard about it on the television. Had television on in my room. I was with a man from Shreveport [Louisiana], and we talked about it past bedtime that night, and he was speculating on what it would have been if it had happened in Shreveport. [...]
> He said that it was his opinion that there would have been more conflict between the federal troops and the white people in the street.

I had asked about Faubus's placing the Guard at the school to prevent the black students from entering the building. But Stan was answering a different question, telling me how he'd felt when Eisenhower sent in the 101st Airborne troops. It was perhaps meaningful that Stan's memory was drawn to that particular moment of crisis. Wanting to be sure I understood the point accurately, I asked:

> *He was saying that people in Shreveport would have fought the troops?*
>
> That was his opinion. And knowing as I did then and knowing as I do now, I wouldn't have been surprised. If it had happened in Little Rock—and I was afraid it might happen in Little Rock—if one shot had been fired, and one soldier had been hurt, there's no telling what would have happened; we'd have had a second Reconstruction.

I puzzled for a few beats about why a second Reconstruction would be a bad thing. The first Reconstruction was a post–Civil War period of political advancement for African Americans, but for white southerners it was also a time of defeat and, in their view, Yankee domination. I thought Stan was invoking this latter aspect, but I was still unclear how he felt about the former. Stan's speculation caused Maddie to reflect on where she had been at the critical moment:

> Now of course, remember, I was home. With kids. [. . .] And it really, as long as everybody was decent and kept their cool, it was okay. And really and truly, I think Little Rock did real well, I honestly do, considering all of it. Now, had it been some other places . . .
>
> *But what did you think when Governor Faubus brought out the National Guard and surrounded the school?*
>
> I didn't think anything about it one way or the other, because, as I said, I was too busy taking care of my child.
>
> STAN: We were under the impression that that was gonna happen, that he was gonna call out the Guard, to keep the kids— well, he had announced it as a matter of fact, that the black kids weren't coming to school, if he had to call out the Guard.

This rendition of events conflicted significantly with Faubus's own version, although it certainly accorded with popular imagination at the time. Publicly, the governor had insisted he'd no desire to keep the black kids out and had only decided to do so late in the game in response to threats of violence.

> *Were you critical of him, Stan, when he placed the Guard around the school? You weren't in a position to speak out publicly, but in your heart of hearts, what were you thinking? Did you think it was the right thing to do?*

> I don't recall what my impression was, I mean my feeling, my impression of that time, now, but I wish he hadn't done it.

> *Because? Why?*

> Well, it was setting the watershed for integration in southern schools, and Little Rock didn't deserve that.

Stan's answer took me by surprise. I had made some assumptions about his views based on his self-definition as a liberal, and I now realized that the story I was writing in my mind was quite different from Stanley's story. I embarked on a series of questions to try to clarify his position:

> *Explain that, because he thought he was preventing integration in southern schools.*

> That's right, he thought he was preventing it.

> *So it's a kind of paradox that you're posing?*

> That's right. It was a paradox. I think perhaps I had a better feel of the situation and the state, the attitude of the state, at that particular moment, than he did. With one or two others, we had communicated that feeling to Governor Faubus. But he was his own man at that particular time, and he figured that he had to do something or surrender politically. And that's what happened.

What Faubus had told me directly about his motivation shed light on Stan's speculation. He did do what he did in order not to surrender politically. But he also did it precisely to engineer the confrontation with Eisenhower Stan feared, in order to get himself out of a political double bind. Based on my conversations with Faubus, I thought Stan was probably right that the governor hadn't been worrying that such a confrontation would hasten forced integration elsewhere, if indeed that was the fear Stan was expressing here. I checked out my perception:

> *So you thought that he was throwing down the gauntlet and that would force the federal government to take a harder stand? Is that what you're saying?*
>
> Yes.
>
> *Why were you upset about that?*
>
> Well, [long pause] I felt then and I feel now that there is no room for human conflict in our society. He didn't have the particular background politically or professionally that I did. See, he was a newspaper man. [As a youth, Faubus had published a small newspaper in his home town.] He just hadn't had the experience in that area that I'd had. He's still my friend, and vice versa.

Stanley was making two statements: first, that he was better equipped than the governor to plan strategy. Most of the people I talked to in Little Rock felt they were better equipped than Faubus to govern the situation. Less clear to me was Stan's second statement, about what exactly his differences were with Faubus and what he would have done instead:

> *I'm confused, Stan. What was the problem with Faubus's having evoked that response from the federal government? Did it make things move too fast? Were you hoping integration would not proceed so quickly in southern schools?*
>
> Yes.
>
> *Why?*
>
> Well, I realized then, before all this occurred, that there was going to be a great deal of conflict. The emotion, everybody that lived in central Arkansas, their emotions were pitched. [. . .] I just didn't want anything to ignite the situation.
>
> MADDIE: I still say I'm proud of what Little Rock did do. I think they did well. I really do and it wasn't easy.
>
> *So, Stan, you were afraid that it would become more violent . . .*

STAN: Yes, uh-huh.

. . . than it did if the federal troops came in?

Yes, uh-huh, that's right.

This goes back to the conversation with the man from Shreveport?

Yeah.

You also thought that integration could or should proceed at an easier pace?

That's right. More slowly. Like, taking the seniors, or start off with the freshmen, I mean, first graders. Integrate a grade at a time, say a semester at a time.

This notion, that another, more gradual plan might have worked better than desegregating Central High, was commonly repeated. Few people, including Stan, seemed aware, or perhaps remembered, that the first proposal by the superintendent of schools had been to start with first graders and work up, and that that idea had been vetoed both by white parents of little kids (who worried that they'd be subject to uproar they couldn't understand) and by civil rights advocates (who complained about how many years that process would take).

Contradiction piled on contradiction. Stan disapproved of Faubus's hard stand because he feared it would result in a confrontation with the federal government, which he feared would elicit more white violence and in turn drive desegregation even faster. In fact, Faubus's actions *did* cause a federal response, the very thing he'd secretly wished would take him off the hotseat. According to both Stan and Maddie, it had *not* caused more violence; in fact, Maddie was proud of how restrained Little Rock's folks had been. Moreover, whether or not the Little Rock crisis in fact slowed down desegregation in the South was moot; historians and analysts still debate that point. Nonetheless, in retrospect Stan stayed true to his critique back then. "Memory collaborates with forces separate from actual past events," wrote Karen Fields, and I was still searching back from the loops and oddities of Stan's account to understand what those forces had been. I felt sure that there was some reason why he failed to integrate his knowledge of what had in fact happened with his fears back then of what might happen to construct a rather different story now. Perhaps he had had other fears I'd not yet heard, ones that had indeed more come to pass. For Stan was still very sure that what had happened wasn't good. But instead of telling me more about his motivation in '57, he instead invoked the present as justification for his position in the past:

As it is now, it still isn't working. It still isn't working.

When a black student can walk into a classroom and stab a white woman teacher, they ain't very well integrated. And that's what's happening in Little Rock today. [...]

You say that as if it demonstrates some failing of integration. Is that what it is, is it a problem of integration?

Well, integration stems from the old thing, we're all for law and order, you know. And law and order ain't taking care of the situation now. Still quite a bit of conflict. And so much of it is racial.

In, I believe it was west Little Rock, one of the districts recently, some black kids drove by and it later had developed they were so-called gang members, and they shot the doors out of an elementary school here. And not only scared the daylights out of all the kids, two or three of the kids were hurt.

What was racial about that?

What was racial about it? Nearly all the teachers there were white. Although we have some great black teachers. [...]

What do you think that's about?

MADDIE: Social unrest.

STAN: There's also a conflict—I guess you'd call it social conflict—between the races, and the little kids themselves don't realize what it is.

They are taught, from the time they are able to learn anything, both sides, that we're better than the other fellow. And one of their basic inclinations is that they set out to prove it, in every form. And the classroom is one of them. "There's just something unclean, physically unclean about the integration of the rest rooms," that sort of thing.

MADDIE: It is not. Some blacks are a lot cleaner than some of those whites are.

STAN: That's right, that's right.

What wasn't working now, as far as I could understand, was that conflict persisted. "I felt then and I feel now that there is no room for human conflict in our society," Stan had said. "As long as everybody was decent and kept their cool, it was okay," Maddie had said. Desegregation had evoked conflict then, and in Stan's view continued to do so now—and a very particular kind of conflict: violence by black youths on whites. In addition, other interests had also been enduringly damaged:

> I don't think [Faubus] would admit it to you or anybody else for the record, but I think that now he's looking back on it, he wished it hadn't happened.
>
> *Why do you think he wishes that?*
>
> I think he realizes now that the effects of it are still lingering.
> MADDIE: That's what's so awful, it still is.
> STAN: It still is, and until the effects of it are gone, we in this state are not going to make any progress economically, politically, or otherwise.
> MADDIE: Oh, I think we're doing all right.
> STAN: Our only hope is for Bill Clinton to get elected. The only way we can get rid of him is to send him to Washington.[3]
> MADDIE: [laughs sardonically as Stanley coughs and laughs] As you can see, I'm not an admirer.

This statement contained hints of the fear that had come to pass, once again couched in terms of a present-day statement rather than a linear account of events back then. In Stan's version of history, the governor (the one back then, not the one perched at the moment we spoke on the edge of the presidency) had acted to protect economic interests in the Delta, but in the process he'd played into a confrontation in Little Rock that damaged economic interests there. Stan had still done little more than suggest what those interests were. But once again, Faubus's actions, to Stan, produced exactly the opposite effects intended. Paradoxically, while the Delta plantation owners had sought to preserve a cheap, uneducated labor force, mechanization had soon made that labor force obsolete (or so Maddie thought) in any case. Taken together, Stanley's and Maddie Jean's accounts were beginning to read like classical tragedy.

Meanwhile, working hard to decipher the twists and turns of our conversation, I had been growing hotter and hotter, shedding clothing, fanning myself and sweating. Now Stan commented mildly, "It's getting kind of warm in here." "I'll turn it down," Maddie said. "It has a habit of going up, particularly when the lights are on." While that business took place, I took stock and realized that I still wasn't clear about Maddie's and Stan's positions on the desegregation of Central High. I turned to Stanley:

> *Looking back on it, you definitely played a role in this history, you were consulting with Governor Faubus, you were advising him. Is there anything you would change of the way you participated in it?*
>
> STAN: [Thinks for a long moment.] No, I don't think that I'd change anything if I had to do it now. If the same situation existed now as it did then, there would be no change. Because from the time I came to Little Rock until I retired . . . , I was not my own man.

Perhaps that was the problem, I thought, with our conversation today. Perhaps Stan was still not being "his own man" and therefore I was having trouble understanding what Stanley, the man, believed:

> *If you had been, what would you have done differently? If you were operating solely out of your heart and your belief, what would you have done?*
>
> Well, I tried to get something done back then, but it didn't take place. The people in eastern Arkansas wanted the governor to do these things and I objected to him taking the lead in that sort of thing, and I was asked, well, what would you do?
>
> I said I'd get a circuit judge in Little Rock, to ask him to call out the Guard, that the situation was so bad that chaos might result if school was integrated at Central High School, where it was to be. And that way, the circuit judge here in Little Rock could have called on, as the chief law enforcement officer in the district, could have called on the governor to bring out the National Guard or to mobilize all the state police, either one.

Now at last I understood that Stan was echoing the governor's own wish that federal intervention would relieve him of responsibility. Where Faubus opted for an out-right confrontation with Eisenhower, though, Stan sought a more subtle, self-protective negotiation. Would he have wanted the Guard to bar the black students? I asked, seeking to clarify his strategy. He confirmed that he'd have used the Guard to "keep the black people away from the school." I asked:

> *Why did you want to keep the black students out of the school? I mean, you said that you didn't object, you felt kindly toward them. Why did you want them out of the school?*

MADDIE: It was the eastern Arkansas people.

STAN: Saying I wanted them out of the school isn't correct. I didn't want the governor to get himself into the position of conflict with the federal government. That was my concern.

> *And that was because of your concern for Faubus, or because of your concern about the repercussions?*

About the repercussions. I liked Mr. Faubus, did then and do now. But I felt then he was making a mistake and some of the people I was associated with and had great respect for felt he was making a mistake if he did this.

He had said offhandedly two or three times, not in my presence but in the presence of some of my friends, that he would call out the Guard, et cetera, et cetera. And so the people in eastern Arkansas, and far eastern Arkansas took him at his word and urged him to call out the Guard. They didn't care what happened in Little Rock, they still don't care what happens in Little Rock, they just didn't want it to happen in their bailiwick.

MADDIE: They're Memphis people.

STAN: They just didn't want it to happen in their neighborhood.

MADDIE: No, they go to the hospital in Memphis, it's closer. Some of those people over there have never even been to Little Rock. They never, they never took an Arkansas paper, they took the *Memphis Commercial Appeal.*

In his advice then as in his recollections now, he viewed matters from the perspective of his employers. What exactly their objectives were he'd still not stated explicitly, but he suggested they clashed with those of the "Memphis people," the plantation folk from eastern Arkansas. At last that began to make sense; profitability for the developers for whom Stan worked lay in an urban, industrial direction, not an agricultural one. They walked their own path, but the direction they walked was toward the growth of business and the maintenance of a climate inviting to capital. That goal led them to support the governor, whose gubernatorial agenda concerning industrialization for the most part coincided with their own, and with whom in any case they had a relationship of mutual aid. What Stan's strategy aimed to do was to keep the governor out of the hot seat by manipulating the courts into doing exactly what he, in the event, did himself: bar entrance to the school by the Nine. To admit them was to risk unrest. But for the governor to be the one blocking their admission was, he feared, to join him politically to the interests of the agriculturists who urged him to that action. It would have looked far better to non-southerners considering doing business in Arkansas if the state seemed to support their moral inclinations around civil rights, and if interference with desegregation were the responsibility of the judicial authorities.

Like Faubus, Stan sought to negotiate power among conflicting interests statewide. By implication, the conflict that mattered for Stan (and Maddie, who formulated her feelings more in terms of her local identity in opposition to the "Memphis people") was not that between blacks and whites but that between people (clearly white people) from eastern Arkansas and people (presumably white people) from Little Rock. That it was indeed white people from Little Rock of whom they spoke was clarified by Maddie. "I certainly do think they did well," she said. I asked her what she meant. "Well, they can fight, and they didn't. They could have all stormed, and they didn't." The "they" to whom she referred were the mob, the whites to whom the man from Shreveport had referred when he'd imagined the carnage that would have taken place in his hometown had desegregation been pressed there.

As my departure time drew near and I prepared to leave, I asked Maddie what kind of discussion had been going on among the mothers of her circle. "Nobody said anything about it," she said. "Uh-uh, there are some subjects you don't discuss." Had she any contact with the Mothers League, I asked? Had anyone tried to recruit her?

> I apologize, I'm not a joiner. About all I can do is take care of, I do well if I take care of my own family.
>
> STAN: Also, it would have been embarrassing in my position if she had joined the Mothers League.
>
> MADDIE: I didn't know there was a Mothers League.

And the women that you were talking to just didn't talk about it?

> Nobody mentioned it.
>
> Because after all, we all had the same problem. I mean, if you had a child over there you had the same problem.

That makes it all the more surprising to me that you weren't talking among yourselves.

> No, uh-uh, 'cause everybody hoped there'd be no problems, big problems. You know what I mean. But, no, if you don't talk about some things you're better off.

Why?

> Why? [laughter from Stan] You need to learn something, see.

Teach me.

> You need to learn something. No, some things are just better not discussed.

Sara Murphy

Stanley Blair, Jimmy Karam, and Orval Faubus, three old white men who'd colluded in making a moment of history, played off each other in the stories they told in the present as they had in their actions long ago. Colorful storytellers all, they told me more or less boastfully of their roles. Taken as parts of a whole, their stories had a deeper meaning as well: how agendas and motivations that had nothing to do with whether it was right or wrong for nine black students to enroll in

Central High School shaped the drama enacted there. Reverend Young, Chris Mercer, and Jerome Muldrew had acted, out of their own experience of injustice, very much in their own interest and in the interest of their race. So, too, had the three white cronies. But there was a significant difference. I imagined lines graphing the connections between motives and goals. For the three black men, the line was bold and straight, from fighting injustice to gaining access to opportunities long denied. For the governor and his friends there were several lines, and they curved all over creation, sometimes vivid, sometimes hazy, sometimes moving in the same direction, sometimes conflicting. They included personal ambition, social acceptance, protecting an economic environment friendly to industry, political expediency, and so on. Nowhere on that list was a principled stand about the rights and wrongs of segregation, often though I pressed the men to tell me their simplest beliefs about racial justice. The story of black Americans was incidental to the stories preoccupying these three political white men. I was not surprised to discover that truth; in the context of their lives and times, their behavior was consistent. But while I saw how their actions grew seamlessly from their biographies, I also believed they had the power of choice. If not, then agency is myth and history is faceless. A large element in my own motivation for this study is to understand how these two truths—that human beings are simultaneously creatures of our social environments and at the same time capable of responsible choice—intertwine to form processes of social change.

For other white citizens of Little Rock did make other choices, many of them working hard to create a new racial order. Sara Murphy was prominent among this group. She was also someone who clearly disagreed with Maddie Blair, a mom who emphatically believed that things are far, far better discussed. Sara's story was appealingly simple in comparison to Orval's, Jimmy's, or Stan's. She was a member of the Women's Emergency Committee, that stalwart group of women who took matters firmly in hand in the second year of the struggle, plunging into the political life of Little Rock out of straightforward conscience and making a very large difference in history.

Harry Ashmore, editor of the integrationist *Arkansas Gazette* back then and the author of many books about the South, told me the story

of how the Emergency Committee came to be. Sitting in a writing stu-
dio behind his home in Santa Barbara, California, Harry was telling
me about how the business leaders of Little Rock (probably some of
those same people who paid Stanley's salary) had gone into hiding
during 1957-58:

> They came back the second year when Faubus closed down
> all the high schools. Now that really put it in the fan, because,
> well, these proper white people had their goddamned teenagers
> at home, and they could stand anything but that! So they began
> to get agitated.
>
> And then of course, Mrs. David Terry—unfortunately, she's
> dead, she was one of the great heroines, and she was the prime
> matron in the town, the oldest family. She owned half the prop-
> erty downtown, she'd been a suffragette, she was a Vassar gradu-
> ate, she'd been in the forefront of every progressive movement
> from time one.
>
> She called me one morning after all this had happened and
> said she'd like to talk to me. And I said, "I'll be right over, Mrs.
> Terry," which is what you said. She said, "No, I'll come to see
> you." So she came over to my office. I'm sure she had on white
> gloves and a hat straight on, ladies still wore hats. She was about
> seventy, I guess.
>
> I said, "What can I do for you, Mrs. Terry?" She said, "Well,
> it's obvious that the men are not going to do anything about this
> dreadful situation in the schools. So I've sent for the young
> ladies," she said, "and we're going to organize a movement."
>
> So all the young ladies came down from the Heights and the
> suburbs in their station wagons to Mrs. Terry's big old mansion
> —it's like a stage set, you've probably seen it, it's now a museum,
> she left it to the city; it's got white columns, it sits on a whole city
> block, right downtown, about two blocks off Main Street. If you
> go back, you must go see it. That's the Terry home place; it was
> built before the Civil War by General Albert Pike. I remember
> her father who was a banker bought it and that's where they all
> grew up.
>
> So anyway, the young ladies came down and they organized
> the Women's Emergency Committee to Open the Schools. Then
> the Chamber of Commerce finally came in behind them. Of

course, the ministerial association, some of the more or less formally moral people had already been out, and they had the schools open; they won a series of elections against Faubus.

And that created a political coalition, really, we used to say between the blacks who were now voting and the country club set, which provided pretty much the leadership. And that became the pattern across the South. That's the Democratic coalition today.

Sara Murphy was a young mother when Mrs. Terry began her campaign. Her children were too little to be directly affected. But Sara did not buy into Maddie's idea that raising kids was enough of a job, that women's place was domestic and men's political. Sara joined the Emergency Committee early on in its history.

I wanted to know why, and I quizzed Sara as she lounged in an overstuffed armchair in her friend and fellow campaigner Irene Samuel's home. Legs slung casually over the arm of her chair, her voice and spirit were nonetheless alert and passionate:

> I grew up in a small Tennessee town, and I grew up in a segregated community. And went to school first in Nashville, then I went to Columbia. It was when I was in New York that I had black classmates in graduate school, and I began to understand that if I went back south, they couldn't come to see me, we couldn't even walk down the street together without, you know, creating a stir. And it, you know, it just flips for you, you realize how wrong it is, and how you really don't want to be part of that sort of thing.
>
> *But there are other southerners who have gone to New York and have come back with their attitudes unchanged.*
>
> Absolutely.
>
> *Was there something in your family tradition that influenced you?*
>
> You know, I think there was. I think my mother was a very open person, and very interested in seeing equal treatment done to all people. She wasn't a crusader in the sense that she got out and joined things, because she was in a little town, but she did do a lot of things to encourage us.

And we were very active in the Presbyterian church and I think some of my conscience came out of that, some of the things that I learned as I came through church. I had this sense, I organized the vacation bible school when I was fourteen for black children in a black community that was not far from there. So it was a thing in growing up, but not understanding the need to, you know, overhaul the whole, um—

I didn't learn a whole lot in Nashville. . . . I hit that agrarian group at Vanderbilt that were writing very conservatively about holding on to the old southern—I don't know whether you're familiar with that, Robert Penn Warren and Oliver Hudson Stroh. They were a bunch of writers, they were really backwards. In fact, I studied creative writing under Donald Davidson, who was one of the leaders. So that didn't help. But I knew I didn't agree with what he was saying, it didn't, you know, fit with what I felt from my deeply religious [perspective], I think.

Like Jane Emery, another transplant from a different American culture, Sara had found herself between ideological worlds. But early in life she determined on a position guided by her religious upbringing and, perhaps less consciously, by a family history she'd only recently come to learn. She went on to tell that story:

Another thing that I've learned, that I'm very interested in right now, because I'm in touch with this woman. I've never been interested in family history, but this woman whose great-grandfather had been a slave under my great-grandfather in Tennessee, who'd come over from North Carolina and brought slaves with him. I've gone back into that and found out that toward the end of his life, he lost his mind, *my* grandfather, and it was partly because he was so distraught over owning slaves. And that is a very interesting thing to me because there's something that did come down to me, through his daughter who was my great-aunt, Aunt Ellen, for whom my daughter is named, and she worked with the black school over there, and did a lot of things in the black community.

There was a history in my family of having—but this woman is, has gotten me to look up my family because she's trying to find members of hers through looking at wills and all that.

As did recollections of maidservants, stories involving slavery recurred in my interviews, one tale echoing others but each told with different style, content, and purpose. Reverend Young spoke of his grandfather, a slave until age twenty-one, as part of a narrative of his origins. Now Sara told me of her grandfather's relationship to slavery as an influence on her own civil rights activism. She went on to elaborate her family background:

> My father was a farmer. And my great-grandfather had the first brick house in Tennessee. He came over from North Carolina. [...]
>
> I've been to the little Isle of Arran, off the coast of Scotland [where they'd come from]. They were Scotch-Irish, they'd come from Ireland over there and then a couple of years, some of them stayed on the Isle of Arran, these were my father's folks, and then they came over to North Carolina on the coast over there.

I might have guessed Sara's origins from her appearance. Starkly thin and angular, she radiated the strong sense of a craggy Scottish hillside. But if her body was spare, her spirit rang with humor and generosity. As she went on telling her story, I felt as if I could see the pages of history come alive in her vibrant person and moving words. She continued speaking of the forebears who set up residence on the Carolina coast:

> They came over to North Carolina on the coast over there. And *were* slave owners, unfortunately, and that's a terrible thing, you know, to have had, I think, in a family. Especially when it becomes very personal and you're going back and trying to establish connections with someone.
>
> But no, I think it was a part of my whole upbringing that we were not—and I remember when I was a child seeing, it was ten miles away, but they were burning down the courthouse because there was a black man that had been accused of raping a white woman in there, and the mob had gathered around the courthouse, and I can still see the sky lit up at night.
>
> *Were you aware of what was happening?*
>
> Oh, yes, I was probably eight or nine or something like that.

My mother and I stood and watched that, and she was telling me
how wrong it was. They got him out of there, got him to Nashville.
I remember I was so relieved. I didn't know it at the time, I just
knew the courthouse was burning. But my family thought that
sort of thing just was horrible. And I think a lot of families in the
South did, too.

I don't think the people who committed those kinds of
crimes, certainly the thinking got prevalent later on, you know
through politicians, and that's why we were so afraid of Faubus
and [other segregationist politicians] because they were saying
to people, "That's okay."

And that's why they were able to organize that Southern
Association of Women against Lynching. It was mostly Methodist
women from the South, and Presbyterian and a few in other
churches, but mostly Methodists and Presbyterians that signed
forty thousand pledges to work on that. And I think in the thirties
that's a remarkable record. And that was when I was growing up
and I didn't know there was anything like that going on. That's
why it's so interesting.

Sara's words tumbled over each other, slow southern drawl and
all. I asked Sara whether she remembered scenes of injustice involving black people she had personally witnessed when she was a child,
and she said something I thought very important:

Oh yeah, yeah, I do. I remember seeing things that I
thought—well, like the lynching, you know, that I knew was a
terrible thing. And I saw people, I didn't see members of my own
family being unkind, my father was very segregationist but he
was not unkind, I didn't see that. I was more aware of acts of
kindness because that was not the norm.

Sara had learned lessons less from overt acts of cruelty she'd witnessed
than from the sense that her parents' acts of kindness were atypical.
How much of what we think about life, I reflected, was born from
sensing such contradictions. In similar vein, Sara went on to describe
how she'd interacted with black people at home:

My mother tended to treat people who worked in the home
as equals. We had a woman who came and washed for us and I

played with her children in the sandpile while they were working over the washtub together. And they talked to each other.
And I remember that, but during the depression we didn't have
a whole lot of help coming in and out, so, you know, I wasn't
aware of a lot of servants in the home or anything like that. But
I would see in the little town instances of people not being
treated well. Somebody, you know, saying something ugly.

When Sara and her husband, Pat, moved to Little Rock from the
East, they sought out like-minded people, "young couples, professionals like we were, who felt very similarly." Nonetheless, they felt
very much in a minority, strongly compelled to do something consistent with their beliefs:

> We realized that the South was an anachronism, and it was
> part of us, part of the new South to do something about it while
> we were here. And that was an exciting thing. [...]
> But, you know, you live in two worlds, is what it's like. And
> if I was going to stay in the South, I had to make my peace with
> how I could be in this place and be a part of it. And so . . .

Sara's voice trailed off. "You seem to have done that, made your
peace with it," I said. "Well, I don't know sometimes," she replied sadly.
"Anyhow, it's been a long, long struggle."[4]

Sara volunteered for that struggle, but there were others who
found themselves in the middle of it through no will of their own.
Inside Central High were two thousand white students, and many of
them struggled against involvement. That was an effort they could
not win.

PART II   Inside Central High

FIVE
Bitters in the Honey

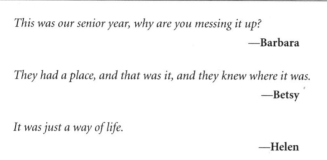

This was our senior year, why are you messing it up?

—**Barbara**

They had a place, and that was it, and they knew where it was.

—**Betsy**

It was just a way of life.

—**Helen**

In the very middle of the struggle over Central High School were the students, some two thousand of them. And in the very middle of the two thousand were nine black newcomers. At the center of the conflict, they were also the definition of outsiders. But if the whites who outnumbered them were the society which excluded them, the white students themselves felt outside the history they unwittingly found themselves making.

As I listened to the reminiscences of white people who had been students at Central High that year, the story of Little Rock's desegregation became many stories. Some accounts had the National Guard arriving sooner, some later. When the federal troops arrived, one person's soldiers were giddy kids, another's were menacing warriors. Most of the white students I interviewed resented the black students for upsetting what they viewed as their enchanted domain. A few described themselves as welcoming to the newcomers that year and horrified at the nastiness of their reception by others. But most insisted that, as far as student behavior went, the year was peaceful; nobody was harassed, beyond the normal razzing of new students by their peers.

In contrast, the black students' accounts, as represented in documentaries, published works, and private conversations, are filled with terror and nastiness. People were kicked, tripped, and sprayed with acid. Thumbtacks were left on girls' chairs. Gym clothes disappeared while boys showered. Dynamite sticks were ignited in their path. They were threatened with violence, vilified, and ridiculed.[1] Comparing one person's story to another, I was amazed that people who had sat in the same classes, eaten in the same lunchrooms, graduated in the same ceremony, could nonetheless have lived such different experiences.

Even among the white students whose factual versions reasonably agreed, the tone and tenor of stories differed. "I went to school, just nothing, no big deal," said **Helen**. "I didn't see if there was commotion going on up here, I didn't see it. 'Cause I came in the side door, went to my locker, did my thing."

Jane, on the other hand, was terrified:

> Front or side, you had to pass through the barricades. And that's when I remember being more frightened. And they would yell at you, and they'd yell things like "Two, four, six, eight, we ain't gonna integrate." And you could hear them in the classrooms. And that went on for maybe a month. . . . Maybe for two weeks they had the bayonets, and that was scary. And then they put the bayonets away, but they were always armed. That was scary. And you never knew what some jerk was going to do. And there were bomb scares. So I remember the first couple months as bad.

How a story is organized is a story in itself. Western culture has accustomed us to stories that begin at the beginning and end at the end, that follow a time sequence with defined dimensions. Almost nobody told me about that year of crisis at Central High in chronological order. Most speakers assumed I knew "the story," the official history (although they were sometimes surprised that my understanding of events contradicted their memories). What they wanted to tell me, instead, was *their* history. Most people therefore emphasized emotional statements that informed me of their attitude:

> *Angry:* I'm bitter over my senior year which was ruined because they were forced on us. It was ruined. [**Betsy**]

Defiant: See, this was my senior year. And it was like, they can't take that away from me. I'm going to school. I'm graduating. [Sally]

Aggrieved: But all we could think about at the time was that this was our senior year, why are you messing it up? This was a year that would be with us forever and you've come in and invaded our territory; why are you doing this? [**Barbara**]

Governor Faubus and Chris Mercer were protagonists in a drama of their composition. They saw events as consequences of their actions, and their actions resulted from thought and belief. The nine black students who integrated Central High participated in events because of decisions they made. "Many of the black families felt that it was an honor and a privilege for their children to be named to be the first ones to go and desegregate the school," Evelyn said. Melba Pattillo Beals writes of the moment she raised her hand to express her willingness to be assigned to Central High:

> As I signed my name on the paper they passed around, I thought about all those times I'd gone past Central High wanting to see inside. . . . I reasoned that if schools were open to my people, I would also get access to other opportunities I had been denied.[2]

People like those in the previous chapters, politicians and lawyers, the Nine and certain adult members of both black and white communities, all engaged history as writers of their own stories, however much it might have felt to them at moments that they were reacting to overwhelming events, that they were powerless to influence the way things happened. Many white students at Central High, in contrast, were taken by surprise when they found themselves in the center of the unfolding drama. Their lack of agency, of a sense of having chosen their roles, was reflected vividly in the ways they represented themselves in their accounts of the times. Universally, the white students' storyline was about how *their* year, *their* world, *their* rights had been violated. They portrayed themselves as non-actors who innocently found themselves swept up by events not of their making.

Helen and Betsy

My first interview with Central High alumnae took me to a tidy suburban house near Atlanta, Georgia. Finding anonymous folk who briefly walked the stage of history more than three decades ago turned out to be no easy task; the methodology I constructed involved a heavy element of luck. Luck it was that led me to Helen, who was a slight acquaintance of a tradesperson who happened to have heard she was a '58 grad óf Central High shortly before I happened to mention my project in the course of an unrelated commercial transaction. This blessed tradesperson proceeded to serve as a connecting link and put me in touch with Helen. We talked several times by telephone before we met. She questioned me about my project, my orientation, my purposes. She was particularly interested in the fact that I, like her, had graduated from a segregated southern high school, and at almost the same time. She said she'd check with some friends to see if they'd talk with me. Finally, she called me and said, "We've decided you're someone who can tell our story. You can understand." We arranged a date for me to meet her and her friend Betsy, another Central graduate who lived nearby.

Now I found myself in Betsy's suburban home a little outside Atlanta. The table at which we sat overflowed with symbols of southern hospitality intertwined with tools of sociological research: wires to my tape recorder snaked past bowls of chilled fruit; glasses of iced tea sweated perilously near the microphone; legal consent forms peeked from beneath decades-old high-school yearbooks emblazoned with embossed tigers. From somewhere in the interior of the house there drifted faint sounds of a football game; Betsy's husband, **Johnny**, apparently watched television somewhere not far away.

We started the interview by chatting about how it felt to be Little Rock expatriates. Betsy said:

> I hated to leave Little Rock. We were thirty-something, thirty-three or whatever, and I really hated it; we both did. That had been our home and we thought would be our home forever. We loved it there. But the job calls, so we moved to Atlanta, and of course I thought I was moving to the ends of the earth. We

learned to love Atlanta, but we did go back three or four, sometimes more, but at least three or four times a year. We couldn't
quite let go. And I still have not let go. I'm still hoping to get back
there.

Helen agreed:

> Oh, I cried, I stomped, I did everything in the world. I just
> hated it, I didn't want to leave—Mother! But I didn't want to leave
> Little Rock, either. I've never changed. We're at the other end of
> it now. We were very young then and now [we're] thinking in
> terms of retirement. I would like to retire back in Arkansas—[to
> Betsy:] you know this, I've discussed it with you.

As the two friends reflected on their feelings about Little Rock, an
emotional portrait of the city emerged, along with some themes that
were to characterize their accounts of the history they'd lived through
there. "Little Rock's a unique place," said Betsy:

> I have a friend down the street here, she and her husband
> had lived there, I think for three years, almost in the same area
> where we were. And they just hated it. They moved back here
> because they hated it so much.
>
> I think in Little Rock it's like there are two—you're either in
> or you're out. There's no in between. Don't you think, Helen?
> Isn't it kind of that way, that in Little Rock there's no in between;
> it's either you're in or you're out. Even with the adults, you know,
> there's no middle.
>
> HELEN: It's a very class system. . . . They weren't accepted.
> They were from outside.

From the outside, Helen and Betsy defined themselves as insiders,
and being inside gave them access to a community life they never
found elsewhere:

> BETSY: It still has that small-town atmosphere, and I miss
> that. Here, you go to the store—[aside, to Helen]: maybe it was
> you I was talking with, and you brought this out, and it hit home,
> it made sense—you go in a store: "May I help you?" They don't
> know you or anything. I could go to Dillard's [the largest depart-
> ment store] in Little Rock and know somebody, I'd know

someone's daughter or something, and you get that personal attention, and they say, "Hello, how are you? Well, what did you do last week?" And I think I miss that a lot.

And it still is that way.

I asked Helen how long she'd been away from Little Rock:

Close to thirty years. I was just figuring here a while ago, I think it was about twenty-eight years.

We relocated down here because my husband being in the furniture industry, and he came to work for a company down here. And again, that was rather interesting. The people in Atlanta were looking for someone they could groom to be their general sales manager.

You've got to understand, this was just going out of the late fifties into the early sixties, and people hadn't really started moving a lot, around the country. And while there was a lot of people that would have loved to have had the job and indicated an interest in it, but they did it inside like, putting out feelers. Because a Yankee, pardon me, somebody from New York, could not sell down here at that time. Well, listen, it would have really gone against their grain; it's just the difference in their techniques.

Helen defined a culture and a community of sorts, very different from the personalized one she and her friend had left, an imagined community of the South, defined in part in contrast to the North. Often people used New York as shorthand for the extremes of Yankeedom and Mississippi as its deep-southern counterpart. How they experienced the South of their youth became clearer as they went on to talk more fully of their feelings about Little Rock and about their family histories. We chatted about the friends and links they'd maintained back in Little Rock, the two women comparing notes on who they'd seen on which visits back. Finally, Helen interrupted the flow of talk:

While we keep talking (I don't know if we're getting in the right vein or not) of what makes Little Rock unique—they are snobbish. A lot of them don't have a right to be. I would call them introverted snobs.

What do you mean by that?

They aspire to be something they're not. Still, I found it to be where you're all one group, if you have money or you don't, you're still one of them. Am I making sense? So when we grew up, there was all kinds. There was maybe fathers that were laborers, fathers that were professors or owned their own businesses, but still you were accepted, we bonded, the kids did.

Helen's theme echoed Wesley Pruden's comments both about life at Central High ("It was really kind of a wonderful, idyllic, Andy Hardy kind of high school. . . . People did very well"), and about the existence of class divisions reflected in the dynamics of desegregation. ("It was felt by the people in the middle-class, working-class neighborhoods that fed Central High School, that Central was being sacrificed on behalf of this new high school out in the richer part of town.") Many people described growing up in Little Rock, and especially their time at Central High, as an experience of classlessness in the same breath that they recalled inequities about which they still felt deep resentment. "You're all one group," said Helen. But at the same time, she expressed a tension between her sense of belonging and her alienation. ("I would call them introverted snobs.") Leaving Little Rock had been hard, but perhaps staying would have had its drawbacks, too. Leaving was the price one paid for escaping a social landscape at once treasured and resented. I was struck by Helen's ability to express ideal versions of her world in the same breath with competing realities. On a theoretical level, the co-existence of such contradictions is meaningful, because it reflects a process by which we negotiate individual locations in a social order, sometimes consenting with good grace, sometimes resisting in this case by "moving on."

My understanding of that process deepened as Helen went on to tell me more about her family background:

> My people, I guess it happened right after the depression, that was before my time, I was born in 1940, and they came from the country (now they consider that a suburb), and moved to Little Rock, and then Daddy went into business with Uncle Dave.
>
> At that time, we had gone through some bad times that had lasted quite a few years. My father had been in business with my uncle, who had a—he started out with one stationery store, he ended up with, I don't want to say a string of stores, but there was several. And my daddy was not a businessman, and they had

a falling out. It was more of a handshaking agreement, and then when it went bitter, Daddy had no papers or anything to go back on, and my Uncle Dave had our money, or my dad's money, because he had put money into that first store down on Capitol Street. [To Betsy:] Do you remember that store, do you? I think there's a high-rise there now.

In any event, we were living in my uncle's house. We did not own that house on Louisiana, that you hear me refer to quite often so fondly, because I spent my formative years there. I think there's a MacDonald's there now.

BETSY: Well, that's sad!

HELEN: Yeah, but it is in the historical home area, the Quapaw quarter area, around the governor's mansion, you know. Betsy had been in and out of my house many times, right? I would say we were middle class to lower middle class, wouldn't you say?

In telling me the story of her father and uncle's business dealings, Helen told me a good deal more: about the passing of her childhood community, about a child's sense of insecurity and injustice in light of her family's dependency, and above all about where she fit and did not fit in Little Rock society. I next asked Betsy where she was while they were growing up:

Helen and I lived on two different ends of town. Hers is more the historical, the older part of town. It's what everybody's wanting now, they're going down there and fixing these houses up, and they're in the Quapaw quarter, and they're on the tours and all that.

We lived out in what was called the Heights area, the Pulaski Heights area; well, a little past that. My house was older, but it wasn't old like that because that wasn't an older area out there. So we come from two different, uh—

HELEN: If you want to say a railroad track, I lived on the wrong side of town.

BETSY: No!

HELEN: They thought eastside was the wrong side of town. Yes, there was eastside, westside, and Pulaski Heights, and we lived on the wrong side of town, so to speak, in that town's way of talking.

BETSY: She's right, so to speak, that's—yeah.

HELEN: But there was many people who lived there on the wrong side of town, of which you know a lot of them. But that didn't make us trash or anything. We just lived in the older homes.

This talk about the right and wrong sides of town fleshed out Helen's angry comment about introverted snobs. It also elicited a sweet but strained dynamic between the two women; Betsy supportively protested Helen's derogatory classification of her part of town, but then quickly agreed that, indeed, it *was* the "town's way of talking." Helen went on to tell me more about her family's roots in rural Arkansas and migration to the city. But when she repeated that they'd come early in the century, Betsy seized the opportunity to bring the conversation back to her previous point:

> See, that's why I say, hers is more historical, that's what I'm trying to say, than mine. Because her family probably lived there a lot more years than mine. We moved to Little Rock when I was in the third grade. [Before] we lived in Green Forest. My daddy worked for a contractor in Little Rock, and we had traveled all over, and finally my mother said, "We're settling. I'm not traveling any more."

History counted in the determination of status, and the history Betsy was reckoning was about longevity of residence in Little Rock. It turned out that most of her family's traveling had been inside Arkansas, but their migratory past weighed in the scales of social position against her living in the Heights, and she used that fine measuring stick to reassure Helen. On second thought, though, she realized she had some credentials of her own:

> *Were your parents from Arkansas originally?*
>
> Well, my mother was. My father was from Mississippi. But my mother's family was from Fort Smith—well, I do have some history, don't I, come to think of it?
>
> HELEN: Yes, you do!

Betsy began to recite her family's celebrity as politicians long ago. As she did so she hit upon an incongruity in what must have been familiar family lore:

So they lived in Fort Smith when my mother was at home and all, and he was in state government. They lived in Fort Smith. I've never quite figured that out; how could he be in state government and live in Fort Smith? But he did.

HELEN: Well, honey, Fort Smith at one time was a very political and influential town.

BETSY: Well, I know, but why wouldn't he live in Little Rock where the state capitol was?

HELEN: Well, way back when, they needed a lot of powerful politics up there because it was a long time before Oklahoma, which is just forty miles across, became a part of the United States. I don't understand it all, but if you read the history that was the entry way, and they had a lot of trouble up there. Outlaws and different things and contraband, and so they had a lot of powerful people there, courts and stuff in Fort Smith.

BETSY: I guess; I don't know.

Having hacked a way through the thickets of Arkansas history, the women moved on to their memories of church and their kids' growing up and the schools and their own current lives. Unlike Reverend Young's story where the subject was very central, race appeared in their reminiscences from time to time, but tangentially. As I neared the point of bringing the interview into focus on Central High, wondering what kinds of beliefs they had grown up with, I asked the two women to tell me what childhood lessons they'd learned about relations with black people. Helen replied thoughtfully:

I would think [my father] wasn't interested. Well, he always seemed to have an opinion on everything. I think it was just getting by and staying out of trouble.

Mother—I have to tell the truth here, don't I, Betsy? Because Betsy knew my mother. 'Course I knew her parents, too—but Mother would have died for shame if her daughter, any of her children, but if I during this period, this integration thing, if my name had been put in the paper, or if I'd gotten in any type of trouble.

While we had our beliefs and our opinions, you didn't voice them to the public. You just didn't do that.

Why not?

It wasn't the thing to do. [. . .] You just didn't, you know, get out and blab, talk about stuff like that.

I was always brought up to say—this carried forth into my first job, Betsy. You remember when I worked for Paramount Life Insurance?

BETSY: I don't think so.

HELEN: Well, in any event, way back then there was no shopping centers. I mean, downtown Little Rock was . . . where all the merchants were, and office buildings and so forth. And this was right central town. And Paramount Life Insurance Company, a lot of the people would come to the lobby—it looked sort of like a bank—and pay their little premiums, whether they were a nickel a week, a dime, whatever; they were very small amounts.

Now most of these type people were blacks—well, a lot of white people did, too, but predominantly they were blacks, and they were just real concerned about paying their premiums up due that would bury them; they were real big on that.

And I can remember distinctly—I can't remember that old man's name that was office supervisor, you'd think I wouldn't forget. But I'd say, "Yes, Ma'am," or, "No, Sir," to blacks, also. Because I was always taught to respect my elders, and Mother didn't differentiate between black and white. 'Cause at one time we did have a maid, Cynthia. Now, although we were middle to lower class, people had maids, right? They came in, and they did the heavy work, and they did the ironing.

BETSY: And your mother didn't differentiate at all?

HELEN: No, no. So I would "Yes, Ma'am" or "No, Ma'am" or "Sir" to blacks, and I got called down for it. Did you know that? Because you did not yes-ma'am or no-ma'am blacks.

What did your supervisor say to you exactly, do you remember?

Roger Michelson, that was that old man's name! I can still see him! [laughs]

BETSY: And we said we weren't going to mention names! [laughs]

HELEN: [. . .] He's probably dead, he was old then. And

another thing from that, you can just pick and choose what you want from this, but this is the same man, the same year, the same whatever—

I was living at home, working, this and that, and going to school, Little Rock University, I went in the afternoon and at night, do you remember? Two years. And I didn't make all that much money. And I did have a car, and I had to make that car payment. And so I'd park and then walk maybe a block, a couple of blocks, to work. Well, many a time, I did not have the thirty-five cents to pay the parking for that day. Now, it's all relative, you've got to understand thirty-five cents would be like maybe five dollars today to park all day.

So there was a black attendant. Mostly blacks did that type of menial type things. And he was a younger guy, more my age, or maybe slightly older, and he was so very nice, and he would carry me. You understand what I'm saying? And then I would pay him, 'cause I got paid every Friday. Well, I thought that was awful nice, now don't you? So come Christmas, I bought him a tie, a Christmas present.

Well, lo and behold! it seems Mr. Michelson parked there, too!

BETSY: Oh, no!

HELEN: And that black boy was so pleased with that tie, he told Mr. Michelson about it. Well, Mr. Michelson just called me in his office, and I got what-for. Because a white girl did not buy presents for a black boy.

Is that what he said?

Yes, Ma'am. And I remember, I was just probably just twenty, I wasn't twenty-one, I was probably nineteen, twenty years old. And I was so mad. But I am, was—you shouldn't use the word waspish, I think that has something to do with races or something, but I mean I might sting.

And even then, and although I was taught to respect my elders, and he was my boss, I can remember I said to him—very well I remember this—I said to him, "You don't have to tell me what to do. I have a father." I mean, I bought the guy a tie! He had been nice to me all year, carrying me, I mean I couldn't have parked! [. . .]

What would your parents have thought if you'd made friends with a young black woman?

Well, I wouldn't have even thought about it. I would not have invited them into my home. [. . .]

Let me go back a little. Remember me saying earlier, you wanted to know how we came by way of Little Rock, and I told you they were farm people. . . . Well, even today, I have country cousins out my wazoo. So we'd go back and visit many times when I was a child growing up to my relatives, aunts, uncles, cousins, great-aunts, and all that, grandfather, grandmother.

So the blacks for the most part, except for one or two families, were sharecroppers. That's big, was then, in Arkansas, and the two blacks that owned their own land, they were considered high class, among their own people even. So I could go play with the blacks.

And this is terrible, but you can—uhn—we called them pickaninnies, now we did not do it to their face, but they were referred to as pickaninnies. And I realize now that is a derogatory term, but I didn't know any better.

BETSY: As what?

HELEN: Pickaninnies. When you were little, you could play with them. I mean, there wasn't anything wrong when you were little; you could play with them. When we'd go visit in the country, oh yeah, I would go to their houses and play and all. I could go in their home, and I never got punished for going in their home, and I want to tell you, a lot of those little old cabins, you could have eaten off the floor. They were immaculate. Even me that small, four-, five-year-old, six-year-old, I can remember that. So I'd go in and maybe sit down. They were always so nice, the mothers were, giving us a little treat, whatever they'd cooked, a peach cobbler or whatever they were eating, or Kool-Aid or whatever.

But by the same token if those same people came to my grandmother's house or my aunt's-uncle's house that we were visiting in the country . . . , they couldn't come in. They came to the back screen door—the screen door, I'm saying, because I always think of this stuff in the summertime. But they were never allowed into the house.

How did you feel about that?

It was just a way of life.

As in Wesley's account, Helen's nostalgia defended an era of inequality. Reverend Young's humor and Jerome Muldrew's dignity had softened the injuries they'd experienced in that era, casting them in a forgiving light. Among them all, black and white, I imagined a sort of collusion of southern manners, a will to excuse the harsh realities of the past, both because the old order had offered up goodness as well as bitterness, and because the old order was old. Helen's experience of race, her relationship with black playmates in a rural setting, was prototypically southern. Betsy's, it turned out, reflected the other side of life in an urbanizing border state:

Betsy, in your family, what did people think about race?

BETSY: It's really, really funny the difference. I'm just sitting here thinking, I just didn't realize what a difference it was. There again, now, I'm thinking I know where it came from. My father now was born and raised in Mississippi, and that carried over into our household.

We had a maid, Marcy, she was the best ole nigger-mammy, is what she was. I mean she was wonderful. We had her almost until she died. She took care of me, she loved me, I loved her. I remember her kids, one time when they got older, her son came to pick her up one day. 'Cause she rode the bus every day, and he came to pick her up, and I went to the door, and I was scared to death.

See, where you had some contact with blacks, I never did. I never had any contact.

HELEN: I played with them all the time when I was little.

BETSY: I just never did. I don't know why, but I just never did, except with our maid. And he came to the door, and I asked him to come in. I said, "Well, come in, she's almost ready."

And, "Oh, no," and those eyes got so big. He wouldn't come in, you know. And I didn't think anything about that.

You said you were scared when he came to the door?

I was scared when I first saw him. I didn't know who he was, and it scared me to see a black person standing at my door.

What was your fear?

I didn't know, I just remember thinking, "Why is he here? What's he here for?" I don't remember if that was before the integration or not. I think it was.

HELEN: Now where was this? Was this in Little Rock up on Beacon?

BETSY: Yeah, on Beacon, where we lived up there. Anyway, about that time she came in there, and I remember her bustling through the living room. She said, "Just get on out! Don't you come in here, boy!" They knew, I want to say where their place was, but that's what it was back then. They had a place, and that was it, and they knew where it was. [...]

I'm even a little afraid when I open the door now, and I see someone from India, or someone I'm not familiar with. Maybe that was it, I just wasn't familiar with them, even though they lived here and I lived here. So, when I saw one at my front door, they didn't come around back then selling door-to-door or anything—

HELEN: He had no business being there.

BETSY: Yeah, that was it. And you were told that. I don't remember any particular thing my parents said. I was just brought up to know you didn't associate with them.

Our maid was wonderful, and my mother took, we took Christmas food and clothing and everything to them every year at Christmas.

HELEN: We took care of them.

BETSY: We took care of them and all that, but, you know, they were inferior. That's all there is to it.

When you look back on that sort of racial milieu, what do you think about it now?

I don't know, back then it was OK. Now, I look back, and I do feel sorry for them. I think it's a shame it has to be that way, but it is and it still is, for the most part.

But then again, and it's like white people, there are some good and some bad, and the bad give the good a bad name sometimes even. It's hard when you've been brought up like that to completely say, I think it ought to be just cut and dried. It's hard for me anyway to feel differently.

I think Helen feels more liberal than I do, but see I always have felt that way, not real liberal. I just really haven't. So we're just totally, not totally, but a lot different.

HELEN: Well, to some degree. Not really. I'm almost hypocritical about it. I say one thing, and then deep down in my unconscious I cringe when I go to the grocery store, and I see a white girl with a black man. It just galls me no end. I can't help it and I think, Why? Why? And these aren't ugly people, either. It's definitely not because they can't get a white boy. I do not believe [sighs deeply] in interracial marriages. I'm sorry, I do not.

What Helen and Betsy sketched as they told their family histories were portraits of a social order, a southern order of which class and racial categories were the building blocks. They wished to speak of racial prejudice as if it were a quaint feature of the past. They spoke honestly of the ways it shaped their consciousness as children, but they also externalized its existence, Betsy by associating it with Mississippi ("My father now was born and raised in Mississippi, and that carried over into our household"), and Helen by placing it in the domain of the country cousins or the outrageous boss. By talking about it in the past and assigning primary blame to other groups, they shaved the edges of their own responsibility because they felt shame about what they nonetheless believed.

As if drawn by an irresistible force, however, the conversation veered toward present times, and the women told more and more troubling stories about their own and their children's feelings on the subject of black America. With the change in grammatical tense there came as well a change in emotional tenor. They lost the protection that came with recollecting something over and done with, and their statements were suddenly hot with resentment and anger. At the same time, they increasingly grew self-conscious about what they were saying. Their speech was dotted with disclaimers: "You must think I'm terrible." "That's enough; I've talked too much." Finally, Betsy connected their current-time racial hostilities with their experiences at Central High:

They think that a lot is owed to them, they do, they think we owe them. And maybe we do, but they're getting more and more, you see it on TV, they're getting, they're getting, they're being given, given, given, and that makes us bitter.

Ours probably started back—Because, like I'm bitter over my senior year, which was ruined because they were forced on us. It was ruined. Now, Helen says she doesn't remember that many bad things, but I do.

There was a marked change in Betsy's narrative. Suddenly, she metamorphosed from observer to participant. I asked her what had been ruined for her. What were the things she remembered from that year that made her feel bitter? "I don't remember not getting to go to the senior prom and all that," she replied, and then went on in a rush with what she clearly did remember instead:

> It seems like it was in the middle of the year, and my husband had a confrontation with one of the blacks going to school. It was no big deal or anything. She also was older, we found out later. She also had a baby in May, or right after graduation. She went in soon after, we knew a nurse that was there, she did have a baby. She was put there to cause trouble by the NAACP; she had to have been. She was not smart, she wasn't even there to study, she didn't try.

I assumed she was talking about Minnijean Brown. As my interviews progressed, there emerged a cast of characters whose roles appeared in many, many accounts with a telling consistency. Prominent among them was Minnijean, the most controversial of the nine African-American students enrolled in Central High that year. The Nine had been instructed to "turn the other cheek" when harassed, theoretically because school administrators anticipated being pressured to administer "equal" justice, to punish both people if a black student and a white student fought, and they wished to avoid that dilemma. Minnijean was the only one of the black students who would or could not comply. Often, she stood on her dignity, talking back, taking action—and eventually getting expelled in consequence.

Although Minnijean embodied a special sort of significance to many of her white classmates, no one presented a more colorful set of conjectures about her than Betsy's: she was a plant, she was older, she was sexually suspect. "What was the confrontation?" I asked.

> He was at his locker, and it was crowded around there, and he was talking to someone back here, and she came along and

said, "White boy, move out of the way." And he started moving
and he bumped into another boy, and he was trying to get out
of the way—He *says*! Now, he might not have been doing it as
fast as he should have. So she shoved him hard.

And so that day after school, they went out, we all went out,
this group went out through these doors every day, and there
were a bunch of the football guys down there, and my husband
was out there, and they all dared him to shove her. Everyone
knew about this, so they dared him. So he shoved her. [...]

Was he reported? Did he get in trouble?

Yeah, I *think* he was suspended at that time.

At this point Helen broke in with what seemed a non sequitur but
wasn't: "**Baby Johnson** did it."

"Did what?" I asked.

"She had to expel him, and she said she didn't want to. She had to,
she was a schoolteacher. She had to do it." Helen, picking up, perhaps,
on Betsy's tentativeness ("I *think* he was suspended . . .") was explaining how Johnny had come to be punished undeservedly. "She had to
do it," she emphasized. "She loved Johnny, but she had to do it."

Betsy, grasping the thread of her friend's defense, elaborated:

In fact, we [...] went to a party [at Baby's home] years later
after we had married and had children, and she remembered us
and took us around her house and everything.

She had to do it. She was out there, and she saw it happen.

Betsy returned to the main point of her story:

Well, anyway, then I started receiving calls. One night someone called, and I remember I was just hysterical because I wasn't
used to having a call from a black person.

They were going to hurt me and they were going to hurt my
family, and, "I better not catch you out!" I remember that. And
so I ran downstairs and told—

Helen interrupted again: "I remember, you thought it was just
white people kidding at first, didn't you?"

"Yeah," agreed Betsy, "and then I realized that it wasn't, that
accent—"

"It was real plain," said Helen emphatically.

"It was, yeah," Betsy agreed.

> And then I ran down and told Mother and Daddy, I was crying and I was real upset, and about that time the phone rings, it was Johnny's mother, and they had just gotten a call, and they were going to kill people, and they better not catch you out and all that. We were both in the house for six weeks, we couldn't go out, we couldn't do anything, you know.
>
> And I'm sure *they* were out running around, whatever. See, it didn't hurt *them*. I don't know, it just seemed like it was just always something that year.
>
> Of course, I was going with Johnny, and he probably was not the most stable person.

"No, no, don't say 'not stable,'" Helen protested. "He was very stable. He was immature."

"Yeah," said Betsy.

I wondered what the deeper meaning might be of this exchange about how to label Johnny's behavior, but bracketed that question and instead asked, "Did Johnny have clear opinions about desegregation, or about black people?"

"He hated them," said Betsy decisively.

"Who did he hate?" I asked. Betsy answered in a more considered tone:

> Well, as I say, none of us really ever thought of anything, he had never mistreated—in fact, he worked over at the ballpark, sold cokes and stuff, and he had friends.
>
> But then when it was forced on us, you see, that's what we're saying. And I guess when I stop and think about it, that's probably the whole thing!

Protest arises from an intricate interaction between what people believe about the world, what they say to each other, and what they experience directly. Betsy had a personal encounter which crystallized her bitterness about the process of desegregation. She also had a belief system which was violated. Her ideological objections (she began and ended saying, "It was forced on us") framed her lived experience, and that interaction resulted in a good deal of ambivalence. Was she protesting the coercive nature of desegregation—or the fact that it had ruined her senior year? Did she support and defend her boyfriend's actions or did she resent them? At one moment she portrays him as the innocent victim of Minnijean's aggression. In the next breath, he was an unstable youth prodded into bad behavior by the dares of the football players—involving her in a whole lot of trouble in the process. If she bore him ill will for bringing trouble to her door, she expressed it only in the most indirect ways. In the end what really mattered, "the whole thing," was what Betsy saw as the injustice of coercive change.

Blame and Consequences

Storytelling is a political act, and the tales the two friends told constructed an argument and revealed a worldview. Taken as a whole, Betsy's story argued for a reversal of victimhood. Desegregation was an action intended to rectify wrongs done to African Americans. But Betsy argues that she, not they, was the one truly wronged: "*They* were out running around. See, it didn't hurt *them.*" Integration was forced on her, ruining her senior year. Johnny was punished, not because he deserved it—after all, he innocently blocked Minnijean's way, shoving her in response to a simple dare; boys do these things —well, maybe it was not so innocent, maybe he was unstable, but really only boyishly immature. He was punished, not because he deserved it, but because a teacher happened to see the incident, and she, too, was forced to do something against her will. In the end, Betsy and Johnny suffered threats to their lives from people they first thought were white jokers but quickly became convinced were seriously violent black people. Rather than accuse Johnny of a wrong which injured not only Minnijean but also Betsy by involving her in struggle she wished to avoid, Betsy protected their couple and argued that they, too, were victimized. The racial conflict was clear to her, but not the gender one imbedded within it.

If Betsy and Johnny and Helen were the true sufferers, who were the villains of the piece? Many culprits emerged as Helen and Betsy continued their story:

> *Let's back up a little bit. When did you first become aware of the fact that there was going to be integration at Central High?*

> BETSY: The only thing I remember was going to school that first day, and we knew it was going to happen. It was kind of exciting.

> *The first day. So you weren't thinking about it before the first day?*

> No.

Helen broke in, protesting with passion:

> No! There was plenty of room for all of us there. Now, I'm not trying to be Goody Two-Shoes, think about it. The school was big enough to accommodate everybody, so who cares? I don't think—Again, it was agitators that provoked things.

"Again?" I wondered if I'd missed some earlier reference to agitators. "Which agitators?"

"Actually, I think the outsiders. If they just let 'em be," Helen began. But Betsy jumped in to set the conversation on a different track: "And let the white people be, too!"

The outside agitator is a common character in histories of social conflict, and one who appears frequently in accounts of Little Rock. Sometimes he is a redneck from the hills who populated the mob. Sometimes he is a crafty, black attorney who engineered Little Rock's shame. Who exactly Helen's agitator might be was unclear. But Betsy leaped into the center of Helen's ambiguity to define with no uncertainty who that mythic figure's victim had been: the white people, *her* people.

Perhaps Betsy's identification of herself and Helen as the victims helped Helen to remember whom she'd blamed for her woes that year. She went straight on to condemn someone who was not an outsider at all: Elizabeth Huckaby, the vice principal who, by her own description in a book[3] she published that became a TV movie, had been assigned the task of keeping order in the school and protecting the black newcomers:

> And one of them is that Mrs. Huckaby. That was the high point of that—and this is my opinion—but that was the high point of her life. I did not like her. She was a cynical, opinionated, [pauses] old bitch.

What did she do that made you so angry?

It was just her demeanor. She made it more than what it was. It's almost like little kids looking for trouble, or looking for something to get somebody else in trouble. She'd go up and down the halls; she didn't have to do that. It was like she was fanning it.

"Umm hmm!" said Betsy in ardent agreement.
"I think she overreacted," Helen went on.

If she'd stayed in her office, pushed her pencil and done what she was supposed to do, taught class, whatever it was, I mean you know. But oh, no! It was probably the high time of her, at that time, teaching career, of her life. I did not like the woman. I just didn't like the woman.

Had you liked her before that year?

Never thought much about her. But you didn't see her a lot either. You didn't see her up and down the halls, and, "You do this," and, "You do that." I mean she was just so pushy!

"If you didn't have any problems," said Betsy, "you didn't see her." Helen raged on:

And I never saw her, like you, 'cause I was a Goody Two-Shoes. I never did, you know. So I never saw her. But then, like she says, she was out in the halls, patrolling around: didn't need to be. I mean, those kids were guarded, for crying out loud. They didn't need her.

I was to hear many versions of who the villain was that year: the black students, the NAACP, the board of education, President Eisenhower, Governor Faubus. For Helen, and once she'd mentioned it for Betsy as well, Mrs. Huckaby was It. It was interesting to me that they put Mrs. Huckaby in that role. As the vice principal for girls, Elizabeth Huckaby had been assigned the task of disciplining delinquent female students. At least, that was the role visible to Betsy and Helen. Suddenly, they saw her protecting those who, in their view, needed no protection, which presumably cast them, the white students, in roles of malfeasance. Betsy and Helen were themselves "Goody Two-Shoes," they insisted. In this context, I translated that as meaning innocents. Yet they stood accused by Mrs. Huckaby's very presence in the halls as being wrong-doers.

Implicit arguments about who was victim and who was villain appeared again and again in my interviews. Many of the white people sought to correct the public record as they understood it: No, no, they argued, you've got it all wrong. The black students were powerful and aggressive. We were innocent, robbed of promised glories of our senior year, and then, to top it all off, regarded as those in the wrong!

> *What did you think that first day when you got there and the National Guard was surrounding the building?*
>
> HELEN: Well, you see, they weren't there in the beginning.
>
> *They weren't?*
>
> No, Ma'am. They came later after all these little, those stupid people, like the one that wrote the sign that plastered, they sent it around the world, I remember it was "goverment," they didn't even know how to spell "government," they left the "n" out.
>
> BETSY: Well, was that whites or blacks?
>
> HELEN: These were whites.

This exchange was interesting on two counts. First, it revealed a little more of the differences between Helen and Betsy. I began to get a clearer sense of what Betsy had meant when she'd called Helen "more liberal": Helen blamed a cast of white characters—Mrs. Huckaby, the mob, perhaps white jokesters threatening Betsy on the phone. Often, Helen's anger had a class tilt, first at affluent snobs, later at ignorant rednecks in the mob. Betsy's focus, however, was more consistently racial; she blamed black actors first and with more vehemence. "The mob," I clarified, "is that right?" Helen continued:

> Yeah, the mob. Now, bear in mind, if you've been there [to Central High] and you started to get the feel of it, although you're not going to get a true feeling of it. I'll never go back again; the school is in pitiful shape.
>
> *It's a grand building.*
>
> Yes, you should have seen it in its heyday, though. There's not a blade of grass, Betsy. The shrubs are all dead. When I was

there, a lot of the windows were kicked out. The beautiful fishpond that was a part of the architecture to reflect the columns
and the statues, they finally had to concrete it in, Betsy, so you
do not get the reflective of the columns or the statues, and it's
cruel now. Because, I mean, that's just the way it is. Blacks, I don't
care, there's no grass around their homes. Now that's—I look at
you and I worry that you'll have contempt for me saying that—
but that's what I observe.

If Helen's terms were primarily class ones, racial feelings followed
close behind. The memory of the misspelled sign evoked images of
the grand building in front of which it had been displayed. And that
memory in turn evoked another that took Helen's narrative in a very
different direction. From criticizing the mob she shifted passionately
to a condemnation of the black community for the run-down state
of the school building and its neighborhood.

The second note worth pursuing in Helen's answer to my earlier
question was a mistake. From time to time in my interviews, controversies arose about seemingly established "facts." Helen and Betsy were
both certain the National Guard arrived several weeks after school
started. All published accounts have them there the very first morning
school opened, an event that is reasonably easy to document and verify.
"Any mistake is meaningful," wrote Karen Fields; what gives it meaning is a context of deeply held beliefs about the world. Providing a
means for interpreting experience, these beliefs in turn shape memory
itself, selecting that which lends consistency to a given ideological argument and thus to a particular picture of the world. What inconsistency
were Betsy and Helen seeking to resolve by placing the Guards in a
timeframe not supported by the evidence? I pursued the question a
little further, and the two friends spoke in emphatic concert:

> *You said that the National Guard was not there at the*
> *beginning—*
> HELEN: No, Ma'am, it was not. It was not there Day One.
> They had to bring them out later because of the, yes—
> BETSY: Yeah, Governor Faubus called them in later because
> the police were not able to control the mobs and all that—

But you had been going to school for some days before they were there?

HELEN [drawing with her finger on a photograph of the building]: If this is Park Street and this is the front of the school, OK? And I don't know if that's Fourteenth or what. But I lived back over in here at that time. [...] I did not have a car till I got out of high school. And so if somebody didn't pick me up I rode the bus, and I'd get off at this block. So then I would walk up one block—

[To Betsy:] Ya'll used to park at, remember the parking lot there, right? And so I just mention this, this is the front of the school, so I'd get off here, walk up here through the parking lot, and I'd go in this door here, Betsy. I never went in the front. And I don't know, but a lot of this you're getting, I think you're getting it from movies you may have watched or pictures you've seen.

Why did Helen address this account to Betsy? I began to wonder what subtext Helen and Betsy were discussing between them in these asides.

BETSY: See, that was the one I always went in, too.

HELEN: So I didn't see the mobs and the policemen the first day of school. I did hear later, like she said, that the policemen were not able to keep these mob people, or irate parents, from climbing up those many long steps. It got so bad that they had to get the 101st Air Force, and all the way around the school, they were. And they did have bayonets fixed. They will try to say that didn't happen, but yes they did. They made them take them off later.

After the first day or two of school, maybe it was the first day, but anyway the first day or two of school, and it was just sort of blown out of propor—. Well, maybe it wasn't blown out of proportion.

Perhaps Helen and Betsy argued against the arrival of the National Guard the first day of school because there had been no mobs to control before the first day. If the Guard had been placed there, not to bar the entrance of the black students but only to "keep order" as both they and Governor Faubus insisted, then it was hard to justify their being there before the trouble began. It made a neater, more convincing story to have the police trying to control those "stupid people" at first, and the Guard arriving (as the 101st Airborne had in fact done) only after the police had failed. At the same time, Helen's elaborate discussion of which door she went in and where Betsy parked served to soften her insistence about when the Guard arrived. If they were at the front door and she went in the side, then she could claim she "didn't see" who exactly was there, even though we'll see below that in another story she contradicted that claim.

If the trouble had all been stirred by outsiders and authorities, what about people who protested desegregation inside the school? The only indication I'd had in the course of our conversation so far that there were people protesting inside the school were some cards Helen had found stuck inside her yearbook. Cards like these had circulated among the students throughout the year. They bore slogans and doggerels:

> That White Trash Mathews [sic] Named Jess [the principal]
> Sure Got *Central High* in a *Mess;*
> The Kids—*If They're White,*
> He *Deprives* of their *Rights-*
> He's a Kansas *Nigger-Lover,* I guess.

Another read:

> Rockaby, Huckaby, betray your own race,
> Get an umbrella smack in your face. . . .

The incident to which that card referred involved the mother of a Central High student who accosted Mrs. Huckaby at a hearing about her daughter's expulsion for misdeeds at school. Betsy continued with reference to that mom:

> Now, I was just going to say, I remember Sammie Dean Parker's mother—Sammie Dean was in the movie, and her mother, and I think wasn't quite in the movie.
> HELEN: Huckaby's [i.e., the film made from Mrs. Huckaby's book, *Crisis at Central High*].
> BETSY: They called one night. Now I don't remember when this was, but it was early on, I think. Her mother called my house.

Now I didn't know her [Sammie Dean], she was pretty, she
was such a little doll, I remember she was so pretty and so cute.
But they were what we considered white trash, really.

HELEN: I don't know why. They were extremely well-
heeled. He was a big railroad man. They had money.

BETSY: Well, probably because of the way she acted and the
way her mother acted.

"Stupid people" in mobs outside the school; federal troops;
imposing vice principals; improperly acting "white trash" classmates:
these were the people making trouble, not Helen, who quietly went
to school through a side door, not Betsy, who innocently was drawn
into trouble by her immature boyfriend. That the two women communicated indignation and resentment about the injustices they
believed done to them that year, wrongs that connected up with the
later indignity of the decimation of school property and neighborhood lawns, seemed to me to be an emotional fact of considerable significance. What they remembered and forgot of that year told a story
in and of itself. They remembered no Guardsmen barring the black
students when school began. They told me no instances, witnessed or
heard, of any of the Nine being hassled or tormented. But the image
of Mrs. Huckaby stirring up trouble by stalking the halls was fresh
and vivid. "Memory 'tainted' by interest is a dead-serious party to the
creation of something true," wrote Karen Fields. When people argue
for a reality that seems unlikely to others, they are in fact arguing some
emotional reality of their own which is not necessarily evident to
others. They tell a hidden story in images and memories and feeling-
tones rather than in words. What story of victimization were these
two friends telling me, I wondered? Why, for instance, did they speak
so angrily of Minnijean, in such a contemptuous and disassociated
way of Sammie Dean?

What was clear already was that they expressed a relationship to
the making of history, one that eschewed responsibility and bespoke
a sense of powerlessness, and that their feelings about that experience
were tangled up in their feelings about two other women students
who *were* responsible and powerfully active.

SIX
Sammie Dean and Minnijean

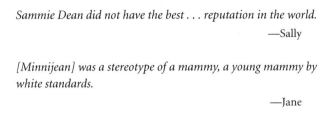

Sammie Dean did not have the best . . . reputation in the world.

—Sally

[Minnijean] was a stereotype of a mammy, a young mammy by white standards.

—Jane

"You know, this will probably be something that I made up in my head," Sally said apologetically, "but I can just remember her attitude. It was just a haughty, snotty, look-down-your-nose-at-me attitude that she had."

She was speaking of her classmate, Minnijean Brown. Sally's recollections of Minnijean echoed Betsy's and many of her white classmates' as I talked with them about their brush with history at Central High.

Their hostility toward Minnijean was matched only by their contempt for Sammie Dean Parker, a member of the junior class. "Who were the segregationist student leaders?" I asked **Nancy**, another senior that year. "Sammie Dean Parker was the only one I knew," she replied. "Sammie Dean Parker was taken to jail that day. She was kicking, spitting, scratching, and the policeman couldn't do anything with her, she was so out of control."

It is tempting to take for granted this archly critical commentary. After all, Sammie Dean and Minnijean were both noteworthy and controversial. But the particular ways in which their women classmates talk about them are significant. They are windows into structures of understanding the world these teenagers co-inhabited. Or perhaps a more dynamic metaphor would better serve: they are screens on which to view moving pictures of the girls' construction of their own identities as southern women in a world in rapid flux.

How we decide who we are as individuals inhabiting a social world is rife with understandings of the significance of gender, race, class, and other social categories. Interlaced with particular ways of being in the world that reflect unique biographies, individual psychology is massively influenced by social identities. Women and men, white people and people of color, children from poor families and rich ones think of themselves differently in any given culture, and act accordingly. Ideas about what is possible and what is desirable, the building blocks of agency, are thus socially and historically determined. While there is a great variation in the identities negotiated and accepted by any given woman or man, there are also very strong commonalties.

In the white students' accounts of desegregation, many strands of identity and agency lie closely intertwined. That gender is fundamental was quickly demonstrated to me: I had a far easier time persuading women alumnae to talk with me than men. The men were more cautious, more critical of my purposes, less personal, slower to build trustful relationships with me. Eventually many did talk with me, eloquently and generously. But Helen and Betsy and their women friends made early and clear decisions to participate in the project and graced me with their stories abundantly.

I have said that within the history of Central High School lie many different histories. One of these is the story of Orval Faubus and Jimmy Karam, a classic example of male interaction—located in the public domain, anchored in negotiations of power, operating through instrumental transactions defined as friendship, a story of white men's ambitions and strategies enacted in a theater of racial change.

I turn now to the particular history of women. Contained within the story of Central High's desegregation is a vivid tale of transformation in white women's lives, a drama interlaced with men's reality but very different. My own memories of Little Rock are highly gendered, although I wasn't aware of it at the time. A teenager fresh from the South, I watched history happening on a television in my northeastern college dormitory. Staunch rows of National Guardsmen sliced statically across the screen, standing militarily erect in front of the magnificent school building. Governor Faubus's serious face appeared, reading earnest messages of resolution to "protect the peace" and prevent the undemocratic imposition of integration on the good citizens of his state. Network commentators, all men, read somber but excited reports of late-breaking news.

But when the cameras turned to the streets around the school, the images were quite different. Girls and women moved through the crowds. Elizabeth Eckford, a frail-looking black teenager clad in the sort of big gored skirt fashionable at the time, clutched her schoolbooks and clenched her jaw as she was turned away from the front door by the Guards. A white girl her age screamed at her, open-mouthed. The mob of women and men noisily hounded her retreat. One gray-haired white woman shielded the terrified Elizabeth, turning to chastise the crowd as she accompanied the girl onto an empty bus.

Over the next months, the news media continued to report an unusual amount of activity by women: Daisy Bates headed the state NAACP, for example, and Margaret Jackson the hastily formed Mothers League of Central High, an offshoot of the Citizens Council's fight to preserve segregation. Inside the school Elizabeth Huckaby, the liberal vice principal, did daily damage control.[1] When the high schools were closed the following year, Adolphine Fletcher Terry formed the Women's Emergency Committee which became a vehicle for women like Sara Murphy to engage the political process.

That women populated the stage on which the drama of Central High was played is not a coincidence. Nor was it altogether new; Chris Mercer, in telling me the story of how the black "do-gooder ladies" brought about school integration in Fayetteville, had told a similar tale. School desegregation was a struggle that especially evoked women's activism; who else could better claim the moral authority to speak up when the site of contention was the domain of children? But the white women who spoke up in places like Little Rock faced a particular set of dilemmas. It was the fifties; the ideal type of white womanhood pictured Mother in the kitchen, tending traditional values along with the home-fires. To enter into public discourse was itself an act of defiance, therefore. That act was especially problematic for segregationist women who, by weighing in to defend the status quo, betrayed it. These dilemmas and paradoxes of women's activism shade and inform the stories white women graduates of Central High tell about those times.

As those stories proliferated, I faced the oral historian's dilemma. If all goes well, you end up with miles of tape and reams of transcripts, a daunting avalanche of data that is both good news and bad. To find my way through the tangle, I devised a method of starting from emotional "hot spots," recurring topics about which people spoke with passion. Never were the white women alumnae of Central High hotter than when they spoke of their classmates Minnijean and Sammie Dean. What exactly did that hostility express, not so much about the women of whom they spoke, but about themselves and about the intense period of history through which they lived?

Sweet Sixteen and Angry

I have said that most of those who were students at Central High School on opening day, like Helen, did not believe themselves to be history makers, even in the midst of mayhem:

> I went to school, just nothing, no big deal. I didn't see if there was commotion going on up here, I didn't see it. 'Cause I came in the side door, went to my locker, did my thing.

Literally sidestepping history did not constitute a position, as Helen saw it. She insisted she was neutral on the question of desegregation itself. "The school was big enough to accommodate everybody, so who cares?"

But some among the students clearly did care, and they protested hard. While grown-up mobs raged outside the building, inside the black students were called names, tripped, kicked, and spat upon. As the year wore on, harassment took a more organized and aggressive aspect. The printed cards bearing racist slogans appeared more frequently, suggesting a network of planners, writers, printers, and distributors.[2] Many people showed me samples they had saved, but all my inquiries about where the cards came from went in vain. Who had brought them into the school? How had Helen come by the ones she'd carefully (but shamefacedly) preserved in her yearbook? Had anyone tried to recruit my interviewees to distribute cards or join other protests? Everybody insisted they knew nothing about it, knew nobody involved, could name no names—except one: a girl named Sammie Dean Parker.

I had first learned that Sammie existed through a series of enigmatic references in Elizabeth Huckaby's book. Responsibly protecting the student's identity throughout, Mrs. Huckaby makes reference to a "small ponytailed girl" who irked the authorities in so many ways, even riling the endlessly patient vice principal herself. As Mrs. Huckaby's account proceeds, this girl becomes "the ponytailed segregationist leader."[3] Years later when I interviewed her, Mrs. Huckaby recalled her student with better humor. But still she referred to her as "the girl who was so aggressive during all of this."

Sammie's peers shared very little of Mrs. Huckaby's reticence as they reminisced about their classmate:

> SALLY: Sammie Dean—this is confidential, right? Sammie Dean did not have the best—how do you put that?—reputation in the world.
>
> *She was a segregationist activist?*
>
> Right. And plus, she also had other, uh, unredeeming qualities.
>
> *Would you say what?*
>
> Well, she was the girl about town, we'll put it that way. And I was Miss Goody Two-Shoes, what can I say? Sweet sixteen and never been kissed and the whole nine yards.
>
> But, anyway, on one of the occasions that happened, they drug Sammie Dean kicking and screaming out of the schoolhouse. Probably the police or the troops or whoever, but anyway, it was one of the, quote, authorities. And she went kickin' and screaming out of the schoolhouse where she crawled out on them and they caught her.
>
> BETSY: Now I didn't know her, she was pretty, she was such a little doll, I remember she was *so* pretty and so cute. But they were what we considered white trash, really.

Sally's reference to herself as "Goody Two-Shoes" reminded me of Helen's use of the same term. Although Helen was talking about her position on desegregation while Sally hinted at sexual matters, both expressed something similar about innocence.[4] They acquiesced innocently to forced desegregation, minding their own business and the letter of the law. They themselves had no beef with black people. They'd always had black people working in their homes, and folks of both races were good to each other. The trouble started, as they saw it, when the black students acted badly.

Actually, it was only one student who acted badly, as they remembered it: Minnijean Brown. The rest were fine, quiet, respectful, demure. If only Minnijean had stayed in her place there'd have been no trouble. Not everyone blamed the Nine for the trouble. But many did, and those who did universally focused on Minnijean.

Said Sally:

> I remember, uh, what was that girl's name? Big girl, Minnijean. She had an attitude, it was like, OK, white folks, here I am. . . .
>
> You know this will probably be something that I made up in my head, that I'm making up in my head now, but I can just remember her attitude. . . . I can't recall words that happened, it was just a haughty, snotty, look-down-your-nose-at-me attitude that she had.

Joyce, a year younger than Sally and the offspring of parents from the mid-West, spoke of Minnijean with more camaraderie, but in similar terms:

> Physically, Minnijean was a large girl. I was a large girl at the time; I've always been overweight. And Minnijean had, I think, more of a presence physically than the other girls did. I also think Minnijean had more, she exuded more of a sense of herself than I remember the other girls doing. It was a confidence-slash-arrogance. The segregationists probably perceived it as arrogance, which they didn't like; I perceived it as confidence in herself, self-assuredness.

Jane was one of very few Central High grads who went on to an academic career. She theorized her classmates'—and her own—view of Minnijean:

> I would describe her unlike all the rest of the blacks. I'd put it in class terms. First of all, she was overweight, so that made her more, what?—easy to tease. She was a stereotype of a mammy, a young mammy by white standards. Remember how there used to be the mammy with the [sketches big belly with her hands]?

OK? Because she was big and she was overweight, and she was more challenging, more asserting, she was more set. Whereas the others were very almost docile.

Mammy and White Trash: Troublemakers Disavowed

What do these descriptions of Sammie Dean and Minnijean tell us about the worldview of the women who spoke them? Although Minnijean is cast as the problem, Sammie Dean, too, is held responsible. Minnijean may have behaved provocatively, but the women of Central High saw Sammie Dean's response as unacceptable, a way of acting that they themselves eschewed. Taken together, these two assessments defined black womanhood and white trash, and in contrast communicated a thick bundle of beliefs about what it was to be white women in Little Rock in the fifties, as well as challenges to those beliefs. Three aspects of the women's accounts are especially vivid expressions of underlying meaning: their references to body image, sexuality, and class.

Right along with the person herself, memories of both Sammie Dean and Minnijean are pinned to body size. Minnijean is large, Sammie Dean small. So central were physical images that they sometimes were the hook for fishing up the controversial classmate's name itself: "What was that girl's name? Big girl, Minnijean." Sammie Dean was small, cute, ponytailed. Minnijean was large, overweight, Mammy-like. Both girls acted in the physical world, and in that respect both challenged rules of femininity. Despite herself, neither one could avoid confrontation. Sammie tangled with policemen, fellow students, and vice principals. Minnijean talked back, pushed back, and eventually dropped a bowl of chili on the lap of a white boy who tormented her once too often. Both girls were ultimately expelled, Minnijean for the chili incident, Sammie for distributing the cards after Minnijean left, saying, "One down, eight to go."[5] Both young women were formidable.

That Sammie Dean's and Minnijean's body sizes were noteworthy speaks of an experience familiar to most women in America. How big we are, how thin or fat, tall or short, compels our consciousness, because physical characteristics are closely bound up with how our femininity is viewed and how, in consequence, we evaluate our own sense of worth. "Physically, Minnijean was a large girl," said Joyce, and then went on to identify herself with Minnijean's size. "I was a large girl at the time; I've always been overweight." Joyce then drew a conclusion about Minnijean as a person in the world: "And Minnijean had, I think, more of a presence physically than the other girls did." As a teenager, Joyce herself was highly conflicted about her own presence in the world.

Said Jane on the subject of Minnijean's size: "I would describe her unlike all the rest of the blacks. . . . First of all, she was overweight." In the context of her remarks, weight distinguished Minnijean not only from all the blacks, but from Jane herself, who was very thin. Like Joyce, Jane too linked size and behavior: "Because she was big and she was overweight, and she was more challenging, more asserting, she was more set." Later, Jane, like Joyce, wrestled with her own choices about how set and challenging to be. For both Joyce and Jane, comparisons with Minnijean elicited a recognition of something about themselves, for Joyce because of their physical similarity, for Jane because of their difference.

When people told me that Sammie Dean was small and cute, they conveyed indirectly a particularly damning critique of her behavior. How striking it was to them that someone who fit the physical standard for American female approval should act in so unwomanly a manner—kicking and screaming and putting herself in the way of being dragged out of the schoolhouse.

Identifying Minnijean as big and overweight similarly served to discredit her, although in this case very directly. Big women are figures of fun, and she was "easy to tease." Mammy carries a particular rhetorical weight. She is one of the few black characters in American racial mythology who is forgiven for being overbearing, because she dominates in the service of motherhood. She can be allowed to dominate, because, unlike a "real" (read "white") mother whose power might be genuinely threatening, Mammy's power is ultimately none at all—she is a slave. All the comfort of forceful mothering is therefore at the service of her white charges, who are nonetheless securely in charge. Indeed, they are in the ultimate control. If mothering is constructed as a natural instinct, the designation of mammy has succeeded in subverting nature itself, severing servant from the mothering service of her own offspring and reconstructing her instincts to the benefit of her white masters. Unlike her charges' biological mothers, she has no choice but to be unambivalently theirs.[6]

But Minnijean could not be tamed by the label "mammy." Her defiance was not confined; it spilled over to become a force in a fierce contest of realities. One white interviewee, searching for a way to explain her hatred for Minnijean, finally burst out, "She walked the halls as if she belonged there."

"There was plenty of room for all of us there," Helen said, more reasonably. "The school was big enough to accommodate everybody, so who cares?" But the implication was strong that it was fine for "them" to come to "our" school. The problem arose if "they" acted like they were there by right, not by generosity.

My white interviewees commonly expressed this idea by reference to concepts of "place":

> JANE: With Minnijean, I remember not feeling very empathetic that she left. Sort of, stereotypically that she asked for it, [that she] didn't know her place, do you know what I'm saying? That kind of feeling.

> BARBARA: I just felt that she was different.... I felt she was probably one of the most out of place people in the whole school.

"They liked us," Evelyn had said, "as long as we stayed in our place." Segregation represented an ordering of the universe, a way of naming social hierarchies and the location within them of every individual, whether black or white. Comments about Minnijean's person and attitude, definitions of her as an individual, combine with comments about her "place" to consign her forcefully to a social position.

Places, Positions, and Power

What place was that, exactly? Overtly "place" was, and still is, a coded reference to racial hierarchy. But there is another sense in which the notion appears in my interviews and in everyday discourse, and that is about class. Significantly, just as often as her white classmates expressed animosity toward Minnijean in terms of her deviance from racial proprieties, they talked contemptuously of Sammie Dean in class terms. Class appeared in the almost universal description of Sammie Dean as "white trash." What that meant was elaborated in the exchange between Betsy and her friend Helen: "They were what we considered white trash, really," said Betsy, and Helen responded, "I don't know why. They were extremely well-heeled. He was a big railroad man. They had money." Said Betsy, "Well, probably because of the way she acted and the way her mother acted." Class equated with women's behavior. Minnijean, too, was considered déclassé—"a more working-class, less-educated type of black woman, a young mammy by white standards."

One clue to the link between conceptions of class and race is contained in things people said about their families' personal relations with black people. Helen identified her family's straitened economic status with dignity: "If you want to say a railroad track, I lived on the wrong side of town so to speak, in that town's way of talking. But that didn't make us trash or anything. We just lived in the older homes." One thing that raised them above the category of "trash" was their ability to employ black servants:

> HELEN: At one time we did have a maid, Cynthia. Now, although we were middle to lower class, people had maids, right? They came in and they did the heavy work and they did the ironing.

> JANE: I grew up in a more working-class neighborhood with middle-class educated parents. But my parents always acted like we didn't have very much money, primarily because my father grew up extremely poor. . . . We did have black help . . . once a week.

Many people emphasized to me how well their parents treated the family servant. Helen said, "I was always taught to respect my elders, and Mother didn't differentiate between black and white." "We had a maid, Marcy," said Betsy. "She was the best ole nigger-mammy, is what she was. I mean she was wonderful. We had her almost until she died.

She took care of me, she loved me, I loved her." But however much Betsy loved Marcy, however much Helen "didn't differentiate between black and white," between themselves the maid was still a "nigger-mammy." That Betsy was unconfused about injunctions against socializing was implicit in the story she'd told me earlier about discovering her beloved Marcy's son on her doorstep. I asked where she'd gotten the message to keep her distance:

> BETSY: I don't remember any particular thing my parents said. I was just brought up to know you didn't associate with them.
>
> Our maid was wonderful, and my mother took, we took Christmas food and clothing and everything to them every year at Christmas.
>
> HELEN: We took care of them.
>
> BETSY: We took care of them and all that, but, you know, they were inferior. That's all there is to it.
>
> Back then it was OK. Now, I look back, and I do feel sorry for them. I think it's a shame it has to be that way, but it is and it still is, for the most part.

Betsy and Helen's stories contained a number of strategic layers. On the one hand, they were presenting themselves in a good light, arguing that white people in *their* South were benevolent, not "trash." Benevolence was a class characteristic. But at the same time, in tone and posture, they also expressed discomfort with the southernness of their attitudes back then. "They were inferior. That's all there is to it," said Betsy in such a way as to suggest that their view back then was not their view now, but that they should be excused for what they thought back then, even though the consequences of what they thought had mostly not yet changed. When she used the phrase "nigger-mammy" she spoke with a certain self-consciousness, mocking herself, but also defying my condemnation. "It was just the way it always was," Wesley had said. "We don't think about it being Sunday morning when it's Sunday morning." Many people protested, "That's just the way it was," in one breath, and in the next defined nuances of their culpability in "the way it was." "I never used the word nigger in all my youth," Sally told me. "If I did I would have had my teeth knocked down my throat;

my parents wouldn't have stood for it." Unwittingly revealing her own
bias, Helen told me how upset she'd been when her father said "nigger" in front of her son:

> He doesn't say Negro, he says nigger. And my son, that beau-
> tiful little blond-headed, blue-eyed boy, I can remember the first
> time he said it, it just killed me. And I said, "Daddy! Don't teach
> him to say that. He's going to have to be around them, and I don't
> want you teaching him that word."

But at the same time Helen and Betsy and Sally defined with
specificity the degrees of their own racism ("I never thought I was a
racist, but . . . ." Helen said, breathing noisily through her lips in per-
plexity, "I still haven't thought about that yet. I don't know if I am or
not"), they argued implicitly that the arrangement back then worked.
Black and white people got along fine before desegregation, they suggested, remembering how they themselves got along with Cynthia or
Marcy. Domestic relations between white families and black maids
were often the only experience white people ever had of occupying
dominant class positions. As members of the white race, they may
theoretically have possessed certain power and advantages. But in
their lived experience that status had reality only at home. "Now,
although we were middle to lower class, people had maids, right?"
Helen said. Out in the world, her people were vulnerable, limited in
their ability to make wishes into commands. "We had gone through
some bad times. . . . My daddy was not a businessman," said Helen
with kindly euphemism. Only when Cynthia arrived at the back door
did her daddy—did she herself—become the boss.

These asymmetrical relationships between white families and
black servants were central in constructing a certain ideology about
the racial order in the South: the proper arrangement of power was
white dominance (in the most benign version, as employers); the
proper role for whites was gentility and for blacks service; the proper
site for interaction between the races was on white domestic territory.
Finally, bolstering this ideology was a prevalent myth (itself bolstered
by the strategic choice of black people to protest mostly "down at the
big gate"): that these relations were equally agreeable to both blacks

and whites: "She loved me, I loved her." Taken all in all, this set of ideas described a social hierarchy and justified punitive acts against black people who failed to play their assigned role, who expressed dissatisfaction with the status quo, for instance, by enrolling in Central High—and acting as if they belonged there.

The other side of the coin, however, was the way in which this prescribed racial order helped to construct a certain moral control of the behavior of disadvantaged whites as well. The very proprieties of white people's treatment of blacks—from generosity toward those who served domestically to intolerance for a lack of deference in return, from a use of derogatory language in private among friends to a show of "respect" in face-to-face encounters with black people—contained within them an underlying set of rules demarcating class among whites. One qualified for "superior" status vis-a-vis black people if, and only if, one acted with gentility. That these white families "took care" of their black servants (that fact associating them with a thick packet of social and ethical standards clustering around acts of generosity) in one sweep both defined black people as inferior and themselves as having standing on the white class ladder. They were "middle- to lower-class" whites, not white trash. White trash behavior—rowdiness in public, loose sexual mores, racist speech, the behaviors on which Sammie's classmates commented in their very first evocations of her—constituted a set of rules that my white interviewees recognized clearly and debated, obeyed and contested in very fine gradations.

Implicit in those rules was a premise of class mobility for whites. For one thing, when white working people employed black domestic workers, they enjoyed an experience of dominance which carried with it notions of rights and possibilities: if they were "boss" material, then they had "boss" prospects. Encouraged to behave in ways associated with higher class status, white working people were solaced by the expectation that these expressions of status would someday become reality, that they could attain a desired class position and leave behind the element of fiction. ("They were introverted snobs," declared Helen, and in the same breath insisted that all the kids, however much or little their fathers earned, were "all one group.") If certain behaviors denoted a certain status, then the opposite was also true: if you behaved in a way associated with a particular place in society, you proved your eligibility to occupy that place. America is unusual in the ambiguity of class-identifying behaviors. In traditional European or Asian societies, for instance, nobody is confused about which place in the class order a given individual occupies. Details of dress, accent, manners, and demeanor express in a very fine-grained way details of social position. While some of these distinctions are weakening in those countries, they have long been muted in the American experience, existing on the extremes of the class spectrum (white trash and high society), but largely homogenized for everyone else. In Little Rock by the 1950s, they did exist on subtle levels; the more affluent an interviewee was, the more likely she was to comment on them. For less advantaged people, their access to public education, ready-to-wear clothing, media-taught speech patterns, education, and, above all, genteel acts of generosity toward black people promoted the notion of the classless society and with it of unlimited opportunity.

Gentility, so central to the construction of the southern social order, was a deeply gendered act; men could be rough-and-tumble while women carried the torch of right behavior. In Arkansas as in many other cultures, power relations in society were signified and transmitted by the actions of women, in ways very similar to the construction of white social life through the control of black people's behavior. Manners were the mode in which Helen and her friends learned and enforced the rules that defined social stratification. What constituted manners were injunctions about sexual behavior; to be "good" meant to be both politically silent and sexually demure. No behaviors were more closely monitored for their implications of status than the sexual activities of women. "She was the girl about town," Sally said of Sammie Dean, putting into words an innuendo that lay heavy beneath many people's stories. Frequently joined with comments on both Sammie's and Minnijean's physical bearing were references to their sexuality, sometimes overt ("she was the girl about town"), sometimes subtle ("she was so pretty and so cute"). Some people claimed Minnijean left school because she became pregnant: "She also had a baby in May, or right after graduation," insisted Betsy. "We knew a nurse that was there, she *did* have a baby."

Other cultures define appropriate femininity in different ways, ranging from the veil to lustful body displays in Rio's Carnival. But whatever the definitions, women's conformity expresses powerfully the degree of control men exercise over their womenfolk, and therefore demonstrates a capacity to enforce a power position in the world. In South Asia, for example, a woman's appearance in the bazaar reflects on the class and social standing of her father or husband.[7] So too in Arkansas, white women's behavior, from the most charged (sexuality) to the most assumed (race relations) to the most banal (salutations), was minutely judged as a measure of the social standing of their families.

Female sexuality, controlled, serves social functions; uncontrolled, it is trouble, whispering of a social order out of order. Unbridled sexuality is a mark of male vitality, not troubling, perhaps even relieving. Boys will be boys, after all, and isn't it better that they blow off steam that way than some others? Gendered double standards are, of course, endemic throughout history, and they are often carried and enforced by women. Here, too, other women were the carriers of Sammie Dean's and Minnijean's reputations and the means of their censure.

Reputation is the child of gossip, a malange of perception, hearsay, and imagination; among women, sexuality is its underpinning. Of all the arbiters of social status, women's sexuality, the most potent is also often the most fictionalized. Sammie Dean's peers disavowed her activism by slandering her reputation. "Sammie Dean did not have the best—how do you put that?—reputation in the world. . . . Well, she was the girl about town, we'll put it that way." Markers of sexual doubtfulness go way beyond sexual behavior itself, many of them looping around to supply implicit meaning to comments about appearance and class: "She was such a little doll, I remember she was *so* pretty and so cute. But they were what we considered white trash, really."

It was not insignificant that Minnijean was large, Sammie Dean small. Mammy is the essence of a de-sexualized black woman. Black women, in the classic southern construction (and its descendants today), are either asexual matrons or super-sexual wantons.[8] Their sexuality is denied or demeaned. Minnijean's sexuality was referenced only in terms of illegitimate motherhood. On the other hand, sexuality (at least heterosexuality) is sanctified for white women if they belong to certain classes and behave certain ways. White trash woman is like thin black woman; she smacks of sexuality, but of a cheap kind.

There are many indications that Minnijean did not have a baby right out of high school (for one thing, she graduated in New York, not Little Rock, and a year later than Helen and Betsy), and Sammie Dean married the boyfriend with whom she had gone steady throughout that time. Their classmates may have known something less obvious about them; rumor generally has some kernel of truth to it, however distorted. But it seems likely that the personal reputations assigned to Sammie Dean and Minnijean served metaphoric purposes. Sally and Helen contrasted their own behavior and status with their classmates', construing themselves as Goody Two-Shoes, the opposite of troublemakers. At the same time that the aspersions cast on Sammie Dean and Minnijean's sexual lives served to contain and trivialize the credibility of their actions in the social world, those same expressions of disapproval also defined the speakers as not-out-of-control, not-rebels, and therefore as eligible for the good life. Social control and opportunity were thus kissing cousins, one the stick, the other the carrot, together keeping white as well as black people contained within a very particular social system.

Acting Inactive

Thus racial identity for the white coeds of Central High was a platform on which were built gender roles and class expectations. Taken all in all, the package enforced a certain conformity on the women, and the terms of conforming precluded taking overt social action. Yet the white coeds did act inside the halls of Central High; their passivity acted powerfully to shape the drama there, and also to construct their own social destinies.

There are many theories about how people come to accept terms of social life peculiar to their societies. Psychologies of socialization range from Freudian conceptions of dynamics innate to biological families, to more political models of internalized oppression and role scripting. Scholars influenced by thinking of the Italian Marxist

Antonio Gramsci write about forces of cultural hegemony that influence individuals to consent to their own disadvantaged social location. Despite these discourses, however, the intersection of individual psyche and social order is largely unexplored territory. When all is said and done, human consciousness consists of identifiable activities, of thought and emotion.[9] How do individuals think and feel about the cultural dynamics with which they grow to consciousness? What exactly are the attitudes, beliefs, expectations, and assumptions that lead us to accept or resist injunctions about social behavior? We are especially lacking adequate understandings of how forces like racism, sexism, classism, and so on shape the psychologies of people in the privileged rather than the disadvantaged groupings. We know more about how women are influenced by sexism, for instance, then men.[10] People like bell hooks[11] and E. Franklin Frazier[12] have given us vivid descriptions of the problems created by racism for people of color. On the other side, we know a good deal about prejudice.[13] What we don't know as well is how racism constructs whiteness, nor more widely how participation in a system of racial injustice serves as a process by which white people negotiate terms of acceptance for their own lives in a stratified society.[14] That some such process was afoot was very apparent in my conversations with white Little Rockians.

It was also clear that southern rules of propriety were central to that process, that they were a vehicle for both conveying and enforcing behaviors that signified social positions both for the girls themselves and for their families. But unlike so many rules, these were internalized by the women not only because they were associated with their elders' strong feelings but also because they were taught for the most part nonverbally, a more powerful conduit for injunctions than are spoken lessons. Silence is eloquent. Children note carefully what their elders don't say and from the contradictions in those gaps draw conclusions: "I would think [my father] wasn't interested," Helen replied when I asked her about her parents' racial beliefs. "Well, he always seemed to have an opinion on everything. I think it was just getting by and staying out of trouble." More eloquent yet, judging from the intensity of emotion behind it, was Helen's next statement: "Mother—I have to tell the truth here, don't I, Betsy? [. . .] Mother would have died for shame if ... my name had been put in the paper, or if I'd gotten in any type of trouble." Shame is the one emotion recognized by many thinkers as being a link between society and individual. Shame is about what others think of you, and its power presumes a need for approval and thus a sensitivity to disapproval so strong that it can modify behavior. Paradoxically, that bond is often cemented by what isn't said. "You need to learn something," Maddie said to me at the end of our conversation. "No, some things are just better not discussed." "While we had our beliefs and our opinions," echoed Helen, "you didn't voice them to the public. You just didn't do that." Why you "just didn't do that" Helen no longer remembered; it simply seemed normal to her. "I don't remember any particular thing my parents said," Betsy mused. "I was just brought up to know you didn't associate with them." So thoroughly do we learn the rules of social interaction and then forget that they are learned, that they appear to be natural truths, like the fact that Sunday morning is Sunday morning.

Having learned lessons early and well, in the moment of crisis Helen knew just how to behave, to go in the side door and do her thing. She took her cues not only from beliefs about racial matters, but even more from interpersonal ones within her family. Helen avoided trouble in order to obey the injunctions of her mother, even though she was critical of her mother, who nonetheless (or perhaps in consequence) influenced her assumptions about the relationship between private beliefs and public exhibitions. This thick tangle of ideas and feelings shaped Helen's choices about many things—how as a teenager she resisted the domination of a boss; how she accepted moving away from Little Rock; and later in life what she taught her son about racial hostility and its public expression. All these ideas relate to the negotiation or acceptance of relations of power. Helen accepted her mother's power to dictate her actions at Central High even while she objected to paternal control.

This aspect of Helen's socialization, the ways in which she simultaneously consented to her social role and resisted it, became clear as she described the growing strife around the school in its opening days that year:

> It was building momentum, and my mother saw and heard
> all that on TV and then the neighbors talking.

So my mother rode the bus with me to school—can you imagine? I can remember it very well, it's vivid in my mind. . . . And Mother walked straight down across there and . . . she saw, the yellin' and the screamin' and all, so we keeept walking, and we went over [to] a porch, a lady let Mother walk up on her porch, there were some other parents up there, too, because Mother wasn't about to get out in it [the mob]. She watched [the rioting] a little while, she said, "Helen, go get your books."

So I went and got my books and came back and went home. And I was a senior! And my mother like would take me by the hand, you know, like you go to the first grade of school—

BETSY: That's what they did back then. Everyone was real sheltered back then.

HELEN: Yeah, but Mother didn't take me to school in ninth, tenth, eleventh grade, then in twelfth grade she took me to school! I don't know how long she kept me home, a day or two, and I was just dyin' to go to school. I'm ashamed to say—I did make good grades, I didn't make excellent grades—but it was a social thing with me and I just wanted to be around my friends.

How long did she keep you out?

I don't remember. It wasn't very long. Because I do remember: "It will be all right. Mother, I want to go, I want to go." I don't remember. It wasn't a long time.

I was struck by the contradiction between Helen's depiction here of standing on the porch with her mom watching the mob, and her earlier insistence that she'd gone in the side door and not seen what was happening in the front. Such discrepancies are common enough, and meaningful, too. Helen's current version expressed a teenager's values, priorities, and sense of justice—a sort of ideology of female adolescence: Mother sought to exercise control in a manner inappropriate to Helen's station in life. "That's what they did back then," Betsy said, identifying the transaction as typical. But Helen disagreed and redefined it as unusual: "Mother didn't take me to school in ninth, tenth, eleventh grade, then in twelfth grade she took me to school!" Her mother's behavior interfered with Helen's interests ("it was a social thing with me and I just wanted to be around my friends") and compromised her autonomy. ("I was a senior! And my mother like would take me by the hand, you know, like you go to the first grade of school.") Helen resisted, defending her values. ("I'm ashamed to say," she said, meaning the opposite, "it was a social thing.") She argued with her mother, assuring her, "It will be all right, Mother," and asserting her wishes: "I want to go, I want to go." In the end, her mother acquiesced, letting Helen return to school.

Thus, while passive on the public stage of history, the women of Central High were actively negotiating power in their personal lives. While being "normal," obediently staying out of trouble and going in the side door of Central High, Helen was simultaneously sorting out her power and rights in another sphere, the family. Socialization is not so much a matter of passive acceptance as of continual, nuanced negotiation. Helen did not outright rebel; she argued, cajoled, reassured, and ultimately did as she pleased. That she was asserting her autonomy with her mother, however, shed a different light on her actions at the school, revealing her to be a creature with will and the power of choice.

Having struck a blow for teenage rights in the domestic arena, Helen also performed a politically relevant act in the civil domain when she went in the side door at school. This double-edged scenario, involving interlocking struggles within the private domain of the family and struggles in the public domain of the school, occurred again and again in the drama of Central High. Teenagers took positions in generational dynamics, fighting parents' wishes about the public drama or allying with their parents, and then acted accordingly to play roles of consequence in the civil rights struggle.

But while Helen's eye was focused on her rights within the family politic, she could not see that she simultaneously exercised power over the rights of others. By taking no position on the controversy, Helen took sides, joining the large majority of students who declined to support or defend the black students and thereby condemned their presence. In this sense all behavior in a society structured by inequality is a declaration of opinion and an exercise of power. Helen may have thought she was simply pleasing herself, but she was also acting out a set of values and priorities that were deeply instilled in her. In their essence those values contained a definition of her place in a social group of her peers, an acceptance and a defense of that place. As a consequence her beliefs were ideologically consequential and, because the group in which she took her place had power in a racial frame, it was also an exercise of dominance that contributed to limitations on the black students' rights.

Helen's story is a paradigm of how roles and rights are negotiated in the dual sites of public and private affairs. But among the alumnae of Central High there were also differences. As Helen and Betsy continued with their story, I puzzled over my sense that I was witnessing yet another little struggle, some controversy they were debating in the present between the lines of what they said to me. I knew there were differences in emphasis in their memories and feelings about their shared brush with history. Helen focused more on anger toward lower-class white "agitators" and on the vice principal Mrs. Huckaby; Betsy was more pointedly angry at Minnijean and the other black students. But neither of those positions seemed particularly charged between them, and yet there did seem to be a rag they were chewing over with some energy. I suspected it had something to do with guilt and innocence, but what exactly was that something? Who was guilty and who innocent of what?

At length the conversation returned to Sammie Dean and Minnijean, and I began to see more clearly. Betsy mentioned that Sammie Dean's mother had called her house one night:

> Now I don't remember when this was, but it was early on, I think. Her mother called my house.
>
> Now I didn't know her [Sammie Dean], she was pretty, she was such a little doll, I remember she was so pretty and so cute. But they were what we considered white trash, really . . .
>
> Her mother called my mother one night, and they had gotten a group of women and they were calling people and saying, "There's going to be a bomb tomorrow in the school. You need to have your daughter walk out." I don't know how it was put, but Mother and Daddy talked to me about it. And they said, "Now, look—" See, 'cause they were in an uproar, they didn't know what to do, they didn't know if there really was, and people kept thinking, "This can't be happening! Well, what is this?"
>
> So they talked to me and said, "Look"—this was before we had the phone call, I do remember that—and Daddy said,

"Look," and they talked to me that night, and then the next morning before we left he said, "Look. You go up to the front hall. If everybody walks out, I want you out of there. I don't want you to stay there." And I said, "Oh, OK."

Well, I remember being confused and a little scared and a little excited, and I had a lot of emotions. But I went up to the main hall, and sure enough there was this huge crowd of people, up there to see what was going on. Well, they started walking out, and I kept watching them and I kept looking around, and everybody said, "Go on. You'd better do it. We need to do it." I walked out, and once you got out the door, you did not come back. And there was fifty of us, that's all.

So I was suspended for three days. Well, that was unnecessary. I mean, there was no bomb, there was no bomb threat. That Sammie Dean's mother, just she and her little group of—and they were part of the mob that would be out there, every day.

HELEN: Well, how come they called you? They didn't call my house.

BETSY: They called a lot of people. [. . .]

HELEN: I didn't walk out. I'm not saying Goody-me or anything, but I didn't know anything about any walkout.

I thought Helen was precisely saying, "Goody-me." Betsy's family was recruited to the protest by the mother of that white trash girl, Sammie Dean. Her parents, moreover, agreed that Betsy should participate in the walkout. To be sure, the mention of a bomb threat was scary and allowed them to protest desegregation while taking the moral high ground of protecting their daughter from danger. But Helen cast doubt on that interpretation when she noted that nobody called her house and that she did not walk out. Along with her subtle air of superiority, perhaps Helen expressed a little hurt as well. "How come they called you?" she first exclaimed, as if she wondered why she had been excluded from that society of protesters.

Almost in the same breath, Helen went on to confess a shade of culpability, and, true to a sweet and subtle competition between them, Betsy seized the opportunity for a wee bit of vindication:

HELEN: [Shows card with racist slogan:] There was many of them. Now I'm not proud of that, but I'm just showing you how stupid the hype, the stuff that went on, that they would pass these out to high-school students.

It clearly made enough of an impression on you that you saved them.

BETSY: Yeah.

HELEN: Whatever. I just stuck these in my annual among other things.

Do you remember what you thought about them at the time?

BETSY: Probably thought they were funny. [laughs]

Betsy was suspended for taking part in the walkout. Nonetheless, she continued to maintain her innocence: her family was given false information by Sammie Dean's mother; her father told her to leave; she was cajoled into it by other kids. Helen, on the other hand, racist cards notwithstanding, had greater claims to innocence. She had not been called, she had not taken part in the protest action.

That Betsy's mother was called by Sammie Dean's mother, that Betsy participated in the walkout and was suspended, placed Betsy in the category of activist segregationist students, despite her protestations. It therefore also created a necessity for her to resist the companion label, white trash. I was to learn that those who participated in such actions represented a range of beliefs and motivations. Betsy painted her own to be benign. But her behavior fit with the attitudinal context in which it took place. Her fearfulness about people of color, her indignation about Johnny's punishment, her protest about integration being "forced" on her, all suggested a frame of reference in which joining a walkout made sense. She need not define herself as a segregationist activist in order to act like one. People often see themselves as innocently swept up in events, but their susceptibility reflects their worldview, which in turn is learned in a greater context of lived experience and social milieu. I asked:

Were you two talking to each other about it?

HELEN: While we did things together, we also had separate interests, right?

BETSY: Um hmm.

> HELEN: I didn't even know what happened until here
> recently, when we were getting ready for you.

Many years after the fact, the two women reproduced (in a very muted vein) what must have been a more overt debate back when they were high-school seniors. Should they stand openly against racial change in their school, or should they accept, however unwillingly, the law of the land? Should they leave the school and join forces with those outsider/stupid/white trash people in the mob? Or should they quietly enter the school by the side door and turn their backs on the whole melee, pretending a normalcy they knew did not exist, pretending a neutrality they could not possibly attain?

They may have disagreed and argued the justice of their stances back then, but in their most essential attitudes Helen and Betsy agreed. If they weren't talking among themselves, I asked, how had they formed their views? Betsy replied:

> I think I already had my own opinions formed, as far as
> them going to school with us. I didn't care. Like what Helen said,
> it didn't bother me. I still had my opinions formed as to whether
> I wanted to socialize with them back then. I would not have.
>
> HELEN: No, I wouldn't have, either. They could have gone
> to school with me, but I wasn't going to go invite them home
> for, we used to call them bunking parties, slumber parties.
>
> BETSY: You just wouldn't do that.

I was struck by the fact that over the years Betsy and Helen had not talked to each other about their shared experience at Central High until my visit created a need and a reason for recollection. If Helen was arguing that Betsy was somewhat less innocent than she herself, if Betsy considered Helen "more liberal" and fought a complicated battle against shame interlaced with resentment and blame, then it was little wonder they weren't talking about all this in the course of normal life. In fact, now as back then, their silence continued to construct a normalcy in which people did not address painful and confusing subjects.

But both the act of going in the side door (in Helen's case) and going out the front one (in Betsy's) did in fact constitute political action. Helen's uninvolvement expressed a very particular—and very common—position: that she would neither aid nor resist the letter of the law mandating desegregation, but that she refused the spirit of the law. "They" could come to "her" school, but not to her slumber party.

When racial change hit, white women students for the first time found themselves on a public stage in which to demonstrate their acceptance or resistance of old behavioral standards through the medium of taking positions, passively or actively, about changes in the racial order. The positions they constructed were consistent with ideologies they had internalized, built out of judgments about things like women's weight and sexuality and class proprieties. How they put the parts together, whether, for instance, they acted as ladies or as white trash as they expressed their attitudes toward desegregation, constituted a rough sketch of their personal life plans, which were actively challenged at that moment in history.

Minnijean signaled that challenge when she betrayed the rules by which her racial "place" had traditionally been assigned—not so much to remain segregated as to remain grateful. At the same time, Sammie Dean challenged the social order, paradoxically, as she sought to uphold it in the form of segregation. It was not that she protested that was most significant, but how she protested—without gentility:

> NANCY: Sammie Dean Parker was taken to jail that day. She was kicking, spitting, scratching, and the policeman couldn't do anything with her, she was so out of control.
>
> She came out the front entrance, the main entrance, and she was screaming at these black students as they were being led away, that they could not enter school. A policeman had walked up to her—I don't know what she was screaming but she was screaming at them. I don't know what she had in her hand, she was throwing something. But nevertheless, he told her, you know, she had to stop and calm down and everything. Well, she kicked him. He grabbed her by the shoulders trying to calm her down, and she cussed him out. And then she started spitting on him and things of that nature, and he couldn't do anything with her so he just took her and took her to jail.

She spit and fought and cussed; she attacked policemen and got arrested. If the old class and race order was continually reproduced through daily acts of gratitude by black people and gentility by whites, if Minnijean's behavior thus stood squarely outside that paradigm, Sammie Dean's both defied and, paradoxically, fit it. By all her physical acts of defiance, Sammie Dean confirmed the caricature of "white trash" behavior at the same time that she demonstrated that what always had stood behind gentility was force, in the form first of legalities and ultimately of violence. When the law failed, people resorted, as they historically had, to physical acts of resistance, as did Sammie. That unpleasant task was traditionally left to "poor white trash," allowing women of the higher classes to keep untarnished the distinguishing customs of generosity and niceness.

Somehow, though, that old design didn't work in 1957. Sammie Dean cut close to her women classmates' bone. Yes, she was acting as white trash is stereotypically known to act. Yet to describe it that way did not resolve a certain discomfort. People talked about her too frequently, with too much contempt, telling thereby another story within their story. Familiar acts in changing times take on new meanings. Like Sammie Dean, other women also made distinct political choices, but different ones. How and what they did sheds light on the peculiar mixture of power and powerlessness that characterized the times for the women of Central High.

SEVEN
Parades and Other Forms
of Political Action

*The challenge is yours, as future adults of America, to prove your
maturity, intelligence, and ability to make decisions by how you
react, behave, and conduct yourself in this controversial question.*

—Jane

*We weren't actually seeking trouble. I think it was just mischief,
you know, more than anything else.*

—Nancy

Despite their identification as "arch-radicals," Minnijean and
Sammie Dean were in fact not alone in acting. Political activism is not
a category but a range. To refuse to answer a heated question is to
express an opinion. Innocent everyday acts in times of trouble con-
vey resistance and protest.[1] Minnijean and Sammie Dean's classmates
responded to the crisis in measured ways, sometimes gaily, sometimes
secretly, but always significantly. Looking outward toward the behavior of their most controversial fellows, Helen and Betsy, Joyce, Jane,
and Nancy revealed very inward things: their definitions of womanhood, of gender identity in a southern context. When, however, they
looked inward and talked about their own roles in the drama of
Central High, they bespoke something situated in the external world,
the nature of political action.

The detailed accounts of how the white women of Central High
decided what to do demonstrate two sides of a totality: their political
choices—whether to enter the school by the side door, whether to join
a walkout, whether to engage in hostilities with the Nine or to look
the other way—derived from very central conceptions of who they
were as social actors: southern women standing on the cusp of a postwar economic boom that promised prosperity to them individually
if they obeyed certain rules of propriety. In turn, the choices they

made became part of the social code to which they adhered and which often they simultaneously challenged. In such daily acts of contradiction, they both accepted a certain place in society and contested the terms of submission. They were both obedient to a social order and resisted it.

Innocent Troublemakers

Prototypic of this dynamic was Betsy's and Helen's classmate Nancy, who gleefully partook in very public protest, but cloaked her actions in charm. If the debate between Helen and Betsy was about innocence and troublemaking, Nancy came from a Little Rock family that typified gendered aspects of those two qualities. Her mother came from a religious family. "There was never any disruption in their household," said Nancy. "I mean, it just ran very smoothly and properly."

But her father was a different sort:

> My dad was a hell raiser. My dad did everything he could possibly do. He smoked, he drank, he ran around with women. He went to the racetrack every time he could possibly get there. Even snuck me in over there when I was thirteen years old, just because I looked mature enough to fit in. Which I did, and it just thrilled him to death to get by with it.
>
> I never heard my mother use a cuss word in my life. My dad, it was just something that came natural to him, it was every other word. Unfortunately, I'm the same way and I don't do it to shock, it's just there. You know, I never did it around my mother until I was married, and one day a word slipped out and she, when a word slipped out, she used my full name, you know.
>
> I had a lot of fun with [my dad]. But I also have a lot of resentments against him for a lot of the things that he did.

If Nancy's parents typified the contrast between a proper woman and a hell-raising man, her own choices in the Central High drama wove a complex tapestry of both traditions:

> The summer before we started in September there was just a buzz around town, you know, just a buzz around town that these Nine were going to be brought in to Central.

The only thing really I remember my mother saying was, "I'm very worried about this because I'm afraid there's going to be trouble." To tell you the truth, at the time I didn't think too much about it. I really didn't dwell on it. My dad didn't really say too much that summer.

Then when we did go to school, they did bring them in and, I mean, all hell broke loose. . . . It just went from bad to worse. Mother was actually afraid for me to go to school. And I was going to go, I wasn't going to miss anything, you know.

But the day that they brought them in, this is the way I remember it: There were so many people out in front of the school, raising hell. And it was parents, it was mainly parents. So I didn't know what was going to take place, no one else did either, and some friends and I left the school.

I went downtown to try to find my dad, and I couldn't find him. He was probably in a pool hall or something, you know. I don't know where he was, but anyway I couldn't find him. I just wanted to let him know that I had left school.

Many parents had instructed their kids to leave the school if the black students came in, either because of fears for their safety or to express opposition to desegregation. I wondered if Nancy had acted independently when she left, or whether she was obeying orders. Had her "hell-raising" father told her to join those "raising hell" in protest?

Yes. My dad had told me to just get up and walk out.

Is that because he was worried about you or was that a protest?

That was a protest on his part. My mother didn't want me to go; it was fear. You know, she was afraid of danger, something was going to happen. She did not want me to go that day at all. But it was left to be my decision. And like I said, I was just dying to get over there because I wanted to see what was going to happen, you know.

But nevertheless, several friends, we left and went down looking for my dad, couldn't find him, and I decided to—I didn't go by Mom's shop to mention it to Mother that I left school because—I don't know why. I just didn't.

It was interesting to me that Nancy grappled (however cursorily) with the reasons she didn't try harder to inform her mother that she'd left the school. It was her own decision, but in its aftermath her impulse was to check in with her troublemaking father, not her proper (and frightened) mother. Failing to do either, she carried on in the flow of her crowd's enthusiasms:

> Anyway, in the meantime, we kind of organized. We had stopped at Fifteenth and Main—it was a little place called Sweet-n-Cream. We had all stopped down there and several cars came pulling up, and I don't even remember who said it but someone said, "Let's have a parade." So we went to the drugstore, bought several bottles of white shoe polish, and we put on the cars "Two, four, six, eight, we ain't gonna integrate." There were about fifteen, sixteen cars. We left Fifteenth and Main and went downtown.
>
> We were shouting this: "Two, four, six, eight, we ain't gonna integrate." And we went across the bridge into North Little Rock. Went to North Little Rock High School.

North Little Rock is an independent city across the Arkansas River from Little Rock. It is a more industrial and working-class community. I asked Nancy why they'd chosen to go there:

> We had no place else to go, I suppose. We didn't want to head over to Central because there was already so much trouble going on over there. We weren't actually seeking trouble. I think it was just mischief, you know, more than anything else.
>
> We were met there by the North Little Rock Police Department. They told us that they could sympathize with us but we had no business being over there and they were going to escort us back across the bridge. As long as we did not try to get out of our cars or cause any kind of disturbance, then we were all right.
>
> So we left. We were not trying to make trouble. You know, it was just, I think, something to do in a manner of protest. So as we came back across, I remember one of the guys—his father was a mortician—and his dad saw him. And you could tell he was furious. When we passed Mom's shop, I would not look to see if my mother was on the sidewalk.
>
> Well, we got back to our little hangout place, which was a

drugstore where a lot of us congregated in the afternoon—before and after school, actually, and then on Saturdays. There was a juke box in there and (you know, kids used to have places to go. They don't anymore. But we did, fortunately) we went to the drugstore and as I walked in the door the owner said, "Nancy, your mother just called. She said that if you showed up here I was to keep you here. You're not allowed to leave." I said, "OK."

So I went to the pay phone, and I called Mother. And this is what she said. She said, "I am so ashamed of you I don't know what to do." She said, "You have besmirched my name, and I'm very, very upset. I'm very embarrassed, and I'm very disappointed." . . .

We were all sitting around talking . . . and having a coke and my dad came in and picked us all up. He was so proud of us, he didn't know what to do. He gave us money for the juke box. So it was just split. I had told him, I said, "Mother called here, and I was told to stay here." And he said, "Well, you can go home with me. I'm headed home."

So I went home with my dad. My mother got off at 5:30. She came in, she would not even look at me. I mean, she was just furious. She was absolutely furious.

But that's the first day that I remember it starting.

Despite the fact that the "parade" made quite a stir in the community ("We did make the national news," Nancy said with some pride, "and that was one of the things that really upset my mother"), Nancy's story is organized around the theme of innocence. "We were not trying to make trouble," she said more than once. She carefully named the action a parade, not a demonstration, suggesting it was light-hearted mischief, not a serious action. Their target was North Little Rock, not Central High where "there was already so much trouble going on."

On the other hand, "it was something to do in a manner of protest." Like Helen when she insisted on attending school, in joining the parade Nancy also took a position in the politics of her family. By leaving school, she might have satisfied both her mother's fears and her father's protest. By taking part in the demonstration, she allied herself squarely with her father:

When I was in that parade I didn't see anything wrong with that. I told my mother, I said, "I don't think I've done anything wrong. I don't want to go to school with them either. So what's wrong with me protesting? I didn't hurt anyone." So that was my answer.

Women's activism always challenges domestic as well as public power relations, because by the very act of taking a position in the public domain women violate their patriarchal assignment to domesticity. This quality of contradictory rebelliousness is a not uncommon characteristic of conservative politics in general. "Right-wing movements hold mixed stances toward prevailing power structures," writes Sara Diamond in her fine study *Roads to Dominion: Right-Wing Movements and Political Power in the United States.* "They are partially *oppositional* and partially . . . *system-supportive*."[2] If conservatism contains within itself this paradoxical quality, so all the more does conservative women's activism, because it is performed in two distinct domains, one public, the other private, and both sites elicit ambivalent attitudes. Like the state, the family too is a power structure that conservative women both defend theoretically and, often, resist in practice. The two dramas, public and private, intertwine, supporting and contradicting each other to weave a tapestry peculiarly gendered and revealingly political.

If Nancy's position was aimed at both spheres, how much was she influenced by an alliance with her father, and how much by her own attitude toward desegregation? Seeking insight into her views about race, I asked what her relations with black people had been before that year, and she added her vivid description of normalcy to Wesley's and others I'd heard before:

> We had all been brought up that the blacks stayed on one end of town and we stayed on the other. Well, to me, that was not our fault. That was the way it was at that time, you know. We came to believe that, that's the way we lived, that's the way we were brought up. I don't ever remember being unkind to any black person, because I never was close enough to one. I mean, we walked on the sidewalk, and if they met us, they got off the sidewalk and walked in the street. And that's actually what it was like.

Do you remember what you thought about that at the time?

I thought it was normal. I thought it was normal. I thought it was normal that they sat in the back of the bus because that's the way it had always been. I'd never seen it done any other way. So to me it was normal.

Jim Crow may have defined normalcy in the past, thereby justifying her participation in the "parade." But to participate without culpability, Nancy's protest had to walk a very narrow edge between trouble and mischief. That her footing slipped from time to time was made evident by another detail she reported, this one overlooked by the written histories of the time. She had described the scene of Sammie Dean's arrest earlier in our conversation, ending up with the statement, "She was so out of control." Nonetheless, Sammie's arrest galvanized Nancy and her crowd:

We all decided that we would go get Sammie Dean out of jail.

Did you know Sammie Dean before this?

Yes.

What did you think about her? You made a little bit of a face when you mentioned her name. What does that mean?

Well, I would say Sammie Dean was an instigator. Her father was one of the top-notch segregationists in Little Rock. He was very outspoken. And therefore, Sammie Dean was. That's what she had been taught. Nevertheless, she was kind of a troublemaker. She was a very cunning person, you know. She could just almost charm the socks off of anyone in order to get her way. You know? She was a beautiful young girl. She was. Very attractive.

But anyway, she was taken to jail. I don't know why, I don't know who decided to do this—I did not run around with Sammie Dean, I simply knew her. We all decided we would go down there and try to get her out of jail. And we went down there, and they told us that she could only be released to her parents. And that her father had already been called, and he was on the way. So we left.

Were you supportive of what she had done?

I don't think it was support. I don't think I would define it as support. Like I said, I think it was just the fact that they had taken her to jail, and we didn't think that any of us should be put in jail. At that age you just think, Well, this is someone I go to school with and how dare they be arrested. Even though she was kicking and cussing and, you know, having a little fit and all. We just decided she didn't deserve being put in jail.

Nancy's story expressed some subtle tensions contained within her assumptions of normalcy. She both sympathized with and condemned Sammie's segregationist prominence. She assumed Sammie's position was a natural reflection of her father's, that she was merely doing what comes naturally to dutiful daughters. "Nevertheless, she was kind of a troublemaker." The word "nevertheless" evoked the conservative woman's dilemma, suggesting duty did not altogether justify the way in which Sammie Dean followed her father's political lead. Her very act of obedience to her father caused her to betray her feminine role. Not only did she cause trouble, but she caused it by using female attributes: her charm, a product of her most gendered quality, attractiveness, a euphemism for sexuality, became a weapon of cunning. Nancy made that observation in a tone at once shocked and admiring. More than most of her classmates, she felt a certain sympathy with Sammie Dean, evidenced by her joining the trek to the police station to free her. But for the very reason that she herself was suspect in the female world of propriety, that she had allied herself with her father, not her mother, she was also careful to distinguish herself from Sammie. Both girls protested, but Sammie caused trouble, while Nancy protested inno-cently. Nonetheless, both took a stand in two closely interlinked struggles: to contest desegregation's challenge to white dominance, and to contest white society's co-optation of female behavior as a signifier of family status. Nancy knew the rules, which she clearly articulated in terms of the contrast between her mother's and her father's attitudes. But she chose to break the rules—somewhat, within limits of inno-cence, not baldly as Sammie Dean did. In making these subtle choices, both girls engaged a set of social relations that transcended status. Because the choices they made constituted political acts in a civil rights struggle, when they opted to obey or break the gender rules defined by their mothers, they helped to redefine both race and gender for their generation. At the same time those redefinitions were going on, others were also unfolding, of the relationship of state and individual, of the rights of individuals to self-determination, of the proper relationship of older to younger generations. Nascent and undefined in 1957, these latter changes became fully elaborated as time went on, appearing in many forms in my interviewees stories of their lives today.

Prefiguring this later narrative back then was the single fact that ultimately justified Nancy's act of support for Sammie: the intrusion of police force into their innocent teenage world. It was at that point that a question of rights arose. Whatever Sammie had done, "she didn't deserve being put in jail." Resisting force was a common explanation given by my interviewees for their antipathy to desegregation. At its core, they claimed, the struggle wasn't about going to school with black children. It was that change had been forced on them:

> NANCY: Everyone was saying, and my dad was one of them, that the government was forcing something down our throats that shouldn't have taken place. I really did not want to go to school with them. I would not have welcomed them, but I would not have mistreated them either. I could have gone to school and gone about my business, had it been that simple. But it wasn't. It just was not that simple.

Resistance to state force is an old theme in white, American, individualist culture. But for white people to construe resistance to civil rights, the imposition of legal power for the purpose of promoting equality, as a response to unjust coercion was to write their own character as victim. It is not that I have perpetrated a wrong that deserves righting, they implicitly argued. I simply, innocently, did that which seemed "normal." What is not normal, what is not right, is that the government is forcing something down *our* throats. Nancy's statement that she would not have welcomed the black students to the school but also would not have mistreated them, was echoed frequently by other white alumni I interviewed. But between welcoming them and mistreating them lay a wide territory of meaning. Others did mistreat them, and when Nancy witnessed her peers doing so, she did not protest. Instead, she voiced yet another complaint, this one about the disruption to her own life:

Central's a very large school, and I was coming downstairs from a class, and one of the black girls was maybe four or five people ahead of me descending the staircase. I don't remember if it was Minnijean or not, but I think it was Minnijean Brown. She was going down the stairs and someone—it was a guy—he tripped her. She fell from maybe the second to the bottom step, dropped all of her books. Someone else came and kicked them across the hall.

Well, there were hundreds of kids out in the hall trying to change classes, you know. And the things that they would holler at her. It was very disruptive. You could then go to class, and you could hear a big ruckus taking place out in the hall. Teacher would get up and shut the door. It was just very disruptive, you know.

I became very disenchanted with the whole thing. I just kept thinking, This is my senior year, and this is not what I was looking forward to. This is just unfair.

The main reason I guess that I resented it so is because it was our senior year, it messed up everything for our senior year. Everybody aspired to get to Central, you know, because it was the only high school, and it was such a beautiful school. It's supposed to be the most beautiful high school in the United States, and the largest. So it was just something to get out of the ninth grade and get to Central. My brother, of course, was in Central ahead of me, and seeing all the things that he did and got to do and the fun and everything—well, that's what I was looking forward to in my senior year.

Well, it didn't happen. See, we had all this disruption. . . . So I just felt like it was unfair that it was done the way that it was done, because it could have been done a better way.

Throughout her narrative, Nancy gave clear voice to her several grievances: her community had been coerced into making unwelcome changes; her classmate had been (shockingly) arrested; her prized senior year had been irreparably disrupted. So when at the end of our conversation I asked her to reflect back on all that ruckus and tell me what in retrospect she thought the upset was most about, she took me by surprise:

> I don't really know exactly what it was other than I do know
> that everyone I was around at that time, they were talking about
> violence, there would be violence. When I look back on it now—
> I didn't think this then—but when I look back on it now I have
> a feeling that [the parents' fear] probably was that it would be
> the beginning of interracial marriage. That's the only thing I can
> come up with. The only thing I can come up with.

It was a stunning and meaningful non sequitur. Having complained
about coercion, unjust arrests, disruption of her senior year, in the
end it came back around to the realm of sexuality. Nancy might challenge her own role as woman-symbol. She might negotiate a complex
balance between her duty to uphold certain standards and her desire
to defy them. But when it came down to it, she joined her elders in
collapsing race and sexuality as a means to describe resentments
which were, it soon turned out, in some part about class. Having told
me that her daughter's most adored teacher was an African-American
woman (a story that seemed intended to point out to me her own
changes of heart over the years), Nancy then described an event at her
workplace that for her was the other side of the coin:

> [A black woman] came and made an application for a job,
> and the salary she asked for to begin with most of us weren't
> even making at that time, and we had been there for years. So
> we resented that. Just things, you know, like that.
>
> But more and more, you would see more and more of them
> shopping, more and more of them downtown than ever before.
> Then, of course, they stopped sitting in the back of the bus and
> things like that. To me, it was just get along in this world, you
> know. This is it.
>
> But I didn't want my daughter to marry one. I still don't. I
> still feel that way.
>
> *Why is that?*
>
> I guess just simply because of my background, the way that
> I was raised. I told Alice that. "You're to be nice to them. Respect
> them. But I don't want you bringing them home to play, and I
> don't want you to marry one." And I guess that's just because
> that's the way I was raised. The only reason I can come up with.

Did Alice ever ask for an explanation of why you didn't
want her to bring black children home to play?

No, she didn't. And I don't know why she didn't, but she
never did.

"I don't know why she didn't, but she never did." Long after our
talk, those words looped round and round my mind. Alice accepted
her mother's rules unquestioningly, as many of Nancy's classmates
did in their time, as Nancy sometimes did and sometimes did not.
Definitions of normalcy are bequeathed by one generation to the next,
dictating more than actions and relationships. Notions of what is normal define the very questions we can ask, ruling out those which
might make visible hidden social structures and allow us to examine
how they do and do not facilitate our own well-being. In her day,
Nancy challenged normalcy as it defined gender rules which constrained her, but not normalcy in a racial realm in which she believed
herself to benefit.

Questioning the Alternatives

Joyce, on the other hand, did raise that specter, and quickly
learned a lesson that shaped her life. If the range of responses to that
moment of history at Central High stretched from Sammie Dean on
the activist segregationist side to a sprinkling of determinedly integrationist students on the other, in between were gradations of conscience and discovery. Sometimes, activism flowed much later from
the lessons of Central High.

I met with Joyce at the social welfare agency where she works. She
sat behind her cluttered desk, apologizing for the scrape, scrape,
scrape of a workman preparing the building's exterior for painting.
Quickly she began to tell me what had clearly been for her the defining moment of that year, when she was a junior at Central High:

One of the things that happened at Central had to do with
a *very* close friend of mine. She and I were just like sisters. We
spent the night at each other's house. We walked to school
together. We studied together. We went to church together. I
would go home with them for chicken dinner after church on

Sunday. She'd come home with me. I mean we were very, very, very close.

I remember one time—have you had a chance to go by Central? Of course people have seen it in pictures and everything. Well, if you recall, the front of the school that faces on Park Street has stairs that go down, and there used to be a fishpond down there that was full of water and had goldfish in it, and so forth. And I remember one day, my friend (her name was Lydia) and another friend of ours, a mutual friend Joanna, the three of us were walking down those stairs, and I was between Joanna and Lydia.

And I don't even remember what brought the conversation to a start or anything, but I made the comment that I just, using the language of the day, I said, "Well, I don't see what's wrong with going to school with colored kids." And Lydia and Joanna both, and Lydia predominantly, got behind me and physically shoved me all the way down the stairs and right to the edge of the fishpond, and I honest-to-god thought at that moment they were going to shove me into that fishpond. And they stopped right there.

I don't remember whether the lesson came to me immediately. I think some kernel of it did, but it has grown over the years to the point that I realize that if you take a stand, if you believe in something that is not popularly accepted, if something like that is in your mind, then you either do one of two things: you either keep your mouth shut, or you be prepared to stand your ground. Because something's gonna happen. And that was a real shocking lesson to me, that even people you consider friends would take something like that so personally and focus so much anger on someone very close to them. That's the lesson I got from that.

What did you do?

I think I kept my mouth shut for the rest of the school year with my friends.

Joyce kept her mouth shut with her friends, but she anguished over what she saw going on at school. I asked her if it had been hard, if she'd had to struggle to stay quiet, and she replied:

Yeah, I think I did. As a matter of fact, there were two other things that happened, one that I did sort of as my way of saying something without confronting the issue directly locally, and the other was an event that happened to somebody else that really made another deep impression on me. I'll tell you the latter first.

I remember, as I said, in September, Central was not air conditioned then, and the windows would be open in September 'cause it'd still be very, very warm. My homeroom—the front of Central faces Park Street, and as you look at it head-on, my homeroom was on the left-hand end of that front part, and the desks all faced in that direction and the windows were to our left.

Every morning, they'd come over the loudspeaker, and we'd all stand up and say the Pledge of Allegiance, and they'd probably have Bible scripture, I'm sure we did at that time, and announcements or whatever. Well, I remember the mobs had been there every day, and I'll admit, I used some of that as an excuse to check out of school, calling my mother saying, I'm scared to be here, and then go off with my friends downtown to mess around. Because every day there were the mobs out across Park Street, they were kept across Park Street and into Park Street sometimes, but they were not allowed on the campus. You could hear them out there and everything.

Well, one day we were standing there, and I had my hand on my heart saying the Pledge of Allegiance, and I could hear the mob, the sound escalating from what it normally was. And as I was saying the words, I turned and looked out the window, and I saw this mob of people chasing what to a sixteen-year-old girl was an elderly black man. I've since found out it was a *New York Times* reporter who was probably forty-five, something like that. I was looking and saying the Pledge of Allegiance, and I was watching them chase him across the yards on that side of the street, and I knew, I really believed that if they caught him they would kill him.

In that moment, while I'm watching this, saying the Pledge of Allegiance, hand on my heart, I'm thinking, There's something wrong here. How can this be happening in a country that we're pledging allegiance to? What's wrong with this picture? And that left an indelible—I can see it today, I will never, ever forget that. I think that, along with my parents' quasi-liberalism, and the experience with my friends, that helped to water the seeds that my parents had planted earlier on about believing in right things and trying to do what was right.

Joyce's first two stories were about matters both nonverbal and starkly communicative. What those experiences stimulated, however, was an act that both engaged the greater world out there and yet remained protectively quiet:

> I wrote a letter to President Eisenhower and said, Do something to make this stop. All I want is my education.
>
> Which was a fairly selfish thing to write about, but as I think back on it, I think it was a fairly activist thing to do at that time, given the fact that I had never done anything before in my life, and to write a letter to the president!
>
> And I got a canned response; I've actually got it framed in my office at home. I got a canned response from some aide, who said, The president's happy to hear from you. We agree with you that the solution has to be found blah-blah-blah-blah-blah-blah. And I remember the day my mother encouraged me to write that letter.
>
> I walked home from school; we lived about eight blocks from school, I guess. And as I got within sight of my house, my mother was out on the front porch waving this letter and telling me to hurry up, that the president in the White House had written me, you know. She was really, really proud, and that memory stays with me.
>
> *Did other students know that you had written that letter?*
>
> You know, I don't remember. I sort of doubt it. I really doubt it. I doubt that I said anything to anybody. And I think that was probably hard, too, because I was so proud and who could I tell?

Why had Joyce drawn such different lessons from the experiences at Central High she'd shared with Nancy and the others? Her family, like Nancy's, was not affluent. Her father came from a small cotton-growing Arkansas town:

> He picked cotton until he got sick of it, and then he lied about his age and took his older brother's name and enlisted in the army. You know, a little bit of a mover and shaker in a way of looking at it.

He was ambitious, rising as high as he could manage in the army. "We traveled a lot," Joyce told me, "had the experience of a lot of different cultures and places and all of that kind of thing." He also married a woman originally from the Midwest. Was her mother an integrationist? I asked:

> It's hard for me to know how to characterize my mother. I don't feel totally comfortable saying that she was a liberal. But I don't feel totally comfortable saying that she was not a liberal. I don't know whether she was or not. But my memory of my mother was in some ways sort of the stereotypical, if not integrationist, moderate on the issue, who says, Some of my best friends are colored people, you know.

Like Nancy, Joyce approached the events at Central High from the point of view of her own needs. "I didn't think of myself as someone who was pushing for integration," she said. "I did think of myself as not having a problem." She echoed Nancy in harboring on-going resentment about the injuries to her own high-school experience, and especially the loss of the year after the drama when the high schools were all closed. I interviewed Joyce shortly before going to talk with Governor Faubus. "Is there any message you'd like me to carry to the governor?" I asked her. "He won't know who the hell I am," she replied, "but tell him I still resent the fact that he cheated me out of my senior year at Central High School."

But after the fact, Joyce made very different choices in her life, attributing their roots to the incidents she'd described to me. Her parents' "quasi-liberalism"—"trying to do what's right" while keeping quiet—was no longer an option. She became an activist on behalf of poor people, "making trouble" in a good cause, and standing up very publicly, in exactly the way she had chosen not to do as a junior at Central High, to promote and defend her beliefs. "You either keep your mouth shut, or you be prepared to stand your ground. Because something's gonna happen." Today, Joyce firmly stands her ground as a religiously motivated activist working with a grassroots organization to advocate social justice.

Walking a Tightrope in the Middle

On the other hand, Jane, the transplanted child who told her story of cultural dislocation in chapter 2, still lives on shaky ground. I asked her when she first became aware that the school was to be desegregated:

> Well, that's interesting because you know . . . , there was no—I know this for sure—there was absolutely no preparation of the schoolchildren, if that's what you want to call us. . . . There was no preparation for schoolchildren.
>
> Again, my father had [just] died, so I was not paying attention much to newspapers, but I remember big headlines. Because they were trying to fight this in the courts, clear through that summer of '57.

Distracted as she was by the personal tragedy of her father's death, Jane nonetheless now registered another contradiction among the many she had confronted throughout her young life, this one between the big headlines and the absence of preparation for the students:

> So there was this kind of feeling, well, maybe it won't happen. And if you look at those newspapers you'll see, it was being battled in the courts. And so there was a lot of feeling that it might not happen. And so there was no preparation for children at all. To my knowledge—and it would be interesting to talk to the teachers—I don't think the teachers were prepared in any sense of the word. If they were, it was at the very last minute, like, "We may have some problems, what is this going to mean, or how are you going to handle that?"
>
> I was very close to the journalism teacher and she was a Daughter of the Confederacy, so you know, she's very opposed to all of this. And I'm just sure in talking to her—we talked a bit afterwards; she died about fifteen, twenty years ago, but you know, about ten years after, I would go back every year and see her—there was just no preparation. There was just a feeling that this wasn't going to happen.
>
> At best, you know, [people wondered] how can we survive? There was not a feeling at all that I felt as a student or through teachers, that this is something we need to do. There was definitely

the feeling, "How can we resist it?" Or, "What can we do to maintain our goal of getting an education?"

I mean, everybody I knew said they were segregationists. I
don't know any white person [who] ever said they were an integrationist. They would say they were moderate, the best was to
say you were moderate segregationist. Versus a radical, a conservative or Citizens Council.

I asked if that were true for kids as well as adults, wondering what
sorts of conversations went on among the students:

Well, I don't remember any white kid ever defending blacks
in that sense, like, "They really should be here," or, "They have a
right for education." Never, OK.

What you did hear was—and I would say this was a majority of the middle-class white kids—a feeling like, "Well, the most
important thing we want to do is finish our high school, and this
is something that eventually the South has got to deal with. And
we really wish it were slower." There was a lot of that feeling like,
"We're not ready yet." "Why should we be the first high school?"
Discussion like that. Like, "What can we do to make sure we can
continue having football games?" because that was so important, or dances on Friday nights.

At best [they wanted to] ignore [it]. I can't remember anyone saying, "I can't wait to be nice to black kids coming to
school." That was never discussed. [. . .] I remember words like
law and order. They would use those phrases: "Are you going to
be a law-and-order kind of person?" Isn't that a phrase that was
common then?

I had very little contact, I remember Ernest Green being
around, but not in any of my classes, so I had literally no contact with any [of the black students]. I mean, how do you see
nine blacks in two thousand students? But I remember occasionally seeing them in the hall, and I certainly felt a need to be
respectful, but not to go out of my way to do anything.

Until this moment, Jane's memories were all about how other
people reacted. Suddenly, she put herself in the story, exempting herself at the same time she included herself: she had no contact, but neither did she go out of her way to be helpful. Thinking I might be

hearing a repetition of the church-attendance theme of dealing with contradictions between her social milieu and her personal beliefs, I asked:

Did you feel discomfort with the way your peers were talking about it?

I didn't like what I considered the cheap kids, the country kids that wanted to be hostile or abuse them or call them niggers or something like that.

Who were those kids?

I had very little contact with them, OK. And I can't think of names, I could probably go through the yearbook and pull them out.

But I have a real sense that there's a social class difference. They were much more what we would call the poor kids, the country kids, the working-class kids, and again I was in a kind of intellectual nerd group. [. . .] My friend [from the plantation] would use words like "nigger" or "nigra," whatever. I would never do that. I would call them colored kids, I guess. So I remember knowing I felt a little different than she did. But if any white kids ever talked with each other, the colored were nigger kids. You could certainly tell racist jokes, that wasn't any problem. No one would ever say anything about that. Racist comments and jokes.

So Jane felt different but kept quiet. Very subtly Jane suggested nuances of her reactions to the use of the word "nigger" by "the poor kids, the country kids, the working-class kids" and by her friend. The former she condemned by her tone of voice and by her statement of distance, both actual ("I had very little contact with them, OK.") and metaphoric ("I have a real sense that there's a social class difference.") Her friend, however, she continued to claim as such, viewing her use of the word "nigger," perhaps slightly softened to become "nigra," as a code for feeling "a little different." Between the lines of these remembrances I sensed, once again, Jane's dilemma as a member of a society about which she cared but from which she felt alienated.

Until this point, her position was not too surprising. She honestly admitted that she was susceptible to peer pressure, that the opinions of her social circle mattered back then. Her tone and manner distanced her from the Jane she was as a teenage southerner, as did her emphasis on the many facets of her alienation and her attempts to fit in with a society with which she disagreed. Our next exchange, however, suggested another Jane, one more unconsciously accepting of her participation in a mainstream of whites, and so it took me by surprise. I started to lead into a question about how things developed over time. "As the year went on," I said, "and the friction grew worse between black and white kids, did you hear stories about . . ." She interrupted me:

> See, I didn't feel that it did. And I'm sure the black kids did. I'm sure they did. I didn't feel it did.
> I felt the worst time was at the beginning of the year when there was much more visible troops. You know, when the Faubus people and the world people in particular. . . .
> Worse at the beginning, because a lot of, a lot of, I want to say poor whites would come up, these were adults, would come up to—see you couldn't get in the school directly. There were barricades, and you see pictures of that, big barricades and the whites, and they were screaming as you went into school.

Helen and Betsy had told me they'd gone in the side door and avoided the mobs screaming in the front. Where had Jane gone in, I asked?

> I was trying to think of that. My mother would often drop me off on Fifteenth Street, so I remember the front door. Not the other door; that's where the kids smoked. And that was where the real rough kids—god, you wouldn't smoke, right! It was real rough kids! So there was a smoking section over there, and I never went in that way.

Rough kids smoked; Jane was not a rough kid (like "cheap kids" and "country kids," another euphemism for class position), and so she was forced to encounter those other "rough" people screaming at the front door. In any case, Jane remembered troops at every door:

> Front or side, you had to pass through the barricades. And that's when I remember being more frightened.

And they would yell at you and they'd yell things like "Two, four, six, eight, we ain't gonna integrate." And you could hear them in the classrooms.

And that went on for maybe a month. The barricades, and then first Faubus's National Guard, and then the federal troops, and then the federalized National Guard.

And then, I would say after about, I'm just estimating, two months, six weeks, two months, you rarely saw guards. They were around, they were certainly available if you needed them, but they weren't all over the place.

And so that's why the first, let's see, month was bad, in terms of tension. And you know, I suppose now you're used to guards in the hallways, but we weren't. And you had to show ID to get in, and they were all in military uniform, and then maybe for two weeks you saw the bayonets, and that was scary. And then they put the bayonets away, but they were always armed. That was scary. And you never knew what some jerk was going to do. And there were bomb scares.

So, I remember the first couple months as bad. I don't remember after November or December that things were bad at all, that things escalated at all. You know it got much better after that. Did you feel it escalated, did other people feel it escalated?

I said that others *had* felt things escalated, thinking both of published accounts—Elizabeth Huckaby's and Daisy Bates's books, primarily—and of other students' stories of hostile encounters they'd witnessed or heard about. Jane assumed she'd see things differently from the black students. But now she tried to sort out why her perception was different from that of her white classmates. When I mentioned Betsy's story of Johnny and Minnijean, Jane commented:

She was kind of a cheerleader and with the football crowd. [...]

You see I never had any classes, 'cause they were all younger. So you would be taking a junior class, if you had them, or a sophomore class. And I was in honors classes, so you know I never had any contact. Now I knew there was some [trouble] when Minnijean left. And Minnijean was considered kind of a joke by most of the whites.

By the time I found myself listening to Jane on the topic of Minnijean, I had heard many others of her white classmates talk about her with severe animosity. So I was intrigued to hear a version of Minnijean by someone who described herself as a liberal. Her version was more theorized, but no friendlier than others':

> I would describe her unlike all the rest of the blacks.
>
> I'd put it in class terms again. She was much more—first of all she was overweight, so that made her more, what?—easy to tease. She was a stereotype of a mammy, a young mammy by white standards. Remember how there used to be the mammy with the [gestures to her belly], OK? Because she was big and she was overweight, and she was more challenging, more asserting, she was more set. Whereas the others were very almost docile.

I asked Jane to explain what she meant by "class terms," and she thought for a moment before she said:

> I would see her more a poor black, and that's not to say poor blacks are always that way, because many times they're much more the Uncle Tom kind of shuffle. But the other black women looked more, some of them were more mulatto, which often meant you had more prestige. And they looked a little more, I would put it a little more brighter, more middle class, more could handle the classroom. I think Minnijean, as rumored didn't do as well in the classroom. Maybe the harassment was more. But the others seemed to be much more scholarly, and she had less of that kind of thing.
>
> So I saw her stereotypically as a more, I don't know how to put it, working-class, less-educated type of black woman.
>
> She was considered much more aggressive and hostile. Let me put it this way: I'm sure if you teased her she didn't just accept it, and maybe you found that from the other blacks. I think when they got kicked or harassed or called names, they were basically, I suppose, trained or told, Don't argue back. Because they'll beat the hell out of you. And Minnijean was the one that, she had more of that posture you see when blacks are angry now. You know, you see it a lot, do you know what I'm saying? And she had more of that defiance. She wasn't going to put up with that bullshit.

So there were jokes about her. [...] People would make fun of her. Nah, Minnijean, or something, I don't know. Let me put it this way, there was no sympathy, there might have been sympathy in whites when they saw another black harassed. There would always be some other whites that might not approve of that. I think what I want to say is, there's a difference in whether or not people wanted them there and whether they were mistreating them.

OK, so I think with Minnijean, I remember not feeling very empathetic that she left. Sort of, stereotypically that she asked for it. That was my kind of feeling, that she fit some kind of black stereotype of what blacks were like or something, [that she] didn't know her place, do you know what I'm saying? That kind of feeling . . .

I didn't have any real empathy for her. I guess I'm embarrassed to say it, but that's what I remember. Like she had sort of asked for her trouble. She didn't play the role right.

No wonder that Jane hadn't seen harassment of the black students increasing as the year wore on, I thought. She, like her other white classmates, was out of sympathy for the one among them who was most publicly tormented. Jane knew it was probably wrong, that the black kids probably were living a different reality. But she still had her view of the matter. I sensed there was some willfulness in her dedication to that view and suspected it grew from her own hard feelings. So I started to ask her whether she remembered feeling resentful about the drama in general, and before I could complete the question, she answered vigorously:

Yeah, I do. I think yes, that's common. Resentful that it, from at least our class's perspective, that it interfered with our senior year.

High school is always, particularly in that vintage, right, and in the South, that was so important. Lot of these kids got married right out of high school. You know, high school, senior year was really a big thing for us. More so than I think it is for kids in the middle class now, don't you? I mean, it was really big, so we felt it interfered.

And certainly it was much more like a prison to see the

guards everywhere when you started school. It had some interference with football games, there were always guards around
there. So I remember resenting—and I guess that may have been
against the blacks—but a resentment that this whole drama took
place. And I guess the blacks, I don't know that I directly resented
them being there, but I'm sure they were the scapegoats of that
feeling, resentment that this had to occur.

Jane had described her family's politics as Republican-liberal. I
asked whether that perspective had influenced the direction of her
resentment. Was she mad only at black people? "I was angry at
Faubus," she replied. "I thought he was stupid that he provoked it."
But the grown-ups she most respected, her father before he died, liberal neighbors, all felt "this was not the time to integrate."

> And the definite feeling among my parents' group was that
> the South wasn't ready for this yet. Even though the medical
> school was integrated, they had black medical students. And
> University of Arkansas was integrated, you didn't want to call it
> that, but there were a few. At least the barrier had been broken.
> But the feeling [was] that the public schools were not ready for
> that.

Her father's opinion was compounded on her mother's part by
fear, the distinction in their responses once again highly gendered.
Men tended to express positions for or against desegregation or how
it was being done. Women, however—the mothers of Helen, Nancy,
and Jane, for example—operated emotionally, most often out of fear
for their children, a more personal reaction. As Jane talked more about
that ("My mother got frightened a lot by it"), she mentioned an event
that gave her mother good cause for fear. She'd written an editorial in
the student paper that had caused quite a stir—the first time in our
long talk that she indicated she'd taken a controversial public stand.
I asked to see it, and she fished out of an untidy pile of papers a yellowed copy of the *Tiger* from September 19, 1957.

The front page was dominated by desegregation—and by Jane
and her co-editor, Georgia, whose photographs accompanied a story
about the new *Tiger* staff. A long article, written by Georgia, factually
recounted events as they had happened up to the moment. Below the

fold was a photo of twenty-five students, crew-cutted boys and rosy-looking girls, accompanied by an elderly teacher wearing a pillbox hat, posed before Lincoln's tomb in Springfield, Illinois. "No prejudice prevailed that August day when Arkansas teachers and students of journalism visited the tomb of Lincoln. . . ." read the caption.

On page two was Jane's editorial, "Can You Meet the Challenge?":

> You are being watched! Today the world is watching you, the students of Central High. They want to know what your reactions, behavior, and impulses will be concerning a matter now before us. After all, as we see it, it settles now to a matter of interpretation of law and order.
>
> Will you be stubborn, obstinate, or refuse to listen to both sides of the question? Will your knowledge of science help you determine your action or will you let customs, superstition, or tradition determine the decision for you?
>
> This is the chance that the youth of America has been waiting for. Through an open mind, broad outlook, wise thinking, and a careful choice you can prove that America's youth has not "gone to the dogs" that their moral, spiritual, and educational standards are not being lowered. This is the opportunity for you as citizens of Arkansas and students of Little Rock Central High to show the world that Arkansas is a progressive thriving state of wide-awake alert people. It is a state which is rapidly growing and improving its social, health, and educational facilities. That it is a state with friendly, happy, and conscientious citizens who love and cherish their freedom.
>
> It has been said that life is just a chain of problems. If this is true, then this experience in making up your own mind and determining right from wrong will be of great value to you in life.
>
> The challenge is yours, as future adults of America, to prove your maturity, intelligence, and ability to make decisions by how you react, behave, and conduct yourself in this controversial question. What is your answer to this challenge?

Although she never mentioned the word "integration," never alluded to race or politics or anything specific about the challenge she addressed, Jane—careful Jane who'd walked that tightrope all her school career—took her place in the circus spotlight.

But having overcome her own fears, she found herself confronting her mother's:

> The . . . editorial I wrote was published in papers across the country. So I started to get phone calls from people in the North wanting to interview me. And then a couple of reporters called and said, you know, "Will you let us interview you?" And, "We'll do a big story, tell us what it's like."
>
> And my mother said, "Don't do that." I think it was AP wanted to do a special, and they said, "You'll get a byline, and you'll get all this," and I was into journalism. And my mother said, "Don't do it." And my journalism teacher said, "My god!"— no way was I to do that.
>
> *Weren't you disappointed?*
>
> I guess I just accepted it, you know, we just accepted parental things. But I remember thinking it would be fun. So, I guess I must have.
>
> But I kept, I was really excited when I got, people sent me copies of it from the *Boston Globe,* for example. . . . I got a lot of recognition.

Almost as if she'd stepped into her alternate persona, Jane went on to tell me with great indignation story after story about racist comments and jokes by teachers and other influential adults in her life. Tale after tale, she built her story of outrage at the constant, endemic lessons in prejudice. Finally, I asked her to assess the effect of all that on her. She replied, baldly:

> I wanted to get out of there, never wanted to, I never wanted to live in Arkansas. My goal was to get out. [. . .]

She went North to college, and went into a sort of hiding:

> I did not want to tell people I was from Arkansas for a while.
>
> *What was your fear?*
>
> Redneck. I changed my accent. I had a very heavy, you grow up there, heavy accent. And I started imitating my roommate

who was from Pennsylvania, who has one of these horrible—
whatever, OK—working-class Pennsylvania accents. So, I felt
really pleased when people would say, "Where're you from?"
They had no idea I was from the South.

As our conversation drew to a close, Jane insisted on telling me
one more story. It was, at last, a tale with no ambivalence, and it helped
to make sense of the contradictions in everything else she'd told me:

> Let me tell the end thing. Helen and I shared it, and I haven't
> told a lot of people, I've sort of forgotten it. And I shared it with
> Helen, and it really triggered something.
>
> Towards the end of the year, graduation, Mrs. Huckaby
> called five of us into her room. . . . and she said . . . the way the
> letters were going to be, [during graduation] one of the five of us
> would be walking with Ernest Green [the only one of the black
> students who was a senior and who graduated that year]. And so
> we could decide what we wanted to do, and Ernest understood if
> we were uncomfortable.
>
> I mean, we literally were going to walk down a path together.
> And whether or not we wanted to walk with him or whether, if
> we didn't feel comfortable doing that, he would walk alone, in
> front of us or behind us or whatever. And I thought that was
> really silly. I thought, I have no problem with that. Didn't think
> anything about it. So I told her.
>
> There were five of us brought in all together. And I was the
> middle person, so of the five people, I would be the one, if every-
> one showed up, I would be the one, and so since they didn't
> know who was going to be absent, they would call five of us. And
> I didn't realize I was going to be it. And I said, "I have no prob-
> lem, I'll walk with him," and I really thought that was silly. And
> I didn't think anything about it.
>
> And I can't remember now, Helen and I were trying to think
> whether it was baccalaureate or graduation. But as I recall, it was
> Friday we were told that. I didn't think anything more about it.
>
> We started getting obscene phone calls [at] my home. My
> mother really got scared. I mean things like—shit! "Are you a
> nigger lover, are you going to walk with him? You want your
> daughter to marry a nigger?" I mean shit, and more obscene than

I even—I've repressed it. You know, "Fuck a nigger" or something. You know.

And it went on 'til late at night, and my mother took the phone off the hook, but she was absolutely scared to death, you know, like the house was going to be blown up. I mean, just shit. I don't remember, I should ask her now more about it. I mean, she was really scared.

So that was Friday, and as I recall baccalaureate was Sunday, and she put the phone back on the hook Saturday morning and it started again. And that went on all weekend. So, Sunday, when baccalaureate occurred, I did walk with him.

And I was angry at the Capital Citizens garbage whites, the low trash whites who did that, who really angered me. So, that just made me more determined that I was going to walk with him. And I walked with him, and I remember maybe saying two or three things to him, that was the first I ever talked to him, because I never saw him. Really angry.

And my mother never told me not to [do it]. That's where the anger was directed towards the whites.

Was your mother angry also by that time?

She was scared, but she was angry at the whites, too, not at the blacks.

Did you get any flak from your peers for walking with him?

No.

Nobody ever said anything?

Never said a word. I don't think anybody really paid attention, so maybe those who were most scared left. And I remember talking to Ernest at graduation, maybe one or two words. . . .

But I just remember that, I mean, I shake thinking about it. So, when you ask me why I wanted to leave the South, I didn't want to be known as one of those kind of whites. You know, one of those angry—I mean I consider that the ultimate racist whites that would say those kind of horrible things.

I thought, I don't want to ever be known as one of those. I put it in class terms, there are a lot of really educated middle-class whites that would—I guess that's the message that I would really like to get across. The majority of the white kids—and

again, I'm coming from a particular perspective; at least, I did
not know any white kids that harassed the blacks. Most of the
white kids that I knew wanted to get through school and make
the best of the year. I can't say I knew any white in my circle that
would do anything hostile to black students. So that's why I did
differentiate them in class, the cheap whites, and I called them
educated middle-class whites.

Jane was very shaken as she told me this story. She grew more and
more animated, more outraged as the distinction took shape between
"the cheap whites" and the "educated middle-class whites." She went
on to describe her reactions to the film made from Elizabeth Huckaby's
book, and as she spoke, she began to weep, harder and harder, until
she could barely speak:

> You know, I'd forgotten a lot of this stuff, and remember
> when Huckaby's thing was on television? [. . .] That was what,
> five years ago, maybe?

By now, she was weeping deeply. I suggested she pause for a moment
to breathe, and I asked her what these memories evoked:

> I just wanna cry, anger.
>
> *The tears are angry?*
>
> Yeah, towards the whites.
>
> I mean, that's what it means to say you're from Little Rock.
> To say you're from Little Rock, people see that cover, that white
> girl hitting that black girl that was all over the place.
>
> So anger, at the whites, and that people would think I'm like
> that. So, when, when, [sobbing] when I saw my high school, I
> just started crying. It just brought back all that stuff. You know,
> I can't say I'm proud of my high school, and there's a real close-
> ness in our class, but when I saw that on TV, I don't know what,
> it's just heavy.

At the very end, as I went to turn off the tape recorder, Jane said:

> So, I think all that needs to come out. And I really feel that
> there were, to me, the majority of whites were very—I won't say
> accepting—but I'll use the word tolerant. And were not harass-
> ing. But all it takes is a minority of course, to make it—

Everything had changed and not much had changed since the days when Jane had lied about church at school, about home at church, about church at home. Jane tried to pass in worlds that repelled and horrified her, but of which she was and was not a part. Her year of desegregation had begun and ended with acts of distinguishing courage, an editorial calling for "right" behavior, a walk down the baccalaureate aisle shoulder to shoulder with a black fellow student. Yet Jane, alien though she experienced herself to be, could not summon up sympathy for Minnijean, another alien, could not allow herself, perhaps, fully to understand how tormented Minnjean had in fact been.

EIGHT
Fathers and Sons

*And I've never made any apology for my father ... who had
attitudes that by today's standards are quite puzzling, baffling,
not even understandable. Because that's just the way it was.*

—Wesley Pruden Jr.

*Dad was a kind of a Harry Truman kind of guy. I mean, he did
whatever was necessary that seemed to be the right thing to do at
the time.*

—Joe Matthews

Jane's reality that year of crisis was very much her own, sometimes intersecting, sometimes diverging from that of Helen, Betsy, and
the others. But every one of the women's narratives had a similar
structure; each speaker was the protagonist in her own story. Among
the people I interviewed were three men who talked about events from
a double perspective: their own and that of a father who played a very
visible role in the drama. If the mothers of Helen, Nancy, and Jane
sought to protect their daughters and keep them off the public stage,
these three men walked the history of Central High in the shadow of
very public fathers: Principal Jess Matthews's son Joe; Wesley Pruden
Jr., the son of a minister who assumed leadership in the segregationist resistance; and Jimmy Karam's son Jimmy Jr. Joe was a senior and
Jimmy a junior in the school that year of crisis, and Wesley had graduated four years earlier. While none of these men's stories was typical,
they form a point of convergence between history as written in the
textbooks and history as lived by ordinary folk, as well as introducing the experience of Central High from a male perspective. Because
their fathers occupied the public eye, the three sons viewed the doings
through a lens of personal concern, involving complicated reactions
to the risks their fathers faced. All three of the fathers were controversial, and all three of the sons were lovingly defensive.

Joe Matthews spoke of his father with respect and sympathy:

There was just three of us, Mother and Dad and I, and Dad was all tied up with that business. It was all he could do to come home and get a little sleep and go on about his business. So except for maybe official functions, I didn't see much of him that year.

I remember he lost a lot of weight. He was a big guy; he weighed about two-twenty-five, and I think he got down to about two hundred. So it was a big strain on him. . . .

All I can remember about that year was a lot of confusion, a lot of comings and goings, a lot of phone calls, a lot of just things going on at all hours, people calling up. Police cars out in front of the house intermittently.

Said Wesley Pruden Jr.:

There is no question that in 1957, attitudes were very different than they are now. And I've never made any apology for my father or for my friends there who had attitudes that by today's standards are quite puzzling, baffling, not even understandable. Because that's just the way it was.

Young people today, in my own family, my nephews, have asked me, "Well, what did you think about segregation?" And the answer is, I didn't think about it. It was just the way it always was, and it was like, we don't think about it being Sunday morning when it's Sunday morning.

But I think it's foolish to judge previous generations by our own. I mean, Jefferson owned slaves. It's true he also gave us our country, you might say. God knows what later generations are going to think about us, some of our silly attitudes.

Jimmy Karam refuted the stories circulated about his dad and indicated no need to justify his behavior:

He was not, in spite of all the stuff in the press, I *know* he was not that active. OK? . . .

He was a friend of Faubus, but what Daddy really likes is a fight. It doesn't matter, and he will invariably take the side of the underdog, it doesn't matter, but he loves a fight, and he'll do that.

I know, for example, for years, he's got his clothing stores. He hired black salesmen when it was unheard of. He wasn't altruistic; probably a third of his business was black. So he would hire, typically it was a good young black football player from one of the local black colleges and so on. I remember him before all this was going on, he'd go out and talk at one of the local black colleges, Philander Smith, and he knew the coaches, knew all the black preachers in town, and so on, 'cause they were business clientele. He did a very good trade and was very active.

Generally, he was a minority—kinda hard to think of a Catholic as being a minority, but he was. He was also a first generation native. So he was a foreign Catholic in a Protestant-dominated, white town, of Arabic descent, funny name, et cetera, et cetera.

So I know both from his business standpoint and his personal interaction he just was not a white supremacist by any stretch of the imagination. There's no way that was his background!

Nonetheless, Jimmy admitted his dad was not altogether unconnected with the acts for which he was condemned:

What I think he was, he was a curious man—and Faubus probably did ask him to go out there and see what the hell was going on. I wouldn't doubt that—we never talked about it, but I wouldn't doubt that. But organize it? Noooo. It was just not his inclination, not his nature.

The Jimmy Karams

I visited Jimmy Jr. at his father's urging, finding him in an upscale home in southern California, where he is an engineer working in high-tech industry. I repeated to him the story the senior Karam had told me about his "prank," sending a black employee out to the new high school to appeal falsely for admittance. Jimmy Jr. listened thoughtfully and said, "I don't remember that." I asked him what kind of talk there'd been about his dad, and he replied:

My father was always notorious by any stretch of the imagination. He had been a football coach, he was always active and so on. But again, it was less than you would think, because having been in it, if that had been the only article that had been in *Life* and *Time* [i.e., the article naming Jimmy Sr. as the organizer of the mob], I'm sure it would have been a lot more negative.

But we all had seen the—"Wait a minute! I was there. It wasn't [like that]. . . ."

So it was very clear to everybody there that there was probably some half-truths [in the accusations], but we all knew it as being half-truths, and a selective collection.

I knew of some stuff that they had missed in some of his skeletons. [laughs] He had done some—you know, after World War II, for a year or two, he had basically operated as a union breaker in the South, he had organized that type of thing. But in the South that's not a bad thing. Bunch of northerners coming down telling us how we ought to live, et cetera, so it wasn't all that particularly negative.

Lot of people in Little Rock didn't know that, because they knew him as a coach out at junior college, most of their first contact with him. And then they knew him as a businessman. And they knew him as someone who was always associated with the power structure, although not a politician himself. I also know he was tight enough he never actually gave any of his politicians any money.

Jimmy finished out his high-school education during the year-without-schools and only much later was awarded a diploma from Central. Like so many of his peers, he insisted that he was mostly interested in his own business—being a good student and getting on with his life—and paid little attention to anything else.

Boys coming of age in the white community of the fifties were brought up to believe they had a clear route to attaining the American dream if they followed certain rules. Their fathers' lives weren't always examples of success; they were, after all, the generation of the depression and the war. Paradoxically, of the three dads whose sons I interviewed, Jimmy Karam most represented the goal defined as desirable: he had risen from immigrant roots to create a sound and profitable business. Morally, however, he was more problematic, labeled by the press a troublemaker and leader of mobs. But his son overcame those problems much as his father had done, echoing the senior Karam's characterization of his actions during the Central High crisis as good-hearted scrapping. Indeed, Jimmy Jr. went further, hinting with humor at some skeletons the journalists had missed.

Joe and Jess Matthews

Central High's principal, Jess Matthews, provided an opposite model, one of rectitude at the cost of financial rewards. His son Joe, a member of the class of '58 in his father's school, is today a physician comfortably ensconced in a private practice. Sitting behind his office desk, he talked eloquently with me about his dad's idealism and dedication. Paradoxically, what made Jess Matthews controversial was what some people saw as his failure to transcend a rigid adherence to educational normalcy, and to exercise instead a kind of moral and practical leadership that might have helped the students and the larger community accept desegregation gracefully. Joe disagreed. To him, his father was an upstanding but very human figure of devotion to his work:

> I felt sorry for him. I would hate to see anybody in that situation that he was in, because, on the one hand, he had his responsibilities, and my dad was big on people, number one; he loved people more than anybody I've ever known before or since. And he truly enjoyed his job over there and getting to see those kids graduate and go on to bigger and better things. That gave him more pleasure than anything.
>
> And I used to ask him, "Dad, what in the, how come you've got more degrees than anybody else around here, and yet you get paid a lot less for it?" And he said he got a lot of satisfaction from his job, and that compensated him for the money end of it. And I think it did, because he's a guy that truly did enjoy his job.
>
> Except for things that one year, and the year the schools were closed and the year the 101st Airborne were out there, and possibly the year he disbanded fraternities and sororities when he first started out there. I guess those were his main stress times. But the rest of it was pretty satisfying.
>
> So I felt sorry for him that he would be in that kind of a position at his stage of life—you know, he might lose his job, I mean I was supposed to go to college. You know, I played football and I was good in school and that might get a little help, but—
>
> I perceived these things, I knew these were some things he was worrying about and that kind of bothered me. But I figured that it would all blow over eventually anyway, and he'd get back

to where he was. Because he was basically a good guy and he deserved it. And I think things generally work out that way.

Out of curiosity, I asked Joe why his father had disbanded fraternities and sororities. Joe talked elaborately about the courage it had taken early in his career to dismantle a system popular among "an elitist group of people" for the sake of promoting equal opportunity at the school:

> He saw this as a major obstacle to creating the kind of environment that he saw as important for educating people, not only in academics but also allowing them to mingle freely, get to know each other, male, female, kids from all strata. . . . That social type stuff, he felt that was important, too, I think, in preparing someone for college.
>
> That's what he thought the whole point of it was about. I guess he felt like everybody needed a college education, I don't know. But that's the way he set up that school, and we got more National Merit finalists and scholarships and academic kudos than any school in this country. We had a mill over there, for sending people all over the country to the best schools.
>
> I mean, *all* over the country and abroad, too. Everybody knew about Little Rock, the high school in Little Rock, Central High, long before the integration crisis ever came up. Because it was known to produce scholars and athletes and good people, people who went on to bigger and better things and a lot of great careers.
>
> That's what my dad was all about. That's what he saw as his mission. Still, it's very painful for me to think about that interruption, and also the way the school is now, where the ability to do that is, because of the political and social machinations, their ability to do that has been hampered.

I was struck by Joe's description of the integration crisis as "an interruption" of his father's agenda to extend quality education to everyone. There was the obvious paradox of how that view of things defined "everyone." But it also made me wonder whether Jess held a view of education as something divorced from social and political life, or whether his resentment of the crisis as an interruption implied a more negative opinion of desegregation than Joe had so far expressed.

Indeed, Joe was reluctant to speak for his father at all, but I nonetheless pressed him to tell me more:

Do you know what his personal views were about desegregation?

Well, I just have to speculate about that, too. I've already kind of hinted around to you that he sort of liked people to mingle. So I think as far as—I'm trying to think of the right word—I think he believed it was probably the right thing to do.

Now, when and how to do it, he might not have been completely clear on that. I'm just guessing. Because the way he was, I never heard in my home a lot of racial stuff: it's us versus them and we're different. That was never a part of my growing up. So I don't think that he or my mom were motivated by either, I don't think they were. I think they felt like it was the right thing to do but they didn't feel so strongly that they were willing to go out and march somewhere or do something like that. I'm sure they felt it was probably something that'd evolve and should be done, but that's about all I can say about it, really. . . .

Do you think your father was critical of the Blossom Plan?

He never talked about it. If he was, he kept it to himself. He wouldn't have said, anyway, because he was one of those guys who just did whatever he was told. He may have harbored some ideas, he may have thought it was great or he may have hated it. I don't know. But I'm sure if it was left up to him, he probably wouldn't have rushed into it quite. I think he would have been more cautious. Because he was really interested in that school functioning, that was his whole thing. . . .

Was he confused about how to keep the school functioning, given what he was being told to do about desegregation?

I don't think he'd ever been confused, because Dad was a kind of a Harry Truman kind of guy. I mean, he did whatever was necessary that seemed to be the right thing to do at the time. That was one thing that I don't particularly like about that movie, that "Crisis at Central High." Because they portrayed my dad as sort of an indecisive guy and Mrs. Huckaby as the force that was really directing all this. And that's a bunch of bull. My

dad was the force and Mrs. Huckaby was his—he told her and
Mr. Powell how to handle the situation.

In her book and the film made from it, Vice Principal Elizabeth
Huckaby carefully refrained from criticizing her boss overtly, while
implicitly consigning him to the sidelines. Her fellow vice principal,
J. O. Powell, was less reticent. The boss was "a shaggy dog type," Powell
said in an interview at the time, "a big, happy man who wants everybody to be happy." Well, maybe not *everybody*, it turned out. Powell
disagreed with Matthews's unwillingness to take a strong stand against
harassment of the black students. "If the white kids want to run them
off next year, let them do it," Powell quoted his boss as saying.[1]

When Joe read this quote in an earlier draft of this chapter, he
wrote to me strengthening his objection to depictions of his father as
anything less than in charge:

> Jess Matthews . . . felt that integration of the public schools
> was the law of the land and should be obeyed by all of its citi-
> zens. If he actually made a comment as quoted by J. O. Powell,
> it was probably made more in frustration than anything else.
> Incidentally, Elizabeth Huckaby and J. O. Powell were definitely
> on the sidelines in the integration crisis. None of these problems
> could rightfully be handled by anyone but the top school admin-
> istrator on the scene. J. O. and Elizabeth might have been asked
> to carry out some of Mr. Matthews's directions, but they were
> certainly not in charge of creating policy or making the final
> decision.[2]

While Joe reiterated his defense of his father's position on law and
order, and his actions as the responsible administrator at the school,
he still shed little light on what Jess Matthews the man felt about the
righteousness and value of racial integration at his school. Jess was willing and capable of taking the heat for things in which he strongly
believed, like the issue of fraternities, which, according to his son, was
for him a class issue. Clearly, the principal was not averse to making
change happen. But when it came to racial equality, his beliefs were
muted. In Joe's view Jess's priority was quality education, and he saw
the disruptions of the year of drama as an interruption, not an educational opportunity. Meanwhile, the principal hovered between

"doing what he was told" and "doing whatever was necessary that seemed to be the right thing to do at the time." What was *right* was protecting his educational program; what *he was told* was to keep peace inside the school as it desegregated. The two agendas merged in a strategy of maintaining silence about the underlying principles of racial justice, a choice that mirrored the behavior of many other prominent men (and many parents) at the time. In a bulletin read to students the second day of school, Matthews called on them to behave peacefully, citing their responsibility to themselves, their school, their city, state, and nation: "Your first and immediate job is to get an education of the highest quality possible. Any disorder, confusion, disagreement, or quarreling at or around school will interfere with classroom work.... We can be known as law-abiding and peace-loving, or as quarrelsome and unintelligent."[3] Carefully he avoided any suggestion that "mingling" with the Nine, not to mention advocating for them, might constitute good citizenship. Implicitly, he drew a clear line between active agency in his small world of the school, which he sought to keep peacefully focused on scholarship, and exercising influence in the larger world, where he declined to side publicly with what he might have personally, but silently, believed to be right. These were scary times, and Jess Matthews, like many others, took the road of caution, never revealing to the world or to his son how closely that route may or may not have coincided with his own objectives.

I thought I could hear echoes of his father's approach when Joe spoke about his own life, telling me how he had constructed a world for himself in which he was effectively in charge for the sake of helping others, while simultaneously insulated from social dynamics:

> I don't see myself as a person strongly motivated toward social change. I like it, I approve of it, but I don't feel like sticking my neck out for it. I figure it's going to happen without my help, where if I do get involved in it, I won't really know what I'm doing, like this interview.

> *I wonder if you went into medicine as your way of making a contribution?*

> Yeah, that's exactly why I went into it. I didn't go into it to make money. And that's turned out to be a wonderful thing,

because if Mr. Clinton and Ms. Clinton have their way, they'll take away a lot of the avenues for making money.[4] I don't care, because I see my job as a way for love and service, just like what my dad did. I know what he was talking about, that's my inheritance from him, is that this is enough for me, to be able to work here and see my patients, see them grow up and their kids come through. I mean, that for me, that's more than enough compensation.

Joe's and Jess's stance toward the world was highly consistent with the personal ideologies of their time and place. "Don't tread on me" mixes freely with a sense of futility about influencing the larger world for the good. Both men opted for lives in which they believed they could do good for those they touched first-hand, while refusing engagement in larger issues which nonetheless refused stubbornly to go away, especially in the elder Matthews's case.

The Wesley Prudens

Wesley Pruden's father, on the other hand, went out to meet history head-on. Unlike Jess Matthews, Pruden did feel strongly enough to act. He believed desegregation was something that decidedly should not be done. If Joe Matthews followed his father's lead by deciding to become a physician, Wesley Pruden Jr., today the editor of the *Washington Times,* faced a more complex task defining himself in relationship to his dad. He needed to find a way to both follow in his father's tradition and simultaneously eschew it. To him, his father was a positive example of both compassion and standing up for a minority position:

> I can remember, it must have been about the sixth grade, and we were living in a town near Little Rock called Scott, which is at the edge of the plantation country. We lived there six years but I consider that's where I grew up because we went there when I was in the second grade and moved back to Little Rock when I was in the eighth grade. So those were the very formative years. . . .
>
> But anyway, there was a girl who had gotten pregnant at the high school and so the school board met, and this was like two months before she was to graduate. And she wasn't showing or

anything, but the school board met and decided that she had to be suspended from school. And my father took it on himself to persuade the school board otherwise, and it didn't split the community, but it was a great deal of talk in the community. And he prevailed; his idea was that it was unfair. I think her family was going to send her away, to an aunt in another state or something, but let her graduate from high school.

Wesley Sr. was an ardent segregationist. So strongly did he feel on the subject that he risked his congregation and suffered consequences:

> My father got interested because he really thought that if the schools were desegregated, they would be destroyed. . . . So, my father got interested in this, and my mother and I tried to tell him, "Don't do it. We agree with you, but you're going to destroy your church."
>
> There were about three times in his life, in his career as a minister (he was a minister for fifty-two years) when he had built up a congregation to a really substantial position. And the first time he did it, I think that was about 1937 or '38, . . . it was inter-denominational, which was part of his problem, because inter-denominational churches don't work in the South very well, where everybody is a denomination.
>
> And it was wildly successful. He had a revival meeting once, and I was only three or four years old, but I got all this from relatives and friends and the lore in the family is quite strong. Church seated about three hundred and fifty people. And he had a revival meeting, and he had a man there named John Matthews, the pastor of the First Presbyterian Church of Los Angeles. He came and spoke and must've been a powerful speaker. And they extended it one week, extended it two weeks, extended it three weeks, and in those days the building codes weren't what they are now, and he built a wooden tabernacle next door to the church that seated a thousand people. Plain wooden benches. He was on the radio every night, on the biggest station in town. And people started coming, the governor came, all the prominent men in town came, because this man was such a powerful speaker. And he had services every night for eight months. A thousand people a night. Now, that was entertainment in those days. Didn't have TV, and in those days not many people went to the movies. . . .

Well, he had that, and then the war came along, and he went to Scott, and he had an idyllic existence there. And interestingly, my father preached in black churches all the time, he was commencement speaker at the black colleges, because he was on the radio, and they loved him. Then he started his church in downtown Little Rock. And it moved to the suburbs, and the church is still there. It's Ridgecrest Baptist Church, it's out on Asher Avenue.

This was the one where he was in 1957, and he was building it up, and he was having big crowds, and they were bringing in chairs. And the fire department came on Sunday to make sure they didn't put too many people in. He was fifty years old, and my mother and I thought this was it, he finally had found, this was what god had wanted us to do all the time.

And then this Little Rock thing came about. And I was working in the paper then in Memphis, and I was going back to Little Rock every weekend, because I had a girlfriend, a woman I later married, over there. The people who started the movement, the resistance movement were, they were not, I mean, racists—we all were, but they were not what we today would call racists. They weren't hard edged. They were ineffectual, they were not substantial people in the community, in the beginning.

I saw that it was going to be trouble for him [his father], . . . that the federal government was not going to let them get by with it. One of the stories I like, in Louisiana they had a wild man who was running for governor . . . and he got up and was making one of these fire-breathing speeches in the Louisiana State Senate, and Earl Long, the governor, was presiding, and he stopped. Right in the middle of his speech, he stopped him and said, "Willie, wait a minute, wait a minute, Willie." He said, "It's too late, Willie, the Feds have got the A-bomb." So, I'd begun to see, they got the A-bomb and we don't, and they could blow us out of the water.

What I was sure of was that my father was becoming controversial in a way that a preacher does not want to become controversial. And I saw it ruining his church, and I knew or felt that this was his last great shot, and he better protect what he had. My mother being a good, cautious wife the way wives often are felt that way strongly. And she was talking to him that way all during the week, and I was talking to him that way on the weekend.

And then finally when he did it, when he and Amos Guthridge and there was a couple of other men. There was a doctor, Malcolm Taylor, whose dad was a physician. They were looking around in the summer of 1957 as the school year was approaching, to find some way to get people fired up. To resist. Because they thought, they were counting on Faubus to do something, if they could make Faubus, who was looking to run for what was then an unprecedented third term as governor, give him reason to resist.

Wesley's narrative switched abruptly from the story of his father's fortunes and his concern for his father, to the politics of the time. Interestingly, his account of those politics revealed the other side of Governor Faubus's coin. Where Faubus saw himself as using the segregationists to further his political ambitions, the segregationist leaders saw themselves as manipulating Faubus into a position of supporting them. Several statements that came next countered claims made to me by the governor, starting with the latter's insistence that violence was a real possibility and the reason why he called out the National Guard:

> They were not thinking in terms of violence, they never believed there was going to be violence, and in fact, there never was any violence in Little Rock, really. The only blood that was spilled in Little Rock High School was when some guy across the street, and I was there that morning, across Park Avenue, didn't move fast enough, and a soldier punched him in the rear-end with a bayonet. That's the only time anybody got hurt. It was not like some of the incidents in the other parts of the South. There was no bombing of the Sunday School like in Birmingham, or there were no lynchings in Arkansas. There have been, back in the twenties and thirties there were, but none surrounding the school desegregation thing.
>
> So they flew up to Atlanta and talked to Marvin Griffin, the governor of Georgia, who was delighted to go to Little Rock, [providing Faubus approved.] "If I can get a letter from Faubus, saying that it's all right with him—I'm not going to go into another state and make trouble for a governor, Democratic governor."
>
> So they went to Faubus, and Faubus said, "I'm not only calling, but I'm inviting you to spend the night in the governor's

mansion," as a courtesy thing. Which he did, and Griffin came
over and made a speech, saying that if he were governor, saying
that if they tried to do this in Georgia, "I know what I would do,
I would call out the National Guard and invoke the police powers of the state."

Well, as soon as he did that, I mean, the state just, the excitement, it was explosive. Because this was the break that everybody
had thought might come. And so two weeks later school started,
and the rest is history.

Faubus had categorically insisted to me he had not invited Marvin
Griffin to the state, that, indeed, he had known nothing about it until
it was a done deal:

> FAUBUS: The segregationist leaders were dubious about
> me, and they never conferred with me in any shape or form,
> directly or indirectly. And I didn't know that the governor was
> coming to Arkansas until it was already announced, that he was
> coming to speak. So, in the somewhat inflammatory situation,
> three or four days after I learned that he was going to be here, I
> called him by telephone, and I advised him that the situation was
> somewhat precarious here, and that I hoped that his speech
> wouldn't say anything inflammatory. And he said, "Nooooo,
> Governor, we're not going to do that." He said, "We're just gonna
> feed 'em the Constitution."

Faubus agreed that he then invited Griffin to stay the night at the governor's mansion, but he insisted that was merely protocol and nothing
of substance happened. "We were walking on soft-shelled eggs.... I tell
you that it wasn't even mentioned." In any case, Wesley was quite right
that "the rest is history," including the fallout in his father's career:

> [My father's church was] destroyed, just about. He went
> down. He had probably a congregation of four hundred people
> when it started and he got down to twenty-five.
>
> *Why?*
>
> People don't want to go to a controversial church. There were
> ministers on the other side, and my father and several ministers
> on his side got very bitter over the years, '57, '58, '59. Nearly every
> preacher that got involved on either side nearly lost his church,

was moved to another town, or the church practically disintegrated. That's a little strong, they didn't disintegrate because churches rarely do, but they were hurt. Badly hurt. People don't want controversy.

Like Joe, Wesley spoke of his father's courage and ordeal with sympathy and defensiveness. Unlike Joe, however, Wesley laced his story with misgivings about his father's actions, not necessarily because he thought they were wrong at the time but because he thought they were fruitless and dangerous. "The feds have the atom bomb," which is to say that Wesley, who was older and more sophisticated than Jimmy Jr. or Joe, recognized where the power lay. Paradoxically, it was precisely to protest the accumulation of power in the federal government that Faubus and other segregationists mobilized to resist desegregation. Wesley saw the battle with realistic pessimism, but he missed the point of the war: to wrest back to the states control that had wandered Washington-ward over the depression years. Wesley's father fought a different fight; a creature of his time and place, he genuinely considered racial mixing wrong. Both battle and war were lost, and the minister, too, went down to professional defeat.

Was Wesley Sr. personally defeated as well? He retired and died four years later. His congregation was given to another preacher who failed to rebuild it. Soon afterward, the building was sold to a different denomination. I asked Wesley Jr. how his father felt about the aftermath, and he replied:

> He wasn't bitter, he never was bitter. He wasn't bitter. He used to worry that I would be bitter or that my sisters would be bitter.

> *Are you?*

> No, not bitter. I'm not bitter at all, I'm angry sometimes. I'm angry, but not at that. What I'm angry about is . . . that our culture's been hijacked. This whole political correctness movement just enrages me because I think western civilization is the best thing that ever happened to the world. . . . This need to judge previous generations by our own standards, I find really remarkable. And I guess the desegregation thing in Little Rock was part of that. Looking back I certainly realize that we were wrong. Wrong morally, wrong ethically.

Wrestling with the problem of how to judge the fathers by the standards of the sons, Wesley took a position in his generation's struggle for social change at the same time that he refused to justify the stance of his father, whom he clearly loved and defended.

So the sons of the leadership in the Central High drama sought to make peace with the actions of their fathers at the same time that they defined their own beliefs and decided their own actions in relationship to them. Ultimately, all three defended their parents by citing the norms at the time. "He did whatever was necessary that seemed to be the right thing to do at the time." "It was just the way it always was, and it was like, we don't think about it being Sunday morning when it's Sunday morning." As I went on to talk with the men and women shaped by the struggle at Central High, especially in those moments when I heard them talking unguardedly with each other, like Wesley I wondered what injustices were invisibly imbedded now in our time's Sunday morning mists?

NINE
Sharing Stories, Shaping History

And he started to get up and hit her, and that's when she called for the guard.

—Dennis

And so this idea about somebody always steppin' on her heels, I don't believe that.

—Nancy

When the white women of Central High and the sons of the leaders formulated their views about what was going on in their school, and about racial matters in general, they drew on a number of sources: conclusions drawn from personally lived experience, a set of beliefs formed through social discourse, and a theoretical understanding of a social world.[1] Woven together, all these threads formed a matrix guiding and delimiting their interpretations of what they experienced, heard, and read. They encountered African Americans in the kitchens of their own homes rather than on hostile street corners, they watched their parents interact with black domestic workers, they played with "pickaninnies" knowing they would receive hospitality in their playmates' homes that their own elders would not reciprocate. These experiences contained within them lessons about relations between the races and about themselves, too, as white southerners. Which lessons the students derived, however, depended on something more, on a frame of reference coming from more abstract and theoretical ideas about the world, concepts like "the southern way of life" and "opportunity for all."

Mediating lived experience and theoretical understandings of the world is a stratum of experience that is crucial to the formation of social roles and identities, as well as to their continual reinforcement and revision. That is talk. How people conversed with each other, the sorts of stories they constructed together in the act of talking, is the subject of this chapter.

Community Talk

All over the United States, I found clusters of Central High expatriates who were aware of each other in a friendly way, but not as a rule in touch. In one such place, Saint Louis, I was invited to a dinner party with Nancy and two other alumni of the class of '58 and two of their spouses. We were gathered in **Annie** and **Bruce**'s dining room, a small formal room adjoining a much larger wood-paneled den, clearly the room more commonly used by the family. I knew it was an act of considerable generosity on Annie's part to have invited us all; a piano teacher, she had told me earlier that she was exceptionally busy getting students ready for a recital. Now, however, she seemed relaxed, dressed casually in well-worn jeans and a tee-shirt, no makeup, simple silver jewelry. Her appearance matched her style of talking: emotive, a little self-deprecating, earnest, and contradictory. In contrast, Nancy, the woman who'd taken part in the "parade" protesting desegregation, knew exactly what she thought and spoke in a clearly articulated way that conveyed a very focused point of view. Stylishly attired in dress and blazer, razor-thin and fragile, she had suffered a series of severe illnesses over the past decade. The third classmate, **Dennis**, was a burly and outgoing man who had insisted on meeting me at the airport and chauffeuring me to my various appointments in town. He was accompanied by **Diane**, his second wife, younger than the others, slender, prettily dressed, an accountant with formidable opinions of her own. Nancy's husband didn't join us. But Annie's husband, Bruce, was there, a year older than the others, a sweet and understated man with a moving story of his own to tell.

Over spaghetti and salad, we talked about memories of their senior year, and I listened, enraptured, as their many stories formed a treatise on the meanings of desegregation. I had talked with each of the three alumni present separately earlier that evening, and so as the conversation progressed I was very aware of how much the interaction influenced each person's story.

The get-together was occasioned in part by the publication of a book by one of the Nine, Melba Pattillo Beals's *Warriors Don't Cry*, an event that provoked high feeling among the Central High community. Word had circulated among the graduates that I was interested in hearing about their experiences, and when Melba's book came out, a woman I'd already spoken with called me and said, "Some friends of mine in Saint Louis would like to talk with you." I'd made arrangements to travel to their city and do just that as quickly as I could. Talking to them separately, I'd asked them each to tell me how they'd felt about Melba's book, and each had insisted, with differing emotional content but intense feeling, that she or he had never seen the incidents reported there.

Annie simply couldn't remember and felt remorse about that. "My regret is my block about not remembering," she said. "It's like some wall is right in front of me, and I do not remember this stuff." She and Bruce had been dating that year, she explained, and her whole focus had been on her future. But she also suggested some more painful reasons for not remembering:

> What I can't understand is why I didn't see all this violence that Melba was talking about.... I think I was just removed from it. I'm just so confused right now. I thought it was all behind me, you know. I thought I would never have to encounter this again. And my husband said, "Well, maybe if you meditate about it you might have some memories," but I didn't, I just didn't have any—

Nancy was resentful, wanting to contest Melba's view in every detail:

> I don't know, when I read her book that must have brought back a lot of resentments in me because she wrote this book to be a factual book, OK? And she said twice in the book that I remember—and it seemed to be kind of like a whine because she would say, "Faubus lived at the governor's mansion," or, no, I take that back, she said, "That was the mansion that Faubus built." Well, *Faubus* didn't build the governor's mansion.

Dennis was forbearing and forgiving. He, too, disputed the reality Melba presented, but he also tried to understand what, as it turned out, he was convinced were her errors:

> I mean, it was so far off from what I remembered that I had to stop sometimes and say, "Look, but man, you saw it from an insider white guy. Hey, I'm sure it was real different from the other side."

At the dinner party, when I opened the subject of Melba's book Dennis responded reflectively but then slipped quickly into argument:

> It was funny, I mean, there was so much I guess I missed because there were so many other things that I wanted to do that were going on. I guess for a while the boy Jefferson, the tall basketball player (and I don't remember which one he was), was in my gym class for a while. And I don't know that he got picked on. I think one time someone took his clothes and threw them in the shower. Maybe I think I remember that from her book; I think I remember, I knew who did that, because I was there.

Dennis's tentative memories ("Maybe I think I remember . . . ") elicited a response from his wife. "But would you have done that to some other white kids, too?" Diane asked, gently offering him a position by invoking a familiar normalcy to counteract Melba's contention that there was harassment. "I know it happened in my school," she said. Dennis accepted her suggestion. "Yeah, it probably would have," he agreed. "I think the guy did it because he was, he was that way."

Dennis continued his story with the usual list of Minnijean incidents that were common knowledge: Minnijean's stepping on the foot of a boy who tried to trip her; two incidents of boys spilling hot soup on Minnijean's neck and back; Minnijean's dumping chili on the head of a boy who blocked her way. All these tales I had heard so often before constituted a sort of Lore of Minnijean and amounted to an exculpation of white misbehavior by casting Minnijean as the instigator.

But suddenly in the midst of this familiar litany, Dennis remembered that he had in fact been present for the last event:

> I mean, I was in the chili incident.

> *How were you involved?*

> I was closer than I am to all of you right now to Minnijean. I mean, I was right there; if the tray had tilted the other way, I would have gotten it, too. I mean, that's how close I was.

Annie sweetly proffered a tentative defense of Minnijean. "Wasn't it more of an accident?" she asked. But Dennis was headed in a different direction, no longer positioned as the good-natured observer:

No. . . . She went through this aisle and the chairs were too close together. And it was not something that a person would normally do. I wouldn't have done it, because I'd have looked there and said, It's too close together. You could have gone this [other] way and made it faster than going through.

And when she came through, they just bumped their chair back [closing the already-narrow space of the aisle behind them]. And then when the next one did it, she just took her tray and just turned it loose, right on his head. And as I say, I was sitting there, and if it'd turned the other way, I'd have gotten the chili. Yeah, they caused it. But I mean, did she have to do it [try to squeeze through the aisle]? I don't know.

But it was interesting to see it from that other girl's [Melba's] point of view of what really went on. And it wasn't at all like that. But I could see how they could think it was that way. If I wasn't there, if I was looking at it from fifty feet over yonder in that cafeteria—

Dennis's process interested me. He sought to reconcile his own first-hand account of events with Melba's second-hand one, and he did so in the context of a series of other stories about Minnijean that were common hearsay in his circle. Any lived moment of experience can be formulated in many different ways. Dennis demonstrated here the premise that the way we articulate experiences to ourselves is a function of how we understand the larger historical context in which they take place. At the moment that Minnijean dumped her chili, Dennis already had a well-formed set of ideas about what was happening in his school and in his world. Those ideas were drawn from many sources: stories he and his classmates were trading about Minnijean, items in the news, and, most implicitly, his own immersion in white southern culture. He read Minnijean's act accordingly, questioning her decision to take a route that challenged the boys seated along the crowded aisle, and interpreting that choice as provocative. I thought his interpretation might well contain a kernel of truth; the most banal of everyday behaviors can become expressions of protest.[2] Under other circumstances Minnijean might have moved down that aisle in such a way as to elicit respectful assistance from the boys. Under other circumstances, the boys might have shifted politely forward or stood to let her pass. Dennis hints at his belief that Minnijean knew they would not, reading defiance in her stance. It is meaningful that Dennis does not reflect on the reasons why the boys did not get out of her way, a reflection of his own perspective. After all, he was one of them; he, too, did not move or stand aside, and the chili could as easily have fallen on his head. What he reveals is his partisan interpretation of the scene; it was normal for the boys to taunt Minnijean by blocking her way. It was noteworthy that she challenged them, not that they challenged her.

Nonetheless, having read Melba's account of her friend Minnijean's version, Dennis claims he can understand how the girls would have seen the incident very differently. But in the next breath he asserts the correctness of his own view as opposed to Melba's, because he was not "fifty feet over yonder in that cafeteria," he was "there."

If Dennis's story is woven of his first-hand perceptions articulated in the context of his understanding of the times, his telling of the story in that moment at that dinner party further shaped its meaning. What ensued was an exercise in group reinforcement of an argument by means of the joint construction of alternative explanations both for their own behavior and for Melba's perspective:

> DENNIS: But I didn't get offended by the book. I read it just to see if I was in it. [laughs]
>
> *And were you in it? Why would you have been in it? What did you do that would have gotten you in Melba's book?*
>
> I was pretty much at the front of the class most of the time.
>
> *What does that mean?*
>
> If there were ten people all standing in line I was number one or number two. I remember being on Douglas Edward's news, because he was broadcasting from there, and I did like this [thrusts his face forward] and going home that night and seeing myself on national news.
>
> *So you were just getting yourself noticed?*
>
> Yeah.
>
> *Did you have opinions about desegregation?*
>
> Not really.

Did you have anything to say when you got on the national news?

No, no. I was just cuttin' up.

NANCY: I made the national news, too, Dennis, but I was in a parade down Main Street. [Dennis laughs heartily.] Besmirched my mother's name is what I was told. [Both laugh.] She was not a happy camper.

Nancy jumped in to associate her own action, identified to me privately as protest, however innocent, with Dennis's "cuttin' up." But Dennis quickly distinguished his own innocence from her more political action:

I was with a group of people who were probably more clowning than doing anything else.

Nancy ignored him, turning to me to argue her case:

You know, that's what I told you today [in our separate conversation], when we decided to do that parade and I couldn't come up with who decided that we were going to do it. It was more or less something to do. . . .

Both of you witnessed incidents in which there was some level of harassment of the black students. . . .

DENNIS: Oh yeah.

NANCY: Umm hmm. [nods affirmatively] I just saw that one.

You didn't see any, Annie?

ANNIE: Umm umm. [shakes her head negatively]

DENNIS: Oh, I was in class when that boy stuck his feet out, and I thought it was kind of funny. And I think it was menacing. But I'm not sure.

I think it was biology [class]. I remember that he absolutely stuck his feet out, cross-legged, and she just absolutely stepped right on his fin.

BRUCE: Serves him right!

DENNIS: Yeah. It really did. I think that's what most people thought. He's a jerk. It served him right. And he started to get up and hit her, and that's when she called for the guard.

I remember, that was kind of an interesting joke that went

around amongst all of us: you know, "Where's muh guawd? Where's muh guawd?" [laughs] They were always going, "Muh guawd."

Dennis vacillated between two rhetorical presentations of his memories. On the one hand, he argued that encounters Melba saw as harassment were in fact just instances of boys being boys. On the other hand, he readily identified the incident in the classroom—another piece of the Minnijean saga he'd mentioned earlier without remembering that he'd been a witness—as menacing. Having given Melba that point, he quickly countered it by ridiculing the black students' reliance on the protection of armed guards. In doing so, he implied that they were overreacting, or that they enjoyed a special privilege in an atmosphere which was, after all, essentially the rough-and-tumble of normal adolescent experience.

I pushed the question, wanting Dennis to declare his position more clearly:

> *Didn't you have any sympathy for Minnijean or for any of the other black students?*
>
> [Pause] Sympathy?
>
> *Did you ever think, "These kids deserve a break; they're having a hard time"?*
>
> I didn't realize they were having a hard time, OK? In fact . . .
> [All speaking at once]:
> BRUCE: Dealing with the National Guard and . . .
> NANCY: . . . protect them.
> DENNIS: If you stop and think, there was definitely two phases going on. Yes, they had a hard time when they were stuck out and couldn't come in, and that was when the National Guard was there. And that lasted two weeks. Then, when the 101st Airborne came in, nobody messed with them. I mean, *nobody.* You remember **Stevie ————**, don't you? Well, he was kind of between us.
> BRUCE: Who was he?
> DENNIS: Well, he was the one that tried to take the gun away from the National Guardsman.
> OK. Well, Stevie was a local thug. Stevie ended up being a

bookie. I knew Stevie; I knew all the thugs. Stevie was one of the ones who was already graduated and was outside. And he tried to take the gun away from one of those guys.

One of the 101st?

One of the 101st, and the guy just did, after now being in Uncle Sam's services I know he just went like this [mimes flipping up the rifle] and caught Harvey with the butt of the rifle right there [points to his chin], and Harvey went off and they took him away, you know, it was bloodied. But that was pretty much a lesson to everybody: Don't mess with these little Chinamen.

It was interesting: there were no blacks, but there weren't many white people, either.

BRUCE: In the 101st Airborne?

DENNIS: Right.

You're saying they were Chinese-American soldiers?

Now I know they were probably Filipino. But they were Oriental to us. There were Hispanics.

NANCY: Umm hmm. I remember that.

DENNIS: And I would say there were probably dark Italians. There were a few that I would consider, back in those days, white people. But there were a goodly number of folks that were dark. And as I say, now I would know that they would be Puerto Ricans or Filipinos, or people like that. But they also wore their little helmets—not little things, but they wore those helmets—and they gave a kid a gun.

NANCY: And they had the bayonets on them.

DENNIS: Well, bayonets outside, but inside it was just that they had the gun. Then they went to sticks, I think; billy clubs.

NANCY: There at the end.

DENNIS: Most people knew, Don't mess with those people!

This treatise on the racial composition of the 101st Airborne troops was fascinating, and something I had not heard elsewhere. It made some sense to me that the troops, drawn from across the country, represented a broader range of ethnicities than were present at that time in Little Rock. But I suspected I was hearing another example of selective perception. Photographs from the time suggest a large majority of Caucasian soldiers. Dennis's memory's eye sketched a reality that corresponded, perhaps, more to his experience of racial division and sense of invasion than to numerical accuracy.

In any case, Dennis was building an argument that Melba's account of harassment could not have been true, because the Nine were under armed protection:

> *Once the 101st Airborne were there, you assumed that the nine black students in the school were not having a hard time?*
>
> That's what I assumed. I do remember the bomb scares. And they were just silly. You know, you had to leave. And I remember one time when somebody spit on one, you know those big stairs you came down. Somebody spit on somebody across [the way], but I think they got about three people. It was like, Fool, don't you do that ever again to me!
>
> NANCY: That happened sometimes when there weren't any black students at Central, things like that; they were just making mischief.
>
> BRUCE: Absolutely.
>
> DENNIS: Oh, yeah.

Here again was the familiar argument that Melba had misinterpreted what was normal teenage mischief. I suspected that people had convinced themselves of this reading long ago, and I wondered whether Melba's book had changed anything in their thinking, and if not, how they reconciled the differences in their remembrances:

> *So now that you've read Melba's book, do you think differently about how much harassment there was?*
>
> [They all shake their heads.]
>
> *You don't? What do you think, then? Do you think she's making it up?*
>
> DENNIS: Either, one, was making it up. Because, you see, that's what I have to ask people. I think the 101st was there the whole year.
>
> NANCY: They were.
>
> DENNIS: That's what I remember now.
>
> NANCY: They were.
>
> DENNIS: I remember at graduation, when we all took our hats off and waved to this battalion that were sittin', or a platoon,

a group of men, that were sittin' down at the far end of Quibley Stadium. I mean, they were recognized as part of our graduation.

You saw them as being the 101st Airborne?

Yeah, and she started talkin' about the National Guard being there. Well, that's just flat not the truth and documentable. And so this idea about somebody always steppin' on her heels, I don't believe that. I don't believe that because what I observed was, as they went down the hall, that guard was never farther than that wall away.

NANCY: That's true!

DENNIS: And most of the time *that* wall. [points to a nearer wall]

NANCY: That's true.

The 101st Airborne had in fact been largely withdrawn from the school on September 30, five days after they first arrived. They were replaced by a federalized National Guard unit, who commanded the area around the school building, and who gradually took over the assignment of personally guarding the Nine from a steadily diminishing number of 101st Airborne soldiers. The last of the 101st remained in Little Rock until late November, when they decamped for their home base. It made some sense that the white students missed the distinctions between armed forces. To the black students, however, the differences were vivid: the Guard were southern youths, often far less than sympathetic to the youngsters they were assigned to protect. Incidents of harassment accelerated, until in October each black student was assigned a personal guard, who, however, was told to maintain a certain distance.[3] It was exactly two weeks after the last federal troop was withdrawn from the city that the chili incident took place and Minnijean was suspended.[4]

DENNIS: And I do remember that the people could go down [the stairs] and get hit with books, and that happened. But that happened to everybody at one time or another. I'm sure with regard to the black people it was malicious. But it happened pretty frequently.

Maybe more frequently to the black students?

I don't remember it being frequent. I remember them being

given a good leaving alone. Which was probably, in retrospect, harder than anything.[5]

NANCY: I think so, too. I agree with that.

DENNIS: And I think it was what they began to understand, and I got it from her book, too, sort of, was the fact that they were absolutely ignored was probably the hard thing because they would have been, had they gone on to Dunbar and been there, they'd have been in our place. I mean, I was one of the senior whatever, recognized; you got your special picture in the yearbook. You know.

So you think that some part of Melba's bitterness that she expresses in this book was because she was ostracized, not because she was harassed?

DENNIS: Absolutely. I don't think ostracized is the right word. I think ignored.

NANCY: Dennis, what do you think about this, when she said in her book, that she really felt lonely because she was never invited to any of the parties, never invited to this, that, and the other. Then she turns right around in the same almost paragraph and says, And also my friends at Horace Mann had stopped calling me, had stopped inviting me, had stopped talking to me at church. So it was not just a one-sided deal; it was her friends, her black friends had left her alone, and then she didn't have any white friends.

DENNIS: Yeah. Wasn't ever going to have any white friends. [laughs]

NANCY: I mean, who's wrong here, who's right here, see?

DENNIS: I don't know that there is a right and a wrong.

NANCY: No, but there's . . .

DENNIS: I think that it is interesting for the first time I began to realize, these people were probably the cream of the crop. They would have been in the same position I was.[6] *The Mikado* that she was talking about: I had a nice part in that. Got to dress up Chinese and wear the long thing. I mean, what fun! They would have liked to have—and if they had been at their own school, they would have been there. And yet, where they were forced to be, and I think that basically after a few weeks of the notoriety and all this began to boil down basically when winter got too cold, and I think that days went by when nobody thought about it.

NANCY: Oh, I do, too.

DENNIS: And that may have been one of the tough things.

BRUCE: Umm hmm.

DENNIS: Because, I mean we had our friends. I mean, we were going to school to see our friends. This was social time. I mean, I don't remember ever having any hard classes. I remember it was the fun of every day going to school. They weren't part of it. They couldn't have been.

Couldn't have been, why?

If they'd been white and transferred in there from Fort Smith, Arkansas, they couldn't have been. Because they were new to the class.

And you don't think that was more so because they were black and there was all this hoopla?

Obviously, it probably was more so. I mean, it was right evident; you just looked in their face, you knew they were new. I mean, you couldn't get around that.

NANCY: It was hard to get included. I mean, it really was.

DENNIS: Sure. It is in any high school. But it would be the same way today! I would say that if a student moved from Fort Smith, Arkansas, to Little Rock, their senior year, they would have been treated virtually the same way. Unless they had sort of made friends with somebody in the class that got them included. It was cliques. Now, I know that's what it was.

Despite an undertow of differences between them, Dennis and Nancy were building a case together, and a fairly sophisticated one at that. Everyone at the table had experienced the politics of adolescent society. We all knew how powerful was the force of group exclusion, and we all had enough imagination to dread the consequences of moving to a new school in the middle of our high-school years. By evoking this commonplace experience, they neutralized Melba's uncommon one, placing it in a context not of historic racial warfare and change, but of normal social dynamics. In doing so, they both acknowledged

Melba's perspective and at the same time discredited it. Now Bruce joined in to support them:

> I remember that real distinctly when I went there in the tenth grade of high school. Because I had moved from Hot Springs, Arkansas, moved to Little Rock, gone into this huge high school, and I had virtually no friends. It was, it was real hard. And a year or two before that, they had fraternities, high-school fraternities, and they really are cliques. I mean, if you weren't in one of these, then you were nobody. So it was, it was real difficult for me to establish my place and find some friends. And it took me three years.
>
> DENNIS: I think they'd of had a whole different outlook, and particularly that woman that wrote the book, if she had had a senior year. But, see, she was a junior; she got that one year, and then they shut the schools the next year. Bingo! She was out.
>
> NANCY: Dennis, I want to ask you something.

The party turned to regard Nancy. Her tone of voice told us she was about to escalate matters:

> I want to ask Dennis something. In Melba's book, OK? She had kept this diary.
>
> DENNIS: Yeah!
>
> NANCY: OK. Do you think—now she was fifteen at the time that she says that she was writing this diary—I mean, I realize she's a smart individual. Her book was very well written, even though there were a lot of inaccuracies in it, it was very well done. But do you believe that a fifteen-year-old had the maturity to write in her diary the things that Melba says she wrote in her diary? Or did she have some help?
>
> DENNIS: I don't know.
>
> NANCY: Did you write like that when you were fifteen?
>
> DENNIS: Hell, no! I couldn't write. [laughs] I still can't!

As Nancy introduced the idea that something more serious than different perspectives or hurt teen-aged feelings were in play, as she hinted at outright dishonesty, I began to register the silence of the third alumna of that class, Annie. I had talked with Annie earlier in the day, and she had spoken of very different reactions to Melba's

book. I wondered what she would say now, in the face of her classmates' growing critique:

> *Annie, you had a more sympathetic response to the book,*
> *didn't you?*

ANNIE: Yeeeees, I did!

> *Would you say a little bit about how you're reacting as you*
> *hear the others talk about it.*

ANNIE: Well, I had two sides. I really responded to her grief.
And I just didn't even see how in the world she could keep going
to school with all this grief that she was going through. I don't
see what kept making them go every day. I even thought, Well,
are they being paid? At one point, I just thought, This is impossible, to keep gettin' up and keep going every single day. And she
didn't ever say, I have—well, she did, too; she had a conviction.
But I just would have given up. I think I would have given up the
first day. And her parents didn't even seem like they were— At
first they were appalled that she was going to be one of them that
was going to go.

DENNIS: The one that got me was Elizabeth Eckford. Now,
if there was any sympathy, it was Elizabeth Eckford.

ANNIE: You didn't feel sorry for Melba?

DENNIS: Oh, yes, I didn't hardly know Melba. Elizabeth
was real quiet. She was one of those that you just felt, That child
needs, she needs the dark.

NANCY: Yeah, she wanted to disappear in the woodwork.

DENNIS: Yeah, I got the feeling that she really wanted,
'cause she was in French class with **Patricia**, my first wife. And
she, I got to know her by that association. She didn't even want
to know how to speak French, and that was their assessment of
it. But somebody'd said, You have to be there. So she was there;
she never got past the first chapter. But she was real quiet.

Dennis's tendency to cast aspersions on Elizabeth's scholarship
was interesting to me, both familiar and a departure. White students
often spoke unfavorably about Minnijean's intelligence, but I hadn't
heard such remarks about any of the other black classmates. Betsy had
commented about Minnijean, "She was put there to cause trouble by

the NAACP; she had to have been. She was not smart, she wasn't even there to study, she didn't try." Jane, struggling to identify a class difference between Minnijean and the other black students, said, "And they looked a little more, I would put it a little more brighter, more middle class, more could handle the classroom. I think Minnijean, as rumored, didn't do as well in the classroom. The others seemed to be much more scholarly."

Dennis had shifted the conversation away from Annie's disagreement with the group, and now I tried to give her back the floor:

> *Annie, will you say more about what you're feeling about Melba's book?*

> I felt a lot of sympathy for her, and at the same time, thinking that she was, feeling like that she must be exaggerating. I don't see how anybody could keep going to school, enduring all that harm. You know, the kids that would pelt her with pencils all the time, and hit her and kick her: I don't think it's possible to do that.

> DENNIS: Well, the truth of the matter was, that simply just did not go on. There were incidences. And I don't minimize that they were probably pretty cruel. But every day! I mean, after reading the book, I felt like she was harassed between every class change, every day, all the time.

> NANCY: And I don't believe that, either. We were all too busy trying to get where we were going and concentrate on what we were doing, there was enough hoopla going on out there in the street.

> DENNIS: Our football team had won thirty-seven games straight in a row, and it was like, you went to the pep rallies and you did all this other stuff, and there was just too much going on. . . .

> ANNIE: Well, another thing that I couldn't understand was why the teachers didn't give them more help, if they were really being as hurt as it sounded like.

I could feel the pull of Annie in the direction of Dennis and Nancy. The very sympathy she expressed increasingly cast doubt on Melba's story.

DENNIS: I didn't do study hall the senior year. . . .

ANNIE: Well, I mean in any class!

DENNIS: Well, she was saying that study hall was so disruptive, and man, the way that I remember it, you didn't talk! You did, and you were at study hall at 7:30 in the morning rather than 2:30 at night.

NANCY: Exactly!

DENNIS: Because there were some real disciplinarian women that ran study hall. I didn't do it my senior year, because I was in the athletic program, which that was my study hall, it was elective period.

NANCY: But the study halls were very large, a very large number of people in them. And for the teacher to keep order, it had to be that way. You didn't open your mouth in study hall. Nothing went on in study hall! As far as I remember, you either did your work, you read a book, or you could lay your head down and take a nap. But you didn't talk, and you did not create any disturbance in study hall.[7]

DENNIS: You know, we had a few juvenile delinquents. I mean, not near probably what they have now. I bet you could name 'em on one hand, the people who would just absolutely go out of their way to misbehave. There were a few with the leather jacket that probably rode a motorcycle or hot rod car. There was maybe five or six. But when we were going to school, most of those guys like that were pretty well taken care of by the football players, too. I mean, if you acted up, they'd beat you up.

NANCY: Yeah, that's the way it was.

DENNIS: It was a lot of self-policing.

ANNIE: Do you think there would have been seventy-five people that were belligerent toward these, that were called segregationist, that were belligerent toward the black students?

DENNIS: In her definition of segregationist, there were probably hundreds. However, the people that were overt and belligerent, I mean, Beth, it just dawned on me, because Matthews [the principal] was still there. He didn't leave until later on. He paddled you. I mean, this was corporal punishment. He and Coach Peters were biiig guys. And that's why we didn't have a lot of people that acted up. . . . They had paddles, and you'd go over in the field house and go into the coach's office, and they'd whack you with it. And so, there wasn't a lot of misbehaving.

NANCY: I saw that one incidence that I told you about, and that was the one and only that I saw.

The conversation went on, replete with memories about the good parts of their Central High experience. They talked with pride about the football team, the musical and theatrical groups, the fun they'd had when exchange students came from another town, and on and on. At length I asked:

So do you have any regrets about that year?

[Long pause]

ANNIE: Well, my regret is my [memory] block, it's like some wall is right in front of me, and I do not remember this stuff. I do wish that, I mean, looking back now, how many years, thirty-seven years? I do not socialize with black people. I don't have an opportunity. I don't take an opportunity. But I am so embarrassed about the way all the white people were acting that I was reading about in her book. I wish that I could go back and relive those things and be a friend to them.

Yet, I'd probably be ostracized myself, from the way it sounded. But I do!

The company were silent. At last Dennis said reflectively:

I guess there were some of them that were taking the position that they didn't want "the niggers" to go to school with them.

In my on-going quest to find more involved students to interview, I asked them to identify those people, and they ran through some names and memories. After a few moments, they shifted gears and began to recollect the other side of the picture, those students who stuck up for the Nine:

DENNIS: Then also, I do remember, I remember my good friend, because we lockered together, **Georgie**, who was in gym with this guy Jefferson Thomas [one of the Nine], and I remember him protecting—and you can't say protecting because Jefferson Thomas was bigger—but like saying, "Cool it; we're going to play basketball. Leave us alone. If you're going to act up, go away."

ANNIE: You mean he wanted to play with Jefferson Thomas?

DENNIS: Yeah. They were playing basketball and somebody was trying to harass them. The way we would say it now, "I don't know what you're into, but you go over there and do it, 'cause we're into this. Just leave us alone."

And Georgie was a big old fat boy who I was surprised would do that.

ANNIE: He's not very tall.

DENNIS: And in those days he was real round! [laughs] He was not an aggressive person.

And I think that I can recall other times when other people would say, like Annie would be saying, "Let's go do something." And he would say, "Nah! It ain't worth it." That sort of deal. Stopping things even before they got started.

I remember one time when somebody whacked one of those girls, and they dropped all of their books, and I saw three or four people pick 'em up and give 'em to them. And it was sort of like, "We're sorry this happened." I don't think there was many words exchanged. But other than them seeing people picking up the woman's books and giving them back to her.

ANNIE: She doesn't have a lot to say about *them* in that book, about that.

BRUCE: That's the kind of thing I think that it would be good if it could be brought out in your book or somebody else's book, that there was a lot of good things that went on that year from the students' standpoint. Everything that's been published is bad.[8]

NANCY, ANNIE, and DENNIS: Yeah. Right.

BRUCE: Central was looked on as just a black spot on the community and on the nation, but there were a lot of good things, I think, that happened, too.

DENNIS: There was one picture that appeared in the *Los Angeles Times* which was a picture of my next-door neighbor talking with one of the girls. And here was this picture, and it made it because it was during one of these bomb scares, and this girl's just lost, and Priscilla was telling her where to go for the next class and how to get there. I mean, just like anybody on a street corner'd say, "Where's so-and-so?"

ANNIE: This is a white girl?

DENNIS: Yeah. That is the good, common, southern manners. [...]

BRUCE: Any time you have that many students, that's a large representative of personalities. You'll have some people that are going to be kind and some people are going to be interested in the black people who were coming into the school. And you have the other element that are going to be totally anti. But you hear more about the anti attitude, because that's the thing that sells.

Disputing Truths, Building Representations

Around that dinner table, five people told five different narratives about Central High the year it was desegregated. As the talk progressed, those five narratives intertwined to form a single story. Let us look at what the narratives were, and how they came to tell a unitary tale.

Diane had least to say; she was a newcomer to the scene and had been least involved of anyone. Nonetheless, she made a clear contribution to constructing the common story. Early in the conversation she articulated the essential theme of the discussion: that interaction between white and black students at Central High was normal and, therefore, that the white students were innocent. "But would you have done that to some other white kids, too?" she asked her husband, Dennis, rhetorically. "I know it happened in my school." Not having been there herself, she drew on her general consciousness of both race and adolescent relations in Arkansas in the period of her own life, and, I imagine, the discourse of her current circle (both the circle in which she lived and the circle around that table) to take a position in an argument that soon was pursued by Dennis.

Of the dinner party guests Dennis had most to say. With humor and volubility, he wove a narrative of opposing themes, a sort of muted one-man debating team. His ambivalent attitude was expressed most clearly when he told the story of Minnijean's stomping on a classmate who "stuck his feet out" in her path. He both thought "it was kind of funny" and that "it was menacing." Who was funny and who menacing was not clear, until Bruce declared a position in that unspoken debate, saying, "Serves him right!" Dennis immediately agreed. ("Yeah. It really did. . . . He's a jerk.") But then he followed that declaration with a comment that allowed for the opposite possibility, by poking fun at the way Minnijean and the others called for protection. ("They were always going, 'Muh guawd.'") It was, he recalled with a chuckle, what he and his friends considered (back then; he still distanced his present attitude from his past one) "an interesting joke."

On the one hand, Dennis agreed with Diane that seemingly aggressive actions directed at the black students were in actuality innocent fun. He cited his own behavior as proof: he was intent simply on "cuttin' up," seeking to be "at the front of the class most of the time." He was not hostile back then, and is not resentful now: "I didn't get offended by the book. I just read it to see if I was in it."

Very subtly, however, he argued with his wife's tone of voice. Where she was indignant, he was sympathetic. It was understandable that the Nine might misinterpret such innocent behavior by the white students, given their outsider status in the school. Although in our private talk he described himself as "an insider white guy" who would naturally see things very differently from a black newcomer, he never made that sympathetic understanding explicit at the dinner table. But he did from time to time suggest that he held a more analytic view of matters than his friends.

But there was another side to Dennis's narrative. In this version, Dennis disputed the truthfulness of Melba's book. He cast doubt on Melba's account of the frequency of incidents. Starting out to suggest that there might be an alternative explanation to outright dishonesty ("Either, one, was making it up. Because . . ."), he instead got caught up in an escalating indictment of Melba's account and never returned to say what "two" might be.

In building the case against Melba, Nancy led the charge, while Dennis, remaining a bit too devil-may-care to share Nancy's indignation and from time to time resisting her momentum ("I don't know that there's a right or wrong here"), nonetheless helped it along. Nancy's position was utterly clear. Melba lied and falsely accused the white students of tormenting her. Nancy was dead set against Melba's version. "I want to ask Dennis something," she said at a key moment in the considerations, stopping the show. Referring to the sophistication of Melba's journal, Nancy asked rhetorically, "Did you write like that when you were fifteen?" Dennis responded with a characteristic joke—"Hell, no! I couldn't write. I still can't!"—apparently agreeing with Nancy while simultaneously undermining her implicit argument. Nonetheless, between them they argued that Melba's book was a strategic construct, designed to discredit the white students, many of whom —Nancy included, despite her lark with the parade—deserved credit for human kindness to the black students. They disputed Melba's facts by inference: the federal troops were there to protect them (white tormentors could not possibly have gotten past the guard). Study-hall teachers ran a tight ship and allowed no misbehavior. (Melba's description of harassment violated Nancy's experience of discipline, although here again Dennis exempted himself from complicity in the argument by mentioning that he didn't do study hall that year.) The principal used corporal punishment which controlled untoward aggression by the boys. (Nobody had the courage to defy the fierceness of the administrators and coaches.)

Finally, Nancy and Dennis sealed their argument that Melba lied by constructing an explanation of why she would do so: she was hurt and resentful because she was ignored. Dennis (helped by Bruce, who contributed his own experience as a newcomer to Central High) went on to argue Melba's discomfiture to be a normal experience for anyone in her first year at a new high school. ("I think [she'd] of had a whole different outlook . . . if she had had a senior year.") Lest ignoring her be interpreted as a criticism of her white classmates, Nancy cited Melba's complaint that her black friends from Horace Mann also ignored her.

Meanwhile, Annie listened intently to her classmates' talk. Privately, Annie had expressed her sympathy for Melba with great emotion. She had been surprised to learn Melba's side of things, abashed at her ignorance, self-critical about how absent she had been. Now, quietly refilling wine glasses and serving dessert while her friends argued a very different perspective, Annie's silence was eloquent. I wondered in retrospect if she would have spoken at all had I not asked her opinion. Not speaking told an ambiguous story, of self-doubt perhaps, or disagreement she was loath to express openly. When I revealed she'd been sympathetic to Melba in our earlier talk, she agreed emphatically she had been. But she also revealed more doubts about Melba's story than she had expressed to me before: "Well, I had two sides." The very persuasiveness of Melba's account of torment made Annie question its veracity, because she could not imagine anyone having the dedication to face it day after day. "I even thought, Well, are they being paid?"

Like Dennis, Annie went back and forth between sympathy and doubt. "I couldn't understand . . . why the teachers didn't give them more help," she says sympathetically, and then appends the doubt, "if they were really being as hurt as it sounded like." Annie told a story of reality challenged. Her view of the world, that people live essentially private lives, that dedication to an ideal so strong that one would suffer daily injury is unlikely, was upset by Melba's book, and she couldn't decide whether she need change her view or discredit Melba's. While her own life focused on family and work, she considered the possibility that Melba's life was different. After all, she herself felt alienated at Central High, so much so that she barely remembered her senior year. But her openness to a dramatic change of perspective lessened as she listened to Dennis and Nancy. If Melba's ardor challenged her to rethink herself, so did her fellow alumni's dynamic creation of an alternative reality. In the end, she genuinely regretted her failure to befriend the black students.

Bruce's role throughout was that of chorus and touchstone. He inserted comments that both moderated Nancy's and Dennis's critique ("Served him right!") and supported it. In the end, he made explicit the picture of reality his wife's classmates implicitly constructed: "Any time you have that many students . . . some people . . . are going to be kind. . . . And you have the other element that are going to be totally anti. But you hear more about the anti attitude, because that's the thing that sells." Imbedded in this statement is a protest, that the good suffer for the deeds of the bad because of a cynical agenda on the part of those who sell the news.

Many other people not at the table complained in like terms, Jane, for example: "To say you're from Little Rock, people see that cover [of a national magazine], that white girl hitting that black girl that was all over the place. . . . You know, . . . there's a real closeness in our class, but when I saw that on TV, I don't know what, it's just heavy." Seeing themselves as decent and law-abiding, many white citizens of Little Rock feel deep resentment when they believe themselves to be characterized as a racist mob: "If I said I was from Little Rock, I mean, it's like they moved over." The desegregation drama created a harsh conflict in the consciousness of the white students between their lived experience of their school community as inclusive, close, friendly, and, in the main, law-abiding, and a sense, reflected back to them from TV screens and the eyes of college friends from other parts of the country that they were somehow complicit in acts they themselves had not performed. And to some extent they recognized that other acts not performed *did* constitute a sort of complicity. Annie cried, "I wish that I could go back and relive those things and be a friend to them." So also Dennis remembered at the very end of our talk one friend, Georgie, who played ball with a black classmate and warned off his hostile white peers, saying, "Just leave us alone." And Dennis associated himself with a widely publicized act of kindness by his neighbor Priscilla. In each of these statements, there is regret about acts not undertaken, pain about the consequent stain upon the speaker's self-image.

Talk can heal pain. If the white students' common story of innocence and victimization is tarnished by those other memories, the stain may be washed away by talk over a generous dinner table. Well, perhaps it is not altogether washed away, merely bleached. Because memory cannot altogether exclude the conflict these people continue to experience. It is a conflict between versions of themselves, as innocent, as complicit.

The white people of Little Rock are not alone in struggling with this dilemma. It is the prototypic dilemma of white Americans. Good people trying to live decent lives nonetheless participate in events and systems that injure others. Moreover, the decent lives of white people do not stay decent. Life's stresses and disappointments push people off narrow paths. Dennis condemned the boy who intentionally tried to kick Minnijean. But he himself sat very near the boys who blocked her way. He did not implicate himself in their wrong-doing, but neither did he challenge his friends and defend Minnijean—a paradigm of many white Americans' relationship to racism.

In the end, the ambiguity of Dennis's position is perhaps most eloquently expressed by a particular contradiction in his story. "There was so much I guess I missed," he said at the beginning of his account. Yet by the end of the evening he had listed many incidents he had not missed. He saw Minnijean tripped in the classroom, blocked in the lunchroom; he saw one of the girls being whacked in the corridor, another being spit on; he claimed he knew from Melba's book about Jefferson's clothes being drenched in the locker room, but he also thought he remembered who had done it.

Stacked against knowledge he did have, sometimes as memories that popped up in the course of conversation ("I mean, I was in the chili incident"), was his unwillingness to believe that his friends—and perhaps by implication he himself—had acted badly. He appreciated his neighbor's public act of kindness toward Elizabeth and perhaps was troubled by the contrast with his own absence of kindness at other moments. ("I mean, that's how close I was.") His belief in the innocence of his white peers is contradicted by that contrast, by the tenacity of his memory itself. Yet he still cannot judge himself and his friends very harshly. For what they did was so "normal," so much in line with boys' mischief, just "cuttin' up." In the contest between self-critique and "normalcy," the latter wins, although not without at least a little bit of a fight.

Memory itself becomes a forum in which contention takes place. Shaped and re-shaped in the effort to integrate lived experience with theoretical knowledge, Dennis's memory of events he personally witnessed clashed with his assumptions on the one hand and his understanding of Melba's experience on the other. In conversation around the dinner table, I could see the contradictions rise and fall in Dennis's consciousness as his conclusions were negotiated by the act of talk with other people.

■ ■ ■

The gulf between Melba's perceptions of the boys who blocked Minnijean's way or tripped her and the interpretations by the dinner guests of those same events was huge. That they saw things differently was due in part to the fact that they had lived different realities. Central High is a huge school; two thousand students roam its halls between classes, congregate in the cafeteria or the yard for lunch, disperse into several dozen different rooms for classes. Many white students told me they rarely if ever encountered any of the nine black students. "It was quite a thing if you saw one in the hall; there were only—what?—eight of them," said Betsy. For the typical white student, on any given day the probability of seeing an act of torment perpetrated on a black student was small, unless that student was himself the tormentor.

But on the other side of the equation, each black student was alone (guard notwithstanding) amidst a sea of white students all day long. If it were true, as Annie hypothesized, that seventy-five from among the white student body were "belligerent," the probability that Melba or Minnijean would find one of them blocking her path or tripping her in the corridors was high enough to make daily, if not hourly, harassment a likely event. Increasing those odds was the fact, widely acknowledged by my white interviewees, that the active segregationists (however many or few they might have been) sought out the Nine to punish them. Hostile encounters, in other words, which were random events for nonactivists, were not random at all for the black teenagers; they were intentional and focused and thus very frequent.

Adding to the difference in experiences between Dennis and his friends and Melba and hers was a perceptual phenomenon that is common and well documented. When an individual has been the victim of an act of violence, more benign acts by the perpetrator or *by others sharing the perpetrator's identity* carry with them active threats of danger. From listening to the stories of sufferers of domestic violence, we know that the threat of violence remains a vivid reality long beyond the moment of physical danger, coercing victims into submission even when nothing apparent is happening. So, too, the Nine lived with a constant threat of physical hostility. It makes sense they would tend to interpret even ordinary transactions as malevolent, even when enacted by people who were not their usual tormentors. The boy who blocked Minnijean's way in the cafeteria and ended up with chili in his lap apologized later. By all accounts, his run in with Minnijean was atypical for him, but all too common for her.

When Diane suggested that the boys soaking Jefferson's clothes in the locker-room shower were only doing what they did to other white kids as well, and Dennis readily agreed, they overlooked the fact that other white children did not daily suffer the hostility of a mob outside the school, nor the frequent hassling of their peers inside, nor constant controversy in the public domain of media and courts about their right to *be* inside. The actions of less "belligerent" students who indulged in "normal" teasing were, in that context, highly political; whatever the perpetrator's intentions, the significance and consequences of their acts were quite otherwise. Most white students loved coming to school, because it was the place they met their friends, found fun and camaraderie, were liked and welcomed by their peers. For the black students, life was very different; most of the time, they were frozen out of social groupings, called names, glared at or looked through, and, often enough to keep the fear alive, physically tormented. Those few like Priscilla and Georgie who showed them kindness, were the minority; all the others, including those who did nothing, merged into a vast hostile majority.

TEN
Boys Will Be Boys

Imagine for a moment that what Melba reported as her daily experience did actually occur in the spirit in which Diane, Dennis, and Nancy cast it—that is to say, that it was good boyish fun. Such a notion of normal adolescent activity is in and of itself significant. "They were just making mischief," said Nancy as Dennis recollected their classmates' spitting on one of the Nine on the stairway. "I was just cuttin' up," said Dennis of his own boisterous behavior at the time. Remembering "the tall basketball player" in his gym class, Dennis recalled, "I think one time someone took his clothes and threw them in the shower." But again, prompted by his wife, Diane ("It happened in my school"), Dennis explained the prank away as boy stuff: "I think the guy did it because he was that way." Nancy's fond stories of her troublemaking father rang in my memory as I listened to her tolerant description of actions that tormented the black students as boys "making mischief." Even Mahlon, himself harassed on the streets of Little Rock, said forgivingly, "I think it was more kids being devilish than anything else."

That spitting on people, knocking books out their hands, tripping them, blocking their passage to a seat, drenching their clothing during gym—all the incidents Dennis and the others personally witnessed—were regarded as normal behavior among boys says something about what it was to grow up male in that place and time. These acts define a set of expectations that are, in practice, lessons about masculinity, just as frightened, protective moms and their shame defined femaleness for the girls. On the level of interaction (all that "cuttin' up" and being "just that way"), on the level of talk (defining one person as a jerk and another as a clown), and on the level of culture (endless images of men who can take the jostling in a spirit of fun, however they may privately feel), adolescent rough-and-tumble conveys a set of ideas that both describe the world and define men's roles and identities in it.

To be sure, white women students were active in these incidents as well. My point is less about behavior than about interpretations, and therefore about what rules of gender are conveyed. Girls who acted toward the Nine with overt hostility were described by their white classmates as aberrant. ("There were some women that were rabid," Dennis said in our private interview. "I'm talking about, 'crazy nigger' and all that. I mean, I don't care how you felt, that was not the way that you behaved. Ladies in the South did not do that. Only those that were the white trash.") Boys doing the same sorts of things were largely forgiven, because they were seen as behaving normally. At worst they were "jerks," but not rabid white trash. It is this contrast between how male and female behavior was read, between the emotional responses of Helen and Betsy toward Sammie Dean on the one hand, and of Dennis and Diane and Nancy toward the boys who tormented Minnijean on the other, that conveys a set of rules about gender. Those rules, internalized as absolute expectations about male and female behavior, contain within them the building blocks of gender identities, which in turn are racially cast and therefore factor into the process and perpetuation of racism.

We have seen how profoundly gender roles were cultivated in the women alumnae, and how much the associated identities shaped their political choices as they confronted the struggle at Central High over racial equality. Despite challenges in recent years in the form of "gender-bending," ideas about what it means to be male or female continue to be enduring and profound.[1] In fact, though, there are multiple gender identities in America. How to be male or female is deeply influenced by race, class, and national origins. As Dennis and

Bruce talked that night over spaghetti dinner, they reflected their particular training to be men. Often when we consider topics like race and gender, we think of them in terms of subordinate groups. Race applies to people of color; white people seem—to white people, that is—to have no race, because, as I've said, dominance tends to define normalcy, and what is normal is unremarkable. "Who discovered water," asked the child, and the wag replied, "Probably not a fish." [2] So, too, concepts of gender are more often used by scholars to investigate the meanings of womanhood than of manhood. But as I ate that spaghetti dinner and listened to the talk around the table, I was very conscious that many of the stories I heard were men's stories, about the lives of white, middle-class men. Because gender identities are influenced by social location (white, black, Asian, and Hispanic working-class men, white, black, Asian, and Hispanic upper-class men, all learn different lessons about how to be men), the opposite is also true: that rules about how to be male or female embody lessons about status and power, and therefore about race relations. At one point in our conversation, Jane said it clearly as she passionately denounced her adolescent training to be feminine:

> And you know what also makes me angry from a sexist perspective? . . . The cheerleaders and the beauty queens get something, but you don't get recognition for anything else, you know. And that's still the case. And girls' sports, forget girls' sports, you could play tennis then, but you didn't dare do anything else. You know? And I loved basketball, and I guess that was grade school, junior high, and you know basically you were discouraged from playing. So, I knew, I didn't keep it up.
>
> But, you know, the important thing was to be some southern lady. We had tea parties; did you do that in high school? Oh, god!

What it was to be male in Little Rock in the fifties, to be the ones who did get to play basketball, is another strand in the tangled skein which is the unrelenting problem of race in America. Let us pull an end of that thread now and see where it leads.

Facing the Future

"Of course, I can only speak from my own perspective," said **Charles**, another member of the class of '58, as we began our conversation. "And there's a lot of confusion in *my* mind about the whole thing." Despite his confusion, he went on to speak in no uncertain terms about his senior year at Central High:

> But it's pretty obvious to me that this whole situation was blown out of proportion. If it'd been just up to me, I don't think anything would have happened because I didn't see it as an opportunity as far as I'm concerned to advance myself or anything like that. I just saw it as just the way things change. I didn't see it as a big deal. And that was my perspective then and to a certain extent it's my perspective now. I don't think it would have been a big deal unless people had other agendas that they wished to pursue to further their own interests.
>
> I will say I was surprised at the hatreds that came out of this thing. I wasn't aware of that.

Charles was the son of well-educated parents. Not wealthy, his family was nonetheless what Helen and Betsy would describe as "well-heeled":

> I can remember reading about that in the paper and hearing about it. The students that I knew and hung out with, we didn't perceive that to be a big deal. Now, I lived out in West Little Rock; at that time that was where the privileged kids or the rich kids were—privileged in the sense that they lived in pretty nice houses, they didn't have to worry about money too much.
>
> And so most of the kids in that area, I think, didn't feel threatened by integrating the schools and didn't see that as a big deal. In that sense, I was surprised at the things that came out of it. I don't know whether Mr. Blossom [the superintendent of schools] was surprised or Mr. Matthews [the principal of Central High] was surprised or any of the teachers. I don't think Governor Faubus or the people who backed him up were too surprised. And I don't know about the national politicians. I doubt it; I doubt if they were surprised.
>
> I guess it just depends on where you were looking at it. I

think if it had been left up to the students, I don't think anything significant would have come of it. You can always talk about conflicts and struggles, everybody has those in their own lives. You know, if I come from West Little Rock, an affluent neighborhood, and another kid comes from a less well, you know, where he has to throw a paper route before he comes to school in the morning, goes hungry or something like that. I mean those are one set of issues. Some people do better in school than others. Some people have more friends than others. Some people are better athletes than others.

From the beginning of our conversation, Charles couched things in starkly contrasting class terms. It struck me as we talked that, where class was concerned, dynamics of visibility and invisibility worked very differently than they did in the cases of gender and race. Upper-class people like Charles, Dennis, and Jane more often commented on class differences; lower-class people described their teen years as classless. Here was a reversal; those with less privilege were less cognizant of the categories, perhaps because they wished to believe that class, unlike gender and race, was malleable as they aspired to upward class mobility, an assumption of possibility that blurred the lines.

From the vantage point of affluence, Charles was very conscious of distinctions. We met in his large, comfortable office in the tall downtown building where he headed his own prospering business. A large man, gray and slightly balding, he wore middle age with comfort, inhabiting his body as he did his office, contentedly. At the moment, he was leaning back in his swivel chair, casual hands behind his head expressing both relaxation and tension. I sat across from him separated by a large expanse of desk. Charles had not immediately agreed to be interviewed, and as we began to talk, I sensed his continuing reservations.

Charles was surprised by the passions desegregation evoked, and also convinced that the adults in leadership had *not* been surprised. Remembering that surprise is a clue to unspoken theories, I wondered what assumptions of his had been challenged. More subtly, I also wondered what his theory was about the assumptions of his elders. Guessing it all had something to do with class and public protest, I asked:

*Were there any people in your circle who by words or behav-
ior made it known they were opposed to integration?*

Hmm. None of them. None of them jumped up on a platform and espoused any—

We were the Eisenhower generation; we did whatever was
necessary. We didn't have an ax to grind or a cause except to do
business as usual and get the job done. That was our philosophy.
And so that was our goal. Dissension and distraction and things
that take your focus off your goal or whatever you were trying
to do, we didn't like those because it was counterproductive.

We had to go to college, we had to grow up and have families and continue the American dream. It was a big responsibility, still is. That's the way we looked at it, I think. Again, that's
the way I looked at it.

Dennis, too, had talked to me about responsibility as a deterrent
to his joining what he characterized as the "redneck protest." "[The
mob] were the people who really didn't have anything better to do.
Whereas most of the folks I knew, well, they had good work, or they
felt the responsibility of 'OK, so this is going on, but I got a job I got
to do.'" Echoing that sentiment, Charles implied a very elaborate set
of ideas: first, that his life plan was described by a straight line to a
future known as "the American dream," via a road called "Business-as-
Usual"; second, that his usual business was to get the job done; third,
that what drove his adherence to the plan was a sense not of promise
but of responsibility; fourth, that social conflict was a distraction from
his goal, not part of the process of attaining it; and finally, that success
and failure were matters of random individual attributes, not background or conditions. I guessed that he was surprised by his classmates'
passionate opposition to desegregation because he had assumed they
shared his premises and was bewildered to learn that, on some level,
they did not. It was one thing for grown men to demonstrate in the
streets—that was what he assumed the leaders assumed would happen. But it was another thing altogether for his peers to protest inside
the school. They had better things to do and, in Charles's view, no need
to kick up a fuss.

As I mused on these qualities of Charles's philosophy, dramatically contrasting stories swam in my consciousness. I thought about Orval Faubus struggling down from the hills and into power. I remembered Jimmy Karam's depiction of himself scrapping and brawling to defend his mother's honor. Reverend Young's description of cussing down at the big gate and Jerome's story of struggling to increase black teachers' salaries rang in my mind. Other men's stories were filled with conflict willingly embraced.

For them, the alternatives to struggle were not positive, as they were for Charles; their alternatives were resignation and powerlessness. Black men had no choice about engaging conflict; conflict found *them*, in the streets and at the front doors of the homes of white people where their mothers' worked. Poor white men, too, saw conflict differently. If Governor Faubus had used the phrase "the Eisenhower generation," for instance, I suspect his meaning would have been something else altogether. Faubus saw Eisenhower as a force to overcome. The president embodied a struggle that was not a distracting sideline but the main event itself. Faubus believed he had to fight for his objectives, to come down from the hills, engage in the political process, and go to the mat with federal authority. Jimmy Karam, too, embraced conflict as a necessary means to protect his mother's honor and his own dignity.

In contrast, Charles saw no need to fight. To him, others' struggles interfered with his path to his goal. He might need to shoulder responsibility if he were to attain the American dream, but he need not fight for the *right* to that dream. Orval Faubus and Jimmy Karam were of a very different time and background from Charles's. In the space of a generation, much had changed. The year Faubus was the age Charles had been at his graduation in 1958, the stock market crashed. Faubus came of age in an era of depression and uncertainty. The teenage Charles, however, lived in postwar boom times, when all the assumptions for people of his class and race were of unlimited prosperity ahead and, as a corollary, of an entitlement to share in the wealth that was bounded only by one's own personal limitations.

Under these two very different conditions, Faubus and Charles formed different ideas of what it was to be men. Those differences were, of course, compounded by their very different origins. Charles came from West Little Rock, the neighborhood of "privileged kids";

Faubus came from the hills. He grew up in a rough-hewn cabin, while Charles lived in a "pretty nice" house. But given all those differences, they also formed some very similar ideas about the meaning of manhood. Both assumed that men who were smart and earnest possessed the possibility of personal success. Both grew up believing in the necessity of competing on a personal level for that success, although how and why they did so contrasted sharply. Faubus, and even more clearly his crony Jimmy Karam, believed that manhood involved plunging into the public arena and, by stealth or by force, fighting for what they wanted. Charles regarded public events like desegregation as not "a big deal" and expressed his competitiveness in more privatized ways. Charles imagined an adulthood lived in an individualized world, while Jimmy and Orval took for granted their place in a political one.

These contrasts cannot be attributed solely to class and generational characteristics. Many men in Faubus's time led very private lives (witness Jane's father and the other fathers who did not take a stand), and enough of Charles's peers entered the public domain to keep politics a well-populated arena. But there is one unusual quality I wish to capture in Charles's narrative, and that is his implicit belief in the possibility of winning without social struggle, of a well-mapped course toward deeply assumed goals, and the resulting vision of manhood as responsible and predetermined. That aspect of his story speaks to something particular both to the fifties and to his class/race location, and also suggests the sorts of topical issues that we all incorporate in our sense of who we are as gendered beings. It typifies the experience of those who belong to a dominant group. He or she who is without power must fight for it, not he who assumes he already possesses it. More accurately, the dispossessed must often struggle to change the rules by which power is won; those from more advantaged groups are more likely to defend those rules passively, often, like Charles, through a "natural" disinterest in conflicts that seek to redefine social relations.

That Charles was unaware of the particularity of his terms of reference is suggested by his use of the pronoun "we." Everyone his age was "the Eisenhower generation" in the sense that they all stood on the cusp of adulthood during Eisenhower's ascendancy. But the attitudes toward life Charles described did not characterize everyone. They pertained to affluent white youngsters and, in a subtle way, especially to boys. That nuance, I thought, was contained in his wording. Injunctions like "do business as usual," "get the job done," and "stay focused on your goal" suggest a masculine voice, not a feminine one. Women's injunctions tend to take a different tone, to be about relationships, not about tasks, about qualities of feeling, not about focus. I suspected when Charles used the word "we," his mind's eye envisioned white boys.

Our conversation went on to elaborate Charles's experience his senior year. I knew that he had been a football player at Central High. Remembering Betsy's account of her husband's run-in with Minnijean —that he had accepted some football players' dare and shoved her— I told Charles the story and asked whether he could confirm it. He replied:

> Well, number one, let me say I don't believe that story, because ... you'd have to know our coach, number one. I mean, you didn't do anything like that to attract attention to yourself. We had an excellent football team. We played an out-of-state schedule. That was a big deal with us. That was one of our biggest things. We were probably the number-one high-school team in the country that year. And Coach Matthews kept us busy with doing football. And between that and being a student, going to school, we didn't have time to get into things like that.
>
> [Quickly] Now I'm not saying it couldn't have happened. Because kids were always being dared to do something. But there wasn't a big racial thing with the football team. Because athletes generally, they may harbor some individual things, but athletes— blacks and other races I think are accepted in an athletic context, as individuals, too.
>
> No, I don't think the football team was involved in any way with any of the social issues or whatever was going on at the time. In fact, that was sort of an asset; we were in our own little thing, when most of the 101st Airborne and all the furor was going on between Faubus and Eisenhower, we were tied up with our deal, playing football, winning games, keeping our thirty-three-game winning streak intact.

Now, *that* was an important thing to me. I didn't lie around
worrying about the integration of Central High, or where I was
going to be twenty years from now. I worried about making the
football team, surviving the two-a-day practices in the heat, who
I'd take to the dance that weekend, trying to win one of those kewpie dolls out at the state fair for some girl.

It was a ringing description of "business as usual" for boys of his time,
all about remaining focused on his "deal," on the normal senior year
he felt had been promised him.

What was your attitude toward the hullaballoo, people outside the school, the National Guard, and so on? How did you feel
about it at the time?

[Long pause] I'm trying real hard to come up with . . .
[another longer pause] Oh, I think resentful would be the best
word. I mean, I'm taking it from my own standpoint. This was
my senior year, I want it to be a big deal, and, you know, all this
is taking the focus off of me.

Charles speaks of responsibility and single-mindedness. The
apparent contradiction between his comment about the Eisenhower
generation's expectations of the future and the football player's dis-
inclination to worry about "twenty years from now" seemed to me to
be easy to reconcile. If you think you are on a straight road to the
future and you assume there are no curves or bumps along the way,
then you can afford to remain focused on the particular spot you tread
at the moment. Winning football games and kewpie dolls helps pro-
pel you down that road, because the whole objective is to win success.
Competitions along the way trained boys to compete in the world. It
is no accident that there were very few athletic competitions for girls
back then, nor that such contests began to proliferate twenty years
later when women had irreversibly taken a place in competitive sec-
tors of the workplace.

But football and state fairs performed another function: to express
something more immediate and exuberant about the boys' spirits. To
take on the responsibility of the American dream so soon, to be under
injunction to focus on a future so thoroughly mapped out, may well

have created conflicts with a young boy's desire for fun and self-expression. White girls could remain carefree longer in the fifties, a paradoxical privilege of subservience. White boys were enjoined to accept adult roles earlier, and paradoxically they also had more permission to act irresponsibly—to "cut up" or "be jerks." The very act of doing so, whether on the football field, or in the locker room and the cafeteria, both let off steam and trained its energy, because the sorts of sport allowed to boys under rules of "normalcy" all involved tolerance of discomfort and all were exercises in coercive power. Charles wanted to concentrate on "surviving the two-a-day practices in the heat" as much as "keeping our thirty-three-game winning streak intact." Those agendas merged nicely with the intense dynamics of sorting out "who I'd take to the dance that weekend, [and] trying to win one of those kewpie dolls out at the state fair for some girl." Relations between boys and girls, especially boys' activism (taking girls to dances and winning kewpie dolls) counterpoised against girls' marginality (cheerleading and having tea parties), constituted another (very important) practice field for life in the American dream.

In all these transactions, at the same time that the boys exercised privilege, they simultaneously were being trained to a certain disregard of their own emotional needs. That dynamic was not apparent in their stories of adolescence (which makes sense, since for many that was the last time they could indulge their needs). But it became clearer when they talked about their lives as men. The theme of self-denial was struck in my conversations with Governor Faubus, for instance. He had been talking for some time about pressures and demands on him in the midst of the struggle, and I heard in his story a note of personal distress. I asked him how he handled it:

> *You told me last time I was here that you had virtually no advisers, no one who was close in, in your inner circle. So I would imagine that you had very little support (you should excuse my language) when the shit hit the fan; you were the center of an enormous controversy. I wonder if you could talk a little more on a personal level about that.*

Well, a lot of people when I was first elected were dubious about my capacity and ability to be a governor. Very often in my

life, I've been underestimated. I found out as time goes on, it's a
pretty good asset when you're in politics and in business.

Why do you think people underestimated you?

Because I never had any close associates. I never bragged
what I was gonna do. I never talked big about rosy things gonna
happen. I waited until I got them done, and then I talked about
them.

Faubus immediately connected his ability to operate alone with
power. I sensed that was because he translated my question about support into a question about alliances. Trained to see human connection in instrumental terms, more as a matter of trading favors than
of healing hearts, he thought I was asking him about political support, even though I had clearly used the word "personal." He had no
frame of reference in which to understand my meaning. He went on
to tell me a long anecdote about a political negotiation involving complex relationships with men in different walks of life. I waited patiently
and then asked again:

What about personal support?

Oh, I had my personal friends. But among the big people
and the moneyed people, friendship becomes secondary. If it's
in their interest to go against you, they will. Now I got so strong
politically that even the big special interests got to be good corporate citizens. Because they found out they couldn't beat me in
the legislature.

He passed quickly over his personal friends and moved on to the dis-
loyalty of "the moneyed people." I let the subject go, and we talked on
and on about various legislation he'd engineered and programs he'd
enacted. An hour or so later, however, he made reference to his friendship with one of those moneyed people, Witt Stephens, and I doggedly
returned to the question. He was telling me why Witt hadn't opposed
him on some issue:

Yeah. He'd evaluated it, and he thought I was too strong
politically. He didn't want to oppose me. But there was also his
friendship.

How did that friendship operate? Did you socialize with him? Did you talk on the telephone? What kind of contact did you have?

Once in a while on the telephone; not very often. I never did use the telephone much. But Witt had luncheons at his office, and he'd invite some people he'd gotten acquainted with, right across the state. Legislators . . . business people in Little Rock. And occasionally I was included. . . . And after all this was over and in recent times, he's had me there along with some of my strongest opponents [chuckle], you know to see if we could socialize and get along with each other, which we did. [. . .]

Did you have other kinds of personal contacts with Witt Stephens? I'm just trying to get a sense of the nature of your friendships.

When he had a problem, he'd call me. Sometimes he dealt with his problem with the departments and administrative aides. He was very aggressive in pushing his interests, his industry.

To be sure, a governor's life is not like the lives of other mortals. But it seemed to me Faubus struck a very common note: friendship was hostage to self-interest, his own need for support denied. Faubus lived life in a political frame, and he spoke more unguardedly than most people about power. Witt Stephens made decisions about supporting Faubus based first on an evaluation of his strength, secondarily on friendship. Witt was "very aggressive in pushing his interests." The governor was wholly without censure for Witt's values, because he shared them. Remember his acceptance of Jimmy Karam's loyalty in the same breath that he defined Jimmy as a "groupie." All these men were cronies; the ability to fold political forces seamlessly into personal relationships is the definition of cronyism. Faubus talked openly about winning and protecting power as his primary objectives in life, and that is understandable for a politician. Politics, after all, is about the exercise of power. But there are many ways to view and to transact power, and the world of modern politics selects for one set of these. That set is characteristic of a deeper social dynamic, one seated in adversarial relations in the context of hierarchies. We "run" for office, unlike some societies where people "stand" for office. We "win" elections, "fight" for legislation, "twist arms" to amass votes. It is conceivable that disagreements could be handled very differently, by dialogue and persuasion, by creative searches for third alternatives. Participatory democracy need not conflict with representation; the road to office need not be paved with wealth. The system within which politicians must work, therefore, is a particular one; it is not naturally ordained even though it appears to be so because it has become so normalized. The dynamics of that system—contests for power based more on criteria of candidates' personhood than on their performances, negotiations of programs based more on the perpetuation of position than on principle—seem normal to us, in part because they reflect ways of being in society that we take for granted.

I suggest that those ways of being are deeply imbedded in ideas of masculinity, and therefore they appear utterly normal beyond the practice of politics. Politicians, like football players, can be read as prototypes of maleness, not as men necessarily live it but as they internalize the rules. When Charles spoke about power, he did so in more veiled ways than Faubus. But it inhabited his view of himself and others just as surely. "Some people do better in school than others. Some people have more friends than others. Some people are better athletes than others." Each of these statements defined a set of powers that a person might have, either by virtue of social position ("... if I come from West Little Rock, an affluent neighborhood, and another kid comes from a less well ...") or by individual character. His very first comment about the desegregation struggle assumed that those who protested "saw it as an opportunity ... to advance" themselves.[3]

While Faubus was speaking of his political friendships in instrumental terms, I thought about his earlier statements about another set of buddies. "Those fellows are looking down on me, up there, that lost their lives. And they say, Yeah, look what we died for, and you son of a bitch, you're betraying us, you know, by taking up with these things." Only in the context of war did Faubus see himself as bonded by ties of loyalty so strong that they could (or should) determine his personal morality. War is an extreme forum in which men learn about manhood—both about displacing empathy for others enough to kill, and about establishing empathy enough to trust someone with your life. Even when men have no direct experience of war, the notion that they could be called upon to soldier is an influence. I remember as a girl during the Korean War having nightmares about being in the trenches and waking up grateful that as a girl I would never be there. If my consciousness was so strongly affected, imagine what boys my age experienced.[4] In fact, most of those boys, Charles, Dennis, and the others, were too young for the Korean War, too old for Vietnam. The men who graduated from Central High escaped combat service, and often even the draft. But connections between a theoretical knowledge of war and everyday experiences brought the lessons home in particular ways. Terry Kupers, a psychiatrist of their generation, for instance, writes about lessons taught by schoolyard fights:

> ... boys are taught on the schoolyard that there are only two positions, top and bottom. Either you fight or you're a sissy. The one who wins is the victor; the loser a weakling. Top and bottom—there is no third alternative.[5]

The boys who soaked Jefferson's clothes in the locker room were laying down lines of power in terms they had been trained to understand and to use.

Between the time when these men were boys and today, major changes in the definition of gender have happened. Women have taken an undebatable position in the workforce. Men now consider a greater range of domesticity to be manly. Along with a larger share of the work of raising children has come a need to have more interpersonal skills, and that need is reflected in, and facilitates, new definitions of relationships between men and women. Those new definitions are often driven by women's expectations of modern marriage: companionship, emotional as well as sexual intimacy, verbal communicativeness, and, above all, equality. The old rules—strong, silent men dedicated to getting the job done (and, incidentally, masters in their own homes albeit occupied most of the time outside them)—suited the needs of men engaged in competitive work situations. War, in a sense, is good training for a life amid the dangers of the corporation or the plant floor. Decisions about trust and mistrust guide one's way through terrain mined with competition. Feeling deeply for others is a perilous mistake.

But the human heart will out, and men so guarded at work need emotional translation and sustenance at home, the traditional role of women like Helen, Betsy, and Sally.[6] As women take on work for wages, they often have less time and tolerance for nurturing menfolk at home, although old habits die hard and too often they carry on in role while accruing thick undercurrents of resentment. Meanwhile, men do more at home, growing more stressed as do their wives. The roles of both grow a little closer to each other, sometimes more in the direction of women's ways of being than of men's, sometimes the opposite. Today, we see the phenomenon of the ruthless woman executive, and also increasingly images of male mothering. At the worksite, large companies adopt team-based structures that require greater interpersonal skills, and they hire expensive consultants to teach those skills at the same time that they downsize employees heartlessly. Men today have more demands on them to communicate, relate, cooperate than before, both at home and at work. Yet they have fewer sources of support, less security, fewer reassurances that they satisfy traditional criteria for manhood that still lie deep inside their psyches in the form of an increasingly archaic, but still relevant, ideology of gender. While all these changes and conflicts develop both internally and in the material world, the old fundaments of social structure remain substantially intact: men still command the lion's share of economic power; women still bear more of the responsibility at home.[7]

"We were the Eisenhower generation," Charles said; "we did whatever was necessary . . . to do business as usual and get the job done." What is necessary is to forego many human connections. What is created is a world in which business as usual is defined instrumentally, as "getting the job done." Attending to injustices—whether they be discrimination toward people of color or the undefined victimization of which so many of my white interviewees complained—has no place along that narrow road to the American dream.

Charles's memory of his agenda as a teenager resonated with stories I heard about the lives of men in their middle years. Together, they reflect an attitude exemplified by their principal, Jess Matthews: that conflictual human relationships are a distraction from the main task, not the task itself. This compartmentalizing of values, objectives, and experiences in which human strife is walled off from individual success and social change from personal security, defines a world in which separations—be they about race, class, or gender—can continue to thrive. By focusing on the task, Charles defended the status quo because he refused to be distracted by injustice; by defending the status quo he made of desegregation "no big deal" and thereby inadvertently abetted the effectiveness of those segregationist students who tormented Minnijean and Melba, even while he disdained them.

Meanwhile, in the process of defending a social order that apparently privileged them by pushing aside the distraction of problems to which they could not relate, Charles, Dennis, and Bruce were continually reinventing themselves as men without problems, men undistracted by their own needs and feelings, men, in short, well suited to the competitive rough-and-tumble of the workplace in which they found themselves. But at the same time they were also preparing themselves very badly to handle social change, and social change that affected them and their families was indeed afoot. Their women classmates may have sensed and feared some such thing long ago, but the men's prescience, blunted by their training to focus on the goal rather than on ephemera like intuition, had failed them. In the event, they were taken wholly, painfully by surprise.

Reviewing the Past

Charles was not present for the dinner party in Saint Louis, in fact had never run with that circle. But many of the themes he struck were very much there that evening. As the guests talked about the twists and turns in their life paths, the conversation inevitably focused on stories of the men's careers. Because they had not seen much of each other over the years, the friends spent a good deal of time comparing notes, especially about why they all found themselves in Missouri instead of Arkansas, a subject which led straight into the heart of the men's stories:

> BRUCE: Little Rock's kind of interesting to me, being that— this is my view of it—unless you were born into a family that had a business, there really wasn't a lot of money to be made

there. That's the reason we came to Saint Louis. We got out of
Arkansas, out of Little Rock, because I couldn't find a job where
I was making the kind of money I needed to be making to support a family. There were many of my friends, I remember classmates in school, came out of families that had a business that
had been there in Little Rock forever. And they expected to pick
up where daddy left off in running the business, you know. I
think that's, maybe that's not that unique, but for that size of
town I think it is. Very little industry; almost none when we were
growing up there.

Dennis was one of those classmates who went into the family
business. He inherited money early in life and found himself without
focus. "I retired for two, three years. I didn't do anything. Ran the
streets, drank a lot. I didn't need to work." Resisting his father's desire
that he enter a profession, Dennis eventually drifted instead into the
family business. Now he waxed eloquent about his good fortune in
managing to be self-employed for most of his working life:

> Except for seven years in my life, I wrote my own paycheck,
> all my life except for when I worked for Uncle Sugar, in the
> army . . .
>
> *Dennis, why is it important to write your own paycheck?*
>
> Nobody can tell you what to do. And you make what you
> are worth. Certainly the tax laws of the United States of America
> are helpful in that regard. And even more so now that there are
> so many write-offs. That's why. And I don't mind taking the
> risks.
>
> The other thing is, when you start talking about retirement,
> I don't know if I'll ever retire. I mean, one of the things we do is
> own real estate, of which somebody right now collects the rent
> for us. But you can just do that as a business until you drop.

I commented on the high rate of failures for small businesses in
America. Picking up on Dennis's comment that "you make what you
are worth," I asked why he thought people so often didn't make it. He
responded that too often people didn't know well enough the businesses
they tried to start. Bruce suggested a more material explanation:

One of the major reasons for failures is not enough cash for your working capital. But one of the other big things is not knowing all the ins and outs of the business. A lot of people get into business, they don't know what they're doing. They don't have the wherewithall to get through it. But you probably got a lot of your, uhh, wanting to go into business from your family, didn't you?

I wondered if he really meant "wanting" or "cash for your working capital."

DENNIS: Yeah. It was the family business.
BRUCE: My family, my daddy worked for somebody else all the time, so I thought that's what I'd do.

Between the lines of this conversation about paths taken and choices made lay a second narrative that echoed my conversations with Helen and Betsy. Dennis and Bruce were overtly talking about why each had chosen a given career. But covertly I thought they were also comparing privileges. Dennis came from a family that owned a successful business, Bruce from a family accustomed to working "for somebody else all the time." Although Bruce now politely described the importance of that fact in terms of his choice of career, I thought about his earlier description of the more material consequences: "Unless you were born into a family that had a business, there really wasn't a lot of money to be made."

Even while citing material factors as a defense of his decision to work for the corporation, Bruce implied that his choice needed defending. He and Dennis implicitly agreed that entrepeneurship was a grander way to go. Indeed, if the paradigm of manhood is all about acts of individualism, then the successful self-employed businessman or professional is the highest prototype of manhood. As if responding to this deeper level of dialogue, Dennis went on to boast, "I always had a company car. I had a company car when I was in college." Perhaps aware of some insensitivity in cataloguing his advantages, however, Dennis quickly, albeit unconvincingly, reassured Bruce that the choice of a corporate route had dignity, too:

I mean, there's some real advantages to working with a big corporation. I saw those in its travel, and its fringe benefits that you don't even have to consider. But still yet, when you travel, they're the ones that tell you where to go. It was fun, but it's something that I . . .

Bruce now interrupted: "All the advantages of working for a big corporation are gone," he said. Soft-spoken as he was, no one at the table missed the emphasis in his voice, and we all fell silent. "What do you mean?" I asked, and Bruce replied:

Because they don't really care about the people that work for corporations anymore. It's just a big game, and you're expendable. Totally. Thirty or forty years ago, that wasn't the case, or even twenty years ago. People were valued for their skills, and if you were with the company for a long time, you had a job. You didn't have to worry about it. I mean, there was probably some abuse of that, but not a lot.

In today's world, I feel sorry for these kids coming into the corporation, because they don't see what it's about, they don't realize that twenty years from now, comes their time and they're going to be out. I really don't understand the mentality of these executive people that run these corporations, because it's no way to run a corporation, just to throw your fifty-year-olds out and bring in some young kids that don't know what they're doing.

Here was the other end of Charles's American dream. Bitterness seeped through Bruce's speech. His assumption back then had been that skill and loyalty would be valued and rewarded by the corporation to which he dedicated himself. Here lay a deepening of Charles's vision of competitive success; a contract was implied: if I shape my life to the interests of the corporation, then I expect the institution to repay me with security and respect. Implicit in this understanding was something quite different from the law of individual achievement. Bruce had assumed there were rules governing the behavior of his employers as well as his own, and his disillusionment was occasioned by their abandonment of the bargain. American men more frequently talk about their individual role in the deal (working hard, being skilled, staying the course) and less often articulate the tacit context for those values, the idea that institutions will play by the rules and hand out the rewards.

I knew from Bruce's hurt and passion that he was expressing a lived reality. "Have you had personal experience in this area?" I asked, and they all laughed. Said Bruce:

> I could almost write a book about it! [laughter]

> *Tell your story.*

> We moved from Little Rock. I always had a job in Little Rock; I was the head of the accounting department at the AMR Corporation.
> DENNIS: Oh, is that right?
> BRUCE: Yeah.
> DENNIS: I'll be darned!
> BRUCE: I was making a piddling amount. I always thought when I was younger, I thought if I ever get to where I'm making ten thousand dollars a year, I'll be in heaven. And I was making ten thousand dollars a year, but I really wasn't happy, we didn't have enough money. I knew that I needed to do something. So I put my name in with some head-hunter agencies.

> And I got an interview here with Better Corporation. I had an accounting background, and I got my CPA certificate. They were looking for someone with an accounting background with possibly a CPA certificate that could come in and be a systems analyst in the data processing group. They had centralized all of their systems and programming here in Saint Louis.

> Well, my last two years with AMR, I was getting into systems design, and I hadn't done any programming, I never was a programmer. And I came down here, and I had a mentor who was the reason I was able to really do, well one of the reasons I was able to really do well in the Better Corporation is 'cause I had a mentor.

> And I spent two years here, and then they wanted me to move to Atlanta and take a managerial job. Which I just thought, that was great, because that's what I really want to do; I want to be in management.

> So I went to Atlanta, and I managed at one time down there. I had responsibility for about seventy-five people. Then we

decided that we really wanted to come back to Saint Louis, and they made a job for me up here.

Earlier, I'd asked Bruce's wife, Annie, who constituted her community in Saint Louis, and she'd sketched an energetic picture of her circle of musicians and artists. Remembering the warmth with which she'd spoken, I listened, moved, as Bruce continued his story of how he contended with the conflicting needs of career and community:

> It's funny how in management in a corporation, I had responsibility for seventy-five people at one time, then all of a sudden I don't have responsibility for anybody but I'm still in management. [...]
>
> In 1984, I'll never forget it, my mentor was kind of graciously booted out of the company, because I think they found out that he had a company that was run by his son that was doing business with Better, and it was a conflict of interest, and they forced him to retire. And he left the company, and there was this guy in Atlanta who used to be an assistant to the governor at one time in Gerogia. They brought him into Better Corporation, and he had these ideas about how data processing should be run. And why, when corporate offices were in Atlanta, why was the data processing group up here, why was it centralized up here? And the president and chairman of the board were always asking questions like, "We're just pouring money down a black hole with data processing, and nothing's happening."
>
> And so in 1986, this was two years later, they decided they were going to move the computer operations from here to Atlanta. And I just throwed up my back and said I'm not going. And they created a position for me here which was just a nothing position. I was supposed to be managerial, but I wasn't really anything.
>
> In 1990, they told me that I was going to start programming. And with no training, and they didn't want to give me any training, and they didn't want to help me at all, they wanted me to program. And then in late 1991, they called me in the office, my personnel director and the big boss and a couple of other people, and they said that I was through.
>
> Fortunately, I was fifty-five years old, and I was ready to

retire. But, that's the way they do things nowadays. You know, I said, "There's gotta be other jobs. I'm a CPA, I've had accounting experience, I have data processing experience; there's gotta be other jobs." "No, there's no other jobs."

The bargain broken, Bruce found himself confronting the unimaginable: unemployment at early retirement age. A part of the failed contract was the demise of his mentor. His mention of this relationship made me think again about how interpersonal relationships work in the public worlds of men. As in politics, they are instrumental relationships, finely cross-hatched affairs of opportunism and heart. Bruce relied on a mentor whose own position was vulnerable, and his departure left Bruce exposed to the impersonality of a corporation that made decisions based not on human loyalties but on the perception that money was being poured "down a black hole."

Where did you go from there? What did you do?

I retired. Well, I've got a small business. I had started a small business in 1986 because I could see the handwriting here. Probably I'm gonna be outta here in a few years and I wanted something to fall back on. So I started a photo processing business, which I still have. I'm in the process of selling it right now.

So you've ended up in the same position Dennis is in, having to rely on your own business?

Yeah. Frankly [to Dennis], I think you're right; I think that's the route I probably should have gone. But see, you look back and you say, "Well, all these people, the corporations, they keep their people on, and they're good to them, and there's good benefits." And it was great benefits. The thing that I failed to see, which, maybe of course a lot of people failed to see, I'm sure, is what most of these big corporations were going to start doing recently here in the last five or six years. It's devastated a lot of people, totally unnecessarily. [...]

There's no more security.

DENNIS: Except from yourself, and that's it.

BRUCE: That's why I think a lot of people are going into their own business.

Caught between the improbabilities of entrepreneurship and the betrayals of the corporation, Bruce described a classic dilemma of the American middle class in the 1990s. Downsizing, the uncertainties of organizational mentoring, the failure of protections promised in return for loyalty, the injuries of repeated dislocation from community, all constituted a tear in Bruce's assumptions about life, about the reliability of his future: "There's no more security." Dennis's conclusion—"Except for yourself, that is"—captures the essence of a lesson he learned well so long ago, a lesson about maleness at its core. That it was also a lesson rife with implications about race became clear with the next turn in the conversation.

I was just beginning to wonder how to bring the conversation back to issues of race when, as if reading my mind, the group did just that. They went on to a more theoretical consideration of bootstraps and responsibility, which quickly raised the topic of affirmative action. I asked what they thought about current controversies over the issue, and there was a silence. At last Dennis said:

> I don't think it makes a lot of difference. Now I really believe, being from the new South, I mean, the [black] agents I have dealt with in real estate, and the brokers to some extent, although there's not a lot, they're good people. I mean, they didn't need somebody to open any doors for them. They just did it. I don't know that anybody needs any doors opened. I'm not sure.
>
> DIANE: They keep fighting for that.
>
> BRUCE (simultaneously): Well, I think you got two sides to this thing. You got a black element that wants the government to take care of them.
>
> DENNIS: There you go.
>
> BRUCE: They don't want any responsibility. Then you got another black element that thinks they're nuts and that they don't want the government bothering them. You know, let us do our thing, we can make it on our own. There's groups now being formed all over the country like this. Like, there's a group here, and they're taking responsibility for the black community and cleaning up a lot of these drug areas and seeing that these young black kids that maybe don't have but one parent or don't have any parents are taken care of. They're really taking responsibility.

NANCY: And I think that's wonderful.

ANNIE: I do, too.

BRUCE: There're two elements. And you've got the Jesse Jackson element that thinks the government owes you a living and needs to take care of you. And then you've got this other element, you never hear anything about them. You don't hear about the responsible black people that are really, "Just leave us alone, let us do our thing, we'll make it." There's a lot of black people that have done well. You never hear about them. All you hear about is the ones that think the government owes them something.

Here again was the theme of responsibility both Dennis and Charles had raised, this time equated with civil rather than state action. "Are you saying," I clarified, "that you don't see a need for affirmative action?"

NANCY: No, I don't.

BRUCE: I think, regardless of what they say, it's a quota system.

NANCY: It is!

BRUCE: It doesn't matter about your qualifications. I've heard so many of these cases, where people are discriminated against, because they had the qualifications—

Where white people were discriminated against?

Yeah. White people are discriminated against.

NANCY: I've seen it happen firsthand.

DIANE: In the system it's easy to get the contracts as a minority in business by joint venture, or being a woman. I mean, I'm also a woman-owned business.

BRUCE: Yeah, I've heard about these deals where they bring in a black or a woman to be a kind of titular head, and they're not really a part of the corporation, but that makes it a minority-owned business.

DIANE: And one out of four contracts had to go to those businesses, and there was a great deal of abuse back when we were in Little Rock last, and those were joint-venture type of things.

I didn't abuse it; I didn't get any contracts.

Nancy, what was the example you were thinking of?

NANCY: Well, it happened when my husband was with a large corporation. This was back in the, oh I'd say, maybe the mid to late seventies and early eighties, you know. The word had come down that they had to hire so many blacks in so many executive positions. And whether or not you were next in line for a promotion was put on the back burner, because a place had to be made for this black individual that was coming in here as an import from another state, you know, whatever. And it happened. It happened. Time and time again, it happened.

Was your husband injured by that?

One time he was, uh huh. And he was very, very upset by this.

In the form you just described? He was passed over for promotion?

Yes, he had already been told the next level was his. He had worked for it, he had earned it, you know. But all of a sudden now, after being told all this, we have new orders in from New York, you know, and this is going to take place, then you will be in line for the next one. OK?

I asked Nancy to tell us the details and, to my surprise, the story had little to do with the headline she'd just given us. Instead, it turned out to be in a category I'd encountered often before, including Betsy's account of her father's career choices and Bruce's explanation of why he'd left Better Corporation. Nancy's story was about the attrition of constant relocation rather than the injuries of racial preference:

Well, when the zone offices closed all around the country, everyone had to go to New York, if you were to keep working for the corporation, everyone was moved to New York. My husband came in one day, and he said, "You know," he said, "they've just jockeyed us all over the country for so many years, and," he said, "I'm up there enough going to . . ." They went every three years, they went back for refresher courses, you know, went back to school, and of course they had a lot of meetings in New York, and everything, and **Ed** told me, he said, "I'm just not going to live there. I'm just not going to live there." He said, "I've got twenty years with this company. We have great benefits; I make great money. But I'm not living there."

So consequently, he resigned. Which he made the decision. And I told him I wanted him to make the decision, because I didn't want to have to live with, "Well, you said this and you said that." Which my husband usually has never been that type of individual. But I didn't want that to ever arise, you know. Because, to me, the happiest time of my life has been my marriage.

So I just stayed out of it. I listened to whatever he brought home, whatever he had to say, and a lot of his business associates would come home in the afternoon, come to our house. Everyone would sit around and talk and try to decide. And it was just a very emotional time, after you've put in that much time. But anyway, he came to the conclusion that the next time he moved it would be because he wanted to. So he resigned.

Contained within Nancy's story of Ed's clash with the corporation was her own story of marriage. She insisted that she didn't herself care where they lived. All that mattered to her was her family; she could take or leave jobs and didn't have a lot to do with the neighbors, anyway:

We sold our home right away, because we didn't know what we were going to do. So we sold our home, and we moved into a townhouse, just to get that feeling of being in that kind of atmosphere. . . .

So we started talking. And our daughter and our grandson were here, so we said, "Well, we'll stay on in Saint Louis." And that's the main reason that we're here, is because of them.

Ed took a new job selling life insurance. Now, it turned out, his boss was in the process of retiring and selling his company to the employees. Hearing where Ed worked, Dennis asked, "Is he going to get to be one of the owners?"

"He doesn't want to be at this stage of his life," Nancy replied, laughing. "No."

"Why not?" I asked.

Well, Ed is fifty-eight; he'll be fifty-nine on his next birthday. And, like I said, we have a lot of things that we would like to do, rather than work. I mean, we've been working since we were teenagers. So we have things that we want to do.

As you know, my health hasn't been all that wonderful the last eight, nine years. And you know, that's why I say, I tried to do, of course, I've done this all my life; you can ask Annie back in school and everything: I try to do every single thing in one day that I can possibly get done. Because I have absolutely no assurance I'll be here to do it tomorrow. So I want to do it today.

I'm used to staying on the go, I'm used to doing something all the time. I sleep very little; I sleep about four hours a night. Because I'm up reading at night. I get up about six thirty or seven o'clock in the morning; I turn my stereo on as loud as it will go, because I love loud music. And almost anything I do I do better to music, you know. I just kind of piddle around my house, and then I'm off to do something. I'm not at home very much, unless I'm having one of my attacks, and I can't walk or [laughs] get around or whatever. . . .

Like I said, we don't want to work until we're sixty-five, seventy years old. We want to play a little while.

Mortality and its twin, a love of life, echoed so strongly through Nancy's words that the group once again fell silent. Dennis reached for the wine bottle and refilled our glasses. "When you were young and starting out," I asked, "when you were in high school looking forward to your lives, did you expect it to be the way it's been?"

NANCY: No, I don't really know what I expected, because back then, I think for most girls, at least the ones that I knew, you expected to get married and have a family. And really, that was your expectation, I think.

ANNIE: It really was.

NANCY: It was just kind of ingrained in us that that was what we were going to do. So I don't really think I had any expectations as far as, you know, business and things like this. After my husband and I were married, I worked for a number of years, and I enjoyed what I did.

Did you work because you needed to financially or because it was interesting to you?

Like I said, I'm never a sit-at-home type person. I mean, you can only polish a doorknob for so long. [laughs] Which I mean, I like to keep a clean house and all that. But that's not my life. I mean, that house is going to be there when I'm dead and gone. And I could care less. So get the house clean and get the hell out of here, is the way I feel about it. [laughs]

But some of it in the beginning was for financial reasons. Because our daughter was ill, we had a lot of medical expenses with her, and everything.

But I always enjoyed working. I've worked quite a bit.

When you think about it now, has it been too much work and too little play?

No, I don't think that for my part of it.

On Ed's part?

I think Ed has worked awfully hard at what he's done to be successful. But he's played a lot, too. He has a good time. He has hobbies. He plays tennis. He used to sky dive. Matter of fact, Ed and I both used to sky dive. I would still be sky diving if I was able [laughs], but I'm just not able to do it anymore. But that was a lot of fun.

DENNIS: You're real daredevils, huh! [laughs]

NANCY: Right, sure! It was just a group we got, we joined it when we still lived in Little Rock. It was quite interesting. We had a ball doing that. We went to Tennessee and some places in Texas, we went to a lot of different states just with the club, just for different meets, you know. So we played a lot, too, along the way.

We've traveled a little bit. We've been to Hawaii four times. We've been to Barbados. We've been to Acapulco. We've been to San Juan, Puerto Rico, twice, I don't ever want to go back there again. [laughter] But we've traveled quite a bit. We've had an enjoyable time.

So, we've worked hard, we've played hard. But you get to a point in your life where you want something other than work. Ed and I had a lot of interests together. So we want to just be together.

Family is the place of refuge. "To just be together" is the reward for all the years of work and disappointment. If men are trained to play on teams but live in isolation, if women are raised in communities of warmth but resigned to leaving them, then enduring human connection, and therefore solace, must be sought in marriage and in children. Buying into an ideology of individualism, men may be able to tolerate alienation, competitiveness, and insecurity in the world. But then at home they need warmth, constancy, and nurturing. In the old middle-class bargain, women were financially supported to stay home in return for their attendance to domesticity, both on material and emotional levels. While it was the idealized bargain of the fifties, it was never altogether successful; many of the coeds' moms were home taking Miltown, their generation's antidepressant, and solitary drinking was a well-kept secret of housewifery. In Nancy's generation, one half of the bargain collapsed. "Back then," she remembered, "you expected to get married and have a family. . . . I don't really think I had any expectations as far as business and things like this." But she had done "business," had worked outside the home. Relieved in part not to be confined to the boredom of "polishing doorknobs," she nonetheless found herself burdened with double duty. Doorknob polishing remained her responsibility, and she was also required to share the task of earning the family living.

For the men of Nancy's generation, there has been a double sense of failure: not only were they unable to support their wives to stay at home, but they also did not achieve lifetime security in the corporation. In many cases, men held their wives, tired and resentful about the "second shift" they must endure, remiss in the nurturing department, and with all the more intensity as they resisted registering fully the self-blame their individualism promoted.

As definitions of gender roles gave way to other realities, as class expectations foundered on rocks of job insecurity, so too did conceptions of race-based rights and responsibilities shift and harden into new forms. How profoundly those changes interlocked became more and more apparent as my talks with the white Central High alumni went on.

ELEVEN
Insecurity and Racism Today

I guess the thing that I resent more than anything else is, it seems to me that the black community as a whole expects the world to give them a living, and the world didn't give me one.

—Sally

The more government gets involved in it the worse it really is.

—Bill

Betsy, Helen, and I were drawing toward the end of our long conversation. Throughout, they'd insisted that they felt no hostility toward the idea of black students attending "their" school back then. Yet, like the friends around the dinner table in Saint Louis, they'd gone on to recount grievance after grievance about African Americans today. At last, Betsy paused thoughtfully and said:

> Maybe I'm antagonistic now. I was not before. I would not have wanted to live next door to one, because I was brought up that way. But I wouldn't have been antagonistic. Now I am antagonized.

Today Central High is thoroughly integrated. Until recently, black and white students attended in near-equal numbers. (Enrollment tipped toward a black majority not long ago.) Central High had then and has now a fine reputation among public secondary schools. Its students regularly win scholarships to the best colleges and universities; its football team consistently wins championships.

But if integrating Central High was successful in academic and athletic terms, clearly it has not managed to open the hearts of Helen and Betsy and Nancy and Bruce to racial camaraderie. What has not happened during these forty years such that Betsy still does not recognize the "antagonism" contained in the statement, "I would not have wanted to live next door to one"? What has happened to cause her to say, "Now I am antagonized"? In her own view of herself, Betsy has become more open-minded, less racist, at the same time she has become more hostile:

> BETSY: I remember, too, when we moved from Little Rock to Atlanta—this isn't so long ago and it seems so funny now, just shows you how you do evolve a little bit—and we looked at this house and we liked it and we were going to put money down on it. I looked out the back yard, and my husband was sitting over, right just ready to sign papers, and I said, "Wait a minute." I saw this black man out there, and then here comes this black woman. And I said, "Is there a black couple live back here?" She said, "I don't know, it could be." And I said, "Really!" Johnny said, "Why?" And I said, "Well, either this is the gardener and the maid just came out, or they live there." And Johnny came over and he said, "We don't want to sign, we'll wait." So we waited.
>
> Now it wouldn't bother me a bit.

> *What's changed?*
> I don't know, unless I've just gotten—
> HELEN: You have. You've matured—
> BETSY:—used to them.
> HELEN:—you were still very young then.
> BETSY: Yeah, yeah. 'Cause that's been fifteen years ago.
> HELEN: You've mellowed.
> BETSY: Yeah, mellowed, that's it, I guess. 'Cause I haven't totally changed, but I have mellowed.

In fact, I thought, it was more the opposite: they had changed but not mellowed. What changed was that now it was no longer about a way of life. ("Back then it was OK. Now, I look back, and I do feel sorry for them.") Now their racial antagonism was articulated less in terms of a social order and more in terms of individuals: "It's like white people, there are some good and some bad," Betsy had philosophized earlier, "and the bad give the good a bad name sometimes even." Through this route of personal hostility, however, the two women returned to a set of statements that were clearly ideological:

> BETSY: I think Helen feels more liberal than I do, but see I always have felt that way, not real liberal. I just really haven't. So we're just totally, not totally, but a lot different.

HELEN: Well, to some degree. Not really. I'm almost hypocritical about it. I say one thing, and then deep down in my
unconscious I cringe when I go to the grocery store and I see a
white girl with a black man. It just galls me no end. I can't help
it and I think, Why? Why? And these aren't ugly people, either.
It's definitely not because they can't get a white boy. I do not
believe [sighs deeply] in interracial marriages. I'm sorry, I do not.

I was struck by the realization that the two friends were discovering things about each other in the course of our conversation.
Apparently they didn't ordinarily talk so deeply about their feelings
in the past or in the present. Over time, they moved tentatively closer
to each other across a breach they had assumed to exist back in high
school. Both women critiqued and simultaneously defended their
deep-seated attitudes. Their ambivalence was not simply confusion;
it was genuinely a case of "feeling two ways." At one moment they tried
to reconcile the contradiction by distinguishing between "good and
bad" people. But at the next, they reconciled themselves *to* the contradiction: "I'm almost hypocritical about it. I say one thing, and then
deep down in my unconscious I cringe...." "I think it's a shame it had
to be that way, but it is."

Seeking more details of that contradiction, and wanting to pursue the subject of race in the nineties, I asked Helen about her son's
feelings. Helen had mentioned her son several times in our conversation, with obvious pride. Now, for the first time in our animated
encounter, she grew still.

"We're supposed to tell the truth, aren't we?" she said uneasily.
Betsy laughed. "My boy's a good boy!" exclaimed Helen. "Let me preface anything I say with that." I promised her I was ready to believe he
is a "good boy" and that she didn't have to tell me anything she didn't
want to. But she plunged on:

You're going to get ideas about me as a person . . . I'm a little
shocked sometimes about my son.
Let me go back a little. I always have to go back a little, I like
to paint these pictures.

She went on to explain that they'd lived in the same place almost thirty
years and that school districts in their area were drawn such that her

son had attended schools that were wholly white. "So my son was never around blacks or anything like that in his formative years," she said. "He didn't go to school with them?" Betsy asked incredulously.

> There was no blacks. That's what I'm trying to say. There was no blacks in Western Hills [the suburb where she lives]. Now they bus them in. But this was even after they integrated, but they did not meet, there was no blacks in the Western Hills school system. And so Stuart was never around them.
>
> Then my father would come and visit, and he uses the term nigger. He doesn't say Negro, he says nigger. And my son, that beautiful little blond-headed, blue-eyed boy, I can remember the first time he said it, it just killed me. And I said, "Daddy! Don't teach him to say that. He's going to have to be around them, and I don't want you teaching him that word." So that was the first that my son, as far as I know, ever heard the word nigger.
>
> As he's gotten older, it didn't seem to affect him coming up through the schools, and not in junior high, but in high school he started being around a few blacks. . . . But it was after he got out and started going to universities (and goodness knows he went to so many of them before he finally settled down) and around black people and all and working, and he has formed his own opinion. Now, you won't mind that I'm talking about my son: he hates blacks! Big time. So I had no fear of him ever dating black girls, I knew he never would. I'm happy that he did not. [. . .]
>
> And I told him he could say that to me in the house, but he'd better keep his opinions to himself out in public. Because they're here to stay, and he's going to have to be around them all his life. He's going to have to learn to not let it show in his face or whatever. I mean, he hates blacks.
>
> But then, my husband does, too. I don't know when this came about. We weren't always that way. I think it's been forced on us. I never thought I was a racist, but [breathes noisily through her lips] I still haven't thought about that yet. I don't know if I am or not.
>
> I never had problems with them till I, particularly where I work now . . . there are unions, and you get 'em in and you're not going to get 'em out. And I resent it very much that I'm working my buns off, and there's one over there not pulling his or her

weight, and you try to get rid of them, and they've tried, and you can't!

"You can't," Betsy exclaimed in agreement. "They'll sue. See, [where] I work . . . it's the same way. And if that were me, you know . . ."

Helen nodded vigorously. "With very few exceptions I haven't met any—they're intelligent, they've got the nohow, they can—That's enough, I've talked too much."

Finally, Betsy summed up their current-time racial hostilities in a voice of sere intensity:

> They think that a lot is owed to them, they do, they think we owe them. And maybe we do, but they're getting more and more, you see it on TV, they're getting, they're getting, they're being given, given, given, and that makes us bitter.

Helen never thought she was a racist, even though she recognized the hypocrisy of her disdain for racially mixed couples. She failed to find the roots of her own attitudes in her parents' beliefs, for in her memory her father never said anything overt and her mother was merely concerned with appearances. Yet she did hold her father responsible for her son's racist language, not recognizing how her own "hypocrisy" may have contributed—not to mention her veiled acceptance of his use of that language. ("And I told him he could say that to me in the house, but he'd better keep his opinions to himself out in public.") Now she recognized *she* may be racist, although she quickly protested "it's been forced on us."

Where she felt it had been forced on her was the workplace, the site in which she did acknowledge her current racial antagonism: "I never had problems with them" until she began to work in an integrated setting. Her complaint, she suggested, is "their" laziness: "I'm working my buns off, and there's one over there not pulling his or her weight." But even more, it was the injustice of the protection "they" received, presumably from antidiscrimination laws ("They'll sue," says Betsy) that evoked her outrage.

That Helen and Betsy moved seamlessly from a discussion of their views on race to stories about their experience of work is not accidental. In today's world, there are three subjects that especially elicit white people's expressions of racial disquiet: the schools, the streets, and the workplace. Indeed, talk about the decline of public education, about violence, and about economic injustices often supplies the coded terms in which racial hostilities are given voice. That is true not only in the South, but all over the country. As Helen and Betsy talked about race in the workplace, therefore, they went from an experience that was very southern to one that is national in scope. Their description of relations between white and black people in the fifties sketched a map of southern social geography, a landscape in which blacks had a well-defined place which in turn defined their own place in society. In that story, they played a role as members of a group: white "middle-class" Little Rockians. When they spoke of their feelings about African Americans today, however, their story was very different. It became a tale of personal competition. They represented themselves, not as settled members of a well-defined social group, but as individual employees aggrieved about injustices they personally encountered. Where yesterday's remembrances were tinged with sentimentality and warmth, today's account was charged with anger and fear and bitterness.

Struggling Upward

Sally expressed that distinction vividly. Months after my first interview with her, we met again, together with her mother and husband. At some point in our conversation, Sally had vividly echoed Betsy's words:

> And all of a sudden, the whole thing is, "They owe us. The white people owe us, the black people." It's like, "The world owes me a living. I don't have to earn this, I have the right to it. I'm black." Well, they don't have the right to it 'cause they're black. I don't have the right to it 'cause I'm white.

I asked for another meeting with her to explore more deeply what she'd meant. On a stormy fall evening, I visited Bill and Sally and her mostly silent mother **Dee-Dee** at the latter's house in an older, modest Little Rock neighborhood. We sat in Dee-Dee's living room over coffee and cake and talked about their various memories of Little

Rock's history. "We used to live right over here, had a pretty little home," said Bill:

> One block from a school. My kids, my oldest one started there, she walked to school every morning, and then in the third grade they bused her to the east side of Little Rock, down south of where you're staying, there on Broadway or Arch, in that area. She was one of three kids in a class of twenty-eight, twenty-five blacks and three whites. Hell, we did, just—
>
> ["Totally black neighborhood," Dee-Dee interjected.]
>
> We, you know, we did what we felt, what we had to do. We pulled up and went to the county. And that's what people will do.

The county is Pulaski where lie the nearest Little Rock suburbs with a school system that is independent of the city's. Sally picked up the story: "Imagine when they call you from the school, and your little third grader's been pushed in the mudhole, you know, by a group of black kids, and she's scared out of her mind."

Sally and Bill's lives read like a paradigm of late-twentieth-century working people. "We didn't have a whole lot," said Bill, "and I made my own way." Sally elaborated:

> You know, you have to work. Everyone wants to start at the top. And so, you know, I picked, I picked it with the chickens [i.e., scratched for chicken feed], it didn't hurt me. It didn't hurt him [gesturing toward Bill], I mean a little hard work, you know. Makes a little bit more appreciation among the kids.
>
> I mean, I didn't have it bad, but I mean when we got married, we didn't have anything. And we scrimped and saved and did without, and he worked two jobs, and I had kids.

Bill worked a series of jobs, in manufacturing, as a trucker, and in the later years of his life as an industrial salesman. At one stage he'd even gone to Law School, "at night, had two kids, with a third one on the way," and dropped out before getting a degree. He'd gone on government loans, they told me, "which we paid back," Sally said emphatically. "Which we paid every penny of it back," Bill echoed.

Sally did more than "have kids." The daughter of a railway worker, she sold retail, worked as a secretary, did light farming.

"Sally went back to school," Bill said, a note of pride in his voice. "And graduated," said Sally.

"Graduated with three kids," said Bill.

Their upward climb started from humble origins. Sally came from town stock, but Bill's people were one step off the farm, which his father had left to join the army. He'd grown up "east of the airport":

> East of the airport, yes, and anytime you wanna go get a look-see at what a real first-class small-town ghetto looks like, I'll take you out there and show it to you sometime. We'll make sure that the car doors are locked before we drive in there. And we used to play with them, one of my best friends who's in business . . . , they have a community grocery store over there, and we used to spend the night over there with them, back and forth, at night playing up and down the street with them.
>
> I used to stay in Miss **Hannah**'s house. Miss Hannah was the black lady that practically raised me, and I spent the night at her house [sometimes]. She used to stand by when I was in my later teens and would get a little too much to drink. She would not tell my momma on me and told me many times, you know, "Don't go home, you come to my house, and I'll call Miss **Thelma** and tell her that you decided to spend the night over here." 'Course Miss Thelma probably knew what was going on. But that was Miss Hannah. I wish she was alive so you could talk to her, 'cause she'd tell you, too, probably what her feelings were about this. 'Cause she used to tell you, she'd say, "We don't, we don't want this."
>
> SALLY: "We don't want to be white anymore than you want to be black."
>
> BILL: "We have this forced down our throats like yours," she'd say. "I don't want my grandkids being bused clear across town." And remember when she used to come out here and iron for us even after we were married, she would catch the bus and come in 'cause Sally was working and I was working, and she'd come over to the house and iron for us.

Sally and Bill knew that I was writing a book about desegregation and race relations. It was not surprising that Bill moved from stories of his family to memories of his relationships with black people in the neighborhood where he grew up, and that those stories formed a defense of their racial attitudes. Over and over in my interviews about Central High, white people protested the injustice of being identified as arch-racists. Again and again people insisted they had been law abiding, and that anyway, people elsewhere were just as bad as they:

> SALLY: And then there are kids like **Melissa**, at the Catholic high school here, was a little black girl here who has the most beautiful voice, in fact she was gonna study at Julliard, and anyway Melissa was, I guess above average, period, not black or white, just above average, and she graduated, and she went north, and she would come back and visit every so often, and she'd come by the store, and she'd stop and she'd talk to us and all, and I asked her how she liked it, and she said, "Miz G., when I finish my studies, and I plan to marry and have a family," she said, "I will come home." She said, "They don't treat the black people up North any better than they do down here, in fact it's worse." She said, "I don't want my children being treated that way anymore," she said. "I'll come home."

Bill followed with a story of his own:

> Well, many years ago I ran a plant for a company headquartered here in Little Rock from Jackson, Mississippi, on a temporary basis until we got a plant manager. And there was an Exxon station not far from the plant that I frequented, and there was a black man that ran it. And he had been from Jackson originally but had moved up North and had gone someplace in Michigan to work in the automobile industry, Flint, or one of those big automobile centers.
>
> And you know, that was notoriously big money, big union money, even back in those days entry level up there was eight, nine, ten dollars an hour, where we were paying a buck seventy-five, two bucks down here. And I was asking him, this has been twenty years ago, so he was probably about my age, early thirties, and I asked him why he came home with all the big money. He said, for the reason Sally just said, he said, "I didn't want my kids to grow up in that kind of mess up there." He said, "This is home." And he said there's a lot more prejudice up there than there is here in Jackson.

Like Bill, Betsy and many other white Arkansas folk invoked Mississippi as the exemplar of what *real* prejudice is like:

> And you know of course, if you've ever traveled in Mississippi, we don't know the meaning of prejudice in Arkansas, compared to what those folks there in Louisiana and Mississippi and southern Alabama are. It's just a whole different world than what we've got right here. But to hear him say that, it always had a profound effect on me, knowing that.

But if Bill and Sally presented their views on race as benevolent, they expressed free-flowing anathema for the federal government, which, in their view, caused all the problems:

> SALLY: [My friend is] one of the teachers at the high school, and she said that the longer she's in it the more prejudiced she becomes. A friend of my oldest daughter's, we saw her in Wal-Mart a couple of days ago, and she teaches in a public school, she said things along the same line of, "The longer I'm there, the more prejudiced I become. I didn't start this way, it just keeps getting worse." . . .
>
> BILL: It's like a snowball, Beth, it just, it started out small and it just, you know, it's gotten bigger and bigger and larger, and the more government gets involved in it the worse it really is. I mean, it started out bad enough as it was, today it's worse than it was thirty years ago. . . .
>
> I don't think it's necessarily black people either, I think that it's the general moral decay of our whole society. I mean, you find the same problems compounded, look at the problems they had in LA. And the problems they've got in Dallas. The problems they've got in, in any other large metropolitan area you wanna look at. They're all the same. I just think that somewhere along the line the federal government has made some grave mistakes in the Little Rock area, and they've pumped untold millions into this mess that they created here, and we still got this mess.

Despite "this mess," Bill and Sally, by their own reckoning, have done pretty well for themselves. They live in a countrified suburb on a sweet piece of land, which they've cultivated and beautified with great creative pleasure. "We didn't have it easy either and it's just, it was instilled in me, it was instilled in my kids," said Bill. "My life is two thirds over, there's not a whole lot that I can do. I'd like to see it be better for my kids and grandkids."

Was it better for their kids? I asked. Were they continuing their parents' upward trajectory? Bill and Sally paused a moment before Bill answered:

> Not all of them have graduated. One has, one's got three years, the other has one year and that's it, but then he opted not to go and we didn't shove him, and we made it available to him, and he's as successful as my other two. He is a production manager in a factory that I'm with.

"But you know, he's more hands-on, he's more geared to that type of thing than he is to academia," Sally interjected—a bit defensively, I thought. I asked where their other kids worked, and Sally related the story of her younger daughter, **Sharon:**

> She's a waitress. And basically she went three years of college and couldn't decide on a major. And decided that there was no sense in going a fourth year because they wouldn't let you major in nothing.
>
> And she went to work. She was tired of us giving her money all the time. She said, "I'm tired of begging off you. I want to make my money in my life." And she said, "Then when I decide what I want to do, I can go back to college because then I'll know, I'm just," she said, "I'm burning out."
>
> So I told her I thought it was a good idea, and she did, and she's working the lunch shift, not every day but a few days a week, when they need her. They give her a teeny salary, and she gets tips. They're not great tips at lunchtime, she's paying her dues. Sometimes she can work dinner, when someone else is gone. She's even bused tables now and then, when nothing else—
>
> And so she piecemeals all these little dollars and two dollars and five dollars together all week long, and that's what she's living on.
>
> And, yeah, we're helping her a little bit because we're paying her insurance for her, but just a little bit. And she's proud of the fact that she can pay her utility bill, and she can pay her rent, and that she can, you know, pay her gas. And she has a little spending

money. And, and she's out there, she's—that's a tough way to make a living. And she's putting it in, and she's not begrudging that she's doing it, because she knows that you have to pay your dues and work your way up the ladder. But she's willing to do it.

As if he'd been listening in on my earlier conversation with Helen, Bill volunteered the comment, "Today, my kids are ten times more prejudiced that I ever thought about being. I never even used the word nigger in my life." "And they do?" I asked. "It's not right, but they use it, and they're very prejudiced." "Why?" I asked. Where had their kids formed their prejudices? Sally recollected a recent conversation with her daughter Sharon:

> We drove past a housing project and there were like three or four young black men, with their shirts off, and they were just sitting around on the porch, and they sat, and we just drove by, and all of a sudden Sharon just got red in the face and she said, "It makes me so mad, I am so mad." And I said, "What's the matter with you?"
>
> And she said, "There they sit, gathering their welfare, doing nothing," she said. "I'm working for nothing, paying my dues." 'Cause she's just gotten out of school, and she's not making much money, and it's hard for her, but she's in there trying. And she said, "And they could be working too, but no, they're sitting on their butt, getting their welfare check."

"I don't blame the black guys sitting on the stoops," said Bill. "That's not their fault; that's our fault. We've let that happen, that's part of what's wrong."

"Why isn't it their fault?" Sally countered angrily.

"Well my god almighty," Bill countered, "it's the way the system is."

"The system doesn't excuse them. There're plenty of people in poverty that will pull themselves up by their bootstraps," Sally said resentfully, citing her youngest daughter as an example:

> She's gonna start at the bottom, and she sees people like those boys sitting around doing nothing, when they could be starting at the bottom somewhere, you know. But it's just not, you know, she's making less than minimum wage, and they could at least make minimum wage doing something.

A long silence followed this breathless speech. At last Dee-Dee, silent until now, chimed in, "Or they could be raking leaves, making four or five dollars for raking leaves."

Bill shook his head reasonably and respectfully disagreed with the two women. The expectation of welfare sapped the determination of poor people to work, he argued. "You can't point the finger at the young black who's sitting on the stoop," he concluded, "any more than you can at the young sorry white doing the same thing. They're going to do what they can get away with."

"I still don't excuse the system," said Sally.

Would Sally and Bill have done "what they could get away with" back when they were starting out? If Bill truly believed it is human nature to take the easy road out, was it then true that he had himself worked so hard simply because there was no alternative? Bill and Sally were people of energy and drive. It seemed unlikely to me that their motivation had been so one dimensional and so negative. They moved toward something, not simply driven by a stinging whip of necessity, but drawn by a vision.

Thinking of the ways traditions of belief and attitude are carried on in families, I wondered whether Bill communicated his moderate philosophy to his children. Had he ever discussed his point of view with his daughter? I asked.

> Yeah, many times. To try to make them understand that, you know, it's not fair to blame all the blacks. But, these kids have had it stuck down their throat so long, and um—

His voice trailed off uncertainly. What exactly had been "stuck down their throat"? I pressed him for an explanation of Sharon's attitude. After all, I reminded him, they'd told me how peaceable their children's school experiences had been, out there in the county. They'd had very few black classmates, and those they had known were middle-class children like Melissa and therefore quite acceptable to them. Where did their resentment come from? Bill responded thoughtfully:

> It's kind of hard to say, Beth, I don't think it came from home. Sally and I don't, we're not vocal about our prejudices. If she's got 'em, I mean, we talk about it from time to time, but not in a

negative term. Mostly I wonder how we can make this better, or wonder why we don't make things better. And not just *my* kids; kids in general in this part of the country are pretty prejudiced.

Like Helen, Bill and Sally made no connection between their own actions, in their case "white flight," and their daughter's "prejudices." After some time, I asked again why they thought their daughter was so angry at African Americans. "Well, I think because when she went to college . . ." Sally began, and Bill quickly interrupted: "That's where I think Dan started picking it up. That's the oldest, and there's seven years difference in their age."

"They see the free ride," Sally declared.

"A free ride in college?" I asked, puzzled. "What free ride do you mean?"

> Well, the free ride as far as, you know, 'course this is all hypothetical, but, the free ride as far as not going to class and, I don't know. I don't know. But she picked it up in college, because I guess, she has a very strong work ethic instilled, instilled, instilled in her. Maybe we instilled it, who knows.

The hour was late, the storm over. As we prepared to part, Sally said thoughtfully:

> I guess the thing that I resent more than anything else is, it seems to me that the black community as a whole expects the world to give them a living, and the world didn't give me one. They need to work for theirs just like I worked for mine. I'm tired of working for them.

After a lifetime of hard work, Sally and Bill contemplate the phenomenon of their children's struggles, and their own, with a good deal of ambivalence. "I'd like to see it be better for my kids and grandkids," Bill said, and that desire is what Lillian Rubin describes (in a fine book about the intersection of class and race, *Families on the Fault Line*) as "the unique and quintessential American promise."[1] "She has a very strong work ethic instilled in her," says Sally of her daughter. "She knows that you have to pay your dues and work your way up the ladder." Sally talks of her daughter's decisions proudly, but pain creeps through her words, and a strong undertow of resentment that Sharon "piecemeals all these little dollars together all week long" to end up with so little. Bill went to Law School at night but could not graduate. What's become of their professional ambitions? What are their disappointments about their daughter's directionlessness ("You can't major in nothing"), about their son's suitability for "more hands-on" work rather than academia?

Through Sally and Bill's determination shine a certain anxiety and a lot of racial bias and resentment: "I guess the thing that I resent more than anything else is, it seems to me that the black community . . . expects the world to give them a living." Why, I continued to wonder, was Sally's resentment directed at black Americans? "I worked for mine," she proclaims. "The world didn't give me a living." Her protestations of pride in her capacity for hard work and perseverance echo meaningfully against her angry belief that someone else refuses to work hard—and can get away with it. Sally's attitude is a mixture of pride in her labors and resentment that she was somehow forced to do them.

It is the final straw, perhaps, that for all that she somehow cannot bequeath her own successes to her children; the world is not giving her daughter a living. Moreover, she has the notion that someone *is* giving "them," a mysterious "them" consisting of unknown young men sitting on a porch, a mythologized "them" seen on TV—someone, she believes, is giving *someone* else a living.

Herein lies a contradiction in the implicit American view of class. On the one hand, success is individualized. On the other hand, we deeply believe we should be able to pass on our hard-won resources to our kids, that our own children, in other words, deserve to inherit our achieved class position. We do not believe class exists when it comes to upward mobility, but we do believe in our right to ensure an advantaged start for our young when we have achieved some privilege.

That Sally and Bill live somewhere on the interstices of these two conceptions is implied by their own confusion about where their family belongs in society. I thought about all those comments I'd been hearing about black people's "place." Where was Sally and Bill's place in today's society? Even on a metaphoric level, Sally's story about her daughter's prejudice expresses dislocation: she and Sharon are passing by, viewing the world from a moving car, while the young black men at whom Sharon rages are firmly situated on their clearly defined territory, the porch. If white working people like these have trouble locating their place, they talk about that fact in terms of rights and privileges, not manners and protocols. In the past, the Central High alumni were deeply convinced—so deeply that they never articulated the idea explicitly—that they were entitled to a share of the country's well-being, that they had a privileged right to an increasing portion of the resources of the economy, not because of who they were in an economic order, but because of who they were in a racial order. Evidence of this privilege was their power to choose to give largesse to African Americans who served them faithfully. Their ability to bestow material rewards as racial actors supported the belief that they would be able to challenge prosperity as economic actors, because the ability to be generous contributed to a sense of power more generally in the material world.

Nowadays, many of them expressed resentment that somehow that belief had been betrayed. Although they had all prospered relatively speaking, they felt far from in control of their material lives. In their view, the power to say who gets what had been taken over by abstract elements—sometimes "the federal government" seemed almost a code for these indeterminate elements—which forced all sorts of things on them: prejudice ("We weren't always that way. I think it's been forced on us"); busing ("We have this forced down our throats"); the presence of blacks ("He's going to have to be around them all his life"); unworthy co-workers ("You try to get rid of them, and they've tried, and you can't!"). They have lost their place in an ordered social hierarchy, control over generosity, the power to launch their children well in life, and what most characterized their emotional relationship to America in their youths, security and a sense of promise about the future. Who is to blame for all that? Sally's earlier remarks echoed in my mind:

> And all of a sudden, the whole thing is, "They owe us. The white people owe us, the black people." It's like, "The world owes me a living. I don't have to earn this, I have the right to it. I'm black." Well, they don't have the right to it 'cause they're black. I don't have the right to it 'cause I'm white.

TWELVE
Victimhood
and the American Dream

I've heard so many of these cases, where [white] people are discriminated against.

—Bruce

Whether or not you were next in line for a promotion was put on the back burner, because a place had to be made for this black individual that was coming in here as an import from another state.

—Nancy

"I don't have a right to it because I'm white." With these words, spoken in a particular tone of voice, Sally summed up an identity and a life plan. She was proud of "picking it with the chickens," proud of her daughter who was "paying her dues." But there was also resentment in what she said. Somehow, I imagined, she *did* think she had a right to something, whether because she was white or for other reasons I didn't know for sure. But reading her remarks against those of her peers, I thought it likely being white played a substantial role in Sally's definition of her rights and expectations.

As I listened to Helen and Betsy, Sally and Bill, the dinner guests and the other white alumni of Central High, I was both moved and alarmed by what they had to say. They talked about their own lives as much as they talked about the history played out at their school, and as much about their views of race now as back then. My role during the interviews was to listen without judgment, and that I could reasonably do because their lives were filled with well-meaning attempts to do the right thing as they had been brought up to understand it. But if I resisted judgment, I could not pretend to hear their stories without emotion. As I listened to these people, loving toward each other and their children, hard working and responsible, speak of African-American people with such deep-seated "antagonism," I felt sometimes sad, sometimes angry, and increasingly concerned. I believed the story they had written in discourse with each other about the experiences of the black students that fateful year of high school was seriously distorted, significantly misinformed. Moreover, that quality of distortion permeated their view of the lives of black Americans now—and of aspects of their own lives as well. After the interviews were over, it became my job to understand what those "mistakes" expressed, what deeper truth they told about an unexpressed reality of my interviewees' experience.

As I reflected on the many hours of talk I'd recorded, I heard again and again fundamental contradictions in the white people's narratives, summed up like this:

- We were not responsible for what happened in Little Rock. Indeed, we were victims of the events.
- We believe in personal responsibility; if you work hard you can achieve the good life, and if you fail to do so, it's your own fault.
- African Americans have greater rights than we white people; they unjustly get rewards they are not owed.

This peculiar mixture of activism, victimhood, and bitterness appeared repeatedly in the stories told me by the Central High grads. Contained within the contradictions lies a web of ideologies about the material world the alumni inhabit and about their place within it, as well as signposts to the dynamics of continuing racial division and hostility in our society. If we are ever to improve the troubled state of race relations that exists in America today, if we are to alter the social institutions that compel racism, then we must come to grips with the mindsets of the ordinary white people who perpetuate it. We must come to see racism not as a sin but as a trap, as a language which is hard to hear, destructive, hurtful, unjust, and therefore too often discounted and overlooked. But using that language, white people express a reality we who seek to undo racism must heed, for if we don't we help to spring the trap, we become complicit in the perpetuation of the very injustices we try to redress.

Mapping the Social World

I start by proposing conceptual tools to address that persistent dichotomy between attitude and social structure dogging the American discourse of race, provoking fruitless debates about whether the problem is one of prejudice or of institutional oppression. In my view, it is both, in intrinsic interaction. Attitudes are artifacts of social structure, the internalization of dynamics of power, which in turn perpetuate those same dynamics. When Betsy spoke of her "antagonism" and Nancy argued that the forces arrayed against the Nine at Central High were just teenagers having fun, it seemed crystal clear to me that their words reflected institutional forces they could not see but had internalized in the form of beliefs and attitudes.

Every human being lives in a social world, in many-layered relationships with others. Every human being also thinks and feels about those relationships in very particular ways. This intersection of psyche and society is poorly researched, in part because so much of psychological theory is focused on individuals outside a social context. Freudian approaches tend to limit the theoretical view to dynamics within biological families; mother and father produce a certain psychology in their offspring by virtue of their genders and the nature of innate instincts and drives. Paradoxically, Freud himself was very interested in how individuals are shaped by social forces. He saw the fundamental drama of psychological development as being about socialization, but because he believed human beings to be bundles of antisocial tendencies, he conceptualized psychological development in terms of taming that which is most animalistic in people, a conflict between biology and civilization. The terms in which he therefore described internal life mirrored that viewpoint. His storyline depicted psychic structures, laid down early in life and relatively static thereafter, unconscious and accessible only through the medium of irrational processes such as dreams, free association, and the projection of early relationships onto an impersonal analyst. While subsequent theorists have sought to use Freud's version of the internal universe to advance social theory, their products have been limited by the vocabularies at their command.[1]

A more useful formulation arose from a different intellectual arena: political action. Anti-colonialists, feminists, black nationalists, and others protesting domination produced theories of internalized oppression,[2] a description of how individuals experiencing power dynamics in the social world come to reproduce them in their own minds and hearts. These theories allow for insight into the most apparent phenomena in the category: colonialist people who identified with their rulers, women who bought into their own presumed inadequacies, African Americans who, under the influence of racist aesthetics, were blinded to their own beauty.

The notion of internalized oppression was further developed by psychotherapists working from a social analysis. A school of thought called Radical Psychiatry focused on it as a cognitive construct.[3] These therapists understand internalized oppression as a way of thinking about self and the world that arises in childhood and continues to be shaped dynamically throughout adult life. Interaction with family is an important source of internalized oppression, but the family is seen as a carrier for particular social relations as well as in its more general biologic relationship to the child. Internalized ideology is formed through a combination of injunctions ("Buck up; boys don't cry!") and attributions ("Why are you crying? You're a sissy!"). Taken together, these messages compel children to socially acceptable behaviors by inculcating certain beliefs and values about the world. The attribution "sissy" defines manhood as unfeeling and, therefore, strong. It also by implication defines womanhood as emotional and, therefore, weak. It also suggests powerful disapprobation to those men who are not real men, who are gay and, by definition, inferior. Typically, in one set of injunction and attribution lie many social messages.

Attached to the beliefs taught in this way are powerful feelings. Shame is central. Shame is the one emotion recognized by many thinkers as being a link between society and individual. Shame is about what others think of you, and its power presumes a need for approval and thus a sensitivity to disapproval so strong that it can modify behavior. In *Microsociology: Discourse, Emotion, and Social Structure*, Thomas Scheff argues that shame is ubiquitous, the emotion underlying many other emotions, and that its force derives from a human need for the social bond.[4] Scheff makes a groundbreaking argument that emotion is a sociological phenomenon, but in an effort to argue the social function of emotion as a whole, he subsumes many emotions within the category of shame, and thus he misses much of the complexity of the social-psychological link. Indeed, shame is more a set of ideas than a true emotion; it is evoked by assumptions about others' judgments which give rise to many different emotions: fear, hurt, longing, anger, resentment, and so on.

Taken together, the theory of the world we internalize is so hegemonic that it appears to be common sense. Contained within that theory are specific instructions about what place we are assigned in a social hierarchy. These instructions are contained in our identities and the roles associated with them. The attributions of a given identity ("I am a white southern woman from east of the railroad tracks") come replete with particular injunctions about how to behave ("You just don't express what you think in public"). Because the world in which social locations lie is highly stratified, with systems of dominance and subordination overlapping and reinforcing each other, the social paradigm offered is one in which power relations are intrinsic. Therefore, the whole package, internalized on both cognitive and emotional levels, constitutes an ideology. This *internalized ideology* is a sort of topographic road map of the social world containing clear signs of how we are to negotiate the terrain, fundamentally accepting the lay of the land, but sometimes seeking alternative routes around its most egregious features.

The construct we internalize locates in our consciousness the intersection of public and private domains. Well beyond spoken messages, the very structure of experience teaches the relevant lessons. I've commented on the significance of where and how black and white young folks encountered people of the other race. For Mahlon the experience was on public territory, on the streets, and it was hostile. For Betsy and all the other white people I interviewed it was at home and was altogether nurturing. Mahlon was threatened and, in a sense, warned off the public thoroughfare, an experience evoking Nancy's description: "We walked on the sidewalk, and if they met us, they got off the sidewalk and walked in the street." But the white children met race in the shape of a warm, complimentary, loyal, helpful servant.

Even when black youngsters like Mahlon lived in protective black communities or in well-functioning biracial environments like Jerome, or when, like Helen, they played with black kids in the country in the summertime, this asymmetrical structure was so universal for children of both races that its significance was unmistakable. To Helen, those playmates were "pickaninnies"; to Jerome, the white boys with whom he played ball were pals/not-pals. The emotional tenor of those two descriptions eloquently describes the map of race relations each child internalized. Again and again, people told me they could not remember any particular message about race relations, but somehow they knew. Said Mahlon, "Even though I was sheltered, you couldn't live here and not know something was going on and what was going on."

Meanwhile, both black and white children were also internalizing a template of the nature of public and private spaces and of the relationship between them. What that template was differed according to the social location of the individual, and in turn helped to define that location. On the most obvious level, white women like Helen learned that home was their dominion and the public world a site for silence and decorum, a place to perform but not to act. For the white men like Charles, however, the public world was their oyster, site of the business they were taught to view as "usual," and a place where conflict was to be avoided. For black women like Marian, private and public spaces merged; white people's homes were their work-sites and in order to make their own homes tolerable they needed to engage in neighborhood political action. Meanwhile, black men like Mahlon sacrificed private lives to play roles in the public domain, achieving success there but eschewing personal credit rather than racial politics for their achievements. Each individual internally located himself or herself in this matrix of gender and race, and was in turn publicly located in a social spot, which might have been contested from time to time but was always clear.

While such internalized ideology serves a clear social function, it also plays a protective role for the individual as well, helping to navigate potential hazards of social existence in a hierarchical world. But there is a large cost. Ideas formed at one moment in life that equip a person to handle specific social conditions become codified—abstracted, rigidified, static—and then impede change at other times when conditions are quite different. In the course of the upheaval they encountered at Central High, for instance, the white students learned from many sources lessons in how to stay out of trouble. Their parents instructed them to avoid the maelstrom by going in the side door; their peers taught them not to speak their minds unless they were prepared to fight for what they believed; their public leaders spun a hegemonic vision that clouded awareness of how familiar actions like hazing take on political meanings in charged social contexts. At the time they learned them, those lessons served them well (and the cause of civil rights badly). But they were fundamental lessons in social powerlessness. Later, when the students, all grown up, were themselves targets of injustice, when they were left unprotected by the removal of mentors, downsized, denied promotions, and so on, they had no faith in the possibilities of protest or collective action, nor had they skills to act effectively in their own behalf in the public arena. As teenagers, they may not have had sufficient power to alter the course of events at Central High, although that's a debatable premise given the impact of youth movements worldwide both before and after the fifties. Certainly, there was little in the culture of the time that would suggest to them their potential political power. But as adults they failed to recognize sources of effectiveness they did have (things like union and political organizing, and collective negotiation), influenced still by lessons of individualism learned earlier in life.

Rather than adults' irrationally "projecting" onto contemporary relationships the experiences of childhood, as psychodynamics would have it, childhood experience models dynamics of competitiveness, submission to authority, and so on, which continue to be very familiar in the grown-up world. What we carry from childhood into adulthood is not so much an unconscious formed in the first years of life, but an emotionally charged paradigm of power and strategies for dealing with power, lying nested in a set of ideas about what to expect in the world beyond the family.[5]

The Postgraduate World of Central High

For the white students of Central High, the expectations of their teenage years seemed clear and simple. They were "the Eisenhower generation," as Charles said, doing what was necessary to get the job done, avoiding dissension because it took the focus off their goal. And their goal was "to go to college, to grow up and have families and continue the American dream." It was a goal they embraced without consideration of alternatives, taking it on even though "it was a big responsibility, still is."

But the reality of the world they were entering was profoundly more complex. Looking backward over the years since graduation, it has been a time of change, decades in which some Americans have migrated restlessly from countryside to city, some from city to suburbia, others from ethnic and racial communities to urban ghettos and individual solitude. Demands for racial and sexual equality have been raised and heeded, at the same time that we've identified things called "glass ceilings" and "underclasses" and seen them stubbornly withstand assault. Class struggle has been replaced with "teambuilding" and "win-win negotiation"—and a vast acceleration in the differential between earnings of those at the top and the bottom of the American economic ladder. Moreover, between the lines of this chapter of American history is written a more subtle and an even more bitter story, of increasing use of street drugs, increasing prescription of psychiatric drugs, decreasing size of households, and decreasing opportunities for entrepreneurship, blue-collar employment, and job security past the age of fifty-five.

"They think a lot is owed to them," exclaimed Betsy. With that simple sentence, she subtly linked her racial antagonisms to economic questions, and thereby to issues of class. Nothing was owed anyone except what they earned by dint of hard work and responsibility. But conversely, *if* one did that work, was responsible, then there *was* something owed: the American dream. I would argue that the two questions Betsy raised—who owes what to whom, and its implicit corollary, what responsibility an individual has for his or her own success—define the nature of economic actors in America. Those two questions are rarely discussed today in any terms other than race. Let us examine the connections more closely.

The myth of Horatio Alger, that every boy (but perhaps not every girl) can work his way to the top, deeply imbues the white American psyche and is central to the ideologies internalized by white youths in the fifties, and still today. Indeed, it creates the terms by which we, men particularly, but increasingly women as well, judge our self-worth. If we succeed in the workplace, then we are successes. If not, we are very sure we are failures in all that matters. What is implied is that the economic actor in America is an individual, that we create our own reality in that arena—which is to say, that he who is responsible to the social agenda deserves rewards.

This theory of meritocracy (the idea that individual merit is the sole criterion for success) is taught to young people on a very personal level, internalized early and well. The Central High grads revealed some of those lessons when they told me about their school. High school was for many of them the essence of promise for the future, that "wonderful, idyllic" place from which anyone could hope to go on to Ivy League colleges and do "very well." This sense of individual promise for the future was compounded by the experience of belonging to a winning group. "Fine athletic teams" contributed to that sense. So did the magnificence of the building: "It was *the* high school . . . , a beautiful school." As I heard stories of their subsequent adult lives, I came to understand that high school was for many the last experience of being clearly and happily part of a distinct and democratic group, of a classless society: "Still, I found it to be where you're all one group, if you have money or you don't, you're still one of them."

The myth of American classlessness is intimately bound up with expectations of individual economic success. We see ourselves, not as members of some group bound to a "place," although in the South of these people's childhood that was, paradoxically, the natural order for people of color. We see ourselves as unfettered humans who can scale whatever heights we are willing to challenge. It is not surprising, therefore, that we don't really know who we are in class terms, that we have only the vaguest of class identities and tend to collapse all classes into one. (Remember my interviewees from very different backgrounds all of whom declared themselves "middle class." Remember Sally, who searched for language and ended up borrowing a signifier from TV: "Probably, oh, I can't think of the names . . . 'Happy Days.'")

In countries with more distinct class systems, a child grows up with a well-defined and more dignified sense of his or her location in a social hierarchy. It is one way of forming social identity, both on a practical level and on a more psychological one, providing signposts to a range of behaviors and expectations, from manners to friendships, to associations, to interests. Class describes a context within which individual acts take place, and therefore a sense of what is individually possible and, more important, what is not. Americans' belief that anything is possible, our deep faith in rags-to-riches as a plausible life plan, at one and the same time requires a diluted sense of the meaningfulness of class and also inhibits understandings of how class is meaningful. Our lack of class identity also helps to isolate us as myths of unlimited opportunity cause us to view others with a keenly competitive eye. Since we can neither measure nor explain our own successes and failures in terms of social location, we watch carefully how we compare to others.

Lacking other signposts to who they were, the class of '58, like other white Americans their age, relied on other definitions of self based more on roles and functions than on social identities. For men, occupation is central to identity—"Who are you?" is often answered, "I am a writer/mechanic/teacher/et cetera"—and accomplishment measures self-worth. Women who came of age in the fifties tended to define themselves in terms of family. "The happiest time of my life," Nancy declared, "has been my marriage." Many of the women I interviewed said clearly that their expectation upon graduating from high school was to marry and follow their husbands "wherever the job led."

There is a strong connection between these gendered self-definitions, indeed, an implied bargain struck between men and women. To work in a competitive world requires a certain disassociation from human qualities like empathy and personal loyalty. If one is to compete, not to mention willingly to be uprooted from friends and community at the behest of an impersonal company, it is not wise to form deep and compassionate human connections. Bonding on a level of projects, fun, shared enthusiasm for sports, provides some human connection. Work relationships may take the form of measured friendships, like Faubus with Witt Stephens more instrumental than loving. But the deeper connections which, I believe, are the true nature of the social bond (and the other side of shame as social control) are sought in an arena distant from the workplace. Home and family are the sites for humanity. Yet people working competitively in corporate milieus have little time or attention to devote to building and maintaining deep relationships at home. In the modern century, therefore, for the white middle-class people who staff the corporation, home and relationships have become the business of women, who consent to another type of isolation in nuclear families, untethered to communities and therefore transferable from place to place. In return, wives like Nancy, focused on their husbands, are supposed to be able to rely on economic support from their husbands.

But in the adulthoods of the Central High alumnae, it hasn't worked out that way. White middle-class women like Nancy and Sally, Helen and Betsy have entered the workforce in unprecedented numbers. Women who graduated from Central High the year it was desegregated are twice as likely to have been employed for wages in their lifetimes as were their mothers. If they went on from Central to graduate from college, they joined a group of fewer than five million women graduates nationwide; by 1995 the pool of women holding bachelor's degrees had almost quadrupled. Over the years they've worked, the female half of the high-school class of '58 have seen their wages increase from sixty cents for every dollar their male classmates earned to seventy-four cents.[6]

As members of a statistical group Betsy and Helen may be doing fairly well, but as individuals they were telling me a different story about life as they experienced it. They did not exactly complain that life was bad for them. But laced through their bonhomie, imbedded in their stories of life since leaving Little Rock, was a sense of disappointment at changes they did not wish and could not fathom. Disappointment, like surprise, connotes some expectation or theory disproved, and it is clear these women's lives turned out very differently from their high-school fantasies. Displaced from home to workplace, in as much need of sustaining relationships as are the men they were supposed to sustain, the women carry with them added burdens from the now-outdated but still highly persuasive training they had for a different role. Their internalized ideology is ill-suited to their actual lives. Strong and feisty as Helen or Nancy may be, they nonetheless continue under the sway of ideas about the importance of body size, rules about sexuality, prohibitions about public expression—the very same mores with which they expressed their condemnation back then of Sammie Dean and Minnijean. "I cringe when I go to the grocery store and I see a white girl with a black man," said Helen. "It just galls me no end. I can't help it. . . . I do not believe [sighs deeply] in interracial marriages. I'm sorry, I do not." Women's sexuality is still the key, where it is bestowed defining social boundaries and hierarchies. The taboo on miscegenation becomes a clear assignment of people of color to the bottom. At the same time it demands of women an acceptance of alienation from their own sexuality, and therefore subordination on the basis of gender. In the fifties and before, the deal was that, in return, women would be economically supported. For the women of the fifties, that bargain has been only partially fulfilled. To make matters worse, the women sympathize with their menfolk's dismay at their failure to perform their end of the bargain. Having been well trained by their upbringing for sensitivity to other's emotional state, the women know how deeply that failure has cut into their husbands' sense of self-worth.

If class and gender identities formed in the fifties have clashed painfully with the reality of life in the nineties, there have also been severe challenges to a third means of locating ourselves in society: by placing ourselves in both real and imagined communities. Being southern was one of these for my interviewees. More specifically, it mattered that they were children of Little Rock, and history, too, helped define them. "Hers is more historical," said Betsy of Helen, and in the next breath discovered her own roots with great relief: "Well, I do have some history, don't I, come to think of it?" Others told me details of their family's migration to America and within the country, before they settled in Little Rock. In one sense, this inclination seemed to me appropriately American. We are a nation of settlers, and how we came to be where we are says something of who we have become. But it does not tell us much about work or money or security or even economic expectations. Stories like these do not have much reality in daily life; they define an imagined community rather than an actual one.

What people describe as their lived experience resonates well with what scholars analyze on a structural level. That so many of the white people in this story left the community of their origins, for instance, is typical of the American experience in the latter half of the twentieth century. Some 43 million Americans moved in 1996, and on average each of us will move twelve times during our lives, more than people in any other country.[7] Ours is a restless population, although restlessness is not really what it is about. Both Betsy and Helen moved because of their husband's career needs. So did everyone at the Saint Louis dinner party. "I couldn't find a job where I was making the kind of money I needed to be making to support a family," said Bruce. "The job calls," sighed Betsy.

In an age of domestic Diaspora, when most people have moved at least once to places away from their communities of origin, Little Rock assumes a symbolic importance. That is to say, the associations Little Rock implies are important for constructing a sense of self and a vision of something desired, however little material reality they may have. To be sure, people occasionally gather together for reunions or to be interviewed by a visiting sociologist. Members of the class of '58 from Boston to Memphis to Los Angeles share memories and traumas. But for most of them, those commonalties add nothing to their store of human resources when they need help with their children, seek companionship to go to a movie, want some extra hands to pack them up and move them to a new house. When people reported having marital troubles or problems with a teenager, they told me most often they turned to religious leaders or therapists. For most, repeated moves or disaffection with the places in which they found themselves contributed to a sense of isolation from community. Some had friends they consulted. But rarely if ever did they turn to their roots in Little Rock, nor to compatriots of their ancestors for help.

Through all these challenges to their sense of self in society, on the levels of class, gender, and community, racial beliefs were reconfigured in new forms and with new emotional consequences. Betsy and Helen, as I've noted, had a very clear, southern-style sense of "place" in both its geographic and its metaphoric senses, and because race was central to that internalized social landscape, it had been in their youths a means of keeping straight on an emotional level the racial hierarchy that was being challenged on a legal one. As such, notions of "place" were a language for social identity for whites as well as blacks. When Betsy said of her family's maid, "They had a place, and that was it, and they knew where it was," she was also saying that she herself had a place and knew where it was. Minnijean "didn't know her place," according to Jane, a place of humility and acceptance, and thereby defined her own position of leadership: she was praised by the world for speaking out in her editorial, yet condemned Minnijean for using the means at her command to speak her piece. Betsy didn't know why she was frightened when Marcy's son appeared at the front door, but her fear defined (on an emotional level) and enforced (on a behavioral one)* a social order which had all the clarity that was lacking in other arenas of life. That order was also invisible to Betsy and to Jane, although not to Minnijean or Evelyn (who said, "They liked us as long as we stayed in our place"). Those social positions which most dominate tend to be least evident to the people who occupy them. Women are more aware of gender than are men, southerners more aware of region than are northerners.

But as the world turned and the women's sense of their own place wavered, so too did their intellectual and emotional construction of their relationship to African Americans shift significantly. How has that happened, and what attitudes have resulted?

---

* In fact, the dynamic of enforcement was more complex. Betsy invited Marcy's son in, albeit hesitantly. Marcy shooed him away. We do not know whether Marcy acted out of an internalization of the white definition of her son's "place," a protective response to Betsy's fear, or her own fear about the consequences of his stepping out of "place." But in any case, adding insult to injury, she was the carrier of the Jim Crow social order.

After the Party's Over

Betsy and Helen's story led away from community, a particularly southern community in which racial hierarchy was central, in which they had little cause to fight for their rightful place, and to a job site in which their rightful place was painfully ill-secured, their experience of class unclear. On one level or another, all of the people who populate this book speak about economic troubles. Helen and Betsy struggle through definitions of class, Bill and Sally painfully recount their hard climb up the ladder toward financial security, Bruce and Nancy speak mournfully of their betrayal in the promised land of the corporation. But there is another theme interwoven throughout, and that is about the quality of their lives: about working hard and playing hard; about being together; about community and roots and identity and investment in the well-being of the next generation. I thought again of the vision I had glimpsed behind Sally and Bill's stories of youth and resentment, and I reflected on Nancy's statement, "You get to a point in your life where you want something other than work. Ed and I had a lot of interests together. So we want to just be together." I wondered if Nancy at the end of her life were not sketching the dream that had motivated Bill and Sally at the beginning of theirs.

All the white people in this book can credit themselves with having made comfortable lives. Most live in homes they own, travel to interesting places, send their children to college, dress fashionably, enjoy hobbies and recreational treats. Yet they portray themselves as victims of something, as people harboring righteous resentment over some injustice. And they suggest that the source of their suffering lies in the black community.

Helen's and Betsy's storyline is that "they" have protection and special privileges, while "we" are exiled from community.

Bill and Sally's text is that "they" have sustenance and care, while "we" work hard without respite.

Bruce and the others at the dinner party weave a tale of "their" freedom from responsibility, while "we" do what we are told only to end up amid the shambles of the American dream.

We could dismiss these complaints as evidence of a psychological fluke, but there are too many white people spinning the same bitter

tale. Nor can we segregate the problem by labeling it southern prejudice. Themes similar in their essentials are struck all over the country.
To dismiss these claims, I believe, is to miss some important truths that
emerge if we ask seriously, without rhetoric, What exactly are they
complaining about? And why do they blame African Americans for
their troubles?

On one level, they do so because of contradictions between the
ideologies they formed long ago and the realities they've lived since.
Hope disappointed is the theme of the emotional story these people
tell. They are weary of constant moves from place to place. They are
bewildered that the resources they've garnered by hard and unrelenting work do not somehow help ease their children into the good life.
They are angry that the corporations they joined with good faith now
betray them, seeming to grant to others privileges they do not themselves enjoy and firing them as they near retirement age. They are
stunned that when they finally reach an age when they expected to
devote themselves to the hobbies and pleasures in which they've
dabbled, they are not sure they'll live to enjoy them.

They've done everything they were told to do—"picked it with
the chickens," gone to school at night, followed jobs and husbands
around the nation, paid their student loans "every last penny"—and
still things have not turned out the way they expected. In the process
of doing all that, they have given up things they've wanted: community, leisure, fun, and family time.

When they talk about these aspects of life, though, there is a
startling difference in emotional tone from the angry and indignant
things they say about African Americans. They complain, but with a
particular flavor, more in sadness than in anger, as if unentitled to their
grievances, as if doubting their own perceptions. There are differences
among them: in general, the men's complaints are more muted that the
women's, the latter tending to personalize their hotter opinions. Bill
blames the system, Sally the young men on the porch. Bruce speaks of
his departure from the corporation in a downcast manner, while Nancy
tells her husband's version of that drama with fire. These differences
of articulation reflect gendered cultures, in which men abstract and
women humanize perceptions, and also differences in how they experi-

ence powerlessness: as an unexpected loss to mourn or an accustomed injustice to protest.

Having followed the beacon of financial well-being away from family and home (not, by the way, a wholly unmixed loss; remember Helen's description of her hometown folk as "introverted snobs"), they found themselves participating in four decades of profound economic change, far from all of it good. They started their careers in a time of economic boom, fueled by wars in Korea and Vietnam which mitigated the effects of a post–World War II downturn. But times turned harder in the seventies and thereafter. I wrote earlier that women's wages relative to men's had improved over the past four decades. In reality, most of that change can be attributed to a decline in men's earning power rather than an increase in women's.[8] A third of all workers were employed in manufacturing in the 1950s, most of them men, most of them white. Today, that figure has dropped under 17 percent, and economists attribute the largest share of the loss to automation (not to foreign competition as popular culture would have it).[9]

Bruce and Ed, however, were never blue-collar workers. They are bedeviled by a new but parallel set of changes: the disappearance of more than three million white-collar jobs. Service jobs began vanishing fifteen years ago, bank tellers replaced by ATMs and secretaries by word processors; now middle management is being decimated, and it is predictable that in the years to come the phenomenon of the vanishing executive will move higher and higher up the chain. "Restructuring," "downsizing," "re-engineering," and most recently the exquisitely euphemistic "rightsizing" have ominously found their way into the vocabulary of the marketplace in a very few years. Computers and new "team-based" management arrangements make obsolete the functions of middle managers who controlled the passage of information and decisions up and down hierarchies. In the past, economists have believed that each wave of automation gives rise to new industries that absorb the workers displaced. In his book *The End of Work*, Jeremy Rifkin, who has long studied the consequences of automation, makes a highly convincing argument that this latest industrial revolution is permanently eliminating jobs. Even when federal unemployment figures are very low (as they are at this moment I write), job insecurity remains very high. "Despite a robust economy," reported a recent Associated Press story, "Californians are working longer, harder and are changing jobs more often.... Among adults who are employed, 45 percent reported working for their current employer for two years or less, while 22 percent had worked less than one year for their employer.... The median job tenure was three years."[10]

Compare this structural view of American economic life with the subjective experiences of my interviewees. They talk about insecurity in their working lives, and they are right: jobs are less secure, especially for older employees. They speak of shock at their vulnerability as managers in America's corporate universe, and they are right: computers are replacing managerial functions, and new-generation machines promise to do so more and more. They express frustration about having too little time for family and fun, and they are right: more and more people work multiple jobs over longer hours than they once did and have less time for leisure and personal connections.

They accuse African Americans (or immigrants or welfare moms) of being to blame, and they are wrong:

> HELEN: And I resent it very much that I'm working my buns off and there's one over there not pulling his or her weight, and you try to get rid of them, and they've tried, and you can't!

> SALLY: And she said, "There they sit, gathering their welfare, doing nothing," she said. "I'm working for nothing, paying my dues." 'Cause she's just gotten out of school, and she's not making much money, and it's hard for her, but she's in there trying. And she said, "And they could be working too, but no, they're sitting on their butt, getting their welfare check." [...]
>   I guess the thing that I resent more than anything else is, it seems to me that the black community as a whole expects the world to give them a living, and the world didn't give me one. They need to work for theirs just like I worked for mine. I'm tired of working for them.

> BRUCE: It doesn't matter about your qualifications. I've heard so many of these cases, where [white] people are discriminated against, because they had the qualifications ...

NANCY: The word had come down that they had to hire so many blacks in so many executive positions. And whether or not you were next in line for a promotion was put on the back burner, because a place had to be made for this black individual that was coming in here as an import from another state, you know, whatever. And it happened. It happened. Time and time again, it happened.

When resources are scarce, competitiveness is an understandable response, although not always the most useful for solving the problem. Good jobs are scarce and getting scarcer. Are more of them going to black workers at the expense of whites? Let us take a look at the particular economic history of African Americans over the past four decades.

Until the end of the Second World War, most blacks were agricultural workers, often sharecroppers, heavily concentrated in southern cotton-growing areas. In 1944, the first automated cotton-picking machine was introduced, and within a very few years an immense migration of black workers from southern farms to northern factories had happened. In the three decades after 1940, more than five million African Americans, close to a quarter of the total black population, had moved north. At first finding well-paid unionized jobs in the industrial workplace, they very soon were hit by the same process of mechanization all over again. Between 1953 and 1962, the manufacturing workforce declined by 1.6 million blue-collar jobs, and black workers bore a disproportionate share of the loss, both because the cutbacks were concentrated in unskilled areas, and because the last hired were the first fired. Black unemployment jumped from 8.5 percent in the early 1950s to 12.4 percent in 1964, while white unemployment rose from 4.6 percent to 5.9. Since 1964, black unemployment rates have consistently been twice those of whites.[11]

It is true that African Americans are beginning to find a toe-hold in the professions and information industries. But they are still severely disadvantaged in terms of how many of them work in those desirable fields and how they are treated once they are there. A mid-nineties census study revealed that 27 percent of white men and women worked as managers and professionals, but only 13 percent of black men and 19 percent of black women. In situations where race was the only variable, in other words where people with comparable degrees held comparable jobs, blacks earned less (about 25 percent less) than whites. Genuine gains have been made by black women in the professions, where they earn just slightly more than white women (about $37,000 versus $36,000) but still somewhat less than black men ($39,000) and substantially less than white men ($50,600) (reiterating the finding that women as a group continue to earn less than men, whether black or white). There are more African Americans with college degrees: about 13 percent now finish college, compared with only 8 percent in 1980. But that compares unfavorably with the U.S. population as a whole, among whom 22 percent have college degrees.[12]

In fact, black family income declined in proportion to white family income in a period of twenty years; from 61 percent in 1969 to 56 percent in 1989.[13] Nearly one out of every three African Americans lived below the poverty line in 1994, compared with only one in ten white Americans.[14] More black men died of cancer than any other population group,[15] and black babies died at rates double those of white babies.[16] African-American women experienced various improvements in their employment opportunities, but still they were half again as likely as their European-American counterparts to live in poverty if they headed families alone, which they did four times as often as did white women.[17]

Although it would be hard to demonstrate by studies, it is not a bad guess that some of the competitive edge white people suspect black people have is real, but attributable less to affirmative action or quotas than to a paradoxical consequence of discrimination. Black workers are cheaper to hire than whites with identical qualifications, a cost-saving bargain for companies which nonetheless continue to reserve the upper echelons for white men (95 percent of senior-level managers of the Fortune 500 companies are men, and 97 percent of them are white).[18] White employees could better protect themselves from the changes afoot if they insisted on an end to discriminatory wage differentials and if they promoted job abundance created by a shorter work week.

The crisis of which Bruce and Nancy complain is real, but they describe it badly. The terms they use were given by an earlier time and a continuing, hegemonic culture built on racial inequality. No wonder that white working Americans, lacking a language for class problems, look for a scapegoat, especially now when worldwide the old languages of socialism and class struggle, never very appealing to most Americans anyway, have failed. In the absence of other ways to perceive and understand a problem, human beings, trying to make sense of the world, seize the means at hand. Concepts of race are deeply imbedded in American culture, constituting a language that works somehow to explain the anomalies created by our classed classlessness. The American system promises a meritocracy; Bill and Sally, Charles and Dennis all described it vividly: you will succeed if you work hard enough and are good enough. All the people in this book have worked hard, but they still do not feel successful because they can neither secure their own futures nor those of their offspring. Control of resources beyond one's wages and possession of inheritable wealth are two criteria by which we might define a certain class position. Why have such hard workers failed to achieve it?

One possible answer is that the system lied: hard work is not necessarily rewarded in America; we are not a meritocracy; there is not endless opportunity for those who try. The problem with that conclusion is that it profoundly contradicts the worldview that motivated the class of '58 and guided them to make so many sacrifices. "We did whatever was necessary," Charles said. "We didn't have an ax to grind or a cause except to do business as usual and get the job done. . . . We had to go to college, we had to grow up and have families and continue the American dream. It was a big responsibility, still is." Packed within the belief that one can make one's own way in life are numbers of other very fundamental notions: that the individual ultimately stands alone; that society is equitable; that each individual stands as good a chance to determine his or her own fate as any other; that human will is the ultimate determinant of reality. To conclude near the end of their working lives that those premises are wrong, that they sacrificed community and fun to pursue a falsehood, is too painful to accept. Internalized ideologies are tenacious. Sally and Bill and Nancy and Bruce search for other explanations.

But the alternative explanation is that right living and hard work *do* lead to success and they themselves are lacking as individuals, that they are not smart enough—or not good enough in some terrifyingly mystified way they cannot begin to understand.[19] It is a very strong element of many Americans' internalized ideologies that our worth is a function of our achievements. To fail, therefore, is devastating; we lose all sense of our right to respect and love. If the first of these conclusions—that the American meritocracy does not exist—is unsettling, the second is intolerable.

It is far more comfortable to look for someone who has stolen the promised rewards. Right at hand are images of black men lying about on porches, co-workers lounging invulnerably in their (well-secured) cubicles, superiors promoted unjustly because of their skin color. Perceptions are often skewed by emotion, and these particular perceptions all contain an important element. The people in them are *not* working hard. Those young men get to sit around all day on a porch, while Sally's daughter is working long hours for scraps. Those young men are together, in their own community, while Betsy had to leave home to follow her husband's job. Those young men are laughing and carrying on, while Nancy and Ed, fun loving as they are, await the day when they need not work hard in order to play hard, fearing Nancy may not live long enough to enjoy it. Envy lurks behind the anger.

And there is a still deeper level on which the people in this book compare themselves to African Americans: the level of rights. Overall, the story told by my white interviewees is a tale of injustice done to their belief in their rights: the right to benefit from hard work, the right to be treated loyally by corporations to which they've given their loyalty, the right to see the fruits of their labors passed on to their children. In the old days in the South, whites had rights to clear expectations, by contrast with blacks who only had possibilities and had to fight to realize them. Whites had the right to be served by blacks, and, conversely, to decide whether or not to be generous in return. Whites had the right to expect a better future, and in return to tolerate "their" presence in "our" school, *if* "they" behaved properly. Whites had rights for precisely the same reason that blacks did not: because of who they were. Now it seems to these people that the equation is reversed. Now blacks have all the rights, by virtue of the fact they are black, while whites have none because they are white. How doubly galling that the change has come about because of something for which they, the whites, are held (unjustly, they believe) responsible, blacks' deprivation of rights in an earlier time.

Moreover, these white people think they are being told that blacks' earlier disadvantages constitute a debt, and ordinary working whites are expected to pay that debt. How have they become responsible, they wonder, when they've simply done the program set out for them back at Central High: worked hard, raised families, moved where they were told, done what they were supposed to? These are the things for which they accepted responsibility—for themselves, not for others. Indeed, they were precisely instructed to take responsibility for themselves and not others, the essential injunction contained in the myth of individualism: You stand alone and therefore can and will be judged by what you do. Although some lived experiences contradict this notion— Bruce had his mentor, Annie her community—nonetheless, it is deeply rooted in the American psyche, lending all the more poignancy to Sally's outburst, "I don't have the right to it 'cause I'm white."

The Central High graduates cannot see their own prejudices clearly (although they sense them on some level) in part because of the mistaken notion that the controversy is about rights. It is not; nothing in the American creed gives white people more rights than people of color. There is much, however, in American history that gives them privilege —a privilege which would trouble most white Americans' conscience, for their identity as Americans still involves concepts of equality and fair play. That paradox is the American dilemma, about which Gunnar Myrdal wrote long ago in the days just before the civil rights movement, and which, on a personal and internal level, is still unresolved. My interviewees could not believe themselves to be privileged and, moreover, they did not feel the spoils of privilege, things like security and leisure. Their lived experience combined with the tangle of ideological beliefs about their country to further bury certain realities. For some people *are* privileged. Inequalities of wealth grow greater and greater in America: in 1997 the top 20 percent of families earned 12.7 times the income of the bottom 20 percent, up from a ratio of about ten to one a decade earlier.[20]

And so Bruce and Betsy, Sally and Helen reverse the statement. Not only do they not feel responsible for racism past, but they feel victimized themselves. If they can't believe the American system of meritocracy has failed, if they can't believe they themselves were inadequate, then what is left is to demonize those they believe to have gotten the rewards they themselves deserve. They know it is not "right" to voice such opinions. They were reared in a genteel southern culture that considered explicit racist expression to be déclassé, the domain of "white trash." They also had positive interactions with black servants and service workers in their youths. Since then, even while direct contact has diminished, becoming confined to workplaces where a certain tension and jealousy prevail, injunctions against racist discourse have been redefined and strengthened. Nonetheless, they give voice to their true opinions piecemeal, at moments of frustration and high emotion, at moments when they most feel victimized.

Talking Code

Over and over again I listened to my white interviewees speak a discourse of race in the coded terms of three heated assertions:

The schools have been ruined by the admittance of African Americans. "I'll never go back again; the school is in pitiful shape," Helen told me. Turning to her friend Betsy, she elaborated eloquently:

> There's not a blade of grass, Betsy. The shrubs are all dead. When I was there, a lot of the windows were kicked out. The beautiful fishpond that was a part of the architecture to reflect the columns and the statues, they finally had to concrete it in, Betsy, so you do not get the reflective of the columns or the statues, and it's cruel now. Because, I mean, that's just the way it is. Blacks, I don't care, there's no grass around their homes.

Glancing my way, Helen said uneasily, "I look at you and I worry that you'll have contempt for me saying that. But that's what I observe."

Sally and Bill did what white Americans do. "We, you know, we did what we felt, what we had to do. We pulled up and went to the county. And that's what people will do." By inference ("you know") and by word ("And that's what people will do"), they declared the naturalness of that act once their child was bused "to the east side of Little Rock." ("Totally black neighborhood," Sally's mother interjected, lest I miss the significance of "east side.") "She was one of three kids in a class of twenty-eight," Bill said in justification, "twenty-five blacks and three whites." Minority status, they implied, is an experience unwarranted to a child of the majority. Nobody enjoys being outnumbered, a familiar position for people of color operating in a white world. But for Sally and Bill the problem was not simply arithmetic; it was about protection and privilege.

That it was about protection was implied by their ultimate justification of the move to the county: "Imagine when they call you from the school and your little third grader's been pushed in the mudhole, you know, by a group of black kids, and she's scared out of her mind." To distinguish ideologically motivated violence from "normal" behavior is difficult in charged times, no matter which side of the experience you are on. Where the dinner party guests were sure that Melba's encounters at Central High were just the usual teasing of teenagers, Bill and Sally were quickly convinced that their daughter's trials were about racial hostility. But third graders do get pushed in mudholes all the time; I remember doing something similar to a dearly beloved but very annoying little boy in my own third-grade class. Sally was so convinced of her racial interpretation that she offered no evidence that the event was racial beyond the identity of those who did it; the point of her story was not that her daughter was pushed, but by whom ("a group of black kids"). Perhaps the more significant point was that Sally and Bill *could* pull out of the school as a way of protecting their child, in contrast to the parents of the Nine, who voluntarily exposed their children to danger in the hope of building a better, safer world for future generations.

Sally voiced the second charge made by my white interviewees: *African Americans threaten white Americans with violence.* Bill and Sally meant to tell me that they were good parents keeping their child safe from physical danger. I did not doubt the genuineness of their protectiveness, but I would suggest that what they protected was a set of privileges to which they believed their child entitled. A discourse of violence lay like rock at the bottom of my interactions with the '58 alumni. It surfaced less in the stories people told of their own lives than in their cautions to me off-tape about how to negotiate my way around Little Rock. Before my first trip there, I contacted an old family friend and asked for helpful traveler's hints, like good places to stay. "Anywhere is fine, downtown or near the university. Just don't stay on the east side of town," he said.

"Where are you staying?" people frequently asked, politely. When I told them I was very comfortably ensconced at a gorgeous mansion in the Quapaw District (precisely in the east side of town), they looked alarmed and said, "Be careful. It's not a good neighborhood."

Yet in the course of researching this book, in all the time I talked with white people about their lives, no one ever told me a story of personally encountered violence. The closest call was Sally and Bill's little girl in third grade. To be sure, people avoided areas where black people congregated. "Anytime you wanna go get a look-see at what a real first-class small-town ghetto looks like, I'll take you out there and show it to you sometime," Bill offered. "We'll make sure that the car doors are locked before we drive in there."

More accurately, white people avoided black men at the same time they welcomed black women into their homes. The theme of violence is laden not only with racial significance, but with gender messages as well and from gender it slides into another question altogether, about rights and debts. If white men are "responsible," black men are shiftless. ("We drove past a housing project and there were like three or four young black men, with their shirts off, and they were just sitting around on the porch.") Worse still, they behave with a sense of entitlement: "It's like, 'The world owes me a living. I don't have to earn this, I have the right to it. I'm black.' Well, they don't have the right to it 'cause they're black. I don't have the right to it 'cause I'm white."

Sally spoke a complex set of beliefs in two simple sentences. She knew she must work hard for what she got; that is part of the myth of the meritocracy. What she resented so deeply was that "they" assumed a right to support that she herself had sacrificed. What she did not say was that she assumed a different right as well: if she worked hard, she had a right to be rewarded. That she had accepted conditions on her right to economic security was an injury to her. I would suggest she was owed a living, not because she was white, but because she was a person.

This question of who is owed what is at root a debate about the basic nature of the human community. It is another aspect of individualism. At its most philosophical, it asks whether we must stand alone in the universe, reliant only on our own efforts (and perhaps those of a mate), responsible for our own fate. Or are we an interconnected society in which one bears responsibility for all? Great thinkers have debated these questions throughout the modern era, and so do alumni of Central High. In the fifties, they bought deeply into the idea of their own individual status. They learned to believe in the correctness, indeed in the moral superiority, of disconnection from community. They agreed to be fitted to a system in which competition determined each individual's right to well-being and security. "And I resent very much," they said at the end, "that there's a black employee over there not pulling her weight."

The third code in which white interviewees talked about race was this: *African Americans are unfairly privileged by welfare and affirmative action.* By extension, white Americans are victimized by black Americans' privilege:

> I guess the thing that I resent more than anything else is, it seems to me that the black community as a whole expects the world to give them a living, and the world didn't give me one. They need to work for theirs just like I worked for mine. I'm tired of working for them.

"I'm tired of working for them." Sally believed she was paying for *their* privilege. She worked hard, was taxed, was convinced she realized no benefits from that levy. Her sweat subsidized their leisure. That equation flew so fundamentally in the face of everything she had been taught that she resented it "more than anything else"—especially since she'd thought she had been working, not for "them," but for her children. Yet her son turned his back on the upward mobility that she and Bill sought in education. Her daughter was waiting tables for almost no money, starting at the bottom just as her parents did. To protest directly the disappointing outcome of her labors would require Sally to question an ideology so deep, to contest social arrangements so powerful—and so powerfully intertwined with her understanding of the world and her self-identity—that she sought another solution to the problem. Her impulses, to protest, to understand, to seek solutions, were human and dignified. The particular explanations she accepted were not.

I have described the dynamics by which Sally located her distress in injustices done her by another, more greatly disadvantaged group, in terms which are specific to a particular time in history. The tangles of identity and ideology involved for her arise out of her historical moment. But the dynamics she exemplifies are far more universal. All over the world, people find themselves pitted against people of other group identities. In moments of felt-powerlessness, some of it perceived, some of it actual, people find control in identities. In turn, those identities and the internalized ideologies in which they are imbedded affect perceptions, creating distortions that divide the races where they might otherwise unite to solve common problems.

THIRTEEN
Building a Relationship
in the Next Generations

See, you have educational apartheid existing here.
                                        —Jerome Muldrew

*My frustration . . . centers around how much effort and how
many people we've put through that process, only to sit in a room
rather than really to enter into a relationship.*
    *I'm wondering how many generations we will lose before we
really genuinely move forward.*
                                        —Mahlon Martin

The world according to the African Americans I interviewed was
a very different place from the one Sally and her peers described. But
there were some striking points of intersection, the most dramatic of
them on the subject of the next generation. When talking about the
children, both black and white voices rang with equal notes of anxiety and grief.

"We had high hopes for the children of the integration process,"
said Marian sadly. "We just thought that things would be much better for the children."

"Both [my kids] went to Central, and it was not a real good experience for them," Mahlon Martin reported. "I worry [about their futures]
every day."

"My life is two-thirds over," said Bill, "there's not a whole lot that
I can do. I'd like to see it be better for my kids and grandkids. . . . Not
all of them have graduated. One has . . . one year and that's it, but then
he opted not to go and we didn't shove him."

"But it was after he . . . started going to universities," Helen began
an account of her son's academic career, but detoured quickly into a
parenthesis: "and goodness knows he went to so many of them before
he finally settled down . . ."

"I was concerned about our oldest son, **Stan**, because he was not doing well in school. He had run away from home once and I knew there was a problem between him and his father," said Dennis's ex-wife. "Stan could make a lot of money if he decides to," said Dennis, sweetly, but suggesting a little of what the problem might have been. "He has talent, and he could any time."

Many of these parents reached for a note of confidence when speaking of their offspring, but in fact each of them communicated doubt and bewilderment instead. Their kids dropped in and out of school, took up the blue-collar trades their elders had worked hard to leave behind, experimented with drugs and unsanctioned forms of sexuality. The parents presented strained grins as, emotionally, they skimmed the surface of their worries.

Parenting is among the most meaningful of human endeavors, and also the most terrifying because it is the very definition of "responsibility." For that reason, emotions evoked by parenting are similar across group barriers; parents of all varieties place great hopes in their offspring and attach to their actions enormous significance. Therefore, problems of parenting have unique potential to elicit a sense of kinship and sympathy between people who are otherwise antagonistic.

Evaluating Desegregation

If the white parents fretted because their kids didn't avail themselves of accessible educational resources, the black parents grieved because of inadequacies in the schools their children did attend. Within the African-American community, a heartfelt reassessment of desegregation was afoot. While no one summarily dismissed the benefits of desegregation, neither did a single black interviewee acclaim the process as a pure good for their children. In this regard, black and white people were in agreement, although for very different reasons. If problems in the schools constituted a code in which white people stereotyped and judged blacks, blaming them for a list of ills, for African Americans the schools were a focal point for assessing recent history, just as they had been for making history in the past.

Marian was a retired teacher and a leader in her all-black community. It was due to her efforts that the streets where she lived were paved. I sat in the front room of her house, one of the many neat, tiny bungalows lining those streets. Beside me was a bookshelf covered with framed awards honoring Marian for her service to the community. Marian was also the mother of seven. We talked about the experiences of her children in the Little Rock school system:

> I have two sets of children, it was about an eight-year span between the two sets of children. So my first set grew up in a segregated school. But the last ones, they were in integrated schools.

> *What differences did you see?*

> Well, my first set of children, they were taught by all black teachers. And the teachers seemed concerned about the children, they worked with the children. There was a lot of competition among the children then, and they just wanted to learn.

> But once the schools integrated and the children started having white teachers, the white teachers did not relate to the black children like the black teachers did. Some of the children resented the white teachers, and they did not do as well as my first set of children did. Because my first set of children really excelled in school, but these last ones who went did not do as well. They did fair, average, but not as well as they could have done.

> *Did that surprise you?*

> Yes, yes it did. Mm-hmm, yes, because we just had high hopes, we had high hopes for the children of the integration process, and we just thought that things would be much better, better than my first set. Because, see, they were raised with all hand-me-downs. But once the schools were integrated, then the children had access to all new materials, to better materials, and it was just a big difference. Big difference.

Jerome experienced the consequences of desegregation from the perspectives of both a graduate of segregated schools and a teacher in an integrated one. As we sat in the counseling room at Central High where he now taught, he weighed the advantages and disadvantages of desegregation for black children:

Right here, we had a desegregated school, supposedly, integrated. . . . And we're segregated within our classrooms, one way or the other [because of] academic skills and preferences on the part of white and black as well. And, of course this is an unwillingness to learn of each other. To me, it is.

He went on to describe to me the failure genuinely to integrate Central High on other levels as well:

Our program in a sense, was better [at Dunbar, before desegregation] in the fact that we taught Negro history, as well as U.S. history and all the social sciences. They didn't teach anything but European history [at Central High]; they didn't teach any Afro-American history. I think they finally got around to teaching some Spanish history—finally! The people of Little Rock School District still have that feeling of, American history, European history, OK, but Asian history, Latin American, African, no. And now when the Pacific Rim has gotten so important, we were way behind as global participants.

I just wish I could serve in a capacity where you could set up an outline of a good program in the social sciences in Little Rock. But it just seems like we don't want to do it. Now, we did add sociology, economics, psychology, and the other social sciences. . . . But the ethnocentricity is there!

I can't understand, I wonder, have we just gone astray on that particular situation, or is this the key, to teach multicultural, or multiethnic education? Is this the key? Looks like the more we try to teach, the more resentful the people get. . . .

I think the people's unwillingness to accept what is happening is a real problem. And we say, Well, OK, next generation will be better because all the old folk will die. Then, those old folks have so ingrained those kids with their prejudices that it is still there.

As we went on talking, Jerome continued to unearth layers of resistance to genuine change. He answered my next question by talking about dynamics that were deeply systemic:

Is there any discussion among the faculty about that problem?

Well, the faculty is divided. . . . And you would think that it shouldn't be. But, the faculty is one of the problems. They try to get around placing black and white kids in the same classes.

You know, you walk through this school this fall and you'll see what I'm talking about. The advanced placement classes are white. . . . And in "gifted and talented" [classes] is, again, up there at 90 percent. And your regular classes, it's the exact opposite. You have 90 percent black in your regular classes, and about 10 percent whites in those classes. Summer school, I just got through teaching it, was 90 percent black.

Are there people complaining about that among the faculty? Is there any discussion about it?

Well, the principal is, he complains about it; he's trying to work it out. But then you have your counselors, and then you have all those complexities dealing with human relations.

Are the counselors mostly white?

Yeah.

Are there any black counselors?

Yeah. Two. You met one in there. You have two black counselors out of eight. You have a school population that's at sixty-five/thirty-five—65 percent black, 35 percent white.

And what is the faculty proportion?

The faculty proportion is 70 percent white, and 30 percent black.

And the administration, also?

No, the administration is three blacks to one white—that's the past year. And, yeah, that's it. See, you have educational apartheid existing here. [laughs] Yeah. [. . .]

And I just say they deliberately try to get around it, and they try to place a white student with [white teachers]—counselors, speaking specifically of counselors in this school, and with the help of the curriculum people downtown, have been able to circumvent this idea of desegregation. Still going on.

It's saddening. I thought by now—I've been in this system thirty plus years—and I thought that we were turning the corner. But seems like it's getting worse.

I've heard stories from recent graduates of Central High School about how segregated social life is.

Yes.

And what you've just told me makes real sense of that. If black and white kids are in different classes, no wonder . . .

. . . they're not social, yeah, they can't talk about things they've done in classrooms. You look at the north side of the campus at twelve o'clock, it's all white, and the south side of the campus is all black. Then you find a few mingling together, maybe, sometimes, in the middle. There again, I thought it would go away, but it hasn't.

It made a lot of sense that it hadn't gone away. The black principal was new. While he energetically tackled some of the problems in the school, he stayed in the job only a short while before controversy overwhelmed him, and he departed for another district. The combination of a system based on different tracks for students of different abilities and the continuing willingness (in Jerome's view) of a mostly white counseling staff to assign white kids to white teachers, doomed efforts to make more meaningful integration happen.

Some months later, I sat in on one of Jerome's classes, and I asked his students how life looked to them in this regard. One white girl insisted she had friends of both races, but most of the black students acknowledged that their lives were very separate. "Everyone has their own cliques," said a boy who was black. I asked how he felt about that and he said, "OK." Someone explained that he hung out with kids who came from his neighborhood, which was not racially mixed. The students were close to monosyllabic; pressing them to talk more fully was an uphill task. At last, one African-American boy burst out:

You know, some whites are more smarter than blacks, but at the same time some blacks are as smart as some whites. Certain people like to hang out, you know, "He ain't that smart," "He all stupid." Some people hang out like this, you know, white or black or whatever.

So, you see some smart people and other smart people [together], not-so-smart people always in trouble, see, you don't hang with them. But I don't think that really matters, it's still, it's still, it's still black and white divided between smart and not-so-smart.

So, I don't think that has anything to do with race, they just say it like it does. The smart people with the smart people and the not-so-smart people with the not-so-smart.

This statement seemed to me to be a prime example of internalized oppression. If the "smart" kids were identified by placement in advanced classes, and if the demography of those classes was overwhelmingly white, then this young man was buying into a very circular reasoning, to his own detriment. Social affinity was based on personal attributes of intelligence, he believed, not race. But the definition of those attributes flowed from a system of classroom assignments imbedded in a social structure that steered white children toward academic success at the same time that it set hurdles in the way of children of color. Race and class are closely associated in America, and children of poverty are less likely to receive the kind of preparation for handling school that those from more affluent families take for granted: books may be lacking at home; parents may have less time or inclination to read; neighborhood peer groups may censure intellectual interests and support nonacademic ones, and so on. Once at a school where the majority of teachers are white, black students must make a cross-cultural adjustment that is not required of white students. Moreover, however unintentionally, white teachers nonetheless carry into their classrooms subtle discriminatory practices; studies have shown that teachers tend to call on students of their own race more frequently, for instance, and to respond to their questions more seriously. "Once the schools integrated," Marian had said, "the white teachers did not relate to the black children like the black teachers did." What the black teachers did was to be "concerned," in her words, "about the children." That focused and nurturing attention was harder for black kids to come by in many white teachers' classrooms.

I remember a story told by a student of mine at the University of California. A creative and sweet-spirited 4.0 scholar, Paul was a young black man from a poor section of a major American city. At age twelve, he was selected for an innovative school program. Participants were drawn citywide and reflected the great diversity of the city. There were some dozen African-American boys included among them.

But by the time Paul graduated from high school, he was the only black male left. No such attrition rate had occurred among any other population group. "I noticed how quickly they expelled us, if we did anything to get in any kind of trouble," Paul said. "The white kids and the girls could do the exact same thing, only we'd be expelled with no second chance." Reading the situation as a challenge, his rebellion had taken the form of a decision to be letter perfect. And so he graduated and went on to the university, taking with him a large rage and a deeply incisive understanding of how racism works.

Were the school authorities implementing a racist policy when they expelled black males but not other students? What they thought and how they ran the institution they headed combined to do serious damage to Paul's peers. It is likely that the individuals making those decisions acted more from fear than maliciousness. When a black boy got in a fight or talked rebelliously to a teacher, they saw, not a child doing what children do, but a dangerous black man in miniature, and they acted to punish the behavior decisively. In doing so, they not only replicated dynamics that lead to a disproportionate number of undereducated black men entering the economy, but they also helped to create the very thing they feared. If they managed to anger mild-mannered Paul, how likely that they caused even more passionate rage in those they expelled.

Dynamics like these, stereotypes influencing institutional policy that in turn evoke emotions and behaviors that contribute to the continuation of the stereotypes, in combination with more direct institutional discrimination, explain why there were substantially fewer black teenagers in advanced placement classes. In turn, that fact was interpreted by Jerome's student as a measure of the black students' "smartness," a categorization that accounted for social groupings and may well have further deflected the "not-so-smart" kids, the ones "in trouble," from acting in ways that would have led to more academic success and thereby challenged the definitions. Round and round the system goes, institutional patterns giving rise to internalized beliefs which are used by those with institutional authority to justify discriminatory policies.

At Central High, even when classroom placement was not based on academic criteria, dynamics tended to keep the races separate, as white parents persuaded white counselors to steer their kids toward white teachers (and perhaps black parents toward black teachers, given Marian's recognition of the hazards involved). Jerome's student commented on the impact of proximity; kids hung out with those they found at hand, in the neighborhood or in the next seat. Diminished opportunities for that kind of intermingling showed up in the lunchtime gravitation to different parts of the school grounds. Added to all these factors happening inside the school were the general attitudes of suspicion and judgment the students brought with them, learned at home and in the larger culture. Little that happened at school counteracted those forces.

Jerome's class actually offered a test of this theory, with some hopeful results. It was part of an experimental magnet program, a concentrated and innovative curriculum in international studies. Designed to draw white students into Central, it mingled the races far more than typical classrooms in the school. The boy who'd commented on smart and not-so-smart kids added:

> I don't think it matters what race you are, what color you are. It's just who you can relate to, who is doing the same thing you are, who you have more in common with. I don't think it matters what color it is.
>
> I am more friends with different people now than I was last year. I mean, I've expanded, I've met new people and I hang out with them more. So I'm still friends with my neighborhood, but—

That dangling "but—" suggested possibilities. Unfortunately, Jerome's class could accommodate only a few students. For too many others, self-perpetuating dynamics constantly re-created and re-enforced segregation and inequity in the school.

Jerome's next comment identified another key part of the problem, adding more depth to the picture and, coincidentally, addressing one part of what Sally and Nancy suspected to be true: that educated black people did indeed have increased choice in where they worked, although not because of the preferential treatment the white grads believed them to be getting:

I think, if we want to make education work, we're going to have to pay comparable salaries to attract qualified teachers. Just look at it now: blacks are beginning to make money, inroads into the middle class, and they're doing that by getting jobs and by starting businesses and so forth. And the people of teaching quality that you had when we began to teach are not, you're not going to get those kind. The guy that's paying the highest salary out here is gonna get that caliber person.

See, we were thrust into teaching. You asked me awhile ago, did I ever think about being something else. Well, economics stopped me. I'm saying that, but I really don't believe that; I believe I could have done anything, if I had the guts to go and do it. But it was a factor. It was a factor.

(I listened with some pain to Jerome's self-deprecation as, in parallel with his student, he wrestled with delineating his own mixture of personal and structural dynamics.)

And that's the same thing that's happening now. It's certainly pulling the black male away from schoolteaching. But when we were [young], in Little Rock, Arkansas, you had three jobs for black people. It was either a schoolteacher, a letter carrier, or a Pullman porter, or you worked as some of that subordinate labor, common labor, unskilled jobs, out there in that area. That would be the job opportunities for the Afro-American in Little Rock, Arkansas, on up to, I'd say, the fifties. This is when the GI Bill helped blacks become more qualified, and the society opened up with the fair employment practices under the Truman administration, and blacks were able to move into, gradually, into these particular areas.

So, you have a drain on qualified black teachers to get in here and teach these kids. I think we're gonna have to really go out and—

You know, they say—and I didn't know anything about this until last year—they say that they've had people that actually try to recruit black teachers, qualified teachers into the public schools in Little Rock. And, I actually don't think they have! I think it's a sham. I think they're just using that for Judge Wright [by whose court the consent decree ordering racial balance in the schools is enforced] or somebody to say, Well, they're trying earnestly to recruit qualified black educators to come to school.

Because, number one, you don't see any evidence. And you don't even know the people who'd even be qualified to go out and recruit people, you know. What are they doing? I don't know.

Jerome grew hotter and hotter as his portrait of the predicament of the schools took on definition. Many of my black interviewees talked about the paradox he articulated: the very successes of racial progress undercut its continuation. Now that talented black youths had more opportunities in life, the black teachers needed to cultivate the next crop of progressive changes were lacking, lured by better salaries elsewhere. To talk about recruitment of black teachers without talking about those economic realities was to Jerome meaningless.

Vanishing Communities

Mahlon echoed Jerome's themes as our conversation returned to issues of community life. Once again, I was keenly aware that some of the underlying problems he named beset my white interviewees as well, and again for very different reasons. Mahlon had told me about the many community influences on his own childhood development (see chapter 2), and we went on to talk about changes in the black neighborhood after that time:

> I can go through the neighborhood now, and while many of them have passed, you can kind of walk through it and see the older leadership, people who stayed in the community, in the neighborhood and provided that.
>
> In turn, you can go into the new neighborhoods now, where we've seen a lot of in-migration from the rural areas, and as a result of folks my age having been given opportunities to move out of the neighborhood, you see decay and you don't see that moral leadership. I think that's part and parcel of many of our problems in our inner cities.
>
> In fact, I found myself saying to Mr. Muldrew [Jerome] the other day [laughs], "You begin to wonder whether integration really was good or bad." And I know a lot of people who think that heresy to even talk about that, but I know a lot of people wouldn't have said that five years ago who are now beginning to really discuss it and wonder about it.
>
> Because when you think back, with the exception maybe of

the church, it was not really integration, it was an absorption of the community into a larger community, and took away many of those institutions, primarily the schools, which had been controlled in those communities and which allowed those neighborhoods and communities to set moral standards and ethical standards, which were different and unique to some extent.

For example, even though everybody (I think this crosses racial lines) misses and now laments the fact that [their children go to schools far from their neighborhoods]—and many are going back to neighborhood schools, particularly at the elementary level, where you actually have some ownership both of the schools but also with the kids in that community. But even though clearly black schools, I think, were inferior in terms of resources provided by the school district, and nobody, I don't think, fooled themselves to think that those schools were not part of the Little Rock School District and that it was bias, generally because of their segregated nature, they were run by minorities, they were part of the neighborhood, part of the fabric of the community and there was a sense of ownership, even beyond the neighborhood level.

For example, Horace Mann High School was the only black high school in Little Rock, and it created an ownership on the part of black adults as well as kids, and allowed for, as an institution, certain morals and ethical standards to be created and implemented and enforced. I think that is missing now. There's not that sense of ownership. And with ownership comes responsibility, and I think that may be the real missing ingredient.

Mahlon echoed an appreciation for the value of responsibility that had been so pervasive in Charles's and other white Central High alumni's stories. But where they talked about it on a moral level, as an individual life plan, Mahlon related personal responsibility to a sense of community ownership, which in turn grew from an institutional reality: who controlled the schools. Power over social conditions, in his view, was a prerequisite for the sort of participation that gives rise to responsibility. He went on to generalize that point beyond issues of race:

I don't think it's particularly minority communities. Number one, it's dispersed, as I mentioned. I no longer live in that neighborhood. I live now out west, I live in a mixed neighborhood....

I think what has happened with integration is, we've taken the moral leadership out of—in large part, not completely, but—out of the minority community. It's kind of like creaming; I mean, those who can afford to get out, get out. . . .

I was talking to somebody the other day and it hits you at some point that the better you educate the kids, the quicker they are to leave. [laughs] By providing the opportunity, you also provide them an escape route. It's not unlike some things I've been reading lately about trying to improve the quality of life in the ghetto, and whether that's realistic, whether ghettos serve the purpose, whether you *can* do that, because when you improve the individual's quality of life, they generally move out. Or is it a holding pattern? Is it a neighborhood, or is it kind of like welfare, where people only are there until they can move out?

And I think, in the neighborhood, if one looks back in terms of what existed then within minority communities, and understanding they were very identifiable entities, the only thing left in terms of an institution within those communities is permanently the church. They don't control their schools. Generally, within what's left in those neighborhoods, there's very little wealth. The wealth has been dispersed with the geographic dispersal of people.

And I'd have to, I guess, hasten to say, I'm not sure the church plays the role, whose responsibility or fault it is I don't know, but if it's playing the role now it played in years back. I think they're beginning to start to do more of that; I know a number of foundations, including ours, have started to look seriously at how we can use the church to do more within the community in terms of a broad array of things.

But I think what integration did generally, and I'm talking beyond schools now, I'm talking about broader definitions, is to pull out of those neighborhoods those things that made them strong. I don't think intentionally, but I think that was the bottom-line result.

I thought about the stories I had heard again and again about white Little Rockians who had lost community as they followed jobs. From their perspective, the loss had been their own. Mahlon, speaking from a very different perspective, suggested the other side of that coin: the neighborhoods white people left behind, not unlike those Mahlon described, were shells of the places the expatriates idealized and longed for. To be sure, community life was different for blacks and whites in the fifties; for Mahlon, neighbors had assumed a much more active mentoring role than they had for Helen or Betsy, out of a sense of protectiveness and identity. The black community, moreover, defined black individuals in a way that was not comparable for whites; when you are a member of a minority group with circumscribed mobility (both socially and geographically), community functions as a tightknit venue for all aspects of life, far more than it does for members of the majority. Nonetheless, the now-lost white communities mattered more profoundly than rugged individualism allows most white Americans to register. "Normal" theories of parenting give mother and father almost all the power to shape who their children become, and with it enormous responsibility. In fact, though, communities matter significantly, in their absence as much as in their presence.

The neighborhoods to which upwardly mobile black people moved were mostly integrated. But what Jerome had called in the old days "salt-and-pepper" areas were now mostly salt with an isolated grain or two of pepper. Mahlon went on to reflect on this aspect of racial change, returning to the question of the schools and calling into question Jerome's advocacy of multiculturalism:

> It will be interesting to me to see where multicultural education takes us. I have mixed emotions about it. Looking back on the history of what happened with integration between blacks and whites, I have some fears. Because I think generally what we saw happen was, with school integration, was an abandonment of black culture and, albeit not conscious, an attempt to force blacks to become part of the white culture. The more they were successful, the more they undid the black folks and regrettably everybody wasn't able to make that transition.

> *Your worry is that this new emphasis on multiculturalism will do the same?*

> Yeah, that that may do the same thing.

Like Jerome, Mahlon saw integration as a one-way street. Black people adapted to white culture and lost something of their own that had served them well in the past. Ironically, Mahlon himself was an example of the phenomenon he cited ("I no longer live in that neighborhood"). We had talked about his own experiences crossing over, moving out of the wholly black community in which he'd been reared and into a largely white world, and the story he told was moving and painful:

If you're willing to go into this a little more, I wanted to know more about the stresses and strains of your position, being a person of color selected for positions of power. I'm sure you were selected because of your talents and accomplishments, too, but in some part because of your race. What are the personal injuries of that?

Oh, I'm sure that had a lot to do with my health. It has been, at least for me, and I guess I can only speak for me, but with each of the positions I've been afforded to hold—being the *first* black city manager, being the *first* black director of the Department of Financial Administration, it's created an awesome kind of responsibility on me personally, and I've held myself responsible for that. Not either that I did not enjoy. But it created for me a need for a conscious, constant awareness of who I was, where I came from, and the need to never be willing to let my guard down.

And I say that because I've also seen on many occasions when forced to place minorities into positions, I've seen people pick minorities they know will fail. So that was something that always went through my mind. And not just minorities; females, too: "We tried it and it failed, so now we don't have to worry about that anymore for awhile." So I've always been conscious of that; I've always wondered when the Peter Principle would kick in.

But even more important, the one thing I've done, and I tell folks this and they kind of laugh at me, but I've always when I get up in the morning and shave or wash my face and look in the mirror, I remember who I am and what I am. I won't go into examples, but there were numerous times I really felt had I been weak enough, I would have easily been set up; you know, people would come in and offer me things, and they'd want something done. If it was the right thing to do, I'd try to do it. But in leaving, they'd say, "If you ever need anything, I want to do this for you, let me do something." Probably 90 percent of it was harmless, but I was so conscious—you know I just had a coined phrase: "One of these days I'll need lunch or I may need a dinner and I'll call you." I actually had one person come in and put a deed on my desk [laughs], and I told him if he didn't get it out of there—

There's this feeling that you're being watched closer and so many people are expecting you to fail that you tend to spend even more effort trying to be successful and not fail.

The question I'd kept asking Faubus about personal support and friendship was in my mind as I listened to Mahlon speak of the stresses and strains of his leadership position. He'd said earlier that he could talk only with his wife, and I asked him now if he'd meant that literally:

Oh, no, no. I've got three or four friends that I feel comfortable talking to. I used to, my mother passed in February, but I'd also talk to her a lot.

The real issue is a lot of the things that I'd discuss or want to discuss are those things that need to and should be kept confidential. And so you're limited in who you want to discuss some of those things with. But I've got two or three friends that I can pretty well discuss anything with and know that when the discussion's over that's where it is. It's not quite just my wife; I was exaggerating when I said that.

Are any of those people similarly situated in the power structure?

There are one or two that way. But—[long pause]

It's been kind of interesting, I find that once you get to that level and if in fact your livelihood depends on your ability to do business within the community, the issues are not as black and white, or minorities versus majorities, at that level.

[Speaking very slowly] Let me see how I say what I'm trying to say. I'm not naive enough not to know I've been selected, maybe because I'm capable, but more importantly because time has tested me, and I've been proven to be steady and not one who would come inside and learn the secrets and go outside and blow you up, play those kind of games. I'm safe, I guess is the word.

And that makes me mad sometimes, even though I know that's part of it. But I've been proven not to be one who's going to play both ends against the middle. I've found out that blacks, many of them, not all, once they reach that level, particularly those once again whose livelihood results from their ability to work within those circles, tend not to be as concerned about the have and have-not issues, as somebody like me might be. In the sense that, even though I work for a board, I'm somewhat insulated; I don't have to go out and sell my services as an attorney or as a businessman to that same group of people I'm dealing with. I go there with some independence that a lot of other folks can't.

So there are a number of people in my peer group that, no, I would not feel good talking about some of these things with, because we look at it so differently. . . .

I've spent a lot of my life, again just as I say I look in the mirror, I spend a lot of my time maintaining my relationships with my roots. For example, once a month I'll go out, there's a group of old fellows who never got much materially in life but who I consider to be just a wise old group of folks, who sit together around a tree and talk every Sunday, and I'll go out and spend a Sunday with them, or a couple of hours. All of my life I've done that. My associates are not necessarily people at my peer level professionally, but people I grew up with. I have to be careful *how* I do that in some instances. But I make it a point to keep in touch with and talk to those folks and it kind of keeps me anchored.

How do you have to be careful?

Only in the sense that some of them have some habits I don't personally condone [laughs], so I want to be with them but not involved in some of the habits, and that's what I mean. And they understand that and respect that, and I respect them; I don't try to change their lives.

But for me that's been an anchor, and the kind of anchor . . . where I feel I know what the issues are outside of my own little environment. . . . And I've tried very hard to maintain both contact and be supportive of and helpful to people at all levels. . . .

Mahlon was being careful as we spoke, constructing his sentences word by word. But now and then a flow of thoughts broke through, and I could hear how much passion lay behind his thoughtfulness. "Aren't there times," I asked, "when you wish you could just kick over the traces and speak your mind freely? Would you say things differently?" He sighed deeply and smiled a little:

I often ask myself that. I'm not sure I'd know how to do that; I've spent my life learning how to do the other, and practicing the other. But I've often wondered.

And I've come close a couple of times to wanting to be able to do that, you know, when your frustration level gets up, and you've been part of the system and you know how it works, and you see so many people who don't know how it works being abused by it, you want to scream out.

And yet I learned long ago that to be successful within a community, or even within an organization, there are a number of factors that have to come into play. I learned, for example, when working within organizations there are limits with what you can do from within an organization; you need outside pressure.

I always remember there was supposedly a meeting that President Roosevelt had with a group of businessmen. After about five minutes they'd convinced him that what they wanted him to do was appropriate. He said, "OK, you've sold me. Now go out and sell the public and make me do it."

So I'm constantly mindful of the various roles we all play within a given community. Maybe it's my way of saying my role and the way I approach it is important enough not to want to abandon that. I've spent an awful lot of time and an awful lot of effort and an awful lot of me emotionally being able to play this role, to be in a position to have some impact. I really think, for example, by being in that inner circle, I've been able when they've really gotten on a tangent, not in any way by telling folks what to do, but to raise issues that cause them to think and really weigh whether that was the way to go. Kind of a gatekeeper role.

I'm always reminded when I want to get up and scream and take a podium somewhere and say something, that I'll throw that away the minute I do that. There are people who are capable of doing that and good at doing that.

The question often is, how many of us understand the roles we play and the important roles other people play, and are willing to openly discuss and accept those others' roles and willing to sit down and talk strategy in terms of where we go with that.

Because it's been my experience that most folks that have the ability to play powerful roles also have very strong egos. Even the thought of somebody else being part of the decision-making process, or a team decision as to where we go, is somewhat offensive. But occasionally that does happen.

And so, sure I'm often tempted to do that. I've been extremely tempted as I've watched the issues revolving around youth and how to deal with gang violence and how to deal with kids. . . .

And so around those kinds of issues I've often wanted to scream out, but then I realize that my ability to play those roles I've been playing almost vanishes when I do that.

Listening to Mahlon talk about the costs to him of being in the integrated world in which he found himself, I wondered how the changes he'd experienced had impacted his children:

Have your kids gone through the school system out in the suburb where you live?

They've both gone through, without much success, but they both went to Central, and it was not a real good experience for them. That's not to say that's typical of all kids; I think some kids, it is a good experience for them.

You have to understand that neither of my kids, and understand my own personal situation, my first wife and I divorced when my daughter was eight and my son was about eighteen months, so even though I've been around them and with them to some extent, they weren't raised in the household with me. Neither, for different reasons I think, both probably out of apathy if nothing else, were real good students.

But watching and talking to 'em, I sensed that there was as much segregation within the school as there was when I went to school with two separate schools. Clearly, they associated primarily with kids of their own color.

A lot of tension, in fact my son was involved in what almost blew up to be a major affair, a major confrontation. One of his best friends had just bought a new car and kids doing some homecoming thing, one kid threw a burning torch on the car and it started a fight and before you knew it there were fifty, seventy-five kids involved. [laughs]

This incident had been the talk of the town when I'd been in Little Rock the year before. I knew it had been reported in the press as an example of continuing racial hostilities at Central High, and the newspaper stories had explicitly linked that interpretation to 1957. Some people had used it as evidence of the hopelessness of integration, while others had disputed that it had any racial character at all. Wanting to know how it had read close up, I'd been searching for someone who'd actually been there, so I asked Mahlon to tell me more:

> [My son] wound up not getting into any trouble, I don't know how. But two kids got expelled as a result of that.
>
> And it showed me how quickly, even though I don't think there was any racial intentions around the incident, how quickly it became a racial issue. It polarized kids. And I guess that's what I'm talking about more than anything. Not that Central *per se* is a bad school; it simply reflected for me that, if one of the goals of integration was to really get people to understand and work better together and become more culturally acceptable, I'm not sure that's worked. Now there are exceptions to that, I'd be the first to admit that. But I think by and large, in the large numbers, that's not been the case, particularly in the South.
>
> *Your daughter's about seven years older than your son. Was the school as polarized during the years she was at Central?*
>
> It was. I have yet to see either one of them bring a white kid home. . . .
>
> I guess my frustration as an individual centers around how much effort and how many people we've put through that process, only to sit in a room rather than really to enter into a relationship.

Mahlon had a unique way of putting his finger on the essential point. How, indeed, had it happened that so much pain and energy had been expended with the result that an internally segregated school had been created? More broadly, how had it happened that people of different races sat in rooms without entering into a relationship in so many places in American life? For both my white and black informants were telling me in vivid detail that they had no relationship, and no ability to make common cause around common problems. The original concept behind desegregation, that proximity would breed respect, now seemed far too simple-minded, undone by the raft of forces continuing to keep the races separate. Moved, I asked Mahlon to talk about his own children's futures. "Are you worried about them?" I naively asked, and again he answered in a devastatingly evocative way:

> Oh, certainly, I worry about it every day. You know, I remember back when, I guess, when the [consent decree] lawsuits were filed and we went from choice to forced numbers, I guess my kids then were young, and I recall thinking that this experiment would probably at least cause us to lose a generation, a large part of a generation, because it would take that long to really work things out.
>
> I don't think I thought at that time that my kids were part of that generation. It hadn't quite rung home. And I look at my kids, and I'm not optimistic now that even a generation later we've—I've got a grandkid now that's started school. So I'm not optimistic; I'm wondering how many generations we will lose before we really genuinely move forward.
>
> Clearly, I now think I was wrong when I thought one generation would do it.

Out of the Mouths of Babes?

At the heart of Mahlon's story lay concerns for his children and their generation. The understated emotion contained in his reflections harked back to anxieties I'd heard from white parents. Like Sally and Bill, like Mahlon, many others hinted at contradictions in their own life-evaluations when they talked about their offsprings' problems. I asked Dennis about his kids, and he told me they had all had "problems with drugs." Both his sons tried college, but neither lasted long. Both joined the military, the elder learning a blue-collar skill that later provided him with a civilian livelihood. The younger, too, worked with his hands as a craftsman. Only Dennis's daughter did eventually finish college and was considering graduate school but not yet going. ("She wanted to go to graduate school, but never could get around to figuring out exactly what," Dennis explained.) Confused about her path, she wandered into a job with some creativity which occupied her still. I asked Dennis what he thought about where his kids were in their lives, and he first said generously, "OK by me." Clearly, he restrained any spirit of criticism for them. Nonetheless, some yearning left untouched crept through his final comment:

> The thing of it is, they all could still—I mean, Stan could make a lot of money if he decides to. He has talent, and he could any time. And one of these days might open his own business and make a million bucks. **Ricky**'s going to do what Ricky wants to do and that's working with his hands, and **Joanie** could be a rock-n-roll star.

Where Dennis's children's choices seemed unconnected with issues of race, Jane spoke of educational problems and race in the same (characteristically honest and self-searching) breath. Parental decisions cause people to reveal and sometimes challenge their principles in a way little else does. As much as Jane espoused justice and equality, she found herself once again conflicted when it came to her children:

> They've gone to private high schools. [...] When the busing got really crazy, I just thought, I don't want them to be with a peer group that's not going to have really good educational backgrounds. So maybe that's why I put them all in private school. You know, I wanted them to have a good peer group. You know, it's just clicking. [thinking back on her own search for a "good peer group"] A peer group where they wouldn't feel such an outsider.
>
> *And has it worked that way?*
>
> It's worked that way. I feel silly saying that.
>
> I guess I, you know, I wanted them to be with kids with the same values. Because I felt so odd with my educational interests. And my one daughter, the one stepdaughter I feel very guilty about, she went to a high school which is one of the worst integrated here in town. She finally dropped out of high school, it was a terrible experience. She was not, and I can't blame it all on busing, but it was, you know, it was Chicano gangs and black gangs, and she had her purse stolen a lot of times. A black girl

came up one time and said, "Let me see your ring," and grabbed it and took it. You know, there really are some ghetto kids—

And her teachers ignored her, because all the other three kids have been in gifted programs. She wasn't in the gifted program, and she wasn't a poor student that had a lot of attention, and her teachers kept saying, "Well, she marches to a different drummer, but she's so sweet." And they just basically ignored her.

I went to see the teacher, because one year she was having so much trouble. I said, "I'm really worried about her, I want to be sure that she has college courses and she really does well," and the teacher said to me, "Well, she's not going to make it at Smith [College]. But she'll do just fine." And I thought that was a real put down, obviously she knew I valued education. So poor **Virginia** quit school.

Finally, she just graduated from the state university, she's doing well, she's going to be a teacher. She's in student teaching, so it's worked out well for her. But I think the peer group is really important.

For the most part, the white interviewees had little permission to speak about their problems. Instead, they complained indirectly, by implication as they made the complaints to which they *did* feel entitled, about African Americans. But they came closest to forthrightness when they talked about their kids. It was through their children that their direct contact with desegregated schooling had occurred. They themselves lived through racial change, but in their pre-college years most had never shared a classroom with a black student, or at least with more than one. Like Sally and Jane, they feared their children would be harmed, and, interpreting every crossed encounter as the harm they expected—much as Paul's teachers interpreted the behavior of their black male students—removed their children as quickly as they could from the dangers they feared. Now in their late teens or early twenties and newly graduated from predominantly white high schools, their children expressed a degree of racism the parents resisted admitting they themselves possessed.

Sally quoted her daughter's wrath at young black men hanging out, "'There they sit, gathering their welfare, doing nothing,' she said. 'I'm working for nothing, paying my dues.'" Bill added, "And not just

my kids; kids in general in this part of the country are pretty prejudiced." Helen's son certainly fit that description. ("He hates blacks! Big
time.") Helen could not make the connection between her son's prejudices and her own. ("So I had no fear of him ever dating black girls, I
knew he never would. I'm happy that he did not.") Perhaps her lapse in
consciousness stemmed partly from her own ambivalence, believing
the conventional judgments, yet socialized not to speak them aloud.
("I'm almost hypocritical.") The youngsters show no such scruples, having missed the experience of either an earlier southern gentility or the
more recent civil rights morality. Reverting to the cruder language of
their grandfathers, "they (pure and simply) hate blacks."

Somehow tangled up with the elders' squeamishness about the
young peoples' racism, there lie all the strands of those issues with
which the parents have struggled throughout their adult lives. What
exactly is their responsibility for the social creatures their children
have become? How much power have they to influence them? If the
parents have not created lives of sufficient security to enable their children to feel generous and accepting, nor succeeded in controlling their
children's embarrassing expressions of unmannerly prejudice, is that
the fault of circumstances or of their own weaknesses? Are perhaps
the children merely echoing their own attitudes, those prejudicial attitudes they insisted they had not had way back then at Central High?
And what, above all, has become of the optimism with which they set
out in life? How has all the hope they entertained devolved into the
bitterness and diminished prospects of their young?

At the end of my talk with Jerome, he spoke, tentatively, sadly, of
hope:

> I feel— [long pause] Well, I haven't lost hope, but I'm run-
> ning out of solutions in my mind [laughter], you know what I
> mean? I say, Maybe so and so and so will help, but when you fig-
> ure one way to alleviate a problem, and somebody else over here,
> the white majority, is figuring out a way to stop the problem
> from being alleviated, you see.
>
> And it's a battle, you know, between the races. We still have
> white flight. We're still living in the run-down, low-economic con-
> ditions, as far as blacks are concerned. I just run out of solutions.

But I do have hope enough not to turn back. I don't want to see it, I don't want to see it like it was when I was in high school, when I was coming up. I think, in the final analysis, even this is a tremendous educational experience. It's a very bold step, even now, to try to get people to respect and love each other.

If you look at it, you see the whole nation's trying this stuff, and that is a hope in itself. At least we're trying. We just gotta find some way to deal with the hearts of man, and it's very difficult to do. And as long as you hand it down from generation to generation, then it's gonna continue. It's a cycle, and it'll drop all the way down to generations to come, unless it's broken.

FOURTEEN
Opening the Gate Wide

With ownership comes responsibility, and I think that may be the real missing ingredient.
—Mahlon Martin

I do have hope enough not to turn back.
—Jerome Muldrew

When Helen and her classmates decided they would allow me to interview them, they said, "We want you to tell our story." It quickly became apparent to me that the story they wished me to tell was of their victimhood. "It was forced on us," said one white graduate after another. "I'm bitter over my senior year, which was ruined because they were forced on us." Not only had they had imposed on them a social change of dramatic proportions, but it had happened dramatically, and right in the middle of their senior year, which they had anticipated as a charmed moment in their lives. To make matters worse, they were held responsible for the drama, for the mob in the streets and for mayhem in the school corridors. Mostly, they insisted, they themselves were blameless "Goody Two-Shoes." They'd minded their own business, gone in by the side door, partied peacefully with their friends, and generally sought to redeem what they could from the disaster. Nonetheless, the world continued to see them as the culprits, as those rough people of Little Rock who'd behaved so uncouthly. Said Jane:

> And when I was in [college], if I said I was from Little Rock, I mean, it's like they moved over. And I would open my mouth . . . , and they would just stare at me. And it was like—I just had that insight—it was like lying to the Christians that I'd been to Sunday School. I had to change my accent, so they wouldn't immediately think I was from Little Rock.

From the beginning, Jane had understood clearly the peril she and her peers faced. In her editorial she had articulated, with considerable prescience, exactly what came to pass: that she and her fellow "law-and-order" white students would be accused of atrocities they had not, in her view, committed. In the event, she resented the world for its viewpoint more than the rowdy mob and segregationist students for their misbehavior.

As feisty, talented, and spirited as she was, Jane saw herself and her classmates as having been acted upon by history. Those who were the history makers resided impersonally somewhere in the "media," Washington, the governor's mansion. To some, the identity of those responsible was personalized in the shape of nine African-American classmates: "... *they* were forced on us," not, "*It* was forced on us." But in its essence, Jane's view of the innocence of the white students was shared by all the alumni I interviewed: they were objects, not subjects, of history.

And indeed it is true that they were not consulted in the decision to desegregate their high school. They were not even included in the plans to do so once the decision had been made elsewhere. A minimum was said to them by the school authorities about how to behave in the course of social change. Their principal, Jess Matthews, exhorted them to behave themselves, but neither he nor anyone else gave them any encouragement to do anything more than stay out of trouble, which, as it turned out, was not untroubled enough.

Even as the white students sought to dodge history by going in the side door, Jerome, a few years their senior and African American, chafed at the bit to be part of making change. "I was anxious to join the fight. I was very anxious, because this is something I wanted to happen." History was on his side; he was not asked to accept something unpleasant but to join something thrilling.

In personal terms, that difference in attitude precisely defines the change that was afoot. For most of American history, black people were required to endure oppression. The civil rights movement of the 1950s changed that necessity, giving them agency to act on remaking the world in a way they believed would be more just. The white students, however, were born into a world that seemed fair enough to them. They "felt sorry" that black people had it hard, but that was just the way it was. They knew their own parents endured some hardships and injustices. Helen's father struggled in vain for an economic foothold. Nancy's mother suffered stoically her husband's trouble-loving antics. But the young people were promised better times; all they had to do to attain them was "business as usual." If they obeyed the rules, different but mutually reinforcing rules for boys and for girls, they would win the prize of affluence, security, and respect. Desegregation was something they might accept, but, unlike Jerome, they did not want it to happen because it challenged rules that suited them just fine. Those rules changed at Central High, and Jerome applauded while Nancy protested and Betsy mourned. But Betsy, Nancy, and the others did in fact unknowingly help to make history. Agency can be a passive matter. Their inaction could not stop the forward movement of racial change in America, but it did contribute significantly to shape the way it came about.

How much responsibility, then, do they deserve for the debacle that was Little Rock? The Central High graduates talk about responsibility in three ways. To Charles it was a positive value, something he took on with pride and confidence. ("We had to go to college, we had to grow up and have families and continue the American dream. It was a big responsibility, still is.") In this sense, the word means a task or assignment, something one is expected to do, an injunction about how to behave: "Be responsible." Principal Matthews instructed the students on their responsibilities when he wrote, "Your first and immediate job is to get an education of the highest quality possible. Any disorder, confusion, disagreement, or quarreling at or around school will interfere with classroom work."

On the other hand, Bruce talked about a "black element [who] don't want any responsibility" but wish to rely on government intervention instead. He used the word in the same sense that the phrase "take personal responsibility" is used in certain quarters, an injunction to act in one's own behalf as opposed to accepting dependency on others. "Taking responsibility" is an act of personal choice, of non-reliance on a collectivity, and thus it contains within it a thick ideology of individualism, deeply internalized, thoroughly hegemonic.

Finally, my white interviewees had a tendency to translate "responsibility" into "blame" and to expend a good deal of energy defending themselves accordingly. They had no wish to be accountable, to be "held responsible" for whatever may have happened at Central High. This last usage of the word makes discussions of responsibility less than fruitful, because it evokes guilt and defensive claims of innocence, neither true, both containing elements of truth, and most important trapping people who seek agency in hopeless tangles of victimhood.

A way out of that bind lies in the connections that Mahlon articulated among responsibility, participation, and control or power. Together, those three concepts define agency and introduce a fourth meaning of the word "responsibility." When Mahlon spoke of the "awesome kind of responsibility" he personally experienced, he referred to the power he had to affect the lives of others. This responsibility was not about a task, individualism, or blame; it reflected a strongly felt sense of possibility and of connection to a community. If you have the power to act differently, if you feel responsible to do so, if you participate in collective activities that can make change happen on a collective level, then you have agency. Seen this way, it is easier to see how the white Central High students did in fact influence history. Going in the side door was an exercise in the power of choice, limited though it might have been, and Helen and the others did indeed play a role by doing so.

The young people had little power, but what they had mattered. The question of who has power to shape history and who is its victim is, I contend, crucial to an understanding of racism as it exists in America today. For while the division of the races involves issues of identity and community, those aspects of it are intricately interwoven with a different reality, a competition for control over the quality of life. "But then when it was forced on us, you see, that's what we're saying. And I guess when I stop and think about it, that's probably the whole thing!" The "whole thing" to which Betsy referred was her resentment about being forced to accept the presence of the Nine at Central High, about having so little say in something that altered her own experience. It also meant her bitterness about disappointments later in life, which she also attributed to the presence "forced on her" of African Americans.

The question we must answer is why she and her friend Helen

connected the two demonstrations of powerlessness, one concretely experienced in the form of Minnijean, the other vaguely felt in the form of uncertain life chances when assured outcomes were promised, with an imagined privilege of African Americans.

Helen's life story is prototypic of the times. Her family was economically tenuous, dislocated from the land, financially handicapped in the city. Her role as a woman was clearly prescribed: keep your head low, observe the proprieties, and marry well. Her male peers, men like Bruce and Charles, were similarly intent on toeing a narrow path. Eyes fixed straight ahead, they had little sense of option and could not lift their gaze from the road they walked to search for an alternate vision. Joyce said it well, recounting the lessons she learned when she dared speak the unthinkable: "Well, I don't see what's wrong with going to school with colored kids." Under the impact of her friends' silent retribution she learned the dangers of going against the grain and concluded quite rightly that she lacked the wherewithal at that moment to withstand the assault. Biding her time, she later joined forces with others of like mind and, with their support, gained the power to assert her beliefs.

Joyce had the benefit of an alternate vision of life, inherited from her Midwestern parents. Helen, Betsy, and the others had neither the sense of personal options to create an alternate vision, nor access to one provided by a forward-thinking leadership. Oftentimes, their ministers reinforced racist messages. Their school administration counseled them on proper behavior but not on visionary thinking. Jess Matthews, the principal of Central High, simply wanted to get on with his life's work—education—and make the interruption of real life struggles for justice go away. The students' political leaders bent in the wind. Indeed, their white elders, who had far more power, acted from attitudes not substantially different from the youngsters'. Governor Faubus insisted he was *forced* to take the action he did because of the passivity of the federal government and the grandstanding of the school board. Jimmy Karam was *made* to act badly by the devil. President Eisenhower himself kept as low a profile as possible until Faubus forced his hand. Criticism was voiced from the left, represented by newspapermen like Harry Ashmore, but Ashmore was widely discredited by the students' parents and teachers. Other critical leadership was silenced in the fifties by the McCarthy witch hunt and a postwar economic boom that made visions of a less competitive, more cooperative society anathema. African Americans, in contrast, were in the process of creating for themselves a language in which to articulate a vision of civil rights, which in turn indicated a strategy for enacting it. Because legal rights were central, Thurgood Marshall and others used the courts as a forum for constructing new law. Because the architects envisioned access to resources and opportunities, they focused on education as a key venue for social action. But nowhere was there a language available to the white students, nor for the most part to their elders, that might construct a framework for insisting with moral righteousness or political acumen on a peaceable progress toward integration.

Perceptual Limitations and Personal Powerlessness

We can hardly blame the students for following a lead so clearly set for them. They were born into a social milieu that provided the very terms of reference that limited them. But at the same time that they accepted those terms, they also resisted them. Nancy chose her troublemaking father's model in preference to her properly mannered mother's. Helen went to school over her mom's objections. The fundamental premise they did accept was that they could do anything they wished, if they were smart and strong enough. What they wished was that the uproar at Central High would go away. But they did not understand that they had power to help make that happen. Their perceptions were limited, for one thing, by the division they were unable to overcome. They could not see that the black students were being hounded and harassed, and so they could not see their own power to intervene, to defend or befriend the Nine. None of us can see the whole of social reality, precisely because we all live in a divided and stratified society. The place from which you look determines what you see, and the white students looked from social locations so severely separated that what they saw bore little resemblance to their black classmates' experience.

In the halls of Central High, Nancy and Dennis saw normal teasing of classmates who happened to be black. Melba Pattillo Beals reported hateful intimidation, painful abuse, and constant harassment.

In the streets around Central High, Helen saw a neighborhood ruined by the neglect of people with no sensibilities about grass. Marian saw a need to fight for amenities, paved streets, and other city services that came by right to white neighborhoods.

On the porches of African-American areas, Sally's daughter saw young men willfully lazy, flaunting their leisure while she worked hard. Mahlon saw a community denuded of moral leadership, struggling to regroup.

To call attention to such perceptual and interpretive differences among racial groups in America is nothing new. Indeed, that the races are divided is a weary truism in our times. Less obvious, however, is the observation that there is an asymmetry in this divide. People of color are far more likely to understand that there is a difference and to find no surprises in the white viewpoint. White Americans, however, often don't know what they don't know. Because their perspective dominates and is more regularly reflected in mass media, because the white world is less confronted with "other" realities than "other" worlds are with white ones, white people are more apt to assume that there is only one reality, and that is theirs.

The invisibility of alternate perceptions of the world, indeed, of very different experiences in it, is a problem not only for people whose truths are disappeared, but also for Nancy and Dennis, Helen and Betsy, for the white majority. We form our views of the world based on our personal experience, on talk with others of our kind, and on ever-present mass media that reflects our world; to believe those views are thoroughgoing is to miss subtexts and complexities of our own reality as well as others'. We never see ourselves so clearly as when we are reflected in the eyes of those who differ from us. The Frenchman Alexis De Tocqueville's *Democracy in America* is standard reading for college freshmen a century and a half after it was written; the Swedish Gunnar Myrdal's *An American Dilemma*, published a decade before the Supreme Court decision desegregating the schools, contributed a provocative analysis of the dynamics of race relations that influenced both law and scholarship for many years hence. Not coincidentally, we accept these views from the outside by two European men, while we resist views from the outside by American minority peoples.

The women of Central High, class of '58, could not critique the construction they inherited of womanhood, even when they sensed on some level its imperfections. Jane protested but did not rebel, and found herself in consequence caught in constant loops of ambivalence. Nancy identified with her free-wheeling father and resisted her convention-bound mother. But with all her spirit, she accepted a helpmate's life that left her with insufficient power to right wrongs done to her husband and herself.

These women's male cohorts, too, bought into a view of manhood that, for many, offered more privileges than it delivered. Bruce and Ed followed the corporation to early and bitter retirements. Bill did everything he was supposed to, going to school to become a professional, paying all his debts, and yet he could not provide for his children what he believed he himself possessed starting out: a certain future.

Together, men and women defined their gender roles in ways that supported a program for class advancement. Women were to stand by men on their way up the ladder, to move away from community, to make self-sufficient mobile families that could supply all needs—for companionship, for economic well-being, for satisfaction, and for fun. Men were told that hard work and good brains would be rewarded by steady career advancement and a secure old age. Both men and women suffered dislocation and disappointment. Having been told they were capable of doing the impossible, when the impossible proved to be just that, they blamed those people of color they saw as competitors. But in their heart of hearts, they blamed themselves.

Herein lies the rub. The most central tenet of the personal ideology Americans internalize is that we are responsible for our own successes and failures, the crucial premise for individualism. There is some truth to that notion, but there is also much falsehood. What any given individual achieves is a product of his or her own will and efforts, but in very intimate interaction with complex social realities. When my student told his story of how his black male classmates were expelled one by one until he stood alone at graduation, he told a tale of agency. His power of decision and self-control enabled him to graduate from his special school and go on to a distinguished career at the university. His decision to exercise self-control was based on a number of personal abilities or powers: to understand what the rules were, to construct an attitude that construed obedience to be the greatest rebellion, to control the anger he felt at perceived injustice, and so on. Each of those elements of his willed consciousness was a way of handling a set of conditions that his white classmates did not face. But they did face other conditions in the form of many unnoticed dynamics and forces. Betsy's participation in the walkout from school was a different act of protest from those of her male classmates, for instance, because she had to contend with her friend Helen's ambivalent disapprobation. Whether through companionable gossip or parental innuendo (remember when Nancy swore and her mother called her by her full name), the white students faced powerful social pressure to conform. Unlike Paul, however, they were unaware of those pressures. Jane, a relative outsider, knew they existed. Joyce felt them literally on her back. But those closest to the social center least knew they were "forced" to be there, and they therefore had no idea there were any alternatives.

They were *responsible* for their actions, but were they to *blame* for the debacle at Central High? It is because the notion of individual responsibility is so deeply internalized that we have trouble distinguishing responsibility from blame. The white students of Little Rock are therefore intent on defending themselves from the accusation that they are to blame for a way of resisting desegregation that they, too, disapprove. Their disapproval is based not so much on the fact that it was resistance as that it was obstreperous, that it interfered with their senior year and broke the rules of propriety. Nonetheless, they insist, it was not their fault that Sammie Dean leaped from the schoolhouse window nor that boys in the locker room soaked Ernest's clothing.

The lessons of Little Rock are identical to the lessons that white people all over America learn from the existence of racism. We learn we must defend against blame, and in the process we disown responsibility—and simultaneously lose the possibility of choice, without which there can be no true responsibility. In part we do so because we do not see clearly that injustice exists, and when we do see it, we cannot see clearly where we have power to redress it, nor where we, too, are its victims.

How much what we see is determined by the veil of culture through which we look was never so dramatically demonstrated as it was at the end of my conversation with Jane. Throughout, she had been warmly honest about her feelings and beliefs, emotionally intense and moving. As our interview ended, while I packed up my tape paraphernalia, she generously pulled old clippings from her files to give me, pointing out photos of people whose names had come up in our conversation. Suddenly, she gasped and grew silent. I looked up from my wires. Once again, she was weeping, her eyes transfixed on a faded photograph on a yellowed page. It was a picture of the Nine, and Minnijean stood to one side, tall and stately—not overweight. On her face was a self-conscious smile; she seemed shy, chin tucked down, perhaps unsure of herself in front of the camera. She seemed very much a fifties sort of teenager, and very vulnerable.

"She was nothing like a mammy," Jane moaned. "How could I have remembered her that way?"

"Memory fails," wrote Karen Fields, "and memory collaborates with forces separate from actual past events...." Jane's memory collaborated with a reputation she'd helped to construct. All that talk among girls had in fact constituted a political act of protest against Minnijean's disturbance of normalcy, against the threat implied thereby to their place in a promised class order. To be sure, that place held them, too, in place, in gendered roles they both embraced and resisted.

"How could I have remembered her that way?" Jane lamented. Participating actively in the construction and defense of their Andy Hardy world, the women of Central High also felt its injuries and rebelled. Lacking clarity on the sources of their own discomfort and hope, they blamed Minnijean and Sammie Dean. In a moment of historic social change, they chose up sides, like Nancy's daughter never asking "why?" Only later could they begin to glimpse their own misperceptions. But they still defended untenable positions of long ago, still were tangled in webs of gender, race, class, of domesticity and political opinion, of ambivalence about their lives, their peers, and their world.

Jane wept, I imagined, in grief not in guilt, and therein lay the power of her tears. So, too, did Annie sigh after reading Melba's book: "How could we not have known?" Helen, so angry at black co-workers she believed to be protected and privileged, could nonetheless reach that moment of reflection in our conversation when she heard her own prejudice and said, "I'm almost hypocritical about it . . . ," and, "I never thought I was a racist, but . . ."

But in the same breath, Helen said, "It was forced on us." If we do not understand the context in which we do what we do, then we blame someone, ourselves or others, instead of accepting responsibility and recognizing what we might do differently. If blame is the issue, then so, too, is defense. If we defend ourselves against blame for racism, we cannot see social reality from the perspective of others, and not only do we lose sight of injustices done to them, but also we cannot truly believe there are injustices done to us, because everything we experience becomes a matter of unbounded individual will and intention, wholly outside the dynamics of social reality. If we do not understand how those dynamics work, we are truly powerless to change them.

Racial division is the prototype for this cycle. For white people race is a paradoxical, ever-present learning ground for an internalized ideology of powerlessness, which in turn is a prison from which we cannot break free to address either racial injustice or dissatisfactions in our own lives. We are taught we are superior, but what we learn is to accept premises that disempower us as well as others. We can move our children away from the multiracial city, accept reassignments by the corporation without complaint, put up brave fronts as we watch our children flounder. But those are individual acts which cannot change the realities we resist. We are caught in a double bind of ineffectiveness because it is only if we can see where we do have responsibility that we can also see where our power lies to make change. Unawareness is our responsibility; blaming and therefore isolating ourselves is our responsibility. If we could hear—if we would listen to—Jerome's analysis of why Central High is racially divided, then we could together do something about it and would not need to move to the white suburbs. Because we are unaware and alone, we cannot do the one thing that would make life better: see the commonalties in the problems of people of all races and join together to solve them.

Just as my white interviewees did and did not have power to determine what happened in their school, so, too, they did and did not have responsibility. The students had less power than Governor Faubus, and certainly bore less responsibility. Where they could have made a difference—in seeing the harassment of their African-American classmates and intervening, in befriending the newcomers instead of participating in their isolation, in believing the stories of the minority instead of disputing them—in these places they were responsible for injustice. Where individual power is limited, however, becomes clear if we look beyond the realm of individual actions and address those social structures that form the context for action. The students, white and black alike, did need to become adults who supported themselves; that is a structural given in America. They did need to work within the framework of a competitive job market. What they did not need to do, however, was to accept that system as normal or right. They do bear some responsibility for accepting a normalcy that includes inequities, both those suffered by black people and those endured by themselves. Do they have power to change that normalcy? In many ways they—we all—do have that capability. But first we must be open to rethinking our own problems and, from there, our world. In doing that, coming to grips with racial hostility is a productive, indeed a necessary first step.

Taking Power, Making History

What can we, especially white Americans, do today to address racial inequities and remake our world in a better image? I offer a few suggestions, not as a perfect program for change, but to stimulate shared thinking.

Let us look first at the levels on which racism operates. While material issues are fundamental to racism's existence, they are part of a dynamic of interacting forces, some of which occur through the medium of individuals' actions, some through the restraints of cultural conventions, some through the impact of social structures.

On an individual level, prejudice is an obvious contributor. Less well understood but, I believe, more profound, however, is silence.

Those who "go in the side door," declining to take a stand in the face of injustice, create a climate that allows wrongs to go on and on. From President Eisenhower to Little Rock's civil leaders, from Principal Matthews at Central High to Helen, those people who failed to speak out were crucial participants in the making of the drama. Joyce learned several lessons at her friends' hands. She learned how strong the pressure is to be quiet when social conflict is afoot. She learned that she should only speak if she were willing to fight for what she felt was right. To take the risk of declaring oneself in a divided society is not easy. But if those white Americans who do not wish to condone racism do not take that risk, change will not happen.

On a cultural level, normalcy is the problem. Doing business as usual at Central High, assigning kids to teachers their parents request on a racial basis, blinking at boyish hazing, continuing to teach from familiar Eurocentric textbooks, all construct a culture in which segregation can not be effectively challenged. Whatever the intentions of the school personnel, the normal way of recruiting teachers, the normal way that classrooms are constituted, the normal way that ideas are talked about have the consequence of perpetuating "normal" racial inequality.

On the level of social structure, there is a long list of factors, some involving social relations, other economic forces, still other issues of political power. Examples very clearly involved in the history of Central High are residential segregation, the existence of exclusionary private schools, the drawing of county lines and the unequal apportionment of public funds to schools, low pay scales for teachers, which taken together construct an interlocking structure of racial inequity.

Many of these dynamics lie invisible behind screens of assumption. We do not usually recognize with clarity how interwoven individual action, cultural habits, and structural forces truly are. Therefore, to ask for color blindness, to be neutral or silent in the face of inequity on unperceived levels, privileges those who already have privilege. It is discriminatory, whatever the intentions motivating it.

So what can we as individuals do to make social change? We can challenge the very premises of individual achievement that motivate and drive us. So long as each individual American seeks to climb the ladder, alone and solely responsible for his or her success, then the very act that might protect the rights of those climbers to true success is foregone. That act is unity. If Bruce and Ed and other men of their age could join in self-protection, the story of job insecurity America reads in today's daily papers might be otherwise. If Betsy and Helen could move beyond their separated homes to make the community whose loss they mourn, the public schools they decry could be made splendid. If all these people were to see their fates as co-joined rather than competitive and separate, then they could welcome the participation of people of color, recognizing what now is wholly invisible to them: that African Americans, immigrants, and other minority peoples are a potential source of shared strength and not the problem. The problem is systemic. The solution lies in acting together to make change, in the corporation, in government, in the neighborhoods, that makes available to everyone, of whatever race, enough resources to secure the good life, enough power to shape community, enough awareness to be able to see, like Jane when she gazed at the photograph of Minnijean after all those years, that "others" are human, just like us.

Notes

One: Stories of Central High

1. F. Hampton Roy and Charles Witsell, *How We Lived: Little Rock as an American City* (1985), p. 191.

2. Andy Hardy was a character in a long series of movies spanning the thirties, forties, and fifties. The son of a poor but upstanding judge in a typical mid-Western town, Andy Hardy was the ideal type of white middle-class America struggling through the depression and achieving respect and solidity in the decades following.

3. This account is drawn from many sources, major among them the following first-hand reports: Virgil T. Blossom, *It Has Happened Here* (1959), Elizabeth Huckaby, *Crisis at Central High* (1980), Daisy Bates, *The Long Shadow of Little Rock: A Memoir* (1962).

4. The new board was elected in large part through the efforts of a group called the Women's Emergency Committee. In the early stage of the history, men's actions dominated the play (with the exception of certain women like Daisy Bates, the chair of the state NAACP). Gradually, however, women came to take more central positions, partly because the action concerned children and therefore women had a certain moral—and increasingly political—credibility. On the segregationist side, the Mothers League, a group of mothers of Central High students, was also influential.

5. What we choose to tell and to omit is often an act of consent to power relations or of resistance. For an excellent discussion of this aspect of story-telling, see Patricia Ewick and Susan S. Silbey, "Subversive Stories and Hegemonic Tales: Toward a Sociology of Narrative" in *Law and Society Review*, vol. 29, no. 2, 1995. I also find useful James Scott's formulation of hidden transcripts, those stories people tell only among themselves, in *Domination and the Arts of Resistance* (1990).

6. Iwona Irwin-Zarecka, *Frames of Remembrance: The Dynamics of Collective Memory* (1994).

7. Karen E. Fields, "What One Cannot Remember Mistakenly" in *Memory and History: Essays on Recalling and Interpreting Experience*, edited by Jaclyn Jeffrey and Glenace Edwall (1984), p. 89.

8. Fields, "What One Cannot Remember Mistakenly," p. 93.

Two: The Big Gate

1. Other sources put the white population in mid-nineteenth century considerably higher. Wesley, I suspect, is expressing a belief about the pioneering character of his ancestors.

2. All quoted by Harry S. Ashmore in *Arkansas: A History* (1984), pp. 53–54.

3. John Gould Fletcher, *Arkansas* (1947/1989), p. 125.

4. Fletcher, *Arkansas*, p. 115.

5. It also provoked a very strong anti-lynching movement headed by a wealthy white woman named Adolphine Fletcher Terry, who later organized the Women's Emergency Committee.

6. Tragically, Mahlon Martin died shortly after our meeting.

7. Mahlon Martin was a highly placed administrator in Bill Clinton's gubernatorial regime.

Three: Inside the Gate

1. Orval Eugene Faubus, *Down from the Hills*, vol. 1 (1980).

2. Ashmore, *Arkansas: A History*, pp. 56–59. Fletcher, *Arkansas*, pp. 89–90.

3. Faubus, *Down from the Hills*, pp. 39–40.

4. *Life* Magazine, Vol. 43, No. 15, October 7, 1957, p. 37.

5. In a literal sense, Reconstruction was never much of a reality in Arkansas, where very few African Americans attained political office even at the height of the phenomenon elsewhere. The classic study of the period is W. E. B. Du Bois, *Black Reconstruction in America: 1860–1880* (1935/1962).

6. Orval E. Faubus, *In This Faraway Land: A Personal Journal of Infantry Combat in World War II* (1971/1993), pp. 4–17.

7. Faubus, *In This Faraway Land*, p. 5.

8. Timothy P. Donovan and Willard B. Gatewood Jr., eds., *The Governors of Arkansas* (1981), p. 211.

9. Faubus, *In This Faraway Land*, p. 16. Faubus's explanation for his speedy departure from Commonwealth College varied from one telling to another.

10. Harry S. Ashmore, *Hearts and Minds: A Personal Chronicle of Race in America* (1988), pp. 253–255. Faubus, *Down from the Hills*, pp. 39–40.

11. Faubus, *Down from the Hills*, p. 37.

12. Bates, *Long Shadow of Little Rock*, p. 62.

13. Blossom, *It Has Happened Here*, p. 74.

14. Brooks Hays, *A Southern Moderate Speaks* (1959), pp. 136ff.

15. Ashmore, *Hearts and Minds*, p. 260.

16. Ashmore, *Hearts and Minds*, p. 261.

Four: Cracking the Gate

1. Blossom, *It Has Happened Here*, p. 38.

2. Faubus, *Down from the Hills*, p. 223.

3. We were talking in late October 1992, a week or so before Clinton was elected president.

4. Sara Murphy was writing a book about the role of women in the Little Rock events. She died of cancer not long after we'd talked, and her book, *Breaking the Silence: Little Rock's Women's Emergency Committee to Open Our Schools, 1958–1963*, was published posthumously.

Five: Bitters in the Honey

1. Major sources: Bates, *Long Shadow of Little Rock*; Huckaby, *Crisis at Central High*; Melba Pattillo Beals, *Warriors Don't Cry* (1994); Ernest Green, "The Ernest Green Story" (film).

2. Beals, *Warriors Don't Cry*, p. 28.

3. Huckaby, *Crisis at Central High*.

Six: Sammie Dean and Minnijean

1. The literature on Central High is blessed with a number of first-hand accounts by women, especially those by Daisy Bates, Elizabeth Huckaby, and Melba Pattillo Beals.

2. A particularly threatening example is this sexualized one:

> Little nigger at Central High
> Has got mighty free with his eye.
> Winks at white girls,
> Grabs their blond curls:
> Little nigger sure is anxious to die.

3. Huckaby, *Crisis at Central High*, p. 135.

4. According to a hard-to-attribute citation on the World Wide Web, the term Goody Two-Shoes derives from an anonymous allegory published in 1766 and entitled:

> The history of little Goody Two-Shoes:
> Otherwise called, Mrs. Margery Two-Shoes.
> With the means by which she acquired her learning and wisdom,
> Set forth at large for the benefit of those,

> Who from a state of rags and care,
> And having shoes but half a pair;
> Their fortunes and their fame would fix,
> And gallop in a coach and six.

Paradoxically, the women of Little Rock dropped the connotation of "do-gooder," but maintained the slight air of self-derision suggested by the original as they used the term to suggest that they *were* good.

5. Sammie Dean and her parents energetically challenged Sammie's expulsion, and with the help of segregationist leaders succeeded in getting her reinstated. It was in the course of that campaign that Mrs. Parker is reported to have threatened Mrs. Huckaby with an umbrella, an event memorialized in one of the segregationist cards circulated among the students. Minnijean was placed in a private school in New York, where she finished out her high-school years.

6. bell hooks, *Ain't I a Woman?* (1981).

7. There is an extensive literature on the link between women's ways and class status, both in the American South and in many other cultures around the world. For two examples, see Kathleen Blee, *Women of the Klan: Racism and Gender in the 1920s* (1991), and Santi Rozario, *Purity and Communal Boundaries: Women and Social Change in a Bangladeshi Village* (1992).

8. Patricia Hill Collins, *Black Feminist Thought: Knowledge, Consciousness, and the Politics of Empowerment* (1990).

9. I am "going in the side door" here, avoiding a major controversy about the nature of cognition and the existence of an unconscious. While I believe this argument is consequential, I do not think it essential to the discussion I am introducing.

10. There is a large literature on the psychology of women, but the psychology of men goes unnoticed as "normal" theory.

11. *Ain't I a Woman?*, *Black Looks,* and many others.

12. *The Negro Family in the United States* (1939/1966).

13. See the classic study Gordon W. Allport, *The Nature of Prejudice* (1954/1958). A more modern treatment is offered by Daniela Gioseffi, ed., *On Prejudice: A Global Perspective* (1993).

14. There is a growing interest, however, in the subject of whiteness. See, for example, Helen Frankenberg, *White Women, Race Matters: The Social Construction of Whiteness* (1993).

Seven: Parades and Other Forms of Political Action

1. See, for example, *My Troubles Are Going to Have Trouble with Me: Everyday Trials and Triumphs of Women Workers* (1984), edited by Karen Brodkin Sacks and Dorothy Remy, and James C. Scott, *Domination and the Arts of Resistance* (1990).

2. Sara Diamond, *Roads to Dominion: Right-Wing Movements and Political Power in the United States* (1995), p. 6.

Eight: Fathers and Sons

1. Interview by Anna Holden, Anti-Defamation League Papers, quoted in "Bibles and Bayonets: The Crisis at Central High School," an unpublished paper in the author's possession by Pete Daniels, p. 59.

2. Private letter to the author from Joe Matthews, dated October 3, 1997.

3. Huckaby, *Crisis at Central High*, pp. 18–19.

4. At the time we talked, President and Hillary Clinton were spear-heading an attempt to reform the health-care system in America. Many physicians, as well as others in the industry resisted, and the White House proposals were ultimately defeated.

Nine: Sharing Stories, Shaping History

1. This formulation draws on George Rudé, *Ideology and Popular Protest* (1980). I have elaborated it in more detail in *Some Trouble with Cows: Making Sense of Social Conflict* (1994).

2. James Scott, *Weapons of the Weak* (1985).

3. Huckaby, *Crisis at Central High*, p. 64.

4. In Melba's account, even guarded she experienced major harassment. As the federal soldiers were withdrawn and replaced by members of the Arkansas National Guard, Melba's fearfulness rose. "On some days," she wrote, "I found myself thinking every waking moment about nothing else but my safety. . . ." Her experience was not uniform, however. Sometimes, she encountered a guardsman who supported her. In mid-October, controversy ran high because Minnijean applied to take part in a talent show. The segregationists objected. One day in school, Melba had this encounter:

> "That nigger ain't gonna sing on our stage. My daddy says he'll see her dead first." The boy shouting this ran past me, knocking my books out of my arms. When I bent over to pick them up, someone kicked me from behind and pushed me over. I landed on my wrist. It felt broken.

"OK. Get yourself up, and I'll get the books." It was a voice I didn't recognize, speaking to me while students rushed past, laughing and pointing as I lay in pain. An Arkansas National Guard soldier was standing beside me, gathering my books and speaking in a gentle tone.

"Can you get up?" I tried to get to my feet, but my head was pounding and my body ached.

"What the hell, gal, take my hand. You're gonna get us both killed if you don't move. We ain't got no help." He took my hand and boosted me upright. It hurt to stand on my ankle. "Let's move outta here, right now!" He was pushing me faster than my body wanted to go, but I knew he was right, I had to move.

When we finally got to a safe spot, I thanked him, blinking back hot tears. That soldier, whoever he was, stayed within full sight of me for the rest of the day. He didn't say anything, but whenever I looked for him, he was there. As I was leaving school, he was standing in the hallway, slouching against the wall like his buddies. But he had been kind to me, and I would remember that not all members of the Arkansas National Guard were of the same character. (p. 183)

More typically, the guardsmen were part of the problem the Nine encountered on a daily basis. "Sometimes we were guarded by the Arkansas National slobs, as we called the federalized soldiers, who, by then, had shown us in every way that they loathed the responsibility and didn't take it seriously. They had become visibly hostile toward us, sometimes whispering threats and taunting and teasing us when they got us alone." (p. 192)

5. Again, Melba's account differed. As the year wore on, she and the other black students noticed "an increasing barrage of injurious activities. What was noticeably different was the frequency and the organized pattern of harassment. Teams of students appeared to be assigned specific kinds of torture. One team concentrated on slamming us into lockers, while another focused on tripping us up or shoving us down staircases; still another concentrated on attacks with weapons. Another group must have been told to practice insidious harassment inside the classrooms. Still others worked at entrapment, luring the boys into dark corners or the girls into tight spots in isolated passageways. Some continued to use the showers as a means of abuse." (p. 213)

6. Dennis reflected back Mahlon's discussion of his reasons for not going to Central two years later. He was precisely in the same position Dennis was, a popular leader in the all-black high school he attended. Melba missed that experience, compounding the sacrifices she endured that year.

7. The study-hall story under dispute here appeared early in Melba's book. Danny, her personal guard from the 101st Airborne, protected her effectively, but he was not permitted inside classrooms:

Entering the door was like walking into a zoo with the animals outside their cages. The room was double the size of the largest classroom
in my old school. I'd never seen anything like it or imagined in my
wildest dreams that an important school like Central could allow such
outrageous behavior. Stomping, walking, shouting, sailing paper air-
planes through the air, students were milling about as though they were
having a wild party. The teacher sat meekly behind his desk, a specta-
tor stripped of the desire or power to make them behave. (p. 141)

I took five steps into the room, and everybody fell silent, abandon-
ing their activities to glare at me.

"Take that seat over there," the study-hall teacher said.

"But I need—" I wanted to ask him for a seat near the door where I
could see Danny, but he cut me off.

"Did you hear me? I said take the seat over there or see the principal."

The teacher returned to reading his newspaper while the students
threw spitballs. They directed only a few at me; mostly they were
involved in their own little games. At one point, they starting passing
notes back and forth. When one was passed to me, I opened it. "Nigger
go home," it read. I looked at it without emotion, folded it neatly, and
put it aside. (p. 192)

8. Paradoxically, of all the first-hand literature I've seen coming out of
Little Rock, Melba's book contains the most vivid anecdotes of helpful behavior on the part of white people inside Central High. One day when she had
missed connections with her carpool, a boy cornered her and threatened her
violently. Another boy appeared with his 1949 Chevy and saved her. "'Melba,'
the blond boy whispered my name, 'listen to me. I'm gonna call you nigger—
loud. I'm gonna curse at you, but I'm gonna put my keys on the trunk of
this car. Get out of here, now. My name is Link, I'll call you later.'" (p. 249)
Terrified, she did as told, escaping in his car. As the year went on, Link continued to give Melba surreptitious information about plans to torment her, helping her to avoid the worst traps.

Several times, Melba expresses appreciation for supportive teachers.
"When I entered Mrs. Pickwick's shorthand class things improved decidedly.
It was like being on a peaceful island. She remained ever in control. . . . Her
no-nonsense attitude didn't leave room for unruly behavior." (p. 136)

It is true that Melba's book is a powerful indictment of the school population as a whole, and that she expresses anger. But it is not true that everything she says about white conduct is "bad."

Ten: Boys Will Be Boys

1. There is a long debate about whether gender or race is the more defining identity. I believe the question is more about power than about something
intrinsic in these identities. Race is basic in societies in which racial inequality
is fundamental; gender is profound in all known societies, because we know of
no societies where men and women are not socially unequal.

2. This phenomenon of "cultural hegemony" (the invisibility of the cultural medium in which we all swim) is described and analyzed by Antonio
Gramsci and his disciples in many places. For a wonderfully vivid exposition
in terms of race and gender, see Patricia Williams, *The Alchemy of Race and
Rights* (1991).

3. See R. W. Connell, *Gender and Power* (1987) for a thorough analysis of
these dynamics.

4. For a vivid discussion of the subject, see Michael S. Kimmel and
Michael A. Messner, eds., *Men's Lives* (1992). and especially Part Three: "Sports
and War: Rites of Passage in Male Institutions."

5. Franklin Abbott, ed., *Boyhood: Growing Up Male* (1993), p. 38.

6. See Barbara Ehrenreich, *The Hearts of Men* (1983).

7. Arlie Hochschild, *The Second Shift* (1989).

Eleven: Insecurity and Racism Today

1. Lillian Rubin, *Families on the Fault Line* (1994), p. 138.

Twelve: Victimhood and the American Dream

1. For an excellent history and overview of the Frankfurt School, see
Martin Jay's *The Dialectical Imagination: A History of the Frankfurt School and
the Institute of Social Research, 1923–1950* (1973).

2. Frantz Fanon's *Black Skin, White Masks* (1967/1982) is a classic formulation of the notion.

3. Claude Steiner, *Scripts People Live: Transactional Analysis of Life Scripts*
(1974).

4. *Microsociology: Discourse, Emotion, and Social Structure* (1990).

5. To track the genesis of internalized ideology necessitates a broadening
of the familiar site of psychological theory, the family. While much of individual consciousness is clearly shaped in and by the family, the sources of internalized ideology are much greater. Indeed, the family is primarily important as
a conduit for social relations beyond the domestic sphere. Friends, neighbors,

teachers, friends' parents and other family members, all contribute to shaping a growing child. How mother and father interact with their children is, of course, biological and idiosyncratic, but it is also profoundly social. Moreover, most families are larger and more dynamic than traditional psychology acknowledges. Siblings matter greatly, as do cousins, grandparents, and aunts and uncles. How all those roles and relationships evolve is complex and deeply illustrative of power dynamics in the larger society.

6. Heidi Hartmann, "The Recent Past and Near Future for Women Workers: Addressing Remaining Barriers," speech to Seventy-fifth Anniversary Conference Women's Bureau, U.S. Department of Labor, Washington, D.C., May 20, 1995.

7. "The Moving Experience," *San Francisco Chronicle*, June 5, 1996. Carol J. De Vita, "The United States at Mid-Decade," *Population Bulletin*, vol. 50, no. 4, March 1996, p. 8.

8. "The Wage Gap: Women's and Men's Earnings," *Institute for Women's Policy Research Briefing Paper*, p. 2.

9. Rifkin, *End of Work*, p. 8.

10. "Californians Found to Be Working Harder," in the *San Francisco Examiner*, September 8, 1998, p. A3.

11. Rifkin, *End of Work*, p. 74.

12. "Census Report Shows Most Blacks Still Earning Less," *San Francisco Chronicle*, June 11, 1996, p. A18. De Vita, "The United States at Mid-Decade," p. 29.

13. "African Americans in the 1990s," *Population Bulletin*, vol. 46, no. 1, July 1991.

14. De Vita, "The United States at Mid-Decade." It is, however, still true that in absolute numbers more whites than blacks live in poverty and receive welfare.

15. According to a National Cancer Institute report for the years 1988–1992. *San Francisco Chronicle*, April 27, 1996, p. A6.

16. "African Americans in the 1990s," p. 13.

17. De Vita, "The United States at Mid-Decade," p. 34 and p. 36. The economic fate of single moms is not a rosy one no matter what their race; 44 percent of them, of all races, live in poverty.

18. *San Francisco Chronicle*, November 26, 1995, p. A9, on the report of the Glass Ceiling Commission of the U.S. government.

19. Richard Sennet and Jonathan Cobb, *The Hidden Injuries of Class* (1972).

20. Richard Pérez-Peña, "New York's Income Gap Largest in Nation," in the *New York Times*, December 17, 1997. De Vita, "The United States at Mid-Decade," p. 40.

Bibliography

Abbott, Franklin, ed. *Boyhood: Growing Up Male.* Freedom, Calif.: Crossing Press, 1993.

Allport, Gordon. *The Nature of Prejudice.* 1954. Reprint. New York: Doubleday Anchor Books, 1958.

Ashmore, Harry S. *Arkansas: A History.* New York: W. W. Norton, 1984.

Ashmore, Harry S. *Hearts and Minds: A Personal Chronicle of Race in America.* Cabin John, Md.: Seven Locks Press, 1988.

Bates, Daisy. *The Long Shadow of Little Rock: A Memoir.* New York: David McKay Company, 1962. Reprint. Fayetteville: University of Arkansas Press, 1987.

Beals, Melba Pattillo. *Warriors Don't Cry.* New York: Pocket Books, 1994.

Blee, Kathleen. *Women of the Klan: Racism and Gender in the 1920s.* Berkeley: University of California Press, 1991.

Blossom, Virgil T. *It Has Happened Here.* New York: Harper and Brothers, 1959.

Bordo, Susan. *Unbearable Weight: Feminism, Western Culture, and the Body.* Berkeley: University of California Press, 1993.

Chernin, Kim. *The Obsession: Reflections on the Tyranny of Slenderness.* New York: Harper and Row, 1981.

Chesler, Phyllis. *Women and Madness.* New York: Doubleday, 1972.

Chodorow, Nancy. *The Reproduction of Mothering: Psychoanalysis and the Sociology of Gender.* Berkeley: University of California Press, 1978.

Collins, Patricia Hill. *Black Feminist Thought: Knowledge, Consciousness, and the Politics of Empowerment.* Boston: Unwin Hyman, 1990.

Connell, R. W. *Gender and Power.* Stanford, Calif.: Stanford University Press, 1987.

De Vita, Carol J. "The United States at Mid-Decade," *Population Bulletin, 50* (March 1996).

Diamond, Sara. *Roads to Dominion: Right-Wing Movements and Political Power in the United States.* New York: The Guilford Press, 1995.

Donovan, Timothy P., and Willard B. Gatewood Jr., eds. *The Governors of Arkansas: Essays in Political Biography.* Fayetteville: University of Arkansas Press, 1981.

Du Bois, W. E. B. *Black Reconstruction in America: 1860–1880.* 1935. Reprint. New York: Atheneum Press, 1962.

Ehrenreich, Barbara. *The Hearts of Men.* New York: Anchor Press/Doubleday, 1983.

Ewick, Patricia, and Susan S. Silbey. "Subversive Stories and Hegemonic Tales:

Toward a Sociology of Narrative" in *Law and Society Review 29* (1995).

Fanon, Frantz. *Black Skin, White Masks.* Translated by Charles Lam Markmann. 1967. 1st Evergreen ed. New York: Grove Press, 1982.

Faubus, Orval Eugene. *Down from the Hills* (vol. 1). Little Rock, Ark.: Pioneer Press, 1980.

Faubus, Orval Eugene. *In This Faraway Land: A Personal Journal of Infantry Combat in World War II.* Little Rock: Pioneer Press, 1993.

Fields, Karen E. "What We Cannot Remember Mistakenly." In *Memory and History: Essays on Recalling and Interpreting Experience.* Edited by Jaclyn Jeffrey and Glenace Edwall. University Press of America, 1984.

Fletcher, John Gould. *Arkansas.* 1947. Reprint. Fayetteville: University of Arkansas Press, 1989.

Frankenberg, Helen. *White Women, Race Matters: The Social Construction of Whiteness.* Minneapolis: University of Minnesota Press, 1993.

Frazier, E. Franklin. *The Negro Family in the United States.* 1939. Reprint. Chicago: University of Chicago Press, 1966.

Freitag, Sandria. *Collective Action and Community: Public Arenas and the Emergence of Communalism in North India.* Berkeley: University of California Press, 1989.

Gioseffi, Daniela, ed. *On Prejudice: A Global Perspective.* New York: Anchor Books, 1993.

Hartmann, Heidi. "The Recent Past and Near Future for Women Workers: Addressing Remaining Barriers." Presented at the Seventy-fifth Anniversary Conference Women's Bureau, U.S. Department of Labor, Washington, D.C., May 1995.

Hays, Brooks. *A Southern Moderate Speaks.* Chapel Hill: University of North Carolina Press, 1959.

Hochschild, Arlie. *The Second Shift.* New York: Avon Books, 1989.

hooks, bell. *Ain't I a Woman?* Boston: South End Press, 1981.

Huckaby, Elizabeth. *Crisis at Central High.* Baton Rouge: Louisiana State University Press, 1980.

Irwin-Zarecka, Iwona. *Frames of Remembrance: The Dynamics of Collective Memory.* New Brunswick, N.J.: Transaction Publishers, 1994.

Jay, Martin. *The Dialectical Imagination: A History of the Frankfurt School and the Institute of Social Research, 1923–1950.* London: Heinemann, 1973.

Kimmel, Michael S., and Michael A. Messner, eds. *Men's Lives.* New York: Macmillan, 1992.

Life Magazine, 43 (15), October 7, 1957.

May, Elaine Tyler. *Homeward Bound: American Families in the Cold War Era.* New York: Basic Books, 1988.

Murphy, Sara Alderman. *Breaking the Silence: Little Rock's Women's Emergency Committee to Open Our Schools, 1958–1963.* Edited by Patrick C. Murphy II. Fayetteville: University of Arkansas Press, 1997.

Pérez-Peña, Richard. "New York's Income Gap Largest in Nation," *New York Times,* December 17, 1997.

Rifkin, Jeremy. *The End of Work: The Decline of the Global Labor Force and the Dawn of the Post-Market Era.* New York: G. P. Putnam's Sons, 1995.

Roy, Beth. *Some Trouble with Cows: Making Sense of Social Conflict.* Berkeley: University of California Press, 1994.

Roy, F. Hampton, and Charles Witsell. *How We Lived: Little Rock as an American City.* Little Rock, Ark.: August House, 1985.

Rozario, Santi. *Purity and Communal Boundaries: Women and Social Change in a Bangladeshi Village.* North Sydney, NSW: Allen and Unwin, 1992.

Rubin, Lillian. *Families on the Fault Line.* New York, Harper Collins, 1994.

Rudé, George. *Ideology and Popular Protest.* New York: Pantheon Books, 1980.

Sacks, Karen Brodkin, and Dorothy Remy, eds. *My Troubles Are Going to Have Trouble with Me: Everyday Trials and Triumphs of Women Workers.* New Brunswick, N.J.: Rutgers University Press, 1984.

Scheff, Thomas J. *Microsociology: Discourse, Emotion, and Social Structure.* Chicago: University of Chicago Press, 1990.

Scott, James C. *Domination and the Arts of Resistance.* New Haven, Conn.: Yale University Press, 1990.

Scott, James C. *Weapons of the Weak: Everyday Forms of Peasant Resistance.* New Haven, Conn.: Yale University Press, 1985.

Sennet, Richard, and Jonathan Cobb. *The Hidden Injuries of Class.* New York: Vintage Books, 1972.

Steiner, Claude. *Scripts People Live: Transactional Analysis of Life Scripts.* New York: Grove Press, 1974.

U.S. Bureau of the Census. *Statistical Abstract of the United States.* Washington, D.C.: U.S. Department of Commerce, Bureau of the Census, 1994.

Williams, Patricia. *The Alchemy of Race and Rights.* Cambridge, Mass.: Harvard University Press, 1991.

Index